Railways and the Western European Capitals

Railways and the Western European Capitals

Studies of Implantation in London, Paris, Berlin, and Brussels

Micheline Nilsen

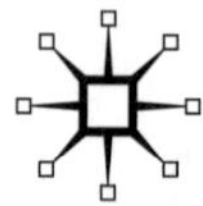

Railways and the Western European Capitals
Copyright © Micheline Nilsen, 2008.

First published in 2008 by PALGRAVE MACMILLAN® in the US - a division of St. Martin's Press LLC, 175 Fifth Avenue, New York, NY 10010.

Where this book is distributed in the UK, Europe and the rest of the world, this is by Palgrave Macmillan, a division of Macmillan Publishers Limited, registered in England, company number 785998, of Houndmills, Basingstoke, Hampshire RG21 6XS.

Palgrave Macmillan is the global academic imprint of the above companies and has companies and representatives throughout the world.

Palgrave® and Macmillan® are registered trademarks in the United States, the United Kingdom, Europe and other countries.

ISBN-13: 978-0-230-60773-6
ISBN-10: 0-230-60773-X

Library of Congress Cataloging-in-Publication Data

Nilsen, Micheline.
Railways and the Western European capitals : studies of implantation in London, Paris, Berlin, and Brussels / Micheline Nilsen.
   p.   cm.
   Includes bibliographical references and index.
   ISBN 0-230-60773-X
   1. Railroads—Europe, Western.   2. City planning—Europe, Western.
3. Capitals (Cities)—Europe, Western.   I. Title.
   HE3005.N55   2008
   307.76094—dc22   2008012346

A catalogue record of the book is available from the British Library.

Design by Westchester Book Group.

First edition: October 2008

10 9 8 7 6 5 4 3 2 1

Printed in the United States of America.

Contents

List of Illustrations

Acknowledgments

Research for this book was supported by an Indiana University South Bend Faculty Research Grant, a Trustee's Merit Citation from the Graham Foundation for Advanced Studies in the Fine Arts, the Kress Foundation for research travel abroad, a Robert T. Silver Memorial Award, an Allen Research Grant, and several travel grants from the Department of Art History at the University of Delaware. For all of these awards, I am deeply grateful.

To the faculty members who provided advice and encouragement, I express my heartfelt thanks. They include Damie Stillman (dissertation advisor), Bernard Herman, Nina Athanassoglou-Kallmyer at the University of Delaware, David Brownlee and John Dixon Hunt at the University of Pennsylvania, Barbara Lane at Bryn Mawr College, Allan Mitchell, formerly at the University of California, San Diego, and David Van Zanten at Northwestern University.

The work of scholars would not be possible without libraries and the many dedicated people who perform the complex tasks needed to make their resources accessible. In this country and abroad, I have encountered a willingness to accommodate a scholar's work, usually more than policies prescribed, in close to 50 institutions, too numerous to list here. At my current home institution, the staff of the Indiana University South Bend libraries deserve special thanks for their tireless attentiveness to the multiple demands I have made on their services. In the complex process of obtaining illustrations, librarians, curators, and archivists have responded resourcefully, promptly, and with enthusiasm to provide high-quality images of sometimes obscure holdings.

At Palgrave Macmillan, Chris Chappell has been enthusiastic, patient, and unfailingly attentive. At IUSB, students and colleagues have encouraged the progress of this work.

During my research abroad I have enjoyed the hospitality of many individuals and institutions. My mother welcomed the frequent European visits due to this project but did not live to see its completion. Closer to home, the South 46th Street back porch or kitchen table advice, and generous assistance from Holly Pittman, Gary Hatfield, Daniel Deudney, and

Donald Jackson was timely, constant, and invaluable. My children Sven and Saskia have been very tolerant and supportive of a preoccupied mother. My grandson Marcel, a fervent disciple of Reverend Awdry, shows significant promise as a railway connoisseur. As for the man I met on a half-hour train ride between Brussels and Antwerp almost 40 years ago, words will not do justice to the patience and caring he has provided over the years devoted to this project.

This book is grounded in Europe, where I grew up in a family of railway men, and I dedicate it to the memory of my parents, Firmin Joseph "dit" Marcel Molle and Marie-José Gillard.

Introduction

We had the century of Perikles, we had the century of the Crusades, the century of the Great Discoveries, the century of the Sun King. Believe me, the nineteenth century will be for perpetuity and for mankind the century of the railways.[1]

La technologie pour eux, c'était le chemin de fer. Et nous, on se passionne pour les ordinateurs.[2]

Emerging among the general public at the same time as the camera, the railways, too, would change the way we see. Not only would the camera become a tool for the railway companies in their engineering and public relations work, but it would also supplant the travel sketch as a means of recording the scenes and landscapes made more accessible and therefore more visible by the railways to increasing numbers of tourists. Early train travelers soon noticed that the railways altered their vision. Victor Hugo, among the first, wrote to his daughter in 1837:

> The speed is incredible. The flowers on the side of the road are no longer flowers, they are spots or rather red or white stripes, no longer dots, everything becomes a stripe; wheat becomes a mass of yellow hair; alfalfa long green braids; cities, steeples and trees dance and mingle madly on the horizon; from time to time, a shadow, a shape, a standing specter appears and disappears as lightning next to the door; it is a road warden, who, as is the custom, gives the convoy a military salute.[3]

The anamorphosis of the landscape seen from the train encouraged examination of the nature of vision, which nineteenth-century artists would explore through their subjects and techniques. J.M.W. Turner's *Rain, Steam and Speed—The Great Western Railway* (1844) depicts a scampering hare about to be overtaken by the oncoming train.[4] John Martin's *Last Day of Judgment* (ca. 1853) hurls a train and its cargo of the damned down into the abyss.[5] Impressionist painters would later try to capture the elusive quality of transitory vision and incorporate the railways in their investigation of modern life.

Study of the railways' urban presence has focused on the front they present to the city, the locus of their relationship with the traveling public: the station. Architectural characteristics of stations have been analyzed, either as chapters in architectural histories or as monographs on specific architects. Carroll L. V. Meeks' landmark study, *The Railroad Station*, expanded the Wölflinian typologies to accommodate a little more than a 100 years of head house buildings.[6] As traveling needs and railway operations evolved, stations became vulnerable to redevelopment. When the first stations fell to the wrecking ball, nascent awareness of their architectural significance sparked protest, and some neglected, dirty white elephants got a second lease on life through classification as historic monuments. The focus remained on the stations or on some of their features, such as their sheds, prowess of nineteenth-century engineering.

Upon closer examination, stations occupy only a small portion of the urban footprint for railway operations, and they have an uneasy relationship with their surroundings, branding them with a distinctive stigma. Lines, yards, and ancillary buildings for freight, maintenance, and other operations command expansive real estate. Out of scale with the urban fabric, these facilities attract industrial, disreputable, unkempt, or disadvantaged neighbors. This aspect of railway implantation has received considerably less scholarly attention. In Britain, two scholars pioneered study of the impact of railways independently. The urban historian H. J. Dyos began to examine the relationship between railway demolitions and lower-class housing in the mid-1950s.[7] Fourteen years later, the economic historian J. R. Kellett published *The Impact of Railways on Victorian Cities*.[8] He focused on available evidence to answer a number of questions on the railways' presence in British cities, such as location of facilities, land ownership, patterns of land acquisition and shift in values, impact on urban fabric, social costs and benefits, as well as promotion of suburban development. Kellett supplements his minute study of extant records with his "back of the envelope" estimations, where documents are elusive, in order to give us a meticulous account of railway implantation in London, Manchester, Birmingham, Liverpool, and Glasgow. In France, Karen Bowie shifted her interest from the architecture of major stations in Paris (topic of her Sorbonne doctoral dissertation) to the urban presence and impact of stations.[9] She has gathered several scholars to reconnect the study of railway facilities to their historical, political, judicial, financial, and industrial urban context.[10] Given the scope and variety of available sources, her team's approach has been to proceed by "soundings," enabling them to elucidate aspects of these questions, rather than complete exhaustive study. Some of the giants, St. Christophers, on whose shoulders this work stands are dead: Dyos, Kellett, Simmons. Others, very much alive and active investigators of the implantation phenomenon, such as Bowie in Paris and Ralf Roth in Germany have not published in English. Their work is meticulously credited, but the scope of this project transcends their nationally or locally based contributions.

This study is similar in focus to the work of Kellett and Bowie in that it asks the question, what was the impact of railway implantation on the city fabric where it claimed vast real estate and changed the urban configuration? It is also similar to the work of Bowie and her team in that it examines selectively aspects of implantation rather than attempt comprehensive coverage. It differs substantially from these studies by removing the examination of impact from the national context and by adopting a more general perspective. Most railway scholarship has remained local or national, and a more general examination opens the possibility of extrapolating general conclusions about the impact of railways on cities.[11] Railway implantation was not an isolated phenomenon in individual cities, but it manifested itself with varying intensity in different modalities, which this book explores. Railway implantation is examined here in four western European capital cities. London, Paris, Berlin, and Brussels were among the first capitals to develop their rail infrastructure in the second third of the nineteenth century. Capital cities were the locus of initial large-scale and centralized railway development. They also experienced more drastic urban impact with several terminals rather than single through stations.

Each of these cities has repaid scores of scholars for a lifetime of study, and a strategy had to be adopted to contend with the potentially crippling volume of material available on the railway history of these four capitals. Each city serves as a case study for one most characteristic aspect of railway implantation: social or urban impact, strategic implications, and connection between terminals. Within each city, closer examination of the selected aspect or facet focuses on one representative station area to allow more detailed investigation. This carefully selected, specific, and logical strategy translates into nine chapters. The introductory chapter weaves a web of common threads from general factors related to implantation in the four countries. The eight subsequent chapters alternate between a chapter on the examination of an aspect of implantation, followed by a chapter with further focus on a specific station area or phenomenon related to implantation. The Berlin and Brussels facets have national implications, whereas the impact of the selected facets for London and Paris remains more localized. The chronological focus is the nineteenth century, but twentieth-century developments are mentioned when relevant. Different questions are thus treated within comparable time frames, except for Brussels. In the Belgian capital, the chronology extends into the twentieth century, because the project examined, which started in 1839, did not reach completion until 1952. This brings the final chapter of the book into the twentieth century, ushering in the conclusion, which provides a brief assessment of the lasting impact of railway implantation today.

This study examines the intense and multifaceted impact of the railways on cities, but it does not attempt to offer a comprehensive treatment of railways in cities: half a dozen books might provide a start for such an agenda. Instead, this work presents various aspects of implantation, highlighting the complexity of the process and the diversity of its implications. Rather than striving to be a classical edifice, this book is a postmodern faceted construct. It is conceived not as a Grand Central, but as a Union, structure, bringing different lines together.

More specifically, Chapter 1 examines manifestations of the impact in England, France, Prussia, and Belgium, primarily the physical urban presence of stations, their location in relation to cities, and the need caused by the railways for updating legislation on incorporation and expropriation.

London invites examination as the capital of the country where the railways were first developed and constructed on a national scale. The first country to open a passenger rail line, England owes the development of its rail network to private initiative sanctioned by Parliament. The free enterprise nature of railway development in that country is reflected in the configuration of its network, which resulted from amalgamation of multiple lines. Impact at the local level also reflects the opportunist tactics that dominated early implantation. Chapter 2 considers the displacement of working-class housing caused by the railways in London. Chapter 3 focuses on how displacement affected the Euston Road terminals—Euston, King's Cross, and St. Pancras stations.

In France, where liberalism and state intervention coalesced, the state determined the general configuration of the lines and regulated operations. The state-sanctioned national network, operated by concessions to private companies, had a strong urban presence but did not fall under the city's jurisdiction. A dozen years after initial railway implantation, Paris was the site of a large-scale urban reconfiguration under the Second Empire. Chapter 4 outlines similarities between railway projects and Haussmann's epoch-defining urban "regularization," which resonated throughout the world. Chapter 5 examines the dovetailing of railway and urban configuration in the neighboring Gare du Nord and Gare de l'Est, which exhibit divergent implantation patterns.

In Berlin, private industry developed the railways under stringent state oversight, but in some cases, usually deemed of strategic importance, the state assumed full responsibility. This resulted in a unique urban network connecting stations with both a circular peripheral line and a direct central one. Chapter 6 examines the gradual incorporation of the railways in the four countries' military arsenal. Chapter 7 considers the relationship between the military authorities and railway development in the Prussian capital, most particularly in the areas of the Anhalter Bahnhof and the Tempelhof military facilities.

Belgian railway trunk lines were initially built and exploited by the state as a means of setting the fledgling country on a respectable footing among European powers. Conceded lines filled in the network between 1845 and 1870, when the state began repurchasing lines from private companies. Brussels, hub of a network conceived as both national and international, saw its role as a European crossroad hampered by the lack of rail connection between its two main north and south stations. The 115-year project to build this connection between two geographical poles through a central core and the ensuing traumatic wound to the city's fabric is the subject of Chapter 8. Chapter 9 argues that the commuting patterns facilitated by this central rail connection encourage the ethnic divisiveness that is threatening the fragile Belgian national entity. The first chapter for each city concludes with a brief section on how the facet of railway implantation examined in London, Paris, Berlin, or Brussels also affected some of these other cities.

In her essay on the state of the discipline of urban studies in the special millenial issue of the *Journal of the Society of Architectural Historians*, Nancy Stieber pointed to the past 25 years as exhibiting "a preference for the concrete over the schematic, an openness to observation, and a distrust of any theoretical construction that might prove constraining . . . a preference for revealing the richness of relationships over the simplicity achieved by systems of abstractions."[12] This describes the spirit of the present study as this investigation of railway impact includes the network of social, political, sociological, and cultural factors surrounding the urban presence of railway stations as they implanted their expansive facilities in capital cities.

Beyond the challenge of developing familiarity with station sites as well as archival and research resources in the four countries considered, this project has demanded forays into disciplines that have only loose connections with architecture history. Geology and geography shed light on the implantation sites, urban history explains the nature of the city fabric at the time of implantation, political and economic history provide an essential context, and sociology probes into local and national factors related to railway development. Specialized studies on real-estate values or incorporation and expropriation laws are directly related to the process of implantation. This contribution from other disciplines should not be discouraging for an architecture historian inspired more by social history than by monument-centered methods.

Shedding light on rail implantation and its shaping impact on the fabric of most cities requires straddling beyond a single discipline. Although accepting the responsibility for stretching beyond the traditional historical methods of architecture history, the methodology adopted here does not lead into practices that can be borrowed from other disciplines, and it is deliberately not comparative. The examination of stations in four different cities might suggest resorting to comparative history, but the strategy to focus on one specific location for each major aspect of implantation considered here precludes systematic comparison.

Michel de Certeau describes historical writing as "the product of a locus." To the extent that everything we do is contingent on personal circumstances and training, that is true; but in the narrower sense of "result and symptom of the group functioning as a laboratory," this project is the result of a solitary investigation that neither distrusts theory nor means to disregard it.[13] Theory is present to the extent that it permeates one's thinking but not as a predictor of methodology. This study is based on empirical observation, examination of primary sources, and literature analysis of a specific process: the implantation of the railways in the modern city.

1

Railways and Cities

For most communities, it was a matter of life or death to be serviced by a rail line. The civilizing potential of the railway generated enthusiasm in the middle decades of the nineteenth century. Intensified contacts would promote general welfare; improved communications would stimulate economic growth, give confidence in the future, and consolidate man's power over the world. As Alexis Legrand stated in 1837, "the earthen roads are those of agriculture, the canals and rivers are the roads of commerce; the railways are the roads of power, enlightenment, civilization."[1]

The increased national cohesion fostered by shortened distances and the advent of universal peace promised by rapid transport were, paradoxically, matched by technological competition for "the first" landmarks of railway development expressed in nationalist terms.[2] Railway construction was a source of innovation and acted as a catalyst for creative solutions to increasingly complex engineering challenges and for the development of industrial production. In the four countries included in this study—England, France, Prussia, and Belgium—and elsewhere, early railway development exhibited common factors.[3] Initial response, general impact, urban presence, and adjustments to legislation follow parallel developments in these four countries. These common aspects are examined in this chapter. International implications of rail transport also surfaced early and will be introduced here briefly to be considered in greater detail in Chapter 6, which focuses on the strategic implications of the railways.

Early Protests

Despite the promise of the railways, the first wave of public reaction was not entirely positive. Concerns for the forceful impact of steam on rail surfaced first in England, where early development of railways was most aggressive. Opposition was voiced primarily on three counts: fear of the unknown, concern for the emergence of a dehumanized civilization, and threat of an economic upheaval with potential impact on social order.[4] Steam intruded powerfully and noisily into a human landscape regimented by the speed and strength of beasts of burden, unchanged for several millennia. Unlike roads, connecting and earthbound, rails would divide and insert themselves conspicuously into the land. An 1835 letter to *The Times* of London cautioned against "[a] compound of the greatest blunders ever to be filiated on the sciences; and which would ride roughshod over the country, reckless of the privacy or security of individual or public property, without an object (beyond the mere making a railway for the benefit of an engineer and a small covey of friends)."[5] The "loco-motive Monster carrying eighty tons of goods and navigated by a tail of smoke and sulphur" would bring smoke, burning cinders, vibrations, frightened cattle, ruined vistas, and divided land to peaceful countryside and towns.[6]

Finding manpower to build railways could present difficulty in the context of shortage of localized farm labor.[7] Social concerns also surfaced, such as the need for a national police to keep pace with the increased speed and territory the railways would provide for criminals.[8] As the 1835 letter to *The Times* suggested, "Radicals, dissenters, and fire-brands of all conditions . . . would come streaming out of the manufacturing towns to spread their poisonous doctrines into the heart of agricultural England,"[9] and, furthermore, "the railway would be very disturbing to the Eton boys" or burn ladies' dresses.[10] Objections were manifested in the press, in parliamentary debates, and in countless pamphlets published by interested parties or observers.[11] Predictions of impending catastrophes abounded, though most did not materialize.

Representatives of other forms of transport voiced their concerns about this new competition. For instance, the Dartford and Strood Turnpike Trust raised objections to the construction of a rail line in northern Kent in 1830, 1837, and 1842. Its petition to the House of Commons against the 1837 railway bill argued that road and water transport were satisfactory, and profit-driven speculative schemes such as the railways offered unjust competition to the investors in the more conservative turnpikes.[12] On the other hand, the preamble to the bill for the London and Birmingham Railway stated that railways were less objectionable than canals, "as the rapid passing admits not of loitering, leaving no one the opportunity to steal or trespass."[13] In France, the first railway theorist, Auguste Perdonnet (1801–67), reported concerns for the livelihood of coachmen and the fate of horses, the latter, according to him, remedied by the diversion of horse meat to food consumption.[14]

The London and Birmingham Railway Bill also stated that the proposed line was drawn not to "encroach on any Park or Gentleman's residence."[15] This fact was echoed by George Stephenson in a letter dated 23 September 1831, wherein he listed the three conditions a line must fulfill: first, remain as level as feasible; second, choose the least intrusive path, even if not the most direct; and third, "avoid Parks and Pleasure grounds in every practicable case."[16] That no such concern was expressed for urban residential districts reflects the target audience of the promoters and the fact that the early lines did not penetrate into heavily settled areas. Stephenson's rule about the least intrusive path no longer applied when the railways penetrated cities.

Among the railways' structures, tunnels were the most maligned and seen as a threat to the health of those passengers they did not engulf entirely. Tunnel entrances were designed to be stately and reassuring, and, on the whole, early railway architects and engineers sought ways to prevent their lines and facilities from striking a discordant note in the landscape.[17] Early views such as those of John Bourne integrated the depictions of railway construction or structures into a well-established landscape tradition. The rails were sometimes barely visible or coexisted with the stock landscape elements of cattle, rocks, sky, and greenery.[18] Despite these reassuring tactics, explosions and speed would cause deadly accidents. As reports of the first casualties reached the public, the cost of material progress might have appeared too high, but as the French poet and politician Alphonse de Lamartine pointed out, "Civilization is also a battle field where many succumb for the conquest and advancement of all. Let us mourn for them, let us mourn for ourselves, and let us march on."[19]

Objections to intrusions into the landscape did not begin with the railways. The development of an extensive canal system in England two generations earlier had drawn substantial resistance from landowners.[20] Land acquisition was, however, more heavily contested for the railways than it had been for the canals, and landowners were the major protesters the railway companies had to reckon with.[21] Intent on protecting their estates from damage, the landowners bargained for higher compensation or other benefits from promoters. This is illustrated by an early 1830s account from the small town of Watford, where the fifth Earl of Essex had prevailed on the London and Birmingham Railway and George Stephenson to avoid his grounds by creating an embankment and a tunnel of "unprecedented magnitude."[22] This account of a landowner's demands goes on to illustrate the intrusive nature of the initial surveys:

> One or two strange faces appeared in the town, and men in leathern leggings, dragging a long chain, and attended by one or two country labourers armed with bill-hooks, were remarked as trespassing in the most unwarrantable manner over pasture land, standing crops, copse and cover; actually cutting gaps in the hedges, through which they climbed and dragged the land-chain. Then would follow another intruder, bearing a telescope set on three legs, which he erected with the most perfect coolness, wherever he thought fit.[23]

The physical confrontation between railway workers and local inhabitants occasionally came to blows, and local folklore points out the irony of the nobleman who owns land because his ancestors fought for it calling the police when a working man wanted to fight him for the same land.[24]

In 1836 the Corporation of London petitioned Parliament against the London and Blackwall (then the Commercial) Railway and against railways in the City. The arguments listed by the corporation were that these schemes would displace 2,800 people, that they would prevent the completion of ongoing street improvement projects, and that "vibrations, smoke and noise . . . would render the occupation of houses in the vicinity of railways scarcely endurable."[25] These stated reasons veiled another: the corporation's concern that the East and West India Docks would, thanks to the railways, gain a competitive advantage over the Pool of London. The corporation's protests only delayed the opening of the railways' extension into the City until August 1841. This early protest illustrates the various counts of urban opposition against the railways: impact on housing, on street traffic, and on physical conditions, with corollaries of economic factors.

The appearance of surveyors and navvies, instructed to go about their business without paying attention to residents, land configuration, or division patterns, did not reassure the uninformed public. As incursions into the landscape became visible, they confirmed suspicions of impending change. Urban landowners also feared the effect the railways would have on their property and its value. This naturally led to resistance as well as financial opportunism. The potentially risky nature of railways also caused three-quarters of the insurance companies to increase their rates for real estate adjacent to railways in the 1840s, a trend corrected by the next decade.[26]

Railways as Instrument of Progress

The railways gradually came to be seen as agents of progress. This change of attitude is evidenced in an 1836 pamphlet:

> On the first introduction of the system it was received with distrust by all, and with aversion by many. . . . These apprehensions, which gave rise to determined opposition on the part of the landowners, have now been proved to be groundless. The experience even of a few years has shown that the value of districts traversed by Railways has been uniformly increased. The evidence given before both Houses of Parliament on this subject is conclusive and unanswerable. . . . Those who but a few years since would have risen en masse to oppose a railway, now come forward as advocates and supporters.[27]

This evolution is connected to the recognition of the positive effects of railways.

After a short initial wave of opposition, proximity to the train lines became synonymous with increase in real-estate values.[28] As opponents of railways saw their protests unheeded and plans ineluctably carried out for rails to trace their line on the open country between cities, they turned their efforts to negotiating the most favorable lines at the most advantageous conditions. By the end of the initial decade of implantation of rail lines, the additional value accrued to property because of proximity to improved streets or railways brought the protest phase to an end. The recognition that railways were necessary for further growth rendered obstructionist tactics redundant and self-defeating.[29] Competition between localities was fierce, with intense lobbying to secure a position on projected rail lines. The rail meant economic prosperity; its absence stagnation and demise. With the shift of public opinion away from protests, railway reporting and literature began to focus on construction, engineering accomplishments, traffic, operations, state intervention in railway affairs, rates, and the guarantees that should be offered to investors.

Development of railways was a risky, dynamic, and, at times, visionary venture. Its players tended to exhibit a pioneering spirit, an almost swashbuckling determination to drive the rails across valleys, through mountains, and into cities. In the words of the French poet Victor Hugo, the ant-like railway workers were doing the work of giants.[30] Financiers risked capital, speculators manipulated the nascent money markets, and engineers found in the railways opportunities for rising to spectacular challenges. The railways were unquestionably a dominant economic force in the nineteenth century. Whether they were underwritten by the state or by private enterprise, railway projects were of such a scale that they had a macroeconomic impact on national, and in some cases international, finances. The capital necessitated by the construction of the iron roads, which were to connect major points of national territories with their capital cities, demanded state involvement and new financing techniques.[31] The railways were major players in a shift from financial backing by banking establishments to much greater reliance on multiple smaller investors through the mechanisms of stocks and bonds. The financing mechanisms refined and regulated for railway construction were in turn applied to other areas of economic activity, such as industry, colonial ventures, and real-estate speculation and development. For instance, the construction projects engendered by Haussmann's works in Paris were financed by Sociétés Immobilières (real-estate partnerships) modeled after the railway investment companies.[32]

Impact of Railways

The impact of railways was measured, and publicized, by the number of passengers conveyed, tons of goods transported, receipts, and returns on investments. Routes, rolling stock, personnel, rates, schedules, and contention with state regulations demanded most of the attention of railway administrators. The physical plant of urban stations took a backseat in executive committee agendas. In the competitive, profit-minded business of early development, there was no room for concern over the nature of the impact the railways had on cities. As Saussay wrote in 1845, "Entirely devoted to their creation, the [railway creators] only ha[d] concern for it, and they willingly sacrifice[d] the present and future of entire neighborhoods of large cities which they service[d]."[33] Also, peculiarities of the approval process could minimize the opportunity for local resistance. For instance, when railway bills were under consideration in England, municipal corporations could voice opposition only when municipal property or streets were involved.[34] Chambers of Commerce were not authorized to make themselves heard until the 1880s. This accounted for a situation where public issues were raised only if they happened to be in concert with private opposition.

The impact of railways was, however, far from negligible. The railways brought a population influx into most large urban centers. The population of Paris increased more during the 25 years that followed the opening of the first station than it had during the eight previous centuries. The population of London doubled in the 40 years between 1811 and 1851.[35] Unlike the automobile, which would disperse population in the twentieth century, the railways at first concentrated populations in urban areas, thereby affecting their morphology. Later, with the advent of commuter services, the railways further contributed to the growth of cities by allowing large numbers of city workers to move to the suburbs.

The railways played a crucial role in the logistics of supplying cities with food, fuel, and raw materials as of the 1840s and 1850s. Milk, fish, produce, cattle, and even flowers reached cities with greater rapidity, thereby revolutionizing the food production and distribution industry. The daily arrivals of fresh food supplies reduced price differences between regions and expanded the supply area of capital cities. Cattle could be brought in fresh from pasture by train rather than driven to exhaustion by road.[36] New slaughterhouses were built within rail access on the outskirts of cities. Railway communication leveled supply and prices, reducing the practice of middlemen who bought cheap at harvest and sold high before the next crops came in.[37] In times of economic hardship, state intervention regulated the freight costs for grain and potato deliveries and eliminated the famines, which had plagued large cities in the past.[38]

The railways also led to regional specialization in food production. The line to Pontoise encouraged the development of a market garden area that supplied, through Paris' Gare du Nord (north station), half of the produce delivered to the Halles Centrales (central market) until 1900.[39] In some cases the railways caused the end of local production. For instance, wines from the Paris and Loire regions were replaced by those from Burgundy, Bordeaux, and the south.[40] More abundant food supply led to some diversification in food consumption for the lower classes, though not necessarily of improved quality. In Paris, lower qualities were substituted for meat and wine, the latter being replaced by an inferior mixture for the poor man who could not afford to buy his *coup de rouge* (shot of red wine) by the barrel.[41] The loss of regional autonomy and decreased consumption of local products was also accompanied by a reduction in the supply of horse manure as agricultural fertilizer.[42]

As early as 1837, the potential of cheap transport for building materials was recognized in London. Rather than local brick, good building stone, Welsh slate, freestone, and a variety of ornamental materials would improve the city fabric. Turnpikes and other roads could be repaired more cheaply and with better materials.[43] In France, the railway made cheap brick available in Paris and replaced the products of depleting local quarries by those from an extending radius—limestone from the Oise and new types of stones from the whole country.[44] In Berlin, the brick of the Schinkel School was replaced by stone when the railways reduced transportation cost and diversified the supply of building materials beyond the local granite and brittle limestone.[45]

For the urban working classes, railway projects translated into much-needed labor, but demolitions in residential areas led to increased crowding in diminished housing stock.[46] The availability of transportation to healthier housing locales did not provide relief to those who needed it most. The inner-city poor, dependent on the proximity to casual unspecialized labor, remained unable to relocate to the nascent suburbs where clerical and skilled laborers were gradually migrating to with their families in search of cheaper and healthier housing.[47] When put in operation, the railways provided employment for a uniformed and strictly regimented workforce. This resulted from the use of former military personnel to operate the lines; from the adoption of military and maritime models for staff regulations, uniforms, and hierarchies; and from the expected military-like dedication of the workforce to a pioneering and challenging industry. There was a bond between those who worked for the railways, and each company or national rail system has its heroes who performed memorable deeds both in peace and during wartime.[48] The British social observer Charles Booth described the 22,000 workers and 6,000 official staff members of the British railway companies as almost all male, most adults, and nearly all permanent employees who enjoyed steady employment and relatively high wages.[49]

In 1859, the French physician Prosper de Pietra Santa examined the health impact of the railways on travelers and employees. His stated goal was to prove that the impact of railways on general health was favorable, their effect on the employees' health was benign, and accidents were less frequent for travelers than in any other mode of transport.[50] In fact, working conditions caused debilitating health problems, and severe accidents could be attributed to long and arduous work shifts.[51] Cost-conscious companies had little tolerance for labor protests and resented state interference in personnel regulations.[52]

Leisure activities expanded their radius and scope due to the railways. From the escape to the country; the organized excursion trains, the so-called *trains de plaisir* (pleasure trains); and Thomas Cooke's tours to guidebook production and station bookstall publications, the ramifications were many and permeated all but the poorest classes of society.

Physical Impact of Railways on Cities

Beyond the significant forms of economic and social impact, the railways would alter the rural landscape with their engineering works. These works were admired for their daring or innovative forms and often enhanced or integrated into vistas. [53] Urban areas were most drastically affected by the construction of stations, marshalling yards, and storage facilities. Up to 10 percent of a city's built-up area could be consumed by railway facilities. As the economic historian John R. Kellett has demonstrated, the 10 percent of land owned by railways had an indirect influence on up to 20 percent of the land area in the centers of cities.[54] Unplanned and opportunist, the implantation of rail lines assumed a recognizable pattern. Long corridors penetrated toward the core of a city, either interrupting the street pattern or hampering its subsequent development. In capital cities, the presence of several lines created radial axes of penetration, often in close proximity to older roads predicated by geographical features. The heavily built core of cities resisted railway intrusion, but the undeveloped peripheral areas with occasional nascent industrial facilities and affordable acreage supplied the expansive needs of growing railway operations.[55] The need to carry freight between radial lines without unloading or penetrating the city core led to the construction of belt lines around the edges of cities.[56] This created a complex pattern of rail systems outside of the area built up at the time of implantation. These encircling rail lines would inevitably be outgrown by suburban expansion. Lines and the maintenance, service, and storage facilities created a distinct railway landscape, industrial in nature and, because of its proximity to the city, more accessible and visible to those who did not reside or work in areas devoted to industrial activity.[57]

The presence of the railways could modify the configuration of an entire urban context. At Chartres, the multidirectional access to the cathedral was reoriented with the arrival of the Paris–Le Mans line. Until the French Revolution, the cathedral's west portal was the ceremonial, royal entry. The south portal, opening toward the town, acted as the main entrance. The north portal, facing the Bishop's and Chapter Houses, provided access to the ecclesiastical community. The railway station was built north of the cathedral, and for the numerous visitors who came by train to view the Gothic monument, access was now from the north. The secular railway tourist, Baedeker in hand, walked in the footsteps of the medieval clerics to approach and enter the sacred space.[58]

The commercial center of communities was frequently displaced by the siting of its station. The access road to the terminal, often named after the station, assumed the same general direction as the tracks and led to the city's center or its business and commercial core. The urban footprint of the railways with terminus, tracks, and ancillary facilities prevented the development of genuine communication crossroads. The immediate vicinity of the station, blackened by locomotive exhaust, plagued with increased traffic, and unfit for commercial or residential settlement, saw the development of the kinds of businesses that cater to travelers: hotels, restaurants, bars, small grocery stores, and red-light districts.[59] This transit activity encouraged a transient residential population. Stable residential settlement was also discouraged by more direct physical impact. The noise and vibrations of the locomotives prevented neighboring residents from sleeping and caused structural damage to adjoining properties. Even most railway employees, who benefited from free rail passes, would choose to live elsewhere.[60]

By the 1860s the railway's urban presence was considered nefarious. Even for the passenger, the initial approach contact was unsightly, as evidenced by an American traveler in 1864:

> You enter the town as you would a farmer's house, if you first passed through the pig-stye into the kitchen. Every respectable house in the city turns its back upon you; and often a very brick and dirty back, too, though it may show an elegant front of Bath or Portland stone to the street it faces.[61]

Originally, station and other railway areas were expected to remain untainted by the industrial nature of the operation, as evidenced by a short article in the 6 October 1850 issue of the *Annales des Chemins de Fer, des Travaux Publics et des Mines*. The author urges the Chemin de Fer du Nord to take the necessary steps to remove a prosperous sewage processing and fertilizer manufacturing plant located within a 100 to 150 yards from the tracks near the Gare du Nord in Paris. The insalubrious odors from the operation were a nuisance for travelers, and this type of facility was legally prohibited in residential areas. The author's expectation was that the railway company would be concerned to maintain the standards of residential districts in the vicinity of the station.[62] Perdonnet provided a reliable indication of the rapid shift in the perception of the urban presence of stations. The first edition of his *Traité élémentaire des chemins de fer*, published in 1855–56, considered the vicinity to stations as desirable and as a cause of increased real-estate value. By the fourth volume of his popular manual's third edition, in 1865, he reflected the stigma imprinted by the railways on the *quartier de la gare* (station area).[63] The term "vandalism" was first used by the magazine *Punch* in 1863 to describe the damage done in the City of London by the railways on Ludgate Hill. The term became commonly used to refer to the damage brought on by railways through their construction in rural and urban settings.[64]

By the end of the nineteenth century, the negative image of the station area would be somewhat tempered, especially in smaller communities. In a 1912 railway encyclopedia, the railway square is described as "consistently the most important area of an entire town."[65] The concentration of street traffic caused by the station had a strong influence on the configuration of the area, which also needed to accommodate local transportation. Presence of the most important public buildings in the station vicinity increased the significance of the area. For instance, the post office, large hotels, banks, and department stores could gravitate toward the station. For suburban developments or smaller cities, the station would supplant the church or city hall as the center around which communities would congregate. During the Belle Epoque, urban life might also center around the station rather than near civic or religious buildings, as it had in the past. Given its importance, the encyclopedia author considered that the station should strike the dominant note for the square, but he granted that this aspect had often been neglected and that the lines of responsibility between cities and railways had not been drawn explicitly.[66] He did, however, reflect an emerging awareness of urban issues, which was not present during the early phases of railway construction.

Developed outside the framework of urban planning, the railways seldom benefited from landscaping. As Lewis Mumford noted in 1938, "The cuts and embankments for the greater part long remained unplanted, and the wound in the earth was unhealed."[67] Smooth and effective operation depended on keeping the rails as level as possible. This predicated following the course of rivers or established roads, which made the lines conspicuous. In low-lying areas, the embankments or bridges used to maintain level made the lines stand out in the landscape. Some embankments were planted with trees, this being cosmetic as well as structural because the roots would strengthen the incline.[68] In the early stages of railway construction, the agricultural potential of the land on both sides of the tracks was considered seriously in France, Germany, and Belgium. Plantings would reduce the impact of snow on the tracks, add profitable forestry or orchard exploitation to the railway operations, and increase the country's lumber and fruit production as well as the railways' revenues.[69] Specific legislation was primarily aimed at preventing accidents caused by cinders, lightning, or fallen trees and branches. It did also regulate the modalities of cultivation near the tracks.[70] However, except as an occasional method for strengthening embankments, plantings were not part of railway construction. Beyond some ornamental gardening by railway staff on station premises, the landscaping activity of rail companies remained limited to cutting down spontaneous vegetation, which a landscape architecture scholar of today qualifies as a "missed opportunity."[71]

For the engineers who designed railways, the challenging step of the operation, where their skill and judgment were called into play, was the location of the line or *tracé* (line configuration).[72] Once the location of the line had been determined (and this could become a hotly contested issue), the remaining steps of surveying and preparing estimates were routine procedures. The configuration of a line was determined by a number of factors, which included geographical features, selection between a direct line and one that would service intermediary towns, proximity to waterways, and scope of engineering works required to run the line. As Perdonnet indicated, a mistake at this stage could prove costly, because to rectify the errors small parcels of land would usually have to be purchased at considerably higher prices than the initial line.[73] As part of the process of determining the line configuration, stations were to be assigned a location at the extremities and at intermediate points of a line.[74]

In France, the location of stations and the configuration of rail lines was determined by the state with company recommendations taken under advisement. There is also a distinction between the French terms *gare* (terminal), for the end of the line where rolling stock would be *garé* (parked), and *station,* where the train would pass through or remain stationary, that is *stationné* (stopped).[75] This points to a distinction between two basic types of stations: through stations and terminals. In capital cities, where lines reached a final point, terminal stations were the most common. Again, according to Perdonnet, requirements for such facilities included office buildings for ticket distribution, shelter for travelers, main and storage tracks, repair workshops, storage facilities, water tanks, and so on.[76]

The tendency of railway companies to focus on movement and operations resulted in an initial vagueness about which premises actually constituted the station. As the facilities would adapt to accommodate expanding traffic, the acceptation of the term "station" would evolve from temporary wooden shacks to palatial and innovative landmarks. As Félix Tourneux pointed out in his 1844 *Encyclopédie des chemins de fer et des machines à vapeur,* "There is nothing fixed in the disposition of a station," which should be predicated by the traffic expectations and requirements of exploitation equipment.[77] The exact configuration of the various station components was not yet fully determined at the time Perdonnet was first codifying his railway principles in the 1850s. He resorted to description of existing facilities, as solutions recently devised by colleagues, drawing from the seminal set of articles published ten years earlier in the *Revue Générale de l'Architecture* by Camille Polonceau and Victor Bois.[78] It was not uncommon to look abroad for examples of solutions that would be, like the domestic ones, accompanied by evaluative comments.[79] Later, authors would exhibit more confidence in outlining general principles.[80] In practice, station building expenses caused the highest overruns above estimated costs. In London, engineers had difficulty estimating station expenses, and the first mile out of London turned out to cost more than any other part of any line. Given this factor, companies might be tempted to share premises. Reasons for or against such a decision were carefully weighed by Perdonnet from the points of view of initial expenses, the expected impact on operations, and the congestion in the areas surrounding the station.[81]

In France, recognizing the different impact stations had from the rest of the line, the Ministry of Public Works required a separate inquest, other than that for the *tracé,* to be conducted for the construction of stations as of 1854. This would also allow potentially affected neighboring communities to register their concerns.[82]

Relationship of Stations to Cities

The janiform urban presence of the railways was noticeable very early, with a sharp distinction between the station, facing toward the city, and the facilities on the line before reaching the station.[83] In 1845, the architect A. Saussay considered that "any railway only results in pouring life and activity downstream from its stations, and upstream in rendering servile and sterile the environments it cuts across."[84] This distinction between "upstream" and "downstream" from the station is clearly illustrated in two 1842 prints of the station facilities for the Berlin-Saxony Railway in Berlin.[85] The first print shows the station as a court or a paved city square with six structures; people in street dress out strolling, riding, or quietly going about their business; and an attentive but calm lying dog. Mature trees are visible between the buildings. There is no indication of the presence of railway on this peaceful urban square. The second print, matching the other in authorship, medium, and size, identifies the station as the central building in the other print. From the back of the central pavilion, a passenger train is pulling away from a platform, where a large number of people are standing. On the earthen expanse between the foreground and the train, workmen are engaged in carting or building. A young, well-dressed couple is walking away from the city, preceded by a dachshund and followed by a servant carrying blanket and bundle, as if on a rural outing. Two masons are visible in a building crowned by the miniature tree from the topping-out ceremony, indicating recent completion of the frame. Stones and clumps of grass stress the unpaved nature of this space, which contrasts with the front of the station. This is the unfinished working space where only workmen and those in search of privacy venture. These two prints illustrate how, early in the process of railway construction, distinction was made between finished urban space, "downstream," and unfinished working space, "upstream." Wolfgang Schivelbusch observes that the upstream versus downstream distinction is reflected in the hybrid nature of station architecture, especially that of terminal stations, "half factory, half palace."[86] The stone architectural treatment of the building, facing "downstream," contrasts with the glass-and-iron industrial shed, leading "upstream." The urban side of the railway, its downstream station configuration, has been privileged by more scholarly attention than the upstream peripheral areas, which, except for engineering specifications or large, undifferentiated footprints on maps, are usually ignored. This privileging or "fetishizing of the façade," as characterized by Henri Lefebvre, reflects, until recently, a reluctance to fully examine the true impact of stations on urban environments.[87]

The extent to which a station would penetrate into the city, into the "downstream," developed area was given serious consideration. Was the expense of urban real estate justified to reach as close to the center as possible? How large should that urban area be? If the station was remote from the center, passengers would be willing to go there only for long journeys and would favor local transport for shorter distances.[88] Intense lobbying and political maneuvering accompanied the choice of location for each station. In 1845, Saussay stated that the prosperity of a railway was not dependent on the location of its station.[89] He advocated locating multiple stations around the peripheral areas to spread activity evenly between various neighborhoods.[90] He also recommended that, given the upstream liability of stations, none be implanted within the area where a city was expected to expand. On the other hand, Tourneux, in 1844, saw the primary cause of high costs in the need to bring the large acreage of stations close to large population centers and to have the lines penetrate as far as possible into cities. He advocated the relegation of storage and workshop facilities to less costly peripheral real estate.[91] In Paris, he suggested making use of those large, yet undeveloped parcels within the city limits to accommodate several stations, which is what would eventually take place.

The solution, as it gradually developed, is described by the Ponts et Chaussées and Compagnie de l'Est engineer M. de Bassompièrre-Sewrin, who reported the observations he made on the penetration of railways into cities during an 1854 visit to eight cities of the British Isles. Although decisions on the location of stations had been made in unchartered territory, and the need to penetrate within cities did not surface until later, "by remaining at the city gates, railway stations seemed to provide centers of activity favorable to suburban expansion and were safer for cities."[92]

The city gates mentioned by Bassompièrre were usually part of fortification systems. This was another factor in the reluctance or prohibition against railways penetrating within cities.[93] Both Bassompièrre and Kellett stressed the importance of the economic pressure to get a return on heavy investment in initial legal and administrative expenses, rolling stock, and acquisition of the line as a factor in refraining railways from penetrating within cities when they could have. As in Paris, large areas owned by a small group of landowners would be targeted by the British railway companies for their urban terminals and rail yards. By the time companies could contemplate extensions toward the center, "the original stations on the outskirts were encrusted, like flies in amber, by the rapid extension of building."[94] The need to attract as much of a city's business as possible would nonetheless drive railway companies to attempt reaching as far as possible into cities in order to position themselves closer to the center than their competitors.[95] This competition between companies was greater in London than in Paris: rival companies operated parallel routes in Britain, whereas in France state oversight had distributed the national network into separate regional companies. Perdonnet approved of the Saint-Germain and Versailles lines' decisions to remain peripheral but condoned the British efforts to reach more centrally.[96] The race was on to reduce the distances between cities, the required accommodations of the urban context being simply the cost of access beyond the metropolis. The density of urban real estate offered resistance to the centripetal driving force of the railways. As further penetration became prohibitively costly or nonnegotiable, railway companies resorted to different tactics to attract patronage. Stations were erected to rival others in both size and technical innovations so as to assert corporate power as close to the core of cities as possible. Station facilities were also repeatedly expanded to meet increasing traffic needs.

Real-estate speculation in the area adjacent to the stations closed in at varying speed to weave or repair the urban fabric near tracks and terminals. The initial period of enthusiasm was followed by disenchantment, as station areas did not yield the expected real-estate boom and their neighborhoods lost prestige. The physical impact of the railways and stations on cities would cause tensions with the communities where this new technology was commanding space and requiring adjustments to access routes.

The municipal administrative structures were not equipped to accommodate the powerful companies without conflicts, which usually revolved around the fiscal responsibilities for costly adjustments to the urban physical plant.[97]

Adjustments to Legislation

Legal Status of Railways

The number and scope of railway projects also prompted adjustments to the legislation regulating their approval, construction, and operation. State involvement and legal framework assumed different forms in the countries considered here. In Belgium and Germany, royal or state initiative was predominant. Established in 1830, the Kindgom of Belgium formulated its railway legislation in tandem with national and international policies. Britain exhibited a more reactive adaptation of legislation in response to problematic developments or abuses. The protracted French July Monarchy parliamentary debates led to a complex structure of mixed state and private sponsorship, which was fine-tuned under the more autocratic and decisive Second Empire. Raising the large capital for railway construction led to the widespread speculation that define modern money markets. State control or subsidy attempted to minimize the disastrous effects of abuses and economic crises.[98]

Britain

British railways were built as commercial enterprises driven by competition. As the number of railway concessions submitted to Parliament increased, the government was compelled to refine existing legislation and procedures in order to manage the activity of a growing industry, but it resisted direct control and intervention. The high number of projects submitted caused unwonted stress on the legal system.[99] Regulation ranged from prescribing the application procedure for concessions, to determining which administrative body had oversight over the railways. In order to harness the companies' profit-minded zeal, a series of Acts of Parliament were devised to represent, at least theoretically, the interests of the public.[100] The railways were granted two essential privileges: the corporate form and the power to acquire property by compulsory purchase. Each railway company was incorporated by a private Act of Parliament, which exempted it from the ban on raising capital from more than six people, dating back to 1720. This exemption placed the railways among the small group of large-scale undertakings considered in the public interest.[101] An Act of Parliament was also required to sanction a railway's recourse to eminent domain for the acquisition of land. Otherwise, it was not necessary to bring a proposal before Parliament; but, in practice, both eminent domain and incorporation were needed by most promoters. As Kellett pointed out, there is an inherent paradox in the fact that private capital in a laissez-faire economy relied on a publicly sanctioned corporate form and on compulsory power to acquire private property.[102]

Investors and proprietors, members of a public that included increasingly large numbers of small shareholders, were concerned about swindling and stock manipulation. As of 1836, standing orders were introduced to submit projects to closer scrutiny. As loopholes were devised around these orders, the 1840s Railway Enactments Committees attempted to devise means to ensure that Parliament approved only railways that were viable.[103]

France

In France, the railway system was defined by the Law of 11 June 1842. This July Monarchy legislation was preceded by lengthy debates in parlement and in countless publications, a flurry of activity that a graduate from the Ecole Polytechnique, Pierre-Edmond Teisserenc-de-Bort, aptly summarized: "In France, we are good at voting, but nothing gets built."[104] The law of 1842 determined the respective responsibilities of the state and of the companies that obtained concessions for railway lines. Following the model of the centralized Ponts et Chaussées (Public Works) for the roads, the state would build the infrastructure (including stations) and prepare the rail beds. The companies were to be responsible for laying rails, acquiring rolling stock, and operating the lines. With state oversight and frequent adjustments, this framework remained in place until the nationalization of the railways under the Société Nationale des Chemins de Fer Français (National Society of French Railways, SNCF) in 1937. The law of 1842 also prescribed the configuration of the major lines as a star-shaped system joining all of the country's borders with Paris at its center.[105] In practice, however, given the large influx of capital required for construction, most infrastructure was paid for by companies. The state's financial role remained limited to subsidies, loans, and interest guarantees.[106] The transition from the July Monarchy to the initially more liberal government of Louis-Napoléon Bonaparte in 1848 favored an increase in the role of private companies (a large number of concessions were granted in 1852, after the declaration of the Second Empire).

A decree of 27 March 1852 initiated successive amalgamations of a number of companies into six large companies (Nord, Est, PLM, Ouest, Paris-Orléans, and Midi). The Law of 11 June 1859 divided each of these companies' networks into an old and a new component. The old network included the established lines between large industrial and commercial centers, which offered good prospects of returns on investments. The more recent lines of the new network promised inferior returns but met the state's objective of rail access to less developed areas. On this new network, the state guaranteed a 4 percent return for 50 years, starting from 1 January 1865. The state retained control over the companies by granting concessions for a maximum of 99 years and through stringent clauses in the schedules of conditions known as *cahiers des charges*. The tug of war between the state and the companies would remain a feature of the relationship between the two until World War I.[107]

Prussia

In Prussia, early railways were regulated by a generic law elaborated in 1836. This law provided provisional guidelines for railway incorporation, and it would not be replaced by general incorporation legislation until 1870. Despite its controversial nature, the law took effect on 3 November 1838, and its stringency did not reflect the favorable attitude of some state officials toward railway construction.[108] Legislation was modulated by the personal interventions of the king. Friedrich Wilhelm III approved guidelines for granting furlough to state engineers to work on private lines in 1838; his successor, Friedrich Wilhelm IV, summoned provincial assemblies in 1842, right after the French railway law was passed, to consider a railway aid package. That year marked a change in the Prussian Crown's state policy of aid for the railways.[109] The Law of 3 November 1838 also provided that a state official be appointed at the expense of each stock-granting railway company to ensure compliance with regulations and statutes.[110] Speculation on railway stocks became intense between 1842 and 1844, but was brought under check by a wave of legislation between November 1843 and May 1844, which put a stop to the railway boom.[111] Prussian policy turned increasingly interventionist during the mid-1840s. Despite the organization of railway administrators into a German association and the upheaval of the 1848 revolution, the Prussian railways were unable to militate against the law of 1838, which remained in power until all lines were gradually nationalized.[112]

Expropriation Legislation

Even in the extremely rare cases of rail lines constructed exclusively with private capital, the state was involved because railway construction required expropriation of private real estate. Increased recourse to the principle of eminent domain caused by railway projects prompted at least reexamination, if not revision, of the legislation on expropriation in each of the countries examined here.[113]

Britain

In Britain, the statutory power of purchasing the land parcels listed in an approved private bill enabled, by compulsory procedure, the railways to acquire the property on which the line was to be constructed, as well as a band on either side, called the "limits of deviation." Once the railway bill was passed, no landowner was immune from enforcement, which gave the companies considerable power. On the other hand, respect for private property was guaranteed by common law, except in the case of public necessity, and it was a serious concern for an influential segment of the voting and legislating bodies. Parliament was therefore under pressure to strengthen procedures for the defense of owners' rights. This pressure was increased by the intensity of railway activity in the 1830s and 1840s. Legal adjustments were made as a result of the actions of the Lords' Select Committee on Compensation to the Owners of Real Property in 1845, which examined the financial implications of loss of property and damage to residences. The ensuing Lands Clauses Consolidation Act and the Railway Clauses Consolidation Act, both also of 1845, clarified compensation procedures.[114] Railway companies were not authorized to deal in real estate. As indicated by the Royal Commission of 1867, if railways were compelled to purchase land beyond that required for their lines (as, for instance, a property they bisected), they could sell or lease the surplus land but not develop it.[115]

Numerous pamphlets suggested improvements to the procedures and modes of compensation. For example, E. Dresser Rogers, in 1864, highlighted the notion, already introduced by the Metropolitan Railway Commission in 1846, that a business involves factors other than real estate, and that compensation should take these factors into account.[116] The report of that commission summed up the government position on railway termini within or in the immediate vicinity of the metropolis:

> The actual demolition of Houses, and the occupation by railways of ground now used for other purposes, may, for the most part, be estimated, and compensated to the owners by money; and although cases will undoubtedly arise, in which the injury sustained being less direct, cannot be so estimated, or redressed, these would be for the special consideration of the Legislature, whenever the projects may be brought before it.
>
> But with respect to the general effect produced upon property in and near London by the passage of a railway through it, we are of the opinion, that although in most cases an injurious one, it is not necessarily and invariably so.[117]

France

In France, the Revolution of 1789 was accompanied by confiscation and redistribution of real estate owned by the nobility and the clergy. Despite these actions, which were carried out without legal sanction, the revolutionary government recognized private property as a fundamental right, which could only be removed in exchange for appropriate compensation.[118] The French Constitution and the Law of 22 August 1795 guaranteed the inviolability of property or just compensation for what had to be surrendered for public utility, if authorized by a prescribed legal procedure. This principle was incorporated in the Civil Code of 1804 with further adjustments in 1807, 1810, and 1814.[119] The Law of 7 July 1833 specified the preliminary procedures required to declare eminent domain and entrusted to a jury of experts the responsibility to determine compensation for expropriation.[120]

The first Paris line, the Paris–Saint-Germain, was built under this 1833 law and highlighted its limitations, which prompted its replacement by the Law of 3 May 1841. This new law maintained the jury procedure for determining compensation, but made expropriation conditional upon a law, that is a parliamentary vote, guaranteeing the public utility of the work to be undertaken. The law of 1841 also outlined the 11 steps to be followed in expropriations for major public works.[121] Extension of the 1841 legislation beyond individual properties to areas of insalubrious housing resulted in the Law of 13 April 1850.[122] According to the Railway Law of 11 June 1842, the state would purchase the land required for railway construction.

In 1836, François Bartholony, author of a number of railway pamphlets, bemoaned the speculation surrounding railway projects, the exaggerated prices demanded by landowners, and the long-drawn legal procedures.[123] By the 1860s, compensation above market value had become customary, and expropriation had become the jackpot of real estate.[124] This opportunity to demand high prices for real estate empowered property owners to exert some influence on the location of stations. The relationship between private property and the railways was still in need of clarification by the end of the century, as evidenced by the attorney Amédée Brun's 1898 publication, which outlined the distinction between direct damage with compensation and indirect inconvenience of proximity, which did not get compensated.[125]

Prussia

In Prussia, state expropriation procedures were extended to private railway construction by the railway guidelines published in July 1836, and reiterated in the Railway Law of 3 November 1838.[126] With right of eminent domain for public utility codified by this law, private industry developed railways under state oversight.[127] Expropriations were performed under government administration, which spared companies the speculation and pressure from neighboring owners.[128] The right to expropriate was granted for any project declared to be of public utility, but it was restricted to the land parcels required. Determination of compensation had to be attempted first by mutual consent. In cases where an agreement could not be reached, the railway company requested a legal decision. If the property owner did not find it satisfactory, the company would deposit the amount specified by the legal decision with the tribunal and could then take possession of the property and proceed with the work. These procedures facilitated rapid eviction of tenants even while expropriation conditions were contested by the owner. The writer Friedrich von Reden did, however, indicate in 1845 that full legal possession of railway land had complex implications in the case of rural parcels with land exploitation covenants.[129] Owners had the first right of repurchase if their property was not used or if the project was cancelled. Later in the century, legislations such as the *Enteignungsgesetz* (law on expropriation) of 11 June 1874 and the *Fluchtlinienegesetz* (law on alignment) of 2 July 1875 constituted the beginning of modern planning legislation in Germany.[130]

Belgium

Annexed to France in 1795, the provinces that would become Belgium in 1830 were subject to the Law of 22 August 1795 and subsequent French legislation until 1815. The principle of inalienable property was included in the Belgian Constitution of 7 February 1831. It was restated in the Law of 17 April 1835, which also shortened the procedure to determine the final amount of compensation. Most of the expropriations for initial railway development were performed according to the procedures set by the French laws of 1807 and 1810.[131] The basic principles of this legislation allocated the prerogative to decide on the public good of a specific project to the legislature or the administrative authority. The courts verified that the required procedures had been followed and then enforced the ruling. They also determined the level of compensation but could not be invoked to question the public utility of the decision to expropriate. Procedural details of this legislation were modified by the Laws of 17 April 1835 and 27 May 1870.[132] Most of the expropriations done during the first half of the nineteenth century for new or improved means of communication allowed the neighboring owners to enjoy the betterment value of their property caused by public works. With the requirements to purchase unneeded parcels imposed by landowners or the courts, this betterment value was a substantial factor in the cost overruns for railway land acquisition.[133]

Urban streets were regulated by the Law of 1844, which enabled enforcement of alignment. With increased prosperity came the need to facilitate communications and to improve insalubrious areas. The Law of 1 July 1858 allowed expropriation of properties intended for public highways but did not allow purchase of properties that were in good condition for large-scale clearing.[134] The most important nineteenth-century public works project in Brussels, the vaulting of the Senne River, was possible because of a liberal interpretation of the 1858 law. It also revealed the shortcomings of this legislation. As a consequence, the Law of 15 November 1867 extended expropriation to whole areas for projects intended to improve or beautify cities or towns.[135] In Belgium, the impetus for modifications to the relatively recent French expropriation laws of 1807 and 1810 (except for the procedural modifications of 1835) came not from the railways and street development or reconfiguration, but from the desire to rid cities of their slums and create in the new country an urban landscape worthy of an energetic and ambitious bourgeoisie, not adverse to making profitable investments with the help of local and national authorities.[136]

By providing a legal structure that accommodated expropriations for railways and for urban projects in the four countries considered here, the door was open for greater disruptive incursions into the urban fabric, that of the highways. As the decrease in railway service as both passenger and freight carrier did not signify retreat of the railways from the sizeable real estate they commanded in urban areas, the impact they initiated in the nineteenth century was to be compounded in the twentieth.[137]

International Context

The international implications of rail development, also a common factor, surfaced in the initial debates about railways, even before any construction had been undertaken. This was particularly true for Continental Railways with long-distance lines. These were expected to "transform the relationships between men and things, to bring province closer to province and people to people."[138] Examples of this rhetoric abound as early as the 1830s: "Lack of communications makes the inhabitants of the same country foreign to each other, fosters hatred from province to province and gives birth to wars between nations. Nowadays, war is no longer a need, the principles of law are discussed more effectively, mores are more sociable."[139] Britain's international position was defined more narrowly by its geographical situation as an island, but this did not prevent heavy British financial involvement in railway speculations all over the world, and most notably on the Continent.[140] Also, British engineers, including Stephenson, were enlisted as consultants or staff engineers for Continental projects.

On the domestic front, the railways soon emerged as a centralizing tool for the progressively more finely tuned political strings of nationalism. Beyond the economic and political benefits of centralization, the strategic potential of this new mode of transport was progressively recognized by politicians and heads of state. The strategic role to be played by the railways was acknowledged even before the first tracks were laid down. It was thought that the railways might allow reduction in military forces as it would reduce the expense and time to move them around. It would also provide decisive first-strike advantage in cases of armed conflict.[141]

The initial rhetoric of the iron road envisioned a bridge between nations, leading to shared, peaceful prosperity and cooperation. The reality revealed by armed conflicts was much grimmer. The Franco-Prussian War and World War I defined a strategic role for the railways in a type of warfare that mirrored society's shift from craft to mass production. The convoys of wounded soldiers from the World War I front lines implicated the railways in the collapse of a vision of progress and civilization.

Conclusion

The common aspects of railway development discussed above are not limited to the four countries considered. They also obtain, with varying degrees and modulations, in the particular circumstances of railway construction in other countries.[142] Although initial response to the railways included substantial resistance, this new form of transport soon became recognized as vital for any community and intimately connected with each country's economic, social, and political welfare as well as with its strategic potential. The physical impact of railways on cities also revealed common factors: the construction of stations, especially the terminals in the capitals, on the outskirts of cities; the detrimental impact of stations on the surrounding areas; and the differentiation between the urban façade and the industrial backyard of urban railway facilities. The legal system of each country required some adjustments to establish the legal status of railway companies, promote their financing, regulate their operations, and enable more efficient expropriation procedures for their construction and expansion. These urban, national, and international aspects of initial railway development exhibited common patterns, which, along with the synchronization of clocks to a uniform railway time, transcended political borders.

2

London: Wedges into the Slums

Where are they all gone, sir? Why, some's gone down Whitechapel way; some's gone in the Dials; some's gone to Kentish Town; and some's gone to the Workus. It's awful; and everywhere the rents is run up so, that where we used to pay two-and-six a week we now has to pay four shillings and four-and-six. It's about time now as the world come to an end.[1]

The railways were not the first agents of slum clearance, but in nineteenth-century London they moved in with such force that their intrusion was compared to the invasion of the Huns.[2] The railways demolished much working-class housing to wedge their way toward the City and to expand their facilities.[3] Between 1830 and 1850, 6,000 miles of railway lines were constructed in Great Britain, providing most of the main trunk lines between the major cities. As the British railway historian Jack Simmons has noted, the speed, power, and ruthlessness of this impetus is hard to fully recover today: "Opposition had to be fought, or bribed or persuaded into acquiescence; obstacles of every kind in the railways' path to be removed. In the process a good many amenities were impaired, and much was destroyed."[4]

By 1890, the railways had spent above £100,000,000 ($486.000.000)—more than one-eighth of its capital—on providing terminals, which occupied 8 to 10 percent of urban land. The scope of railway development rivaled that of great estates and contrasted sharply with the predominant patterns of small-scale land speculation and construction. The economic historian John R. Kellett characterizes this as "perhaps the greatest single influence of the period upon the national land market."[5] In London, it is estimated that more than 76,000 people were driven out of their homes owing to railway expansion between 1853 and 1901.[6] The urban historian H. J. Dyos argues that the financial and legal interests of the companies in laying their lines through the "fissures" or "wedges" of poor districts resulted in more substantial damage than would otherwise have been the case.[7] Dyos and Kellett provide solid evidence for the impact of the railways on London housing, but it needs to be considered within the context of a more comprehensive urban reconfiguration. Kellett acknowledges the impact of cheap fares and workmen's trains on the development of the London suburbs in the last two decades of the nineteenth century. This impact affected the geography of suburban development and the social makeup of communities. His claim that "the main physical impact of railways upon the heart of the Victorian city and upon urban property was over by the end of the 1860's" needs to be modulated.[8] Without the extensive slum clearance projects that accompanied railway expansion of the 1860s and continued to resonate in the subsequent decades to increase public consciousness of the plight of the displaced, it is unlikely that workmen's trains and eventually subsidized housing would have evolved to the extent they did. If the rail assault on the urban core began to move underground in 1863, the impact of suburban growth, development of commuting patterns, rise of organized labor, and its corollary of increased wages or social costs to management continue to affect the demands on the urban physical plant even today. The railways were, willy-nilly, gradually enlisted to participate in providing a solution, which, by 1905, had changed London into a metropolis with a commuting working-class population. This chapter focuses on this evolution from population displacement and slum clearance to suburban development in London.

Railway Impact on Housing

Railway Demolitions and Slums: Demolitions and Wedge Strategy

Demolitions for public improvement projects had become widespread with the construction of the canals beginning in the 1750s, but their impact would be magnified by the railways during the next century. When St. Katherine's Dock was built near the Tower of London in 1825, St. Katherine's Hospital with its fifteenth-century chapel was demolished. The strongest protests did not bemoan the loss of architecture but came from the inhabitants of the 1,250 houses that were destroyed. Among railway intrusions into London, the earliest large-scale displacement was caused by the London and Blackwall Railway in 1836, when its extension from Blackwall to the Minories claimed the housing of 2,850 people.[9] To put this and subsequent figures in context, the population of England and Wales grew from under 9 million in 1801, to 18 million in 1851 and 32 million in 1901. London, home to just under a million in 1801, had engulfed surrounding areas to include the 6.5 million of Greater London by 1901. Each decade between the 1861 and 1901 censuses saw a 50 percent growth in London's outer suburbs.

By the 1840s, the attempt to build central rail terminals was proving to be sound competitive strategy, and 19 projects driving into the heart of London were put forward in 1846. The potential impact of these combined bills was such that a Royal Commission was appointed to consolidate the work of the Select Committees considering separate railway bills. The 1846 Metropolitan Railway Commission, also known as the Royal Commission on Metropolis Railway Termini, was to examine how the proposed railways would affect traffic, real estate, and overall urban configuration.[10] It also considered the social impact of expropriation by railways. Charles Pearson, progressive member of the Common Council and solicitor for the Corporation of London, testified eloquently to the commission on the social consequences of population displacement: "A poor man is chained to the spot; he has no leisure to walk, and he has not the money to ride. They are crowded together still more, they are pressed together more densely in a similar description of houses to those which they formerly inhabited."[11] The commission's report acknowledged the immediate hardships caused to lower-class districts and the fact that railways did not facilitate necessary improvements. New streets, improved housing, drainage, and ventilation tended to be obstructed by a railway. The commission also considered the impact on adjacent businesses, "especially trades of sound character, and rooted as it were, to a spot, no reasonable compensation does pay them. . . . With regard to parties on the opposite side of the street, or in the neighbourhood, whose property is not touched, they do not get paid, and their trade is damaged to a great extent by sweeping away their customers."[12] The commission was thus recognizing diverse forms of social impact. Its recommendations stressed the importance of considering the railways as part of an overall plan for the metropolitan area. Its most lasting impact was the establishment of a central exclusion zone not to be penetrated by railways.[13]

Thoughtful as it was, the commission's report did not prevent the surge of metropolitan railway construction that took place between 1859 and 1867 and displaced an estimated 38,000 Londoners, or between 1.1 and 1.5 percent of the city's population.[14] One of the strategies developed by the railway companies in the 1830s to avoid resistance from property owners was to seek large land holdings belonging to small numbers of proprietors, preferably in the poorest districts.[15] Until the 1870s, Select Committees responsible for approving railway bills seemed ready to accept unquestioned the statements of promoters that the displaced would cause no difficulty when the proposed construction claimed slum areas rather than industrial land. In a society where the lower classes had no political representation, housing needs did not warrant attention as long as they remained invisible. If property owners were compensated as provided by law and even, in some cases, more generously, weekly tenants were not. Only those in possession of a lease were entitled to making claims. In 1861 Lord Derby stated that the Metropolitan Railway Bill had received no opposition because "there was not a single person of sufficient means to petition against it."[16] In some cases, railway companies resorted to the expedient of paying residents, who often would be willing to settle for a modest sum or payment of rent arrears. Dyos interprets the readiness of tenants to accept such modest cash payments, which the companies considered more than adequate, as an indication of the degree of poverty, not of the adequacy of compensation.[17]

Some Specific Causes of Slum Development

Conditions such as overcrowding, health hazards, or poor physical status of structures might cause an area to be labeled a slum, but the designation remained subjective in the absence of legal definition for the term.[18] Beyond ease of purchase from a limited number of owners and appropriate location, the land-leasing pattern in London contributed to making some areas more vulnerable to railway acquisition. Most of London had been developed over the preceding two centuries on land made available on long-term leases (usually for 99 years). Subleases were granted for shorter periods in a process that could be repeated by the sublessee, leading to a complicated legal framework of land and property use. With expiring lease terms, no reasonable profit could be expected for investment in building or maintenance. Slum dwellers were frequently third- or fourth-generation occupants in hand-me-down space not intended for current use. If first-generation compliance with building regulations had been minimal or nonexistent, conditions could deteriorate rapidly with intensive use and lax maintenance. As the last phase in a "cycle of human occupation," which could run from "meadow to slum in a single generation," the slum could only be followed by a clean sweep.[19]

Some physical conditions, such as poor drainage, isolation, and proximity to waste- or odor-producing industries, predisposed certain areas to becoming slums. Dead ends and back alleys were favored by criminals "whose professional requirements were isolation, an entrance that could be watched, and a back exit kept exclusively for the getaway."[20] Conditions encouraging deterioration could occur in areas isolated by docks, canals, rail lines, or streets, so aptly described by Dyos as gangrene-causing "tourniquets."[21] Charles Booth described crossing the "barrier formed by the Great Eastern Railway" as "pass[ing] into another world."[22] By the

1860s, areas in close proximity of terminals or rail lines, even if developed after the coming of the railways, could have deteriorated enough to provide prime terrain for further railway expansion.

Indirect causes of deterioration included displacement of evicted tenants into already crowded areas. A long chain reaction of displacements set in as improvements, such as docks, railways, and streets, were being made to accommodate the increased traffic of prosperity. If clearing the slums was part of the implicit or explicit agenda of transportation infrastructure development, the process aggravated conditions as the supply of lower-class housing diminished either in number or in condition.

From *Punch* to Dickens, anecdotal material on dire housing conditions is abundant.[23] Publications on urban blight are attributable less to scientific curiosity than to a concern about the danger caused by this condition "on the doorsteps of the respectable classes in the 1840s."[24] Actual data are harder to come by. Journalists' figures often reflect the heat of their argument and need to be taken cautiously. As Dyos indicates, the annals of the London poor are buried deep.[25] He also considers that figures used by Parliament were more a "challenge to government to produce better ones than an accurate testimony of verified facts."[26] In 1851, Charles Pearson already mentioned the unreliability of census data, with discrepancy between the active population and night residents.[27] The *Transactions of the National Association for the Promotion of Social Science* reports 20,000 people dislodged by metropolitan engineering projects, including railways, before 1864. *The Builder* mentions 50,000 displaced by 1867.[28] Such figures are conservative. Demolition statements, which were required from railway companies as of 1853, were also considered to yield questionable figures.[29] Useful in examining the impact of railways on residential areas is the study of London poverty by Charles Booth (1840–1916). As a businessman who refused to believe that the conditions of the London poor were as dire as depicted, Booth set out to investigate them. Booth and his team gathered field work data over the whole metropolis. The results of these investigations were published between 1889 and 1904 in 17 volumes, where he acknowledged that the situation was actually worse than he had assumed. The maps accompanying his publications invariably show areas of concern in the vicinity of railway terminals. Although prepared a generation after the most intense wave of displacements, the maps illustrate their lasting impact in terminal areas[30] (see Figure 3.1).

Public Opinion and the Railways' Positive Urban Sanitation Role

Public opinion was alerted to the plight of displaced inhabitants as early as the 1840s by concerned observers and journalists. In an article titled "Attila in London," Charles Dickens protested against demolitions with characteristic poignancy: "Pigsties, dung-heaps, dogs, children, and costermongers' refuse, jammed together into a heterogeneous and inextricably confused mass, fringe all the squalid homes . . . [But] standing with your back to the entrance of any of these courts, you look far away across the line of railways over a vast and desolate waste."[31]

In *Dombey and Son,* published in 1848, Dickens depicted the assault on north London as "the first shock of a great earthquake [that] had just . . . rent the whole neighborhood to its centre."[32] The "Journeyman Engineer" Thomas Wright described the plight of an evicted working-class family in his 1868 narrative, *The Great Unwashed.*[33] Pamphlet literature also contributed to and reflected increased public awareness of slums and railway displacements.[34] George Godwin, editor of *The Builder,* published an enthusiastic endorsement of the railways in 1837, but by 1845 he advocated more 'doing' and less talking for rehousing the displaced.[35] His appeals, repeated in 1854 and 1864, echoed in much contemporary press.[36] During the Lords' Debate on Metropolitan Railways in February 1861, such prominent figures as Lord Derby, Lord Shaftesbury, and the bishop of London spoke on the impact of street projects and railway demolitions on displaced populations seeking refuge in already congested areas. Debates in Parliament used projected demolition figures to advocate greater state control over railway development.[37] Only in the 1860s, when a large number of projects were carried out and reporting on them increased, did the public begin to respond. Between 1859 and 1867, the railways' role in the destruction of working-class housing drew more public attention than the engineering exploits, which had previously been the stock-in-trade of most publications about railways. Also, the considerable demolitions undertaken in Haussmann's Paris as of 1853 were reported in the British press, although accounts of those spectacular public works tended to leave out their social implications when they crossed the Channel.[38]

Despite greater public exposure of the impact of railways, the laissez-faire had strong support among the powerful railway companies, public opinion, and politicians. The ruling classes saw the housing conditions of the poor as reflecting their debased nature. The assumption that the displaced poor simply moved to the suburbs allowed complacent inaction. This attitude would have been challenged by a closer, honest examination of the situation, but, as Dyos demonstrated, blindness to these issues existed even on the part of institutions and individuals looking into them.[39] He also pointed out that the various reports published in *Punch* on the tightening noose of the railways around St. Paul's in the early 1860s reflected greater concern for the impact on the City's architecture than for the plight of the displaced.[40]

Dyos suggests that, given the abundance of public information, the permissiveness about slum destruction was deliberate on the part of the authorities.[41] Slum ownership was a real-estate investment, which was expected to provide returns just as any other commodity. As middle-class investments shifted toward the suburbs, they also had an impact on the areas left behind. The large houses vacated by the well-to-do were subdivided to maintain profitability, thereby ensuring more rapid deterioration. The incision of the railways would clear the urban abscesses and benefit everybody; it was part of the cycle of development. As *The Times* reported in 1861, "As we cut nicks through our woods, and roads through our forests, so it should be our policy to divide these thick jungles of crime and misery. Much has already been done to tempt these people to purer air and better habits. Thousands of cottages are springing up yearly in the suburbs."[42]The role of the railways in slum demolitions was welcome, and witnesses were more aware of the fact that slums were being cleared than they were of the plight of the displaced.[43] *The Times* editorials of the early 1860s reflected the callous attitude resulting from laissez-faire policies and practices:

> If the working people of the city are compelled to find room at a greater distance from their work, there will be builders and speculators ready to supply their wants. This is not an affair for railway companies. . . . Government has nothing to do with providing dwellings for the poor, and has no more right to impose an obligation of this sort on railways than anybody else who pulls down a dwelling-house to build something else—a church, for example—in its place. The interference is both idle and contrary to the usages of this country. It can end in no good. We accept railways with their consequences, and we don't think the worse of them for ventilating the City of London. . . . You can never make these wretched alleys really habitable, do what you will; but bring a railway to them, and the whole problem is solved.[44]

A Slow Path toward Solutions

Social and Real-Estate Factors

During the railway construction boom of the 1860s, it was assumed that those displaced could take care of themselves and take advantage of the "thousands of cottages [which were] springing up yearly in the suburbs."[45] This callousness, which left the displaced poor to their own devices, also ignored the fact that slums were not mere physical entities. Social ties, relationships, and support systems existed in these communities.[46] Slums were not restricted to one location but distributed all over the metropolis, where the poorer districts had close economic ties with the more well-to-do areas nearby.[47] Another crucial fact, already pointed out by Pearson in 1846, continued to be overlooked: the poor did not remain in London by choice; they remained to be within reach of the work they needed to survive, in order to be "near their bread."[48] In the absence of cheap, dependable transportation to and from the suburbs, walking distance from casual or regular employment formed the radius of the poor's habitable circle: "I might as well go to America as go to the suburbs," stated a workman in 1882.[49] In 1866, about 680,000 workers depended on casual labor in central London alone.[50] The limitation imposed by distance from work forced the displaced urban poor to crowd into already severely overpopulated areas. The recognition of this fact was crucial to enable change.

Real-estate trends also aggravated the housing situation of the London poor. After 1861, metropolitan ground rents rose as more houses were converted into offices or warehouses. Real-estate market forces placed the working man out of competition for decreasing residential space. Besides the inability to obtain land, rise in building costs and tightening of building regulations made it difficult for housing companies seeking a 3 to 5 percent dividend to build affordable working-class housing. Also, land within proximity of railways could, in some cases, increase in value beyond reach of the working class due to convenient access or other amenities.[51]

Demolitions, the social activist William Denton pointed out in his *Observations on the Displacement of the Poor*, might find favor with local authorities, who welcomed the increase in ratable values caused by shifts in land use and the decrease in poor relief.[52] On the other hand, demolitions reduced the incomes of parishes and District Boards of Works, placing extra burden on other ratepayers, an argument that was used against some projects but was seldom invoked in the case of poor districts. Railways were not alone in causing house demolitions; some commercial and public works, such as streets and schools, also claimed housing districts.[53] Considerable amount of slum clearance was also caused, for instance, by the building of the West End shopping district toward the end of the century.[54] These projects compounded the problem by failing to provide rehousing as well. The Metropolitan Board of Works (MBW) provided rehousing for only 13 out of the 50 improvement projects it carried out.[55]

Advocacy and Demolition Statements

The poor working man's helplessness in making his housing needs recognized and supported did not originate from flawed genetics or behavior but was caused by circumstances he could not control and had no agency to influence. The people displaced by the railways had no political voice. An Evicted Tenants' Aid Association originated in the 1860s with MPs and clergymen among its ranks.[56] Their delegation found a receptive ear in the prime minister at the time, Lord Derby, on the issue of deteriorating urban living conditions caused by multiple railway projects.[57] Government was, however, not in a position to control a situation caused by private companies, with powerful connections, in a laissez-faire political environment. In this context, state and local authorities were slow to understand that they had a responsibility to remedy this situation. As early as 1853, the philanthropic member of Parliament, the Earl of Shaftesbury, chaired a committee to consider the financial, housing, and additional impacts of taking working-class housing.[58] Lord Shaftesbury did not necessarily see the effects of clearance as deleterious; he saw benefit in having those displaced move to the suburbs, into "new and better tenements."[59] He was, however, instrumental in having the House of Lords accept a standing order (S.O. 191), which mandated the inclusion of demolition statements in the documentation provided before the first reading for proposed railway bills as of 1853. These statements were required to list the properties to be demolished and their residents. They were mandatory for bills that necessitated the demolition of 30 or more houses located in the same parish and inhabited by members of the "labouring classes."[60] The initial committee recommendations also included that, for the 30 houses, "adequate provision be made by the undertakers within three years and within a convenient distance," but this wording did not remain in the standing order.[61] Promoters were also required to indicate what steps were planned to remedy the situation caused by the demolition and displacement. The promoters' obligation was limited to supplying the information, and enforcement was nonexistent.

Demolition statements were inaccurate. As Dyos indicated, their apparent meticulousness was deceptive and no checking mechanism existed as part of the procedures for deposit of private bills. Also, practice varied among promoters. Some statements included all the property potentially affected, although the actual demolitions would only affect between a third and a fifth of the area. Others listed only the demolitions actually intended, but the method selected was not always explicitly stated or inferable. In addition, the compiling of these statements relied on flawed data and procedures. The data were derived from the railway bill's Books of Reference, which listed owners, lessees, and occupiers for the properties within the boundaries of the proposed project but did not include any information about their "family members, lodgers and casual occupiers."[62] Estimates derived from these statements were therefore very conservative but nonetheless indicative of substantial impact. Flawed as they were, demolition statements provided some evidence to those concerned about the displaced poor. More recent estimates state that 69 separately approved schemes involved the displacement of more than 76,000 people between 1853 and 1901, with 51 of these schemes before 1885 displacing 56,000 people. A relatively short period of peak activity between 1859 and 1867 displaced 37,000 people, with 70 percent of total activity taking place between 1859 and 1879.[63]

Starting in 1874, clauses began to be inserted in railway bills requiring rehousing of the displaced listed in demolition statements. The standing order's lack of enforcement power had not remained unnoticed. Some statements prior to 1874 would even state that they did not expect difficulty in relocating the displaced to "suburban parts of the Metropolis not at present overcrowded with houses and population."[64] In 1874, the council of the Charity Organization Society formed a committee, chaired by the Lord Mayor, to attempt to find solutions to the working-class housing problems. Thanks to lobbying and support from House members, the committee's work yielded new standing orders that year, which required companies to give eight weeks' notice for evictions and to provide replacement housing.[65]

The plight of the displaced then began to receive more attention from philanthropists and other concerned influential parties, who advocated that the promoters assume responsibility for rehousing those whose homes they destroyed. Placing such demands on the railway companies, which were adept at protesting any kind of state interference in their affairs, did not result in their building satisfactory accommodations, even when required by law. Also, even when abided by, legal provisions did not stipulate equitable treatment of owners and occupants. Between 1874 and 1885, companies became creative, acquiring the land prior to introducing bills or purchasing and emptying properties of residents before 15 December, the date when the inhabitants were counted. The companies could also make private agreements with landlords to clear the property of tenants for them.[66] In some cases, projects were broken down into segments involving fewer than 30 houses. One of the most devious evasive tactics was the Metropolitan Railway's 1859 purchase and conversion of housing units, a court in St. Bartholomew, to demonstrate its ability to rehouse those it displaced and reduce objection to its proposed scheme. Two years later, after the bill had been passed, the rehoused tenants were evicted and the buildings converted into warehouses.[67]

The 1882 report of the Select Committee on Artizans' and Labourers' Dwellings and the Royal Commission on the Housing of the Working Classes (1884–1885) both highlighted the inadequacy of the demolition statement process. No railway company had rehoused those it had displaced before 1885.[68] Measures to remedy the railway companies' tactics were included in standing order 184, which recommended gradual clearance and local and simultaneous rehousing of the displaced. It also gave local authorities the responsibility for long-term monitoring. Loopholes were thus addressed in 1885, but enforcement was not uniform by the end of the century. For instance, the documents for the Manchester, Sheffield, and Lincolnshire Railway's extension to Marylebone Station during 1893–97 listed 4,448 persons to be displaced, who were allegedly rehoused. When, under its new name, the Great Central Railway obtained powers to make enlargements at Marylebone in 1898, the 1,750 persons listed on the project's demolition statement crowded into the neighboring Lisson Grove slum area because the company had not provided a timely rehousing plan.[69]

Even when enforced after 1885, rehousing requirements did not help those who needed it, for accommodations for the displaced were not made available before demolitions. Because of the time elapsed between eviction and availability of replacement housing, the occupants of the new housing were usually not those who had been displaced. Also, in the absence of subsidy for this housing, London market forces could drive rents beyond the means of the evicted, ensuring social sanitizing of the new housing units.[70] In 1905, after some railway rehousing had been carried out, the Select Committee on Workmen's Trains recommended exonerating railway companies from rehousing in exchange for fare concessions that facilitated suburban migration.[71] Charles Booth, writing in 1901, acknowledged the failure of rehousing and pointed to a more appropriate role to be played by the railways: "It is found that the people actually displaced never do occupy the houses built for them; and as it only touches those who require Parliamentary powers of purchase, it presses principally upon the railways, whose projects and extensions, as facilitating the spread of population over a large area, rather deserve encouragement."[72]

Other Measures

The aggravation of working-class living conditions caused by railway demolitions had led to the appointment in 1866 of a committee by the Department of Economy and Trade of the National Association for the Promotion of Social Sciences, to be chaired by the progressive and the then-retired sanitation commissioner Edwin Chadwick.[73] The committee's work led to the McCullagh Torrens original bill to promote slum clearance. The resulting Torrens Act (1868), which gave local authorities the power to demolish individual insanitary houses, was followed seven years later by the Cross Act (1875), which expanded the power of the Torrens Act to larger areas.[74] Local medical officers of health were charged with recommending demolitions of insanitary houses to the vestries. They were reluctant to do so because they understood that further demolitions would aggravate the problem rather than bring remedy. Also, the number of officers was insufficient to keep pace with the increasing population.[75] The implementation of other forms of housing legislation, such as progressively more stringent building codes, was also a double-edged sword with the potential to aggravate overcrowding.[76]

Not directly related to railway displacements, philanthropic endeavors to provide housing for the dispossessed were limited in scope and did not address the magnitude of the problem. These efforts included the projects underwritten by George Peabody (and, after 1869, the Peabody Trust) or sponsored by Octavia Hill and the work of other charitable bodies. They did not help those who needed it most, those who could not afford the rents in model housing. Also, such housing might come with stringent regulations, which the slum dweller might find coercive.[77] New housing might attempt to reshape the dwelling patterns and habits of its inhabitants, and such adjustments might require education or at least a change of mind-set as suggested in 1886 by Joseph Corbett, sanitary engineer and architect:

> Thanks to the rapid progress of national education in the widest sense of the term, the difficulties formerly arising from the miserable ignorance and apathy of the poorer classes are rapidly passing away; and now that third-class railway carriages are cushioned, and picture galleries opened freely to the masses, without receiving any damage, it is safe and practicable to provide in even the smallest dwellings various fittings, promoting health, economy, and comfort, which some years ago would not have been duly appreciated, or even tolerated, by the poorer classes.[78]

Up to the 1880s, housing was seen not as a separate issue but as a component in public health problems, which included water, sanitation, lack of ventilation, and disease-breeding promiscuity. These problems attracted more attention than overcrowding until the last two decades of the century. These conditions improved over the century, whereas overcrowding became more severe until at least 1891. The extent of one-room living even among regularly employed workers was not common public knowledge until the findings of the 1884–85 Royal Commission on the Housing of the Working Classes. Figures for person-to-house density showed an increase from 7.03 in 1801 to 8.02 in 1896.[79] Recognition of the housing problem as a discrete issue was necessary for government to assume a role and eventually allocate subsidy.

Railways and Commuters

The 1882 report of the Select Committee on Artizans' and Labourers' Dwellings and the Royal Commission on the Housing of the Working Classes of 1884–85, which encouraged enforcement of rehousing provisions, also began to present cheap transport as a complementary rather than alternate method of dealing with the working-class housing problem.[80] Suburban growth remained connected to the social and economic conditions of the urban area it expanded.[81] The Georgian model of town planning facilitated a form of social segregation, with upper-class residences on squares and main streets, middle-class dwellings on back streets, and the lower-class courts and alleys out of sight.[82] Suburban retreat from this diverse and promiscuous city housing pattern was taking place before the Victorian era and was primarily a prerogative of the well-to-do.[83] Middle-class migration began and continued through the Victorian era as improved transport afforded greater mobility and urban conditions worsened. For the populations displaced by the railways, slum conditions were a more powerful incentive than the health, moral, and aesthetic ideals driving the middle class out of the city. Housing requirements for the working class called for affordable prices within manageable distance from place of work. As mentioned earlier, it became increasingly difficult for the landowners, investors, and builders of the traditional London building industry to erect and manage working-class housing profitably.[84] By the end of the nineteenth century, suburban migration was deliberately encouraged as the most promising solution to the working-class housing problem. This population migration would put an end to the social contacts between the different classes, which had taken place in the inner city. The suburbs would gather together families of comparable means in spatially discrete developments, which fostered social homogeneity. The railways were key players in this segregation process.

The extensive demolitions of the 1860s hastened the adoption of workmen's fares in London. These fares had been acquiring favor by the late 1850s, and by the 1860s suburban lines began to be considered as promising investments. Many of the new schemes proposed for London in that decade were for suburban lines. Cheap train fares had appeal for a number of constituencies. The displaced workers considered it fair to receive something in return from the companies that destroyed their homes. Working men had called the railways to task: "Why don't they build us a great village or town out Epping Way . . . and then let the railways bring us backwards and forwards for a trifle? They take our homes; let them give us something in return."[85] Those concerned with urban conditions saw that cheap train fares had potential for improving slum conditions. The railway companies saw a smaller portion of their profits evaporate in reduced fares than in replacement housing. Parliament, unwilling to restrict economic activity, saw the fares as the expedient solution, easier to legislate than having to fund allocations for building housing. Workers' trains were therefore the most suitable solution and the one adopted first.

In 1860, the London, Chatham and Dover Railway was required to offer workmen's fares, as were most of the companies submitting bills to build or expand lines into London after that date.[86] Some, however, escaped this requirement.[87] The Cheap Trains Act of 1883 increased the availability of workmen's fares by doing away with passenger duty on all fares at a penny a mile or lower. It also gave the Board of Trade the authority to require companies to offer workmen's fares. By the end of the century, workmen's trains had encouraged a huge migration toward working-class settlements in northeast London, Essex, and, to a lesser extent, south London.

Suburban railway lines went hand-in-hand with land speculation, and the building of estates for the middle class followed an expanding course along the lines. Development was encouraged by issuing free railway passes during the 1850s and 1860s for persons intending to build houses in designated areas.[88] Development of suburbs for lower-income commuters followed a different pattern. Once the removal of working-class families to the suburbs had been recognized as the most realistic solution to the housing problem, the provision of adequate service became a concern. The more-or-less voluntary compliance with the Cheap Trains Act of 1883 did not constitute an obligation for companies to build train lines where there were no customers. On the other hand, the extreme dependence on train conveyance to get to work prevented lower-class workers from settling in areas where there were no trains, thus creating demand for new lines.[89] This resulted in compact working-class suburban development along the lines that provided the most workers' trains. In addition, some inner suburban zones became accessible by tram or bus, which competed with the railways; for every passenger on the urban railways, two rode the horse-tram or omnibus.[90] The economist John R. Kellett estimated that, at the turn of the century, 250,000 people commuted by rail out of a population of close to 6.5 million.[91]

In 1905, the Royal Commission on the Means of Locomotion and Transport in London opened its report with a strong acknowledgment of the shift to a commuting population:

One of the most important features of the problem of London locomotion is the movement of the population from the suburbs towards the centre every morning and back again in the afternoon and evening, so that, in any general examination of the means of locomotion and transport required to meet the wants of the public, the area taken into consideration must include the districts in which persons dwell, who, for the purpose of their work or business, move every day into and out of the central portions of the Metropolis, and must be wider than that contained in the Administrative County of London.[92]

Beyond advocating encouragement for the railways to provide cheap transport, Booth also pointed to the interconnection between the means of communication available and the movement of people to affordable housing, "gathering its strength from overcrowding at the centre, aggravated by demolitions, . . . depend[ing] upon motives which are common to all classes, whatever may be the circumstances of their lives, in the pursuit of happiness, comfort and health."[93]

Railways and Housing in Paris, Berlin, and Brussels

In Paris, as in London, the railways adopted a strategy of acquiring large tracts of land. They purchased properties reclaimed from religious orders during the Revolution, where initial attempts at development had been unsuccessful, as, for instance, the Quartier de l'Europe and the Faubourg Poissonnière.[94] Like the London slum real estate, the land had few owners; but, unlike London, it was not developed. Population displacement did occur as a result of Haussmann's reconfiguration of the city during the Second Empire, but the railways did not contribute significantly to that phenomenon. Haussmann's projects did, however, attract large numbers of immigrants, who came from the provinces to meet increased labor needs in the capital.[95] To the extent that the railways facilitated that transit, they did contribute to population displacement, though not by their construction but by the services they provided. The plan for a rail line to the Halles Centrales (central market) could have compounded the effect of that large urban renewal venture, which was responsible for the demolition of a large number of houses, but the rail component of the project was not implemented.[96] The large acreage of rail facilities developed in the Battignoles, La Chapelle, and La Villette districts had configuring power on these suburbs, which were annexed to the city in 1860. The presence of rail in these peripheral areas affected the socioeconomic level of their development, but it did not contribute to the kind of overcrowding and aggravation of slum conditions that occurred in London.

As for suburban rail services, yearly and six-month season passes were introduced in France as of 1850 on the Paris–Saint-Germain and Paris–Versailles (right bank) lines, emulating the British practice for developing districts. As mentioned in Chapter 5, the lion's share of suburban rail activity took place through the Gare Saint-Lazare, which contributed to an ongoing displacement of activity toward the northwest of the city. However, when the Paris-Vincennes line opened in 1859, its trains included, at the request of the emperor, third-class carriages, which would enable workers to settle in the less densely populated eastern part of the city and commute to work in the center.[97] Dormitory communities developed outside of the city along the rail lines, where population exhibited substantial growth.

In Berlin, as mentioned in Chapter 7, the large size of the city and the location of stations outside of the inhabited areas accounted for minimal impact of railway implantation on residential areas. For the construction of the western loop of the second belt line around the city, put in service between 1871 and 1877 as a double-track line, the authorities purchased land for a four-track line. This was intended to provide the kind of transit services that would encourage working-class settlement southwest of the city.[98] The years of prosperity after victory in the Franco-Prussian War attracted many working-class immigrants to the city, which aggravated housing shortages. In 1893, the British city planner Arthur Cawston commented that there were no slums in Berlin; poverty did exist, but the filth characteristic of London or Paris slums was absent.[99] The infamous *Mietskasernen* (rental barracks) of the Prussian capital included substandard housing with unheated, below-ground, or attic spaces in poorly lit and ventilated courtyards. Some of them, following industry that settled near rail lines, were in close proximity to the railways, but these housing conditions could not be attributed to the railways.[100]

In Brussels, the impact of the nineteenth-century railways was felt primarily outside the central pentagonal area delimited by the fourteenth-century fortifications and did not cause significant population displacement. The Senne River vaulting project, begun in 1867, brought to the fore the insalubrious housing conditions of the working class. Slum clearing was part of the agenda for this project, as well as for the numerous plans for a direct rail connection between the capital's two main stations, north and south of the pentagon. Legislation was passed in 1844, 1858, and 1867 to facilitate urban sanitation.[101] The issue of workers' housing in Brussels was the object of a report by Burgomaster Buls, published in the 1891 *Bulletin Communal*. Buls highlighted the severity of the problem, the inadequacy of measures taken so far, and workers' preference, as in London, for remaining close to their work in the city. He added that the city poor were reluctant to move outside the city limits and lose their right to municipal public assistance, which was considerably less developed and less substantial in the outlying communities.[102] According to Buls, only 5 to 6 percent of inhabitants displaced in Brussels opted to settle in the suburbs. In the last quarter of the nineteenth century, real-estate investments were increasingly successful, and for landlords, workers' housing constituted conservative long-term secure investments. Buls had a great deal of sympathy for the displaced poor and for displaced businesses, which never returned after improvement projects. He was opposed to the construction of workers' barracks and recommended subsidy for workers' houses with garden plots, built in the outlying communities, accessible by cheap public transportation, and where residents would remain eligible for the same municipal poor relief as in the city. As examined in Chapter 8, large-scale urban reconfiguration would take place in the twentieth century, between 1911 and 1952, for the construction of the rail connection between Brussels' main stations. Some lower-class residential areas were eradicated, and Buls' recommendations for working-class housing were widely implemented, with significant political consequences.

As this brief summary indicates, the impact of railways on housing in Paris, Berlin, and Brussels did not assume the same intensity as it did in London. Brussels experienced a substantial railway-related population displacement in the early decades of the twentieth century, somewhat mitigated by access to commuting, housing subsidy, socialist political advocacy, and a more developed social safety net.

3

London: The Euston Road Terminals

The three main-line terminals north of Euston Road—the Euston, King's Cross, and St. Pancras stations—create the densest cluster among the 15 terminals constructed around London by the end of the nineteenth century. Their north London location is near the natural Fleet River and the man-made Regent's Canal. With their dependencies they claim more than 300 acres north of Euston Road.[1] They were the result of three consecutive and progressively more invasive campaigns of railway implantation and impact as they were built in a gradually more developed area north of central London. During the 40 years spanning the construction of these three terminals, the surrounding areas became part of the metropolis. Euston was built among fields. King's Cross cleared an "awful rookery"; rubbed elbows with gas works or tile kilns; and replaced a smallpox-and-fever hospital, a facility relegated owing to danger of contagion to the outskirts of habitation.[2] St. Pancras, built as the public and the authorities were becoming aware of, if not sensitive to, the disastrous human cost of displacements, nonetheless continued the favored pattern of thrusting rail lines through areas inhabited by the poor, which were easily obtainable from a small number of landowners. These large estates, which had survived undivided until the nineteenth century, simplified the acquisition of the land needed for railway projects.[3]

Where upper-scale development had already taken place, owners and managers of estates were careful to stay away from railway construction or insisted on conditions that would minimize the impact of the line on their property.[4] Measures were taken to keep street traffic to the stations out of exclusive residential areas. Gates were erected at the northern entrance to Bloomsbury to deviate carts, carriages, and public transport out of the estate during the day and all traffic at night.[5] More vulnerable were the areas devoted to lower-class housing, where owners were equally well or better served by selling land to the railway companies than by continuing to collect ground rent. As those displaced by railway construction began to find solutions in subsidized housing and affordable transportation, the physical configuration of the metropolitan area was also undergoing adjustments. This chapter focuses the examination of railway impact outlined in Chapter 2 on the area of the three Euston Road terminals, one of the densest railway landscapes in London. A walk in this area reveals the inescapable presence of the railways interwoven with some remnants of surviving lower-class housing or their twentieth-century alternatives. This walk through Camden's industrial landscape could easily miss the handful of structures remaining from Agar Town, one of the communities eradicated by the Midland Railway Company. With a recent study as guidebook, a closer examination sets an agenda for further investigation on the nature of the demolished urban fabric in areas claimed by railway expansion.

From the New Road to the Borough of Camden

In the mid-eighteenth century, Oxford Street was London's northernmost east-west road, and there was no direct connection between the parishes of Paddington and Islington. Some Middlesex property owners proposed a road that would intersect the northern access roads and go from Paddington to Marylebone, Tottenham Court, Battle Bridge (King's Cross), and on to Islington and Old Street. This road would open communication between east and west, divert cattle from Oxford Road and Holborn on the way to Smithfield Market, and provide a strategic loop around the city. This first city bypass was put into use in September 1756 and had its first omnibus on 4 July 1829.[6] On this road, Euston Square was built in 1827 and named after the ground landlords, the Earls of Euston. The New Road became Euston Road in 1857.[7]

The main northern turnpikes were supplemented by new roads in the 1820s, with Caledonian Road, Camden Road, and Finchley Road providing access to the west of the City and encouraging northern development. When the North London Railway line was constructed in 1850, it enclosed a developed area.[8] The former Borough of St. Pancras, which covered land mostly north but also south of Euston Road, included the localities of Camden Town, Chalk Farm, Kentish Town, and Somers Town. Since 1965, it has been part of the London Borough of Camden.

The geographical configuration of a south-southeast Fleet River valley created an approach to the metropolis, which the three main-line railways followed to a flat clay area of the middle valley, where they established their terminals in close proximity to each other.[9] In order to reach Euston Road, the three stations required engineering know-how to compensate for the geographical accidents of the terrain. The lines came toward London from the chalky high ground of the Chiltern Hills toward the gravel and sand of the Northern Heights. An inclined plane and a canal bridge brought the London and Birmingham Railway to the Euston Grove terminal in 1837. The Great Northern Railway (GNR), the fifth line into London, reached King's Cross Station in 1852 by tunnel under the Regent's Canal. This increased the line's climb out of the valley to a grade of one in 107, which, unlike those of the 1830s, the locomotives of the 1850s were capable of ascending. And the Midland Railway, after reaching London first on the London and North Western and later on the Great Northern lines, opted to build its own access to Euston Road in 1863. The St. Pancras terminal is reached by an elevated line over the canal and into the raised station.[10]

The text accompanying John Bourne's prints of the London and Birmingham Railway published in 1839 describes the growth of the suburbs and the incorporation of detached villages in the metropolis. The almost five miles from Highgate Hill to Tavistock Square are now fully developed and "the valuable property of the railway has, since that time, come into parochial assessment, and thereby greatly augmented the rental of the parish."[11] In 1854, the Frenchman de Bassompièrre-Sewrin provided an accurate description of the railways north of London:

> The three main lines which reach London on the left bank of the Thames are the Great Western, the London and North Western and the Great Northern. The colossal stations which the companies have built for these main trunk lines of the English network are located at the limit of the agglomeration of squares and new districts which constitute the new London. It would not be possible for the companies I have just mentioned to have the heads of their lines step closer in toward the City, hence their decision to settle permanently in their present location.[12]

The short-lived 1866 publication *The Working Man* gives a vivid account of the Midland Railway's irruption in the area and the destruction of Somers Town and Agar Town. The author estimates that 32,000 people were turned out of their homes, "the population of six fair-sized provincial towns":

> This district has been a stronghold for the working man; rents have been proportionately low, and the houses small—hence, the working classes have sought it for their home; . . . the thin end—nay, the very broad end—of the wedge was inserted by the Imperial Gas Company a few years ago, who increased their works by making a great sweep, and erecting those vast gasholders. Then the Midland Railway encroached farther north; the Bass's large stores were erected; and inch by inch the dweller has been beaten back, till the Midland Railway Company makes its grand assault, storms the place, and spares nothing; for it is not to be expected that home and hearth can be

studied, when consecrated ground is disturbed, and the rest of the dead invaded by the pick and shovel of the navvy. . . .

Somers Town partly taken, and Agar Town demolished, where are our working classes to dwell? Model lodging-houses have been erected, but they are as but a drop of water in the ocean; the railways are beginning to think of providing accommodation, but as yet little has been done to make up for the losses sustained.[13]

Dickens wrote about the area more concisely: "There was even railway time observed in clocks, as if the sun itself had given in."[14]

When he made his inquiry of the outer ring of London, north of the Thames, in 1897–98, Charles Booth remarked on the area west of Gray's Inn Road that two or three vicious spots remained north and south of Euston Road, after massive clearance by the Midland Railway. Some residents had left, but those who remained degraded the adjoining streets by increasing overcrowding. He illustrated this point with a description of Somers Town, located on either side of Euston Station from Regent's Park to St. Pancras Station:

Somers Town was the work of speculative building early in the last century [early 19th c]. We read that "Everybody who could obtain the means turned builder, each contrived to raise his house or houses, and every street was lengthened in its turn; and herein is to be found the cause of many of those evils which have been a scandal in our day."

The degraded poverty that remains, both in Somers Town itself and in the parallel districts lying further West, is undoubtedly of long standing, dating back to the time when Russell Square was a center of fashion and wealth. The place seems to have had no special industries, but was largely occupied by those immediately supported by the expenditure of the rich. Into this region of back streets and small houses thronged with poor people, whose living depended on irregular work eked out by charity, a wedge was driven by the great railways which successively sought entrance to London from the North. Slice after slice has been taken, and the part of Somers Town now occupied by the railways is about as large as that which we have to deal. . . .

The result has been to raise site values, and of late there has been little or no fresh building. Extravagant claims are made by the owners of slump [sic] property, and every scheme of improvement is hampered. Crowding is chronic. . . . In many cases no shelter but the workhouse has been available for people turned out into the street with their belongings, in the execution of sanitary orders. . . . In Somers Town one infant in five dies within the year.[15]

And, he added,

This corner of London, including a portion of the parish of St. Pancras, is cursed by the street-walking form of prostitution, for which many of the small hotels in the neighbourhood of the railway termini offer facilities. The lowest of these women used to live in the vile quarter off Cromer Street, which has now given way to model buildings, and some still live near, but women come here from all parts.[16]

The railways thus constitute a running thread of Booth's account of Somers Town with their impact on housing conditions and the corollaries of low life expectancy or prostitution. They were also responsible for the decrease in parish land.

Booth's initial investigations of the 1880s were condensed into one of the most striking documents resulting from his project, the 1889 *Descriptive Map of London Poverty*.[17] The map indicates by color coding the economic conditions of each street in the metropolitan areas (except the City). From dire poverty (in black) to affluence (in yellow), with intermediate shading, this map is a vivid testimony to the impact of railways on adjacent areas (Figure 3.1).[18] It reveals visually the extent of railway intrusion into the area of the three Euston Road stations. It also indicates poverty by the presence of dark-colored pockets in their immediate vicinity. Booth's first two projects (the first eight volumes of the *Life and Labour of the People in London* and the map) were followed by a third series of investigations between 1897 and 1903 (published 1902–4) on the work of the local churches.[19] A comparison between the two projects reveals that in the span of 10 to 12 years, many houses between Euston Road and Camden Town (northwest of Somers Town) had deteriorated enough to warrant a darker color on Booth's revised maps.[20] A second team of investigators compared current conditions with those in the previous survey and commented repeatedly on housing conditions. Somers Town was the worst area, owned in great part by the railways, which made no improvements on properties it might reclaim at short notice.[21]

In the 1952 volume of *The Buildings of England,* devoted to London beyond the City and Westminster, Pevsner concurs with these descriptions and adds: "Just N. of St. Pancras and King's Cross is the most intricate and noisy railway landscape of London (with the exception perhaps of some parts of Southwark)."[22] The lasting impact of the railways on the area is further confirmed by the juxtaposition of two documents dated 1860 and 1991. In November 1860, a memorial signed by 80 residents was delivered to the directors of the London and North Western Railway by inhabitants of Adelaide Row, on Haverstock Hill, complaining of the constant pealing of a very large and sonorous alarm bell; the ordinary use, in fine weather, of very powerful detonating signals; the prolonged use of the steam whistle; and the illegal consumption of coal in the locomotives.[23]

The second document, a press release from the Borough of Camden, dated 23 January 1991, relates the attempts of Councillor Graham Good to make

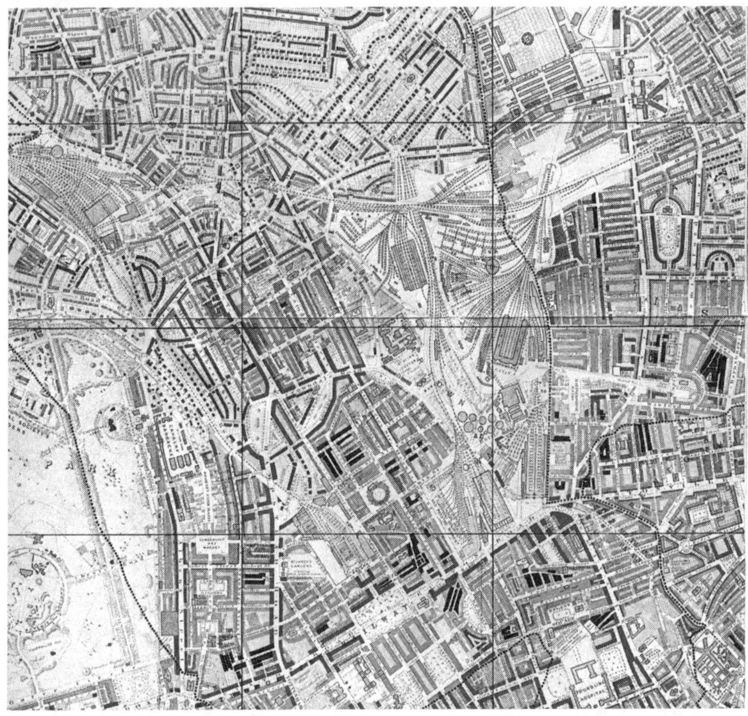

Figure 3.1   Inner northwest London, 1901. From Charles Booth, *Life and Labour of the People in London*, 3rd ser., *Religious Influences* (London: Macmillan, 1902–4), final volume, map E, after p. 196.

British Rail (BR) "take responsibility for vibration disturbance to people's homes caused by the passage of heavy freight trains" in the Camden Road area near the North London line and near the Belsize Tunnel.[24] The document states that the introduction of new freight rolling stock may be responsible for the increased vibrations, which have been investigated and determined as not likely to cause structural damage to houses. The increased noise, however, remained a concern. BR (in an appended letter dated 1 November 1990) stated its right to run trains at night and denied any liability to adjoining landowners for the noise and vibration caused. The press release remarked on the change of attitude on the part of BR since its reconfiguration into more profit-driven groups. The new BR appeared less willing to talk with the council and attempt to solve problems. The press release concludes that local authorities have no legislative power over railway companies and can only hope to persuade them to act honorably. These two documents 131 years apart testify to the continued impact of railways in the St. Pancras area.

The 125 acres of the King's Cross railway lands have been under study for redevelopment since 1987, and a number of proposals were submitted in 2004. The area has also been the object of an industrial archaeology study.[25] A rich industrial and technological history lies dormant, and threatened, in the acreage of buildings and structures crossed by the Regent's Canal, bounded by York Way on the east, Euston Road on the south, the rail line out of St. Pancras on the west, and the tracks of the North London Railway on the north. With a number of listed buildings, from St. Pancras Station to the 1824 gasholders; the Regent's Canal; a plethora of industrial archaeological sites; John Soane's memorial; the new British Library; and traces of the presence of Lenin, Dickens, Rimbaud, and Verlaine, the area is attempting to attract its share of London tourism. The King's Cross Partnership publishes and distributes attractive brochures of walks in the area.[26] And while the stations remain in active domestic use, the area has again been reshaped by extensive railway work for the Channel Tunnel Rail Link (CTRL). On 14 November 2007, St. Pancras became the London terminal for the Eurostar high-speed trains to Paris and Brussels.

Euston Station

The arrival of the London and Birmingham Railway in London in 1838 was hailed in heroic terms:

> The London and Birmingham Railway is unquestionably the greatest public work ever executed, either in ancient or modern times. If we estimate its importance by the labour alone which has been expended on it, perhaps the Great Chinese Wall might compete with it, but when we consider the immense outlay of capital which it has required . . . together with the unprecedented engineering difficulties, which we are happy to say are now overcome,—the gigantic work of the Chinese sinks totally into the shade.[27]

The railway required lifting 67 million cubic feet, more than for the Great Pyramids of Egypt. About the station, a contemporary guidebook comments: "This is a Roman Work, conceived in a Roman spirit, and accomplished with Roman perseverance and determination . . . in which the Roman deification still presides."[28]

When the London and Birmingham Railway designed its first London station, the first main-line terminal in London, the question of what a terminal should look like was far from settled. The choice of a gateway with Doric columns emulating the Propylaea of the Acropolis in Athens reveals awareness of the importance and outward orientation of the operation.[29] The impact of the railway was yet to permeate society in 1837, but it was anticipated. The dynamic corporation that could undertake such a forward-thinking project as a railway line had to impress customers, and shareholders, of its power. It also needed to woo customers with the reassurance of an architectural form that evoked security, safety, and stability. The 72-foot-high Doric gateway of the Euston Arch designed by Philip Hardwick met these criteria with its four solid Bramley stone columns taller than those of any other building in London at the time[30] (Figure 3.2). The £35,000 expense for the embellishment was justified to shareholders by the directors as "opening immediately upon what will necessarily become the Grand Avenue for travelling between the Midland and Northern parts of the Kingdom."[31] Like the Athens Propylaea, the station was to act as the Gateway to the North, a portal to the country's most valuable assets, the northern industrial heartland.[32] The railway looked toward Birmingham, Liverpool, Manchester, and Newcastle and to the engineering works that would tunnel through mountains and fly over rivers. With such wealth and challenges at hand, the undeveloped area on the outskirts of London seemed inconsequential, except for the price needed to acquire it freehold.[33]

The Euston Grove area was at the time "a quiet scene of nursery gardens," which could be improved by development.[34] The railway company did not yet know how much land it would need to meet operational requirements, and it had acquired twice as much acreage as its facilities occupied. The other half was to be let to the Great Western Railway, but that company opted to settle on the Paddington site off Praed Street, and the London and North Western Railway soon occupied the entire space as traffic expanded rapidly with the connection to the Yorkshire lines in 1840.

F. R. Conder, a civil engineer, writing in 1868, 30 years after the opening of the London and Birmingham Euston terminus, comments on the changes that had taken place in the area: "Since that date a new city has arisen on the site of fields and parks," and the few buildings north of the Regent's Canal were pleasant, "far from presenting their present dingy and depressing appearance."[35] In 1839, John Bourne qualified the area as a "garden and nursery."[36] The area toward Hampstead had a "thin crust of houses" along the roads, as well as pastures, small ill-tended market gardens, a small colony of fireworks makers, a milk producer, and a school.[37] Landmarks included a cottage that had been inhabited by Sir Richard Steele and frequented by the literati of the Steele and Addison circle, the Old St. Pancras Church and churchyard, St. Katharine's Hospital, and Regent's Park. Past the 30-acre Camden depot were the Chalk Farm spot favored by duelists, Primrose Hill, and Barrow Hill with the West Middlesex waterworks reservoir. A little further off, Hampstead and Highgate, on high ground with Kenwood between them and the Primrose Hill tunnel, indicated a landscape progressively marked by more geographical features than human settlement.

Figure 3.2   Euston Station, entrance, lithograph, 1839. From John Cooke Bourne and John Britton, *Drawings of the London and Birmingham Railway* (London: J. C. Bourne, 1839), title page.

The original Euston Station buildings did not match the scale of the Doric portico. Pevsner calls them modest, "a remarkable anticlimax to passengers."[38] The Great Hall, Grand Staircase, and Board Room of the second station built between 1846 and 1849 were on a grander scale, but they were not on axis with the portico. The arrival of the Midland Railway down the block in the 1860s provided incentive to clean up the station's Euston Road presence. Access was improved, and the portico axis was stressed by the addition of a drive flanked by two hotels in 1870. The linking of the two hotels by a corridor, decided in 1878 and completed in 1881, negated the approach created a decade earlier and made the portico a redundant feature. Impossible to view at an appropriate distance, the columns seemed to be underfoot without purpose. During the planning stages for the 1878 construction and again for the third station in the late 1950s, moving the portico as a gateway on Euston Road was proposed— and dismissed.[39] As with the demolition of Penn Station in New York in the same decade, the demolition of the Euston portico in 1961 raised consciousness of the need to preserve architectural landmarks. Ironically, as Pevsner pointed out, the current arrangement at Euston could have accommodated the "arch."[40]

Travelers and historians have focused on the portico with its command-ing presence but limited footprint. This has diverted attention from the steady growth of the station facilities. From the original 200 x 50 foot two-story building along the departure platform, the station now occupies an entire block, which has incorporated two neighboring streets and adjacent buildings. With each subsequent stage of rebuilding, the railway laid claim to additional land, spilling beyond and reconfiguring its eastern and west-ern boundaries and pushing its southern approach toward Euston Road.[41]

For the opening of the new Euston Station in 1968, its architect, R. L. Moorcroft, commented on the complexity of the context and the impossi-bility of accounting for all factors in the planning process.[42] This awareness of surrounding factors marks a shift from the total blindness to context encountered in the early years of railway construction. Except for minor adjustments, the new station remained confined within available land. For the first main-line terminal to be rebuilt in London since the building of the last London station, Marylebone, in 1899, probably the most characteristic development was that the new Euston Station did not displace any residents.

King's Cross Station

A small village named Battle Bridge existed where the New Road (now Euston Road) and Pentonville Road met in 1756. The name Battle Bridge, a corruption of Broad Ford Bridge, refers to a ford on the Fleet River, which ran west of Pancras Road. The name King's Cross, which replaced Battle Bridge, refers to a monument topped by a statue of George IV erected in 1836 at the junction of Euston, Pentonville, and Gray's Inn roads. The name remained, but the statue was taken down in 1842 and its base, in use as a public house, demolished three years later. Between 1746 and 1846, the location of King's Cross Station was occupied by a smallpox hospital.[43]

King's Cross Station, London terminus of the GNR, was designed by Lewis Cubitt (1799-ca. 1883). When it opened in 1852, it was the eighth London station and the largest in England. It also accommodated the Midland Railway until St. Pancras opened in 1868. The plain, functional design of the yellow brick façade evokes the sheds behind with its two rounded arches sep-arated by a 120-foot-high central tower (Figure 3.3). The 105-foot-wide sheds extend 800 feet northward parallel to York Road (then Maiden Lane). The Italianate station hotel, also designed by Cubitt, was opened in 1854 on the curved corner of Euston and Pancras roads, west of the station.[44]

Unlike the Euston portico, which relied on tested associative symbolism, the Cubitt design stated the function of the building explicitly. The engineer-ing requirements of the sheds dominate the façade and assert the building's main purpose. The building's confident presence does not reveal its adjustments to a location with stringent constraints. On the front of the station, which aligned with the road until adjustments were made for the Midland Railway terminal, several attempts have been made to optimize use of space with various outbuildings and, later, the underground station.[45] The 1973 single-story concourse, with shops and service spaces, was not any kinder to the building façade than the preceding encroachments, but its demolition and subsequent replacement by an open-air piazza was approved in 2005.[46]

The King's Cross Station site extends only 600 yards from north to south and is confined between inflexible boundaries: the Regent's Canal and the Euston and Pentonville roads. The Maiden Lane (or Gas Works) Tunnel is only 250 yards away from the northern end of the train shed, which restricts maneuvering space. Inclines downward to the tunnel, then upward underground, also complicate operations. Large goods-and-coal depots are located north of the canal, and both passenger and freight traffic converge on the longer and equally steep Copenhagen Tunnel, heading northward after crossing the North London Railway line.[47] A travel guide description written at the time of the station's opening considers that, for the traveler, the location "at the hub of newly formed arteries" offers convenient access, the "abodes of disease and infamy" are making way for a direct route to the North, and the "very equivocal sobriquet of Maiden-lane has been metamorphosed into the more appropriate name of 'York-road.'"[48]

Unlike Euston Station, built on market garden acreage, the construction of King's Cross Station in 1851 necessitated the demolition of "the awful rookery at the back of St. Pancras Road."[49] The international exhibition, housed in the Crystal Palace, erected the same year, provided an added incentive to clean up a city that expected large numbers of visitors. The "vast,

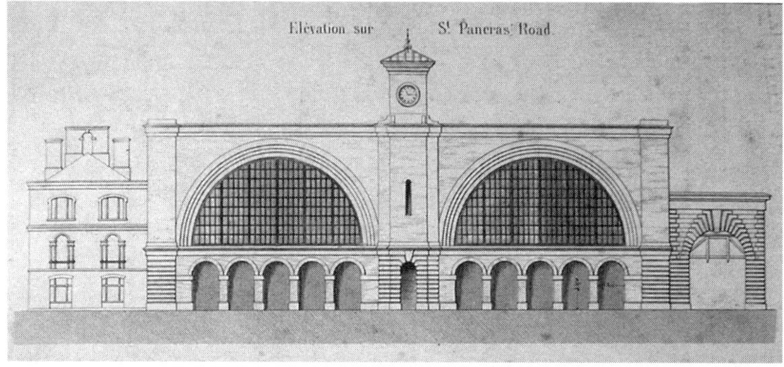

Figure 3.3 King's Cross façade. Auguste Perdonnet, Camille Polonceau, and Eugène Flachat, *Nouveau portefeuille de l'ingénieur des chemins de fer* (Paris: Lacroix-Comon, 1857), pl. K 18–19.

howling wilderness" that the GNR had acquired in an outlying district already suffered from the mixed blessings of industry and urbanization.[50] The Imperial Gas Works was surrounded by the courts of working-class housing. Brick works, with or without kilns, exploited areas where clay lay on the surface. A plan labeled "GNR Kings Cross Passenger Station and Line Extending to Junction with Main Line at Copenhagen Tunnel, 1852" shows a dense residential area in the crook of New Road, the smallpox-and-fever hospital buildings, the Imperial Gas Works south of the canal, and the brick fields and tile kilns beyond, straddling the line between the parishes of St. Pancras and St. Mary Islington along Maiden Lane.[51] The line is driven through industrial and residential areas alike, inexorably straight.

A later plan shows the line in a cleverly folded format that follows the contours of the terrain.[52] The area of this map representing the goods-and-coal station shows the line emerging from the Copenhagen Tunnel, branching toward the Caledonian goods-and-coal yard, passing east of the village of Belle Isle, and fanning out into the curve of the Regent's Canal. On the eastern side of Maiden Lane (crossed out and replaced by York Road on the map), the residential grid of recent development remains clearly visible under the dendritic pattern of the line. The houses, meticulously numbered to correspond with a Book of Reference, and possibly (depending on the actual date of the imprecisely marked plan) a demolition statement, are on narrow lots, along a rectilinear street checkerboard. The irregular structures show piecemeal development of houses, modest and varied in size, some in rows, or twins, with the characteristic residential ell extension or satellite outbuildings. The rail lines leave untouched small remaining areas of houses in the east and the west. A hatched pattern and neat, rounded hand annotations record purchase of areas adjacent to the line. In the numerous documents generated for the almost yearly bills submitted by the railway companies for expansion between 1850 and 1900, seldom is the relentless implantation of the railways in residential areas so graphically illustrated. The enormous space commanded by the railway facilities makes the traces of modest, vernacular, and idiosyncratic human habitation appear hopelessly vulnerable. In corporate memory, however, the area had been "little more than a gigantic dustyard,"[53] where one encountered a "long battalion of rag sorters and cinder sifters . . . the dull heavy thuds of the North London carpet beaters . . . the stray cats with wicked propensities . . . snapping at a dead sparrow or fighting fiercely with each other over the latest sample of fish bone."[54]

A bit further down the line, the landscape changed more slowly: the area around the first station remained rural ten years after King's Cross opened. Two miles north of the goods yard, the Seven Sisters Station, a modest pair of wooden platforms, was opened in July 1861 at a point where the line crossed over a minor road. With the acquisition of Hornsey Wood by the Metropolitan Board of Works (MBW), this station was upgraded to a waiting shed with footbridge in 1868 and the name subsequently changed to Finsbury Park, which became a tube-railway connecting hub at the beginning of the twentieth century. By 1872, Hornsey (four and a half miles from King's Cross) was receiving suburban service from the GNR. When the Alexandra Palace public entertainment center opened in 1873, a journalist commented that fields and hedges did not begin to appear until the train had passed beyond Finsbury Park.[55]

Most historical accounts, including that of the railway historian Jack Simmons, depicted the GNR as enlisted against its will into suburban service.[56] Kellett agreed, stating that the GNR expended more than £1,000,000 ($4,830,000) on adjustment for suburban traffic to get rid of what their historian C. H. Grinling called "the suburban incubus."[57] In 1985, Simmons reviewed his position. He documented that the GNR went into the suburban traffic business early and without statutory obligation to do so because it found the business profitable.[58] Whether the GNR adapted to suburban business out of foresight or obligation, the increase in suburban passengers between 1867 and 1881 from 1.7 to 12.9 million reflects the railway's impact on the growth of London's northern suburbs.

St. Pancras Station

First known as Longwich Lane, then as King's Road, St. Pancras Way followed the course of the Fleet River. The Old St. Pancras Church was built along this ancient northern road out of London. Edged with "dust heaps and open drains" in 1760, it remains industrial today.[59]

A dominant feature of this area is the terminal of the Midland Railway Company, St. Pancras Station. The Midland Railway was the only company to serve all seven largest provincial towns in England, but it did not develop its own London approach until the 1860s and was sharing London terminal and access facilities with the GNR until 1868.[60] At this late stage in railway development, the separate terminal was a costly venture. As railway historian William Acworth stated in 1888, the first half of the 100 miles from Leicester to London cost £1,700,000 ($11,611,000) while the second 50 miles cost £9,000,000 ($48,780,000). This figure included St. Pancras Station and Hotel, goods depots, and other facilities in addition to the line.[61]

The Midland Railway Company's bill for its London extension was one of many such bills proposing additions to the London railway network. The aggravation of social conditions due to the railways' practice of building through lower-class housing areas had prompted the establishment of a special Metropolitan Railway Commission in 1863 (reappointed in 1864).[62] In its report the commission recommended proceeding with a number of projects "being only improvements of existing lines or works; connecting links of a very limited extent, or enlargements of existing stations in no way conflicting with any comprehensive system of Metropolitan Railway."[63] The Midland Railway's St. Pancras branch appeared to meet these criteria, and the bill was approved on 22 June 1863.[64]

From a technical point of view, the extension presented challenges to the engineers employed by the Midland Railway, who sought imaginative and unprecedented solutions. The proximity to Regent's Canal and the Fleet River bed made it necessary to raise the tracks 20 feet above the level of Euston Road (12 to 17 feet higher than other adjoining roads). As pointed out in an early history of the Midland Railway, written when all the trenches had barely been filled in, the station buildings were just "like an iceberg, the greater portion [being] below the surface."[65] The connection with a branch of the Metropolitan Railway (opened in 1863) ran under the station. The Fleet River, running from north to south, was channeled into a subterranean sewer line and diverted from a decaying brick casing to an iron culvert running at an angle from the original sewer. The arched vaults below the tracks rest on iron pillars and were designed as storage for Burton ale from Burton-on-Trent. In order to maximize storage space, the size of a beer barrel was used as module to determine the distance of 29 feet and 4 inches between the 720 supports.

The single-span arch of the shed, then the widest in the world at 243 feet, rose to 100 feet for a length of 689 feet over a total surface of close to 4 acres[66] (Figure 3.4). Designed by W. H. Barlow and executed by R. M. Ordish in 1866–68, it was hailed as an engineering virtuoso performance. Affixed to a massive underground and below-passenger-track-level structure designed to counter the effects of downward, upward, and lateral thrust, and stabilized by the floor level acting as ties, the ribs of the depressed Gothic arches are free to rise unobstructed. The entire shed surface is unencumbered by support columns, giving maximum versatility to the covered-track arrangement.

The Euston Road frontage, the Midland Grand Hotel, was built between 1868 and 1874, after a competition won by Sir Gilbert Scott in 1865 (see Figure 3.4). The Gothic inspiration of the design has been extensively discussed with admiration, contempt, and the deference due to a structure classed Grade I, a designation reserved for buildings of exceptional interest. John Summerson contrasted the two components of the terminal "as a highly rational feat of 19th-century technology" juxtaposed to "a product of the most utterly irrational episode in English architecture, a kind of thing which, having been done once, should on no account ever be done again."[67] Jack Simmons is more complimentary for both the "logical exactitude of the train-shed and the rich exuberance of the hotel."[68] As the new CTRL terminal, the hotel and shed structures are gaining a new lease on life.

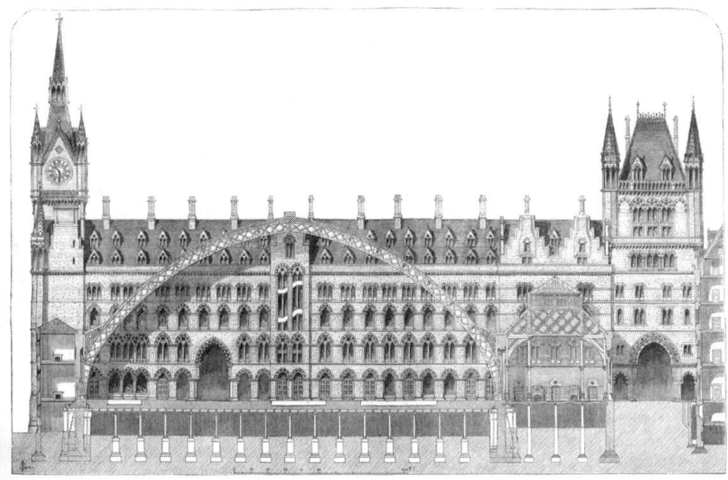

Figure 3.4   North elevation of Midland Hotel with outline of St. Pancras train shed, London. From "Midland Railway Extension: St. Pancras Terminus Hotel," in *The Engineer* (London), 23 (14 June 1867): 540.

As plans were moving forward for the construction of the passenger facilities on Euston Road, additional property was acquired for satellite facilities. In 1864, the Harrison Estate between Kentish Town Road and the embankment of the Hampstead Junction line was purchased for "goods and coal station, carriage sidings and engine sheds."[69] Excavations for the engine shed and workshops were started in 1865. The original goods yard reached by the GNR line was reorganized and reoriented toward the new northern approach in the spring of 1866. It was at that time that Agar Town was demolished,[70] as examined in the following section, "Agar Town." A decade later, the goods facilities ceased to meet traffic needs, cramped as they were by the gas works and the GNR facilities. The construction of the additional goods station in Somers Town (approved in 1877) necessitated the displacement of another 10,000 people in the area immediately west of Midland Road.[71] In his "Description of the St. Pancras Station and Roof, Midland Railway," the engineer William Barlow mentions that "when the Company were offered an estate adjoining the Euston Road on advantageous terms, they lost no time in making the purchase," an acquisition that determined the site of the new station.[72]

The social historian A. S. Wohl presents this transaction in a different light: "In the 1870s . . . the whole of Somers Town, a densely populated working-class district, was torn down to make way for the railway construction. . . . Despite the protests of such groups as the Somers Town Defence League, the working classes were helpless in the face of the onslaught."[73] The goods station occupied the block bordered by Euston Road, Ossulston Street, Brill Place, and Midland Road. It was demolished in the 1970s for the construction of the new British Library, though some fragments are preserved at the corner of Brill Place and Ossulston Street.

Agar Town

The Midland Railway Company's terminal and additional extension projects would require demolitions in Somers, Camden, and Agar towns. The station and its dependencies were to straddle over two districts, Somers Town and Agar Town, and two estates, that of the Skinners and the Brewers' Companies. According to *The Working Man,* 4,000 houses, home to about 32,000 residents, mostly working class, were demolished.[74] E. G. Barnes, one of five historians of the Midland Railway, described the land negotiations with the vestry of St. Pancras as "exceedingly difficult" and further indicated that "within days of the contract being let," sidings were installed for the contractors,

> and thereafter Waring Brothers' demolition teams moved in against Agar Town. During March and April 1866 those hideous slums, sprawling between the new goods station and the St. Pancras gasworks, were swept away for ever, and with them disappeared a menace to public health. During May and June 1866 the equally sordid slums of Somers Town vanished in the same way; and with the whole length of the Pancras Extension then completely cleared, Waring Brothers made ready to tackle the general constructions works.[75]

Barnes also mentions that the 1866 displacements caused for "thousands upon thousands of ordinary working-class people in the parish of St. Pancras . . . a particularly loathsome and disastrous year. During the spring and the summer the desperate wretches displaced by those operations simply herded into the nearby districts, where overcrowding had already reached simply alarming proportions."[76]

The number of people receiving relief in London had risen from 90,000 to 103,000 over the previous year, and a cholera epidemic broke out in 1865, lasting into 1866. It caused 300 deaths, including that of the parish Medical Officer of Health. The Midland Railway was enlisted in the new MBW's efforts to enclose London sewers, a project reported to have been of great difficulty and danger and which the company executed successfully in November and December. Barnes thus credited the Midland with providing the service of clearing the slums and participating in the metropolitan sanitation efforts.[77]

What do we know of these areas eradicated so quickly and efficiently? Somers Town began to develop as a community north of the New Road in

1783, less than a decade after Bedford Square in Bloomsbury, south of it.[78] It had been built, in part, by refugees from the French Revolution, whose settlement included modest houses; their Catholic chapel, built in 1808; and their tombs in the St. Pancras graveyard. The Old St. Pancras Church, rebuilt around 1350, on one of the oldest Christian sites in Europe, had been inactive after the completion of the new Inwood-designed Greek Revival parish church off Euston Road in 1822. Restored and expanded in 1847–48, the Old St. Pancras Church served as a chapel-of-ease for the parish. The churchyard had been the primary burial place for north London, and some of its residents had acquired notoriety during their lifetimes. Overcrowded, the burial facility had been expanded from one and one-half acres to five in 1792.[79] Near the deceased French refugees also stood, in the adjacent St. Giles burial ground, the memorial John Soane designed for his wife in 1815, where he joined her in 1837.

The railway's southward path from Kentish Town to Euston Road could either pass though the gas works of the Imperial Gas Light and Coke Company or through the churchyard. Both alternatives were fraught with difficulties. The churchyard was the cheaper of the two options and the one selected. The cemetery turned out to include several layers of graves, which caused the railway's excavations to be more invasive than initially anticipated. This clearing of the burial grounds was condemned as dese-cration, drawing protest and giving rise to anecdotes of local folklore.[80] The public outcry over digging below the Old St. Pancras burial grounds deferred the decision of the Select Committee reviewing one of the bills for extension under consideration. The bill was nonetheless sent to the Lords, where the Midland prevailed.[81] According to Jack Simmons, the "unfortu-nate proximity" of the gas works and the graveyard increased the difficul-ties to be surmounted by the company and has hindered its operations permanently.[82]

North of Somers Town, Agar Town was developed after 1810, along the canal. Jack Simmons, adopting the conventional descriptions of the area, has described the whole area as optimal: "It was occupied by a canal, a gas-works, an ancient church with a large and crowded graveyard, and some of the most atrocious slums in London; and through it all ran the Fleet River. . . . Agar Town was never anything but a slum from the first."[83] Its residents had been displaced by the construction of New Oxford Street and were extremely poor, weekly tenants. The freehold for the land was attached to the prebendary of St. Pancras in St. Paul's Cathedral.[84] As Agar Town was demol-ished by the Midland Company and, "apart from Agar Grove, which passes under the railway a little north of the canal, and the tiny Agar Place leading off it, nothing remains to recall its horrors," Simmons credited the railway company with performing "real Metropolitan Improvement" and redressing the evils brought upon the poor by ecclesiastical slum landlords.[85]

This account of Agar Town illustrates a position common among railway historians: the conviction that the railways' actions were justified in the name of progress and in order to run the trains effectively. Admittedly, Simmons was writing as the future of St. Pancras Station was in question, but also more than ten years after H. J. Dyos had published his landmark article "Railways and Housing in Victorian London" and while Kellett was at work on *The Impact of Railways on Victorian Cities,* published a year later.[86] The attempt to draw a more accurate picture of the railways' impact had been initiated, and even such a railway advocate as Simmons would gradually give increasing attention to the social considerations surrounding land acquisition and slum clearance.[87]

As for Agar Town, all published accounts appear to be in agreement about the nature of the community: it was a slum, called by Charles Dickens "an English Connemara" and similarly described in a number of contemporary sources.[88] These descriptions point to an area between Maiden Lane (York Road) and St. Pancras Way, which becomes Pancras Road (aka King's Road) as it proceeds northward. The site is described and illustrated as the seat of "Councillor" Agar in "The Kentish Town Roll," which is a panorama of the road from Kentish Town to Old St. Pancras Church, done in the 1840s by J. F. King, but depicting the area around 1820.[89] King indicated that the property extended between the ruins of the Old St. Pancras workhouse and Cook's Row, a row of 17 three-story attached houses, and that it was bordered along the road by a large number of poplar trees. The lease of the estate, a little more than 70 acres of the Manor of St. Pancras, was purchased at auction in 1810 by William Agar. Agar was born in 1767 in a Yorkshire family, was called to the bar in 1791 as lawyer in the Court of Chancery, practiced at Lincoln's Inn, was made King's counsellor, and died in 1838. According to King, Agar appears to have been a colorful character, hospitable, involved in parish affairs, and sufficiently influential or persistent to prevent the Regent's Canal Company from building the canal through his estate. In 1816, Agar leased the land he already occupied directly from the prebendary of St. Pancras. By 1820, Agar built a mansion house named Elm Lodge, surrounded, again according to King, by "coach-house, stable, yard and large garden, pleasure ground, plantation, a Lawn, East Field and Near Field."[90] Two additional leases were taken by the Agar family, in 1822 and 1839. At Agar's death, his son, William Talbot Agar (1814–1907), assumed the lease.

According to King, since the time depicted in the Kentish Town Roll, the poplars

> have all been cut down and two- and four-roomed cottages have been
> built by Working Men at a ground rent, on the road side, payable weekly
> or monthly. The leases terminate at the end of 21 years, which have

brought together such a variety of poor of every description known as Agar Town extending to the Gas Works in Maiden Lane . . . to make it a second St. Giles, it being very hazardous for any respectable dressed person to pass or repass without insult or annoyance, as that locality received most of the refuse which the forming of New Oxford Street swept away to improve that previous impure district, so long the pest of the Parish of St. Giles.[91]

After Agar's death, his widow and children began to lease the land in 1840 for 21-year terms, the longest possible for ecclesiastical lands. The leases were for very small plots, which, along with the short term and proximity of industrial and graveyard odors, discouraged solid development. Clauses regulating drainage, repairs, and appearance were nonetheless included in the leases.[92] Out of the 72 acres, 40 were leased by 1842, and most of the estate, except the Elm Lodge grounds, was leased by 1844, but some leasing activity continued until 1850. This meant that all leases were to expire between 1861 and 1871. The ecclesiastical commissioners became owners in 1847 after the death of the last prebendary of St. Pancras, but this did not affect the Agars' right to grant leases. Although Elm Lodge must have been closely surrounded by road development and the north London viaduct, the 1861 census lists the Agar daughter as still residing there. Other documents, however, indicate that by 1860 the family had relinquished all interest in the estate.[93]

The geographical conditions of Agar Town did not predispose it to slum development. The area was not poorly drained, nor was it initially isolated by the railways. It was, however, in close proximity to industrial activity in the nearby town of Belle Isle or at the gas works, and the neighboring burial grounds of St. Giles and Old St. Pancras, filled beyond capacity, did release noxious odors. The original development occurred on a small scale mostly in the southern part of the estate, by craftsmen who built their own residences or by small developers. Larger-scale development started in the north around 1855 on large tracts leased for 99 years directly from the ecclesiastical commissioners by developers. Peak expansion was reached by 1860, when the commissioners agreed to sell the freehold to the Midland Railway Company. With a London average of eight pounds rated value for rental housing in 1850, Agar Town houses ranged between five and 18 pounds, with the lower values in the south, the higher ones in the north.[94] Some even reached 24 pounds in 1863, the year the Midland mapped out the area, as required for its extension bill. Paving and lighting were brought to the area by 1860 after much wrangling between the vestry and the ecclesiastical commissioners, who, by that time, had other plans for the land. In 1861, the census shows 553 inhabited houses with 4057 residents (2071 males, 1986 females), 2062 north and 1995 south of the canal. Most had some form of employment, and Agar Town residents accounted for a very small portion of St. Pancras poor relief records. Health records are equally benign.[95]

As it was considering its London extension, the Midland Railway settled on a site for its goods facilities on the northern half of Agar Town between the North London Railway, the goods area for the GNR, and the Regent's Canal. It began negotiating with the ecclesiastical commissioners as early as 1859 to purchase 27 acres for £8,000 but did not close on the deal until 1863, after sanction of the Bill for the London Extension. Additional powers were sought by the Midland Railway in 1860, 1861, 1863, and 1864, accompanied by further negotiations on less advantageous terms, for other portions of the Agar Town estate, which were secured for less than £50,000 ($498,500). The vestry attempted to protest the loss in rates and the disruption of the Old St. Pancras graveyard. It also sought to obtain some compensation for its paving expenses. The London extension from Bedford into London, sanctioned in 1863, drove the line through the remaining southern part of Agar Town. Compensation for the rest of Agar Town and for the area of Somers Town necessary for the construction of the station were higher than expected and not made public. A sum of £2,150,000 ($15,222,000) was requested from shareholders.[96] As the Midland Railway assumed the expiring leases, it allowed occupied properties to become dilapidated, deserving the qualification coined by Dyos of "meadow to slum" in a single generation.[97]

A contemporary account, which precedes demolition, gives contradictory assessments. In *Ragged London,* published in 1861, John Hollingshead described Agar Town as "the lowest effort of building skill and arrangement in or near London—[which] arose upon church property." He mentioned decayed habitations but improved roads, with a marked distinction between the poor laborers or costermongers in the south and hardworking mechanics, railway men, or wives of sailors in the north.[98] He mentioned that plans for higher quality development on land leased for 99 years were stopped by the purchase of the land by the Midland Railway and described the deplorable condition of the houses in the lower portion, where dogs and alcoholism were rampant and plumbing nonexistent. He qualified the overall area as a "stepping-stone to and from the workhouse,"[99] and added: "No known thieves or prostitutes are found in the neighbourhood—its lowest part is too poor and miserable for that; and what vices it has arise largely from overcrowding."[100] On the positive side, Hollingshead described a well-run soup kitchen providing inexpensive food, cleaner air than in most slums, and a dedicated clergyman whose ministry had brought improvement over the past ten years—school, maternity society, mother's society, Sunday school, penny bank, and day care—all of which exhibited high levels of participation.[101] Hollingshead's account is consistent with the physical layout of the area divided by the Regent's Canal, and his overall evaluation makes a distinction between the two sections. The area south of the canal, developed earlier and piecemeal, was more dilapidated than the northern section, developed later by larger-scale developers.

In his 1994 University of London thesis and subsequent publication on Agar Town, Steven Denford attempts to go beyond the "recycled Victorian accounts" of modern historians.[102] He refutes the image of Agar Town as the dwelling place of a lazy, drinking, Irish population: "Agar Town, for all its faults, was—by the standards of the time—a realistic response by working men to a chronic housing shortage."[103] Drawing from local library collections, local newspaper accounts, the national and architectural press, vestry minutes and other parish records, deeds, census, poor law and health reports, and such parliamentary records as the 1851 Report of the Board of Health, Denford reconstructed the community eroded by the railway over several years and eradicated in less than two months.[104] The careful examination of remaining records for a community that has been swept off the map suggests convincingly that Agar Town was a poor working-class community, not a slum. What can be pieced together about the housing units suggests that they resulted from attempts at solving the severe housing problem in metropolitan London with individual initiative, trade solidarity, and ingenuity. This raises the more provocative question of whether this reassessment can also be applied to other so-called slums of Victorian London, and to the other poor areas the railways acquired to wedge their way into the metropolis.[105]

The difficulty in understanding the conditions of the lower classes in London, which Dyos began to investigate, has been a challenge for the past generation of social historians.[106] Many details of the relationship between tenants and landlords remain elusive to us. Building conditions and practices cannot always be documented precisely, but some clues do exist.[107] In his 1901 article, "The Jerry Builder Considered in Relation to the Housing of the Poor," E. Gwynn, Medical Officer of Health for Hampstead, comments on the failure of London County Council and charitable programs to keep up with the housing demands of a growing population: "In other words, whilst the various bodies already named, with all their resources, during the past decades provided house accommodation for thousands, the jerry builder has succeeded in housing tens of thousands."[108] For the jerry builder, who built cheaply and flimsily, the cost of housing per inhabitant averaged between £15 and £20, and for the other building concerns, between £45 and £100.[109] Other historians have demonstrated the resourcefulness of the working classes in making accommodations to their living conditions.[110] John Summerson raised the question of what we can know in his introduction to Dyos' study of Camberwell:

> I write this in a house built in 1849 and through the window the life of a London suburb takes its Sunday-afternoon course. . . . On paper I know all

the people who lived in my row and the row opposite a hundred years ago; I know . . . their names and occupations, the children and servants they had and something of their wealth. . . . They are all dead. . . . I know far less about the people who live there now. . . . The Registrar General and the Inland Revenue know but will not tell—at least not for a hundred years.[111]

Our view of the present may suffer from blinders we cannot remove. Similarly, the Victorians who lived where the diseases breeding in densely populated areas were a threat to the well-to-do and to the destitute alike were not inclined to see vernacular adjustments and ingenuity in substandard overcrowded housing. They saw a slum that could most easily be improved by being first destroyed. The extensive records alluded to by Summerson have enabled Denford (and Linda Clarke for Somers Town) to remove some blinders and exhume part of the slums the railways buried. Their work suggests that the evolutionary forces swayed by a rhetoric of progress relied on power and economic momentum to drive wedges into lower-class neighborhoods it was expedient to label as "slums."

The more than 300 acres of railway land north of Euston Road have had a configuring impact on their surroundings. Booth documented the evolving and lasting nature of this impact on adjacent residential areas during the course of the nineteenth century's last decade. Today, what remains of Agar Town is a residential area showing signs of incipient gentrification. West of St. Pancras Station, on the site of its former goods depot, the British Library brings a distinguished, civilizing presence to the area. St. Pancras Station is reconfigured into a high-speed train terminal, hotel, and residence. The extensive works involved in this conversion further eroded built areas or remaining park and cemetery land. The King's Cross development site remains in limbo, with some industrial use, prostitutes along the road, and neglected industrial archaeology structures, which are unlikely to survive the successful development plan for the area approved in 2005. The tension between progress and preservation is played out in a context with more developed social, environmental, and cultural safety nets. Nonetheless, the railway's economic momentum, even if less forceful than in the nineteenth century, remains a dominant and shaping agent of the urban landscape north of Euston Road.

4

Paris: Haussmann, the Railways, and the New Gates to the City

In 1848, Charles-Louis-Napoléon Bonaparte (1808–73) returned to Paris from exile in London. He arrived inconspicuously at the two-year-old Gare du Nord (north station).[1] The short, modest-looking man in bourgeois dress hardly knew the city. He would quickly get to know it very well and place its reconfiguration high on his agenda.[2] Four years later he would assume the imperial throne as Napoleon III. By the time Georges-Eugène Haussmann (1809–91) was appointed Préfet de la Seine in 1853, the emperor had drawn a color-coded map of the city. Blue, red, yellow, and green lines reflected the priority the monarch assigned the streets to be opened through the urban fabric.[3] On 29 June 1853, Haussmann's second day on the job, Louis-Napoléon handed the new prefect the map and gave instructions to carry out the projects.[4] The emperor had already expressed his convictions about the importance of the railways as the new highways of the future. On 9 October 1852, before his assumption of the title of emperor in December, Napoléon had included the railways in his program for the country: "We have immense uncultivated lands to clear, roads to open, harbors to excavate, rivers to make navigable, canals to finish, our railway network to complete."[5]

The railways were present on the emperor's map, which was to act as the basis for the reconfiguration of Paris over the next decade and a half, and the monarch demonstrated awareness of the circulation problems caused by the new stations. Merruau, secretary of the prefecture, wrote in 1875:

Individuals who had access to him [Louis-Napoléon] often found him penciling lines on a map of Paris. He paid special attention to the railway terminals as points of departure for what he planned; he saw them as the real approaches to the city instead of the old "barrières" which, though they led to the national highways, would in his opinion eventually become secondary lines of communication. That is why it was of major importance to him to link these new terminals in such a way that the traffic flow between individual stations and hence between the various regions of France could proceed promptly and efficiently through their common center. It also seemed indispensable to him that broad arteries lead from these terminals directly to the center of the metropolis.[6]

In the program elaborated by the emperor for the short-lived 1853 Commission des Embellissements, the railways were explicitly mentioned in the first agenda item: "That all major arteries lead to the railways."[7] Chaired by Henri Siméon (1803–74), the commission worked for five months after its institution by Napoleon III on 2 August 1853, producing a final report in December 1853.[8] Haussmann, who considered such commissions cumbersome and inefficient, claimed to have rendered it ineffective, although some of its recommendations surfaced in the prefect's subsequent projects.[9]

The railways retained a high priority for the emperor. For instance, in his speech for the opening of the 1858 legislative session, he stated, "In the domain of public works, the most important results are 1,330 kilometers of railways put in service in 1857, 2,600 more kilometers conceded, new roads built, etc.,"[10] again placing the railways as a first priority. The notion of the stations as gateways, as it had been made explicit by the emperor, was well accepted by the end of his reign. As Léon Say wrote in the entry on railways for the 1867 *Paris Guide,*

One enters Paris through fifty-one gates and four posterns, when one comes from the few villages which encircle the big city, and by twelve railway stations when one comes from the rest of the world. Thus one can say that the stations are the real gates to the city. The others are only service entrances for the market gardeners, the quarriers, a few mail coaches behind the times, and all those whom a horse and cart can bring in, in the morning and back out in the evening of the same day. The traffic coming through the gates only stretches twenty or thirty kilometers, while that coming through the stations goes to the end of the world.[11]

The prominent and peripheral rail terminals, the emperor's new gateways of Paris, had configuring power for the city. But their impact was primarily dispersed and localized around the core of the older city, for no railway company succeeded in driving a rail line into the core of the city.[12] The growth of the railway companies created increasing needs for real estate in order to accommodate traffic and space-consuming technology. Access routes to the stations were gradually reconfigured to accommodate steadily expanding rail transport. Haussmann's projects, which implemented a major urban reconfiguration, were aimed at creating the most beautiful city in the world by opening circulation and strategic axes into and around the older center. They attempted to approach the city in a systemic and global manner.[13] With the exception of the *petite ceinture,* or inner belt line, approved by the emperor in December 1851 and partially operative as of 1852, the railways did not operate on a city-wide scale.[14] As with many of the Second Empire projects, the pattern and mode of railway implantation in Paris were inherited as a fait accompli by Haussmann. Confronted with the Herculean task of implementing the emperor's vision of an accessible, open city, Haussmann's work intersected with that of the railways, which provided access to the city. Forced to reckon with private companies operating under state oversight, Haussmann assumed an opportunist relationship with the railways. He used them if they dovetailed with his plans, accommodated them as minimally as possible where they did not. For instance, major stations such as the Gares de Lyon and d'Austerlitz were given no significant role in the Second Empire reconfiguration.[15] As powerful entities he could not control, the railways subverted the prefect's implementation of a single commanding vision. There is, however, a significant similarity between Haussmann's and the railways' mode of operation. This similarity reflects pervasive nineteenth-century cultural and economic changes, and it is within this context that they will be examined in this chapter.

Paris and Haussmann

Paris and Haussmann are indelibly associated as a model of city planning that was emulated over the world. This influence did not usually take into account the fact that the reconfiguration of Paris under the Second Empire continued projects already in process. Recent scholarship has highlighted the contributions of Haussmann's predecessors and the Paris urban projects begun during the first half of the nineteenth century.[16] The notion of a rupture with the past was cultivated by Haussmann, most prominently in his *Memoirs,* where he highlighted the innovations, ingenuity, and problem-solving approach of his work and that of his associates.[17] When he assumed his duties, Haussmann outlined the four basic principles of his work to the city council. These included disencumbering monuments for aesthetic, practical, and tactical reasons; improving health conditions; creating large boulevards to permit the circulation of air, light, and troops; and, lastly, "facilitat[ing] circulation to and from railway stations by means of penetrating lines which will lead travelers straight to the centers of commerce and pleasure, and will prevent delay, congestion, and accidents."[18] We notice here that the stations, first priority on the coeval program created by the emperor for the Commission des Embellissements de Paris, have been relegated by Haussmann to the fourth item on his own agenda.[19]

As evidenced by the recently resurfaced papers of Henri Siméon (chair of the emperor's commission), the major elements of the program for the reconfiguration of Paris had been conceived by the emperor prior to Haussmann's appointment as prefect.[20] Haussmann's contribution was primarily to steamroll procedures or legislation and to strong-arm the banking establishment into adopting more dynamic practices in order to finance the project he had been assigned and made his own. The Duke of Persigny (Victor Fialin, duc de Persigny, 1808–72), minister of the interior who recommended that Haussmann be hired, suggested to Haussmann that he undertake no project without the emperor's sanction, or, as he phrased it, "without having the project drawn by the emperor's hand on the map of Paris," a suggestion the prefect appears to have heeded in most cases.[21] But, as Brian Chapman suggests, Haussmann considered that Parisians did not have a civic commitment to their city, which justified his strategies to give them "what they ought to want."[22]

The extraordinary effort required for the reconfiguration of Second Empire Paris took place within a national strategy of economic development fostering rapid economic growth and improved communications. The Paris works fitted within both facets of this agenda: a network of new streets would improve communication and stimulate building, economic growth, as well as employment.[23] The arteries driven through the center would open up volatile overcrowded areas and would be lined by uniformly regulated construction under stringent aesthetic control. The axes and inner boulevards that linked them were connected with radial routes reaching out toward new districts where speculators could profit from residential construction on cheaper undeveloped land.[24] Communications also included the country's railway network, as laid out by the July Monarchy. Much self-conscious nationalist debate had led to the Law of 11 June 1842, which codified the building and operating conditions of the French railways.[25] The resulting combination of state infrastructure operated by private companies would remain operative until 1937, when the Société Nationale des Chemins de Fer Français (SNCF) was created.[26] The state was to provide the infrastructure of track beds and all constructions, including stations. The companies would obtain concessions to supply rails and rolling stock and to operate the lines for a determined number of years.[27] Construction was to be carried out under the supervision of engineers from the national corps of civil engineers, the Ponts et Chaussées, to ensure safety.[28]

For strategic and economic reasons, Paris became the hub of a star-shaped network of nine lines, the "*étoile* Legrand."[29] The Second Republic and subsequent Second Empire inherited the configuration of a radiating national network of trunk lines connecting all frontiers and major industries through the capital. The Paris terminals were built outside of the city core between the Grands Boulevards and the *octroi* (toll) walls of the *Fermiers généraux* (tax collectors).[30] The first Paris stations included the Gare Saint-Lazare (temporary, 1837; permanent, 1841), Gare du Maine (Montparnasse, 1840), Gare d'Orléans (Austerlitz, 1843), Gare du Nord (1846), Gare de Sceaux (Place Denfert-Rochereau, 1846), Gare de Strasbourg (de l'Est, 1847), and Gare de Lyon (1849). The decision to build multiple terminals rather than a single one or one on each bank (as lobbied for by the companies) would compound the urban impact of the railways. The stations were poorly sited, inserted at the edges of a tight urban fabric, and did not have convenient access, either from the center or between stations. The railway companies attempted to bring their lines into the center of Paris with intermediate stations on the urban portion of their routes, but the city, the national government, and expropriation costs prevented this development.[31]

Beyond implanted terminals, Haussmann thus also inherited the need to improve circulation between the railway stations and into the city center. The stations were creating a strain on the thoroughfares in their proximity and adjustments were needed.[32] Under Berger's prefecture (1848–53), Louis-Napoléon had persuaded the city council to build the Boulevard de Strasbourg, linking the new Gare de Strasbourg (later Gare de l'Est) to the Grands Boulevards, and offered a subsidy.[33] The first demolitions for the construction of the Boulevard de Strasbourg were begun before Haussmann's appointment.[34] The opening of the north-south and east-west axes, Paris' *cardo* and *decumanus,* or *grande croisée* (great crossing) initiated by the Rue de Rivoli and the Boulevard de Strasbourg remained to be completed.[35] Haussmann was aware of the mandate to accommodate traffic from the center to multiple railheads by opening additional arteries. The 55 kilometers of boulevards, which he initiated, addressed this need to a certain extent.[36]

Haussmann and the Railways

Haussmann's *Memoirs* gives some indications of his thoughts on the railways. His peripatetic career up the administrative ladder of the July Monarchy exposed him to the difficulty and danger of travel through the French territory prior to the construction of rail lines. He also noted how his contacts with the capital benefited from the expediency of rail travel where lines did exist. A leitmotiv in his *Memoirs* is the increase in Paris' population attributable to the railways, which also contributed to the migration of unwed mothers or welfare seekers and increased the demand for cemeteries.[37] The prefect thus appears to have recognized the importance of the new means of transport both as a convenience and as a significant demographic agent. To the extent that Haussmann's priorities included traffic and communication, rather than housing or industry development, for instance, the railways were germane to his primary concerns. He approached his "regularisation" of Paris as engineers did a new rail line, by conducting a survey.[38] Haussmann was also in a position to incorporate or eliminate railways from city projects. The most striking instance of his attempt to incorporate a railway in his plans was the unexecuted project for a large cemetery in Méry-sur-Oise near Pontoise. This new facility was to be connected by dedicated rail line to the three main cemeteries in the capital, which were to be equipped with a station.[39] As for eliminating a project, Haussmann supported Baltard's involvement in the design of the Halles Centrales (central market). He discarded the project commissioned by the government in the summer of 1853 from the engineers E.A.J. Brame and Eugène Flachat with the architect Alfred Armand, which included an underground rail component to the Halles and a planned central post office.[40] However, as already noted, the state-regulated, privately owned railway companies were not under Haussmann's jurisdiction, and, more significantly, no office in his tightly run operation had responsibility for working with them.[41]

The prefect does not seem to have recognized the similarities between his operation and that of the railways. The development of the rail network and the reconfiguration of Paris sped up and facilitated the pace of communication and development. Immigration, as well as commerce and industry, were stimulated by the railways and by the city works. Both the railways and Haussmann relied more on engineers than on architects, both developed centralizing goal-oriented management practices that broke away from the administrative model, and both invested and speculated on large amounts of capital from multiple sources with the expectation of returns. Railway construction required energetic intervention and abundant manpower in a manner comparable with the extraordinary effort put forth by Haussmann, his staff, and the thousands of construction workers kept employed by his city projects. And, when new streets were inaugurated, the ceremonies bore considerable resemblance to those conducted for new railway lines.[42]

Reliance on engineers by Haussmann and by the railways reduced architects to ancillary status and contributed to a widening gap between the disciplines of engineering and architecture.[43] A number of architects mastered the use of metal, which relied on engineering techniques, but this attempt to bridge the gap was short-lived.[44] Haussmann benefited from the increase in the number of engineers that took place during the 1840s to work on the railways and fortifications.[45] He had a poor opinion of the quality of the work performed by contemporary architects, especially those already holding appointments when he arrived. He attempted to create a corps of architects working exclusively for the city, as the engineers did, but although he had a team of architects working for him, he was unsuccessful at incorporating them in the city hall organization chart on a permanent basis. According to Sigfried Giedion, architects in Haussmann's Paris were "prepared at best to design single buildings, for erection on sites pointed out by someone else."[46] This was also precisely the role reserved for them by the railways. When architects worked for railway companies, they did so under the supervision of their engineering department.[47] Only occasionally would a railway company hire a prominent architect to design one of its terminals, most station design being performed in-house.[48] The first Paris terminals were entrusted to the state elite corps of Ponts et Chaussées engineers, who were at the time the only group capable of undertaking projects of such magnitude. Their solutions exhibited technical know-how and frugality and were promptly executed.[49] There is no indication that Haussmann deliberately adopted the modus operandi of the railways, but the prevalent climate might have fostered the similarity for efficient project management of public works, whether performed by the state, the companies, or the city of Paris. On the other hand, if Haussmann did emulate the practices of the railways, he did not acknowledge any influence that was likely to diminish the originality and stature of his accomplishments.[50]

Haussmann's impact, like that of the railways, transcended the purview of the architect. His predilection for geometric design is germane to engineering with its reliance on mathematics. The French urbanist Pierre Lavedan described Haussmann's preferences in urbanism as classical.[51] Haussmann favored rectilinear streets, regulations, and perspectives (*rectitude, ordonnance, perspectives*). He went to great lengths to implement these principles, despite the emperor's willingness to tolerate irregular alignments that spared significant structures. From Sixtus V's baroque planning of Rome, he retained arteries connecting two poles, but for the basilicas that acted as visual focus at the end of these arteries, he substituted railway stations and strategic rond-points.[52] As stated in his *Memoirs*, "I have never determined the course of a street and all the more so of a major artery without being concerned by the vista it could be given."[53]

Haussmann bemoaned the fact that the alignment of the Boulevards de Strasbourg and Sébastopol could have been adjusted slightly eastward to focus on the Sorbonne dome on the left bank. As a substitute, he had an awkward dome incorporated into the design of the Tribunal of Commerce on the Île de la Cité to provide the boulevard with a visual pendant to the

Gare de l'Est.[54] This concern for vistas and their visual focus gave the circulation objective a lesser priority and impaired rather than facilitated the objective of improving traffic.[55]

Another similarity between Haussmann's projects and that of the railways was the need to refine existing expropriation legislation and its implementation. Besides the Laws of 3 May 1841 and 13 April 1850 (Armand de Melun Law) mentioned in Chapter 1, a Senate order of 25 December 1852 authorized expropriation by executive decree rather than by parliamentary vote. This allowed expropriation of properties in good condition along the intended layout of new streets. Further legal adjustments in 1858 and 1860 deprived the city of betterment values on unused land and enforced tenant compensation, even in cases where leases were being honored. By the 1860s, property owners were receiving compensation above market value or tried to obtain compensation they were not entitled to.[56] For instance, The Chemin de Fer du Nord records in the Paris archives contain evidence of legal activity about a property located at 22 Rue de Saint-Quentin, one block from the Gare du Nord.[57] Between 1875 and 1878, M. Radiguet, owner of the property, requested damages of F35,721.50 ($109,970) for expenses and F8,750 ($26,937) for loss of rent caused by the street-level modifications performed in 1844, 1846, and 1858 to build the first Gare du Nord, and later after the opening of the Boulevard Magenta. Radiguet claimed that street-level modifications caused a drop in rental income and loss of property value because the drop in level prevented the construction of one additional story above the existing structure. Legal proceedings were delayed by a number of factors, including prescription rulings affecting the timeliness of the claim and the lack of specificity as to the responsible agent: the state or the city of Paris. However, the work performed in 1844, which placed the responsibility beyond prescription delays, did not come within 100 meters of Radiguet's property. His claim was therefore rejected. The record does not reveal why Radiguet decided to initiate legal action when he did, but his general motivation is clear: he wanted compensation for what he presented as wrongful interference with his property. Court and legal expenses would be his only reward. As this episode illustrates, the increased costs and legal implications of acquiring real estate reduced considerably Haussmann's elbow room in financial maneuvering as they increased the railways' expenses for urban expansions.[58]

For financing purposes, Haussmann divided his projects into three *réseaux* (networks).[59] For projects that could be justified by their strategic, military, and civic importance, in that they crossed poor districts or linked barracks and railway terminals, funding was easier to obtain from the legislature than for reconfigurations with more localized impact. The first network, submitted in 1855, included continuation of the Rue de Rivoli and the Boulevard de Sébastopol, the cardinal axes or *croisée parisienne*.[60] A F60 million ($185 million) loan was secured without difficulty. The second network included the streets agreed on by the city and the state in the March 1858 *Traité des 180 Millions* (180 Million Treatise). Haussmann used access to the railways to justify state funding for this second network, which provincial deputies considered a lesser national priority. He also claimed that it contributed to "national security by facilitating public order in the capital." Of the 180 millions ($554 million) requested, the state was to provide a third; and the amount, doubled by 1860, was obtained in 1865 under the same conditions as in 1855.[61] Beyond financing considerations, the first and second networks followed a logical sequence. The first network drove axes through the old, crowded city surrounded by Louis XIV's boulevards; the second increased the street network between the boulevards and the toll wall, opened up crowded areas in the east, and created communication between the center and the periphery. This included access to national highways, thus creating connections between the city core and the areas to be annexed in 1860, as well as links between the stations.[62]

The third network included various projects, some relegated to lesser priority from the second network and others mostly resulting from the 1 January 1860 annexation of the surrounding communities between the toll wall of the *Fermiers généraux* and the Thiers fortifications of 1841–44.[63] This annexation, stipulated by the Law of 16 June 1859, took effect on 1 January 1860, and resulted in the redistricting of the city from 12 to 20 *arrondissements* (districts), which required, beyond a street network, new *mairies* (town halls), churches, schools, and other public facilities.[64] Attempts to fund this third group of projects in 1868 occurred as Haussmann's financing practices were drawing public attention. Haussmann prevailed and obtained an F300 million ($923.5 million) loan, but his days in office were numbered. Conservative financiers and politicians were unprepared to consider the enormous debt Haussmann had run up for the city as an investment in expected higher taxes rather than as a mere loan with interest.[65] Total rebuilding expenditures between 1853 and 1869 amounted to F2,553,668,424 ($7,861,544,853), as much as the total budget for the country. The city's annual budget was then 55 million ($169 million). The city's debt was 163 million ($502 million) in 1852, 2.5 billion ($7.7 billion) on 1 January 1870. Haussmann had been encouraged in his financing practices by the concept of productive expenses advocated by Victor Persigny, minister of the interior, who had recommended the prefect's appointment.[66]

The increasing financial needs of the network sequence point to Haussmann's most ineluctable and formidable challenge, the need to raise the capital for the projects he had been assigned. The railways shared this need for capital, and the initial nine lines of the Legrand star were developed by 20 companies financed by 72 banks.[67] Haussmann's financing predicament reflected the changing pace of economic development, which had not yet been matched by supportive financial institutions.

The years of expansion of national railways (after 1838) and the Second Empire brought about tension and struggle between two forms of banking.[68] The first, commonly referred to as *Haute Banque* (high banking), is exemplified by the operations controlled by James de Rothschild (1792–1868). Developed under Restoration France, it was a family concern, working discreetly, relying on personal contacts and practicing conservative finances tied to gold as standard. The Rothschilds, and the small group of traditional banks to which they belonged, monopolized credit, which they extended to underwrite the government and the capital needed for large enterprises while weathering political changes. This form of banking remained prevalent under the July Monarchy.[69]

Under the pressure of expanding markets and Saint-Simonian ideology, a second, credit-oriented form of banking began to develop more flexible borrowing and lending terms to support more dynamic and diversified business and industry.[70] The Péreire brothers attempted to introduce a more responsive credit system, essential to economic development and social change.[71] They operated with publicity, to mobilize savings from all sources into credit institutions capable of financing large-scale projects for extended periods. They applied the principle of association of capital to perform large-scale speculation in future development. Their Société Générale du Crédit Mobilier, founded in November 1852, was an investment bank, the first such banking establishment, initially developed to finance railway construction and the industries on which it relied, such as metallurgy. This and other similar institutions helped consolidate the savings and investments of the smaller investors to support railways, industry, agriculture, and commerce, which experienced unprecedented growth during the Second Empire.[72]

Haussmann, as most of the railway lines, had to rely on collaboration with operations such as the Péreires' to supply the huge capital influx needed by his projects, and he resented the influence Rothschild had over the emperor.[73] In 1867, the Péreires' overextended speculation brought on their collapse, and, with them, Haussmann lost his most solid financial support.[74] Traditional banking had, however, not remained impervious to the new financial requirements of modern capitalism and had begun emulating the Péreires by 1856. And, although the Rothschilds experienced a loss of influence during the early years of the empire, they were too powerful and tactically adept to remain eclipsed.[75]

Beyond funds for the city's projects, Haussmann depended on the work of operations capable of financing, carrying out, and managing the building opportunities he created. For instance, the Péreire brothers set up the Compagnie de l'Hôtel et des Immeubles de la Rue de Rivoli in the early 1850s (renamed Compagnie Immobilière de Paris in 1858) as a development company to undertake construction along the Rue de Rivoli.[76] The profits of this and other real-estate companies that originated at the same time were derived increasingly from speculation. Haussmann was also aware of the challenge his practices of capitalist property presented to traditional forms of private ownership. He managed to remove institutional opposition by remaining as the sole member of the city's planning commission and ensuring that the appointed municipal council only included supportive members. He was, however, reluctant to give property owners reasons for objections by raising taxes. He therefore favored creative financing and speculating on expected returns from an expanded tax base rather than increasing the rate of taxation.[77]

For both the railways and Haussmann's Paris, the state or the city were neither disposed nor able to pay for the projects, but they provided a framework for speculators and corporations to consolidate the savings of all levels of society, give acceptable returns on investments, and make large profits.[78] The similarities between Haussmann's operations and that of the railways reflected the dynamic forces of mid-nineteenth-century society. It is surprising that Haussmann did not recognize the kinship between his operation and that of the railways, implanted in the capital during the decade preceding his appointment as prefect. As mentioned earlier, his *Memoirs* testify to his knowledge of railway projects and of their impact, but he does not refer to them as models or precedents. The parallels drawn here between Haussmann's modus operandi and that of the railways, especially pertaining to design methods and financing, put in question Haussmann's claims to resourceful originality. Like the recommendations of the Siméon Commission des Embellissements, the precedents set by the railways did not surface in Haussmann's *Memoirs*, his most carefully crafted and unduly influential public relations document.

Railways and City Planning in London

The extensive urban upheaval caused by Haussmann's projects in Paris were followed from the other side of the Channel, where the resulting transformations received more attention than their social cost.[79] Traffic problems in London were as serious as in Paris, but transformation of the city was more gradual, although the 1860s did not have much to envy the French in number and impact of building work sites for improvements.[80] In addition to railway and station building, Holborn Viaduct and the

Thames Embankment, the latter with its railway component, brought construction sites to the central areas. Railway builders were soon followed by invasive sewer projects. By the 1870s, the increased circulation to railway terminals required costly realignments and improvements, which were almost as extensive as the railway projects but barely kept pace with road traffic.[81] Independent of railway construction, slum areas were claimed for new streets. As mentioned in Chapter 2, the shopping district of the West End also required considerable amount of slum clearance toward the end of the century.[82] By 1893, the railways were incorporated in urban planning considerations by the British city planner Arthur Cawston in his general London improvement plan. Cawston's description of railway facilities in the urban context stressed the need for creating convenient access in light of the fact that "the railway companies have been allowed admittance to central districts on terms easy to themselves but not advantageous to the convenience of the public."[83] That Cawston's suggestions for London exhibit great similarity with Napoleon III's and Haussmann's programs for Paris, albeit 40 years later, is significant. The process of London's adjustment to the demands of increased traffic caused by the railways, and by urban growth, did not occur as the assertive program of a controlling political regime but as a longer evolutionary process under a long-established constitutional monarch. The mechanism of a laissez-faire economic and political environment responded more gradually, and less radically, than the forceful, autocratic, and short-lived regime of Napoleon III.

5

Paris: Gare du Nord and Gare de l'Est

The dynamic potential of the railways at the service of communication and circulation inside the capital is harnessed very differently by two of Paris' stations located in close proximity to each other: the Gare du Nord (north station) and the Gare de l'Est (east station). Both stations were built under the July Monarchy and subsequent significant adjustments were made under the Second Empire. They are now part of the same neighborhood and administrative subdivision or *quartier* (quarter), but they exemplify two distinct modes of relating to the urban configuration[1] (Figure 5.1). The imprint of the adjustments made in the area of these stations during the Second Empire, more than a decade after initial railway construction, remains to this day (Figure 5.2). The Gare de l'Est figures prominently at the end of the city's north-south axis, whereas the Gare du Nord is wedged awkwardly between the angle of the Rue La Fayette and Boulevard Magenta. The two stations were built in distinct administrative units of the city and were shaped by the actions of two different companies. After construction of the second Gare du Nord, both stations, which serviced the greatest number of international passengers in Paris, were consecrated as monuments worthy of a visit, rendered convenient by their proximity.[2] Today, the two stations constitute one of the major poles of communication in the capital in what has now become the *quartier des deux gares* (ward of the two stations), recently connected by the new underground EOLE-Magenta Station.[3] With 700,000 passengers per day, it is the most intense traffic hub in Europe. During Haussmann's reconfiguration of the city, his relationship with the two railway companies and some of the persons affiliated with them left a perceptible and lasting imprint on their urban presence.[4] In spite of the railways ranking high among the emperor's priority projects for the city, Haussmann's implementation of this aspect of the program exhibits arbitrariness and inconsistency. Following the pattern of

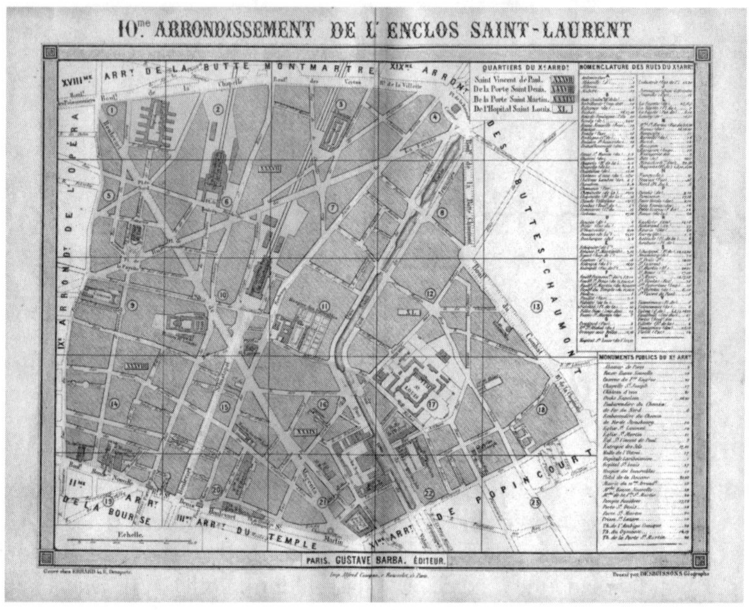

Figure 5.1   Tenth *arrondissement* (district) after 1860. From Emile de La Bédollière, *Le Nouveau Paris: Histoire de ses 20 arrondissements*, cartes topographiques de Desbuissons (Paris: Gustave Barba, 1860), unnumbered map.

closer focus on a more limited geographical area, this chapter examines the two closely located stations in the northeast of the capital and Haussmann's role in the disparity between the two.

Line Configuration and Terminal Location

The first rail line out of Paris was inaugurated on 24 August 1837. The Paris–Saint-Germain line was one of two lines proposed in 1834 to bring passenger railways to the capital.[5] At that time, most lines in the country had been designed primarily for coal transport within the industrial Loire region and in the south.[6] The first railway experiments in Paris were "leisure" or advertising lines intended to develop public confidence in the new mode of transport.[7] The promoter for Paris–Saint-Germain, Emile Péreire, had Saint-Simonian enthusiasm for transport projects. After the project was sanctioned by the Law of 9 July 1835, the Rothschilds and other financial concerns were brought on board to supply required capital. Emile Péreire considered Rothschild participation crucial for the enterprise and for the future of the industry.[8] The initial project, with the rail

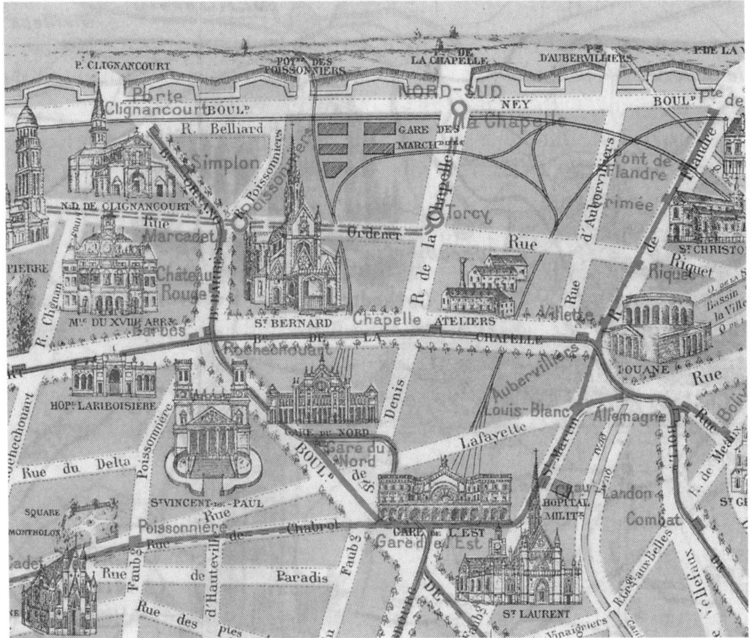

Figure 5.2   Map of Gare du Nord and Gare de l'Est area, Paris, ca. 1900. From L. Poulmaire, *Nouveau Paris monumental: Itinéraire pratique de l'étranger dans Paris* (Paris: Garnier Frères, imp. Dufrénoy [ca. 1900?]), detail. With permission of the Harvard Map Collection, Harvard College Library.

line departing from the Place de l'Europe, was revised to move in closer to the center near the Place de la Madeleine. The station was eventually built between the two proposed sites, on the Rue Saint-Lazare, at the site of the current Gare Saint-Lazare, inaugurated in 1842.[9]

The urbanist Pierre Lavedan considered the July Monarchy's handling of the location of rail lines as general territorial dispositions, whereas the stations were primarily a Parisian consideration.[10] However, without negating the importance of local power struggles, which did take place in the case of the two stations examined here, the location of a station reflected both line engineering requirements and local forces.

For the city, the location of a terminal was a political decision with financial implications. As prescribed by the railway law of 1842, the Paris prefecture was responsible for selecting and ceding the necessary land to the state, which would build the facilities to be entrusted to the companies for exploitation.[11] The municipal council anticipated that stations would alter their surrounding area and the urban geography of the capital. Therefore, the council decided on the location and construction of six terminal stations on 29 June 1844.[12] Unlike in London, where private initiative had been kept in check by Parliament, in Paris, the solution was in response to public pressure to spread the "benefits" of the new stations throughout the city. Confronted with the need to locate six sites between 350 to 400 meters in length (to accommodate sheds of 200 meters) on an average surface area of 40 hectares, the city claimed convent grounds and market garden lands, mostly within the toll tax area. In Paris, most of the large land areas available during the first half of the nineteenth century had been confiscated from émigrés or religious orders during the Revolution.[13]

For railway builders, determining the location of a terminal included a number of complex factors, such as the availability of suitable acreage, the estimated expropriation costs in built-up areas, and the pressure of interest groups operating through political and legal systems. Besides a large area and convenient access to the city, stations required suitable topographical features. These needed to accommodate a rail line with minimal curves and crossings, and adjustment to ground-level changes such as cuttings, embankments, and tunnels. The location of terminals was thus predicated by local geography and the *tracé* (layout) or configuration of the line.[14] Early debates on the configuration of rail lines revolved around the choice between running straight, strategic lines on plateaus, where no communication lines existed; or longer lines along rivers and canals, duplicating existing routes, diverted through more populated areas, which reflected concern for profit or the public good. The latter was encouraged by the Saint-Simonian progressive social theory, which permeated early railway development.[15] Engineers sought to determine the optimal ratio between length of line and traffic predictions. Despite the engineers' predilection for a rational approach, location became politicized, with communities lobbying intensely to be included on the *tracé* of projected lines.[16]

Within cities, the scale of intervention shifted from the national context of the line, to the general urban configuration, and to the urban real estate of the station and its access routes. The engineers who devised the configuration of a line operated on all three of these scales, which are interrelated. They were usually sensitive to the factors influencing them. Topography, for instance, a factor for the design of the entire line, does not cease to be operative as the line enters the city. In Paris, the rail lines enter through valleys, and on the right bank none of the five stations penetrated beyond the old meander of the Seine, north of its current course. Despite the engineers' ability to operate at different levels and to respond to local circumstances, the implantation of the *tracé* within cities was more frequently imposed on rather than integrated within the urban fabric.[17]

Like the routing of a line, the response of the city to building railway facilities also operated at different scales. Considered primarily for their local impact under the July Monarchy, terminals assumed city-wide dimensions under the Second Empire. Also, at the time of initial railway construction, under the July Monarchy, property owners had more power than either during the Restoration or under the Second Empire, and voiced their opinion through petitions or directly to their elected representatives in the municipal council.[18] For instance, when John Cockerill attempted to gain a concession to build the rail line between Paris and Brussels in 1837, Emile Péreire tried to persuade him to share the terminal for the Saint-Germain line and for those planned to Chartres, Tours, and Rouen. The companies were in favor of building two stations, the Gare d'Austerlitz on the left bank and the Gare Saint-Lazare on the right. The Péreires advocated a single "union" station at the Gare Saint-Lazare. This drew protest, which was expressed in a document addressed to both Houses of parlement by most Paris *arrondissements* (districts).[19] The need to counter a displacement of Paris' center toward the northwest and the need to acknowledge the function of each *quartier* (ward) within the city were stated in this document. Industry and commerce in the Saint-Denis and Saint-Martin areas with freight activity and warehouses justified the placement of the station in their proximity, an argument that eventually prevailed.[20]

Also, debates on common stations, which would have reduced the need for a belt line, were balanced by the military authorities' preference for multiple stations, which would be more conducive to rapid mobilization. Shared station facilities were considered undesirable from the outset because the savings achieved on construction costs would be offset by operational hardships. They were, however, given serious consideration because of their potential to reduce expense for cost-conscious companies, which progressively assumed more responsibility for building their stations. Yet other factors would also influence the configuration of installations. For instance, as the early railway theoretician Auguste Perdonnet wrote in 1856, in order to minimize cost, Paris passenger terminals were built at considerable distances from the center, and to avoid tolls on freight, goods stations were built outside of the toll enclosures.[21]

Area of Implantation for the Gare du Nord and Gare de l'Est

The Gare du Nord was built inside the Clos Saint-Charles (an extension of the Clos Saint-Lazare), and the Gare de l'Est was built on the location of the Saint-Laurent market. The Rue du Faubourg Saint-Denis runs between the two stations, and during the first half of the nineteenth century it separated the third and fifth *arrondissements*. The stations were thus originally built within separate administrative units. The 1860 reconfiguration of the city would place both stations in the tenth *arrondissement* and the Saint-Vincent-de-Paul quartier (see Figure 5.1).

The large undeveloped area known as Clos Saint-Lazare and its northern extension, the Clos Saint-Charles, located between the Grands Boulevards and the toll wall, had been owned by the Lazarist brothers, where they ran a leper house since the Middle Ages. The religious enclave had been enclosed, and it was represented on eighteenth-century city plans.[22] After nationalization of religious properties during the Revolution (1790), most of the confiscated land was ceded back to the city of Paris in 1811. Part of this land was intended for the construction of a hospital, which had been planned since the eighteenth century. The Hôpital de Lariboisière would eventually be built between 1846 and 1854 on land adjoining the toll wall, obtained in exchange from James de Rothschild in 1845. The land acquired by Rothschild would enable the future expansion of the Gare du Nord.

The railways did not initiate real-estate activity in the area. The Nouveau Quartier Poissonnière or southern area of the site had witnessed development attempts in the early nineteenth century. As part of Restoration development projects, which combined private and state capital, two societies were founded in the area to install new streets and to subdivide the land into building lots for resale. Both societies were dissolved by 1836 without performing the intended street development. The city (under Chabrol as prefect) demanded considerable contributions from the developers: ceding the land for streets to the city at no cost, edging them with stone sidewalks on both sides, and providing paving and lighting. Such conditions would create a precedent for the disputes between the city, the railway companies, and property owners about the responsibility for street development and maintenance around stations.[23] In 1847, the prefect did not consider it necessary to adapt the street network to accommodate station traffic. At that time, the area remained undeveloped, and large infrastructure development projects were initiated. These included acquisition of large holdings by the Compagnie des Entrepôts du Nord et de l'Est, the Compagnie du Chemin de Fer de Paris au Havre par les Plateaux (which failed to secure the concession for the line), and, later, the Compagnie du Chemin de Fer du Nord. Railway projects were thus among a second group of plans for this unbuilt site, where large parcels were available at low cost. Its geographic configuration between the two hills of Montmartre and Belleville (Buttes Chaumont) made it the logical northern route out of the city.[24] As of 1843, the state began to expropriate land for the station for the line from Paris to Belgium, which would be conceded to James de Rothschild in September 1845 as the Compagnie du Chemin de Fer du Nord.[25]

Initially lukewarm about the railways, James de Rothschild did not begin to see the Northern Railway as a *belle et grande affaire* (nice and big business) until the 1842 railway legislation was in place. As the debate on its implementation was taking place, he rekindled negotiations with the government about the Northern line. Unlike his involvement in other rail lines, where he remained only a financial advisor and sponsor, in northern France and southern Belgium he became directly involved in railways, navigation, mining, and metallurgy and invested considerable effort to place the company in a competitive position for the international connections to England and northern Germany.[26] Returns for investors in the Compagnie du Chemin de Fer du Nord were 8.5 percent in 1847. As a result of the financial crisis of 1847 and the revolution of 1848, Rothschild railway activity assumed a low profile between 1848 and 1854. By 1855, the Péreires' spectacular rise due to the Crédit Mobilier, founded in 1852, caused Rothschild to assume a more visible role. The Péreire-Rothschild rivalry lasted between 1855 and the Péreires' financial collapse in 1867. Until his death on 15 November 1868, James de Rothschild was actively involved in the affairs of the Chemin de Fer du Nord as chair of its Board of Directors. His reports to investors testify to the expanding nature of the railway operation in Paris.[27]

Gare du Nord

Station Site

As prescribed by the law of 1842, the Chemin de Fer du Nord was built by the Ponts et Chaussées (Administration of Public Works) corps of engineers. The Ponts et Chaussées engineer Louis Vallée had considered seven sites in 1837. All these sites drove the line into the city near the Porte de la Villette, the traditional route out of Paris toward the east. Vallée's projects, which also proposed lines to the center of the city, already demonstrate concern for connecting the terminals of the national rail network, an item Napoleon III would later incorporate in his program. The site selection was not settled until January 1843, and the reasons for the final choice remain obscure.[28]

The site eventually chosen by the government, the former Saint-Laurent enclosure, was located north of the Church of Saint-Vincent-de-Paul, between the *Fermiers généraux* (tax administrators) wall, the Rue du Faubourg Poissonnière, and the Rue du Faubourg Saint-Denis. The site was near established communication channels of the Saint-Denis and La Villette toll stations, the Saint-Martin Canal and La Villette Basin, the Montmartre and La Villette slaughterhouses, and the three parallel north-south streets of the *Faubourgs* (suburbs—Poissonnière, Saint-Denis, and Saint-Martin, the old Roman road). In addition to available acreage at low cost, the location offered good communications with the city, enhanced by the main artery of the new Rue La Fayette, which connected the Rues des Faubourgs. At the site where the Rues La Fayette and Faubourg Saint-Denis intersected, the Rues de l'Abattoir (de Dunkerque), Barrière Saint-Denis (de Denain), and Magasins (de Saint-Quentin) multiplied access routes and would prevent congestion. Primary access to the main artery of the Rue La Fayette would be provided by the street renamed de Denain in 1847. The site also offered close proximity to the customs warehouses and neighborhoods of commerce and transit activity. This site had been among those suggested by Vallée and was also in the Bourla Project devised in 1837–38 for a railway to Belgium by the John Cockerill Company[29] (see Appendix A). The communication advantages of the site were also evoked again in 1843 by the Ponts et Chaussées engineer Onfroy de Bréville (1799–1889) in his 23 January 1843 report for the Chemin de Fer du Nord.[30]

The Compagnie du Chemin de Fer de Paris à la Mer, which had been granted the concession to build a rail line to the Atlantic across the plateau rather than through the Seine Valley, had purchased almost half of the Clos Saint-Charles real estate in 1838 for its Paris terminal. The company was liquidated in 1839, and the aborted project enabled the Public Works Administration to purchase some of the company's land and the remaining Clos Saint-Charles for the Chemin de Fer du Nord. An 1843 surveyor's report attempted to reconcile for the Compagnie du Nord the conflicting plot and street boundaries resulting from earlier development plans. A protracted legal battle ensued to determine the status and ownership of the real estate planned for street development. This affected some of the parcels required for the station and it appears to have been resolved in favor of the railway.[31]

In 1845, the year the Chemin de Fer du Nord was conceded to James de Rothschild, real-estate activity became intense and complex. The Rothschild Notarial archives reveal the acquisition by James de Rothschild of close to eight hectares in the Clos Saint-Charles some months before obtaining the concession of the Paris-Nord line.[32] In 1846, Rothschild purchased additional land originally intended for the Hôpital de Lariboisière located next to the station. Rothschild further acquired a large area in 1853, part of which would be resold to the Compagnie du Nord in 1854. Development of the area lagged between 1845 and 1855. The 1855 universal exposition encouraged some activity, but the city, the railway company, and Rothschild did not appear eager to invest in improvements, even those mandated by prior agreements.

A decree of public utility dated 19 November 1855 prompted large-scale exchanges, which took place on 15–17 May 1856, between Rothschild, the Compagnie du Nord, the city of Paris, and the Assistance Publique in order to facilitate access to the hospital and to the railways by opening and widening streets. This included the opening of a section of the Boulevard du Nord (Magenta), the enlargement of the Place de Roubaix, and other adjustments. Rothschild became responsible for street development (including paving, sidewalks, gas, sewers, etc). He would also assume responsibility for building, on Boulevard Magenta, houses with freestone façades of specified height and configuration.[33] Subdivision and development of the area would then become more active after the construction of the hospital (completed in 1854) and expansion of the station. Between 1857 and 1865, with peak activity between 1860 and 1862, Rothschild began to build income-generating buildings (apartments, stores, storage) on Boulevard Magenta and nearby areas. He also leased some of his land to other builders and continued acquiring real estate in the area. At his death in 1868, he owned more than 40 houses on Boulevard Magenta built between 1857 and 1865 and a large number on Rue de Dunkerque, Rue Saint-Quentin, and Boulevard de Denain, which were reconfigured for the expansion of the Gare du Nord between 1859 and 1865. This substantial activity around the Gare du Nord had remained undiscovered, and it was commonly assumed that Rothschild had not dealt in real estate. Recent research shows that the area around the Gare du Nord and the Lariboisière hospital was built at James de Rothschild's initiative, in part by architects who had been hired by his family for other projects.[34]

First Gare du Nord

The state Ponts et Chaussées engineer Onfroy de Bréville was in charge of building the first segment of the Chemin de Fer du Nord between Paris and Amiens. His 1843 report, submitted before a final decision had been reached on the station, considered two projects of different sizes—4.5 and 5.5 hectares—in the Clos Saint-Lazare. The least extensive was selected, although the problem of outgrowing initial stations had already surfaced in London and Brussels. De Bréville expressed confidence that the initial, smaller project was more than adequate for rail transport and preferable for its impact on the neighboring street traffic. The second project was presented almost as a reluctant afterthought, prompted by unrealistic estimates of growth potential. Although the second project only required one additional hectare of surface, it involved more costly real estate and would thus increase expenses more drastically. De Bréville's cost-conscious recommendation prevailed, an understandable error of judgment given the lack of track record for these facilities at the time.[35]

The first Gare du Nord was designed in 1843–46 by engineer-architect François-Léonce Reynaud (1803–1880). Primarily an engineer, Reynaud had been a student of Durand and reflected his teacher's functionalism in his design. The sober design of the station fronted a 35×133 meter shed divided into two naves and constructed with cast-iron columns and wood trusses. The zinc-covered shed sheltered six tracks and two large platforms. A large side courtyard accommodated vehicular traffic. A distinctive feature was the use of the hollow shed columns as rain drain pipes connected to the city sewers.[36]

The *Journal des Chemins de fer* regularly reported on progress in the construction for this second station in the capital. In August 1845, the station appeared entirely adequate for the passenger and domestic freight traffic. The decision of the Chemin de Strasbourg to build a separate terminus, and the construction of a 14-hectare freight facility outside of the city walls, made the choice of the smaller project appear as a judicious one. Located on a square bordered by shops and placed on an incline, the station was reached by ascending streets, but it was built below grade and could only be seen completely from close proximity. It did not constitute a focal point, such as the Church of Saint-Vincent-de-Paul at the end of the Rue de Hauteville.[37]

The station was opened partially in September 1845, completed in January 1846, and inaugurated on 14 June 1846, at the same time as the rail line to the Belgian border, with splendid festivities organized by the Rothschilds.[38] This first station proved insufficient to accommodate the growing traffic by 1854. Several expansion plans were proposed between 1846 and 1857. Authorization to enlarge the terminal was given and decision to proceed was reached in 1857. Although most Paris stations were reconfigured with varying frequency during the nineteenth century, the first Gare du Nord's 11 years of service were remarkably short.[39]

Second Gare du Nord

A site near the heart of the city was briefly considered for the second Gare du Nord, but land next to the first terminal was purchased for the expansion, at high cost. The new terminal was located slightly to the south and west of the original one and accommodated continued operations during construction.[40] Plans were drawn and dated during the summer of 1858 by a company architect, Lejeune, and later by an independent architect, Ohnet.[41] The plans were deemed unsatisfactory either by the company or by the Conseil des Bâtiments Civils.

The station was replaced between 1861 and 1865 by the monumental terminal designed by Jakob-Ignaz Hittorff (1792–1867). The timing and scope of Hittorff's involvement in the project is debated. According to the historian Karl Hammer, Rothschild admired the Church of Saint-Vincent-de-Paul and wanted to hire its architect, Hittorff, for the terminal, but the Paris railway station expert Karen Bowie indicates that this fact is unverified.[42] Hammer and Donald Schneider date the association of Hittorff with the company architects to 1859, and Hammer indicates that Hittorff would later be given full responsibility for the project.[43] Karen Bowie bases the date of Hittorff's beginning involvement with the project in January 1861, on the evidence of a signed contract dated 16 January 1861.[44] Thomas von Joest adds to the argument in favor of Hittorff's late involvement the fact that some of the drawings held in the Hittorff archives at the Wallraf-Richartz Museum in Cologne are unsigned, reflecting Hittorff's respect for the work of colleagues rather than an omission.[45] The January 1861 contract stipulated that Hittorff would be responsible for the design of the façade, the building to a depth of ten meters, and the inner and outer lateral façades. Work would be performed by the company and its personnel.[46] However, working drawings for the shed trusses and columns bear the name of Hittorff and his son Charles, which indicates that the architect's responsibility must have been redefined at a later date.[47] Because the station was under construction as of the spring of 1861, a January 1861 contract would have given Hittorff very little time to provide a complete design, and he would have had to rely on work done previously.

Bowie indicates that the reason for Hittorff's involvement in the project remains obscure. Company records do not shed light on this; in fact, they contain the text of a 11 May 1860 decision not to build the station as a monument with sculptural decoration. This was in order to assume a low profile and to avoid pressure from a cost-conscious and aesthetically concerned public to make changes.[48] The project begun a year later would include 23 statues.[49] The 1862 shareholders' report indicated that the economy-minded company had reserved for the façade the "architectural and artistic forms which we could not do away with entirely" for an "edifice [...] worthy of the head-house for the Northern Railway."[50] The same report commented on the size of the station. Current progress already enabled the determination that it would be sufficient for current and future needs. The fact that the architect is not mentioned in the 1862 report, when he had to have been involved since construction was in progress, and that the report downplays the importance of the terminal's architecture suggest that earlier company documents may have also omitted the name of the architect when he was already on board in order to avoid unwanted publicity. It does seem likely that, in light of the Rothschild-Péreire rivalry, James de Rothschild would have been concerned to assert his presence on the Parisian streetscape at the site of the company that he controlled and that was considered the "jewel on his crown."[51] Several factors point in this direction. Emile Péreire had stated that he wanted to write his ideas on the landscape, and the Péreire real-estate involvement in the Rue de Rivoli and Parc Monceau areas gave them more visibility in Paris than the Rothschild industrial investments (Rothschild real-estate investments in Paris having had no public exposure).[52] If the Rothschild family had not benefited from the transformation of Paris to the extent the Péreire brothers had, because of their perceived financial conservatism and residual affiliation with the preceding parliamentary regime, their ability to operate on a grand scale without direct imperial support remained unimpaired.[53] James de Rothschild wanted to make an assertive, monumental gesture.[54]

Rothschild's need for the grand station and its sculptures justified overriding the board decision and bringing in an internationally known architect. The resulting terminal would set a precedent for subsequent luxuriously decorated Belle Epoque stations.[55]

Completion of the design by the end of February 1860 had been announced in *The Builder*'s 3 March issue, but a year elapsed before final approval and beginning of construction in the summer of 1861.[56] During that time, the façade designs were modified at least six times, due to Haussmann's interventions.[57] Because part of the land was under the city's jurisdiction, Haussmann had the legal right to intervene in decisions about the terminal, and his interference with the station design is reflected in the multiple versions of the façade. The first drawings are dated 1858, 14 March 1859, 20 March 1859, April 1859, and 11 May 1860. Haussmann rejected the May 1860 design in a letter to the company dated 28 January 1861, objecting to the decorative elements and double pilasters. Revisions were dated 20 March 1861 and 4 May 1861, the final design submitted to the prefect with a letter. This was presumably approved because construction followed within 60 days.[58]

Haussmann disliked Hittorff, whom he had inherited from the July Monarchy. Haussmann's *Memoirs* describe the architect as inflexible, given by some the nickname of "Prussian," which alluded to his Germanic origin.[59] Besides some disagreements about the Place de la Concorde and the Avenue Foch, the Church of Saint-Vincent-de-Paul had also been the terrain of a power struggle between the architect and the prefect. Hittorff, who had done archaeological work and published on the chromatic decorations on ancient monuments, had devised a decorative program for the church.[60] Haussmann saw the exterior polychromy proposed by Hittorff as

> a great shame to hide thus the simple and noble beauty of the materials used in construction. And when various ornaments adorn this casing, which remind me of the tattoos used by barbaric peoples to cover their nakedness instead of clothing, I cannot help but find grotesque this pretentious form of decoration.[61]

Haussmann's irritation with the Gare du Nord area had surfaced earlier. He considered the monumental staircase with driving ramps leading to the Church of Saint-Vincent-de-Paul out of proportion with the building, but he nonetheless had the ground in front of it lowered by Baltard to reduce the incline from the Faubourg Poissonnière to the Gare du Nord.[62]

As for the Gare du Nord, wedged between the northern obtuse angle of the Rue La Fayette and the yet-to-be-constructed Boulevard Magenta (originally Boulevard du Nord), Haussmann relates:

I only had further dealings with Mr. Hittorff on the occasion of the station for the Chemin de Fer du Nord, which the Baron James de Rothschild had hired him to build. I determined, in consultation with the architect, the layout of the three access routes to this station: the Avenue de Denain, which runs toward the Rue La Fayette at about the middle of the Place de Roubaix [now Napoleon III], laid out in front of the façade, the Rue de Compiègne leading to the departure court; the Rue de Saint-Quentin, leading to the arrival court. I had these two streets opened according to his indications, and he played me the trick of changing the entrance to the departure and arrival courts, which are no longer in front of the streets leading to them.[63]

Haussmann had thus another reason to be ill-disposed toward Hittorff: the architect had been hired by James de Rothschild to design the Gare du Nord. Beholden to the Péreire brothers, Haussmann was wary of Rothschild influence.[64]

The Compagnie du Chemin de Fer du Nord's Paris terminal would be a suitable monument, achieving dimensions close to those of St. Peter's in Rome, 36,000 square meters, to house station facilities and company headquarters. Forty meters in height at the top of the statue of Paris on the central portal, the façade would be 180 meters long (40 meters wider that the Avenue Foch). The U-shaped terminal building fronted a shed of 200 meters in length. The shed was built using the gabled truss system invented by Polonceau in 1837 with a span of 36 meters and two side aisles of 18 meters. Departures were located on the left, arrivals on the right, and suburban traffic in the center.[65] The masonry façade was erected between 1861 and 1863, when the sculptures were completed. These include Mercury, Neptune, and Jupiter, and personifications of 23 cities—Paris, 8 foreign cities, and 14 domestic cities served by the Chemin de Fer du Nord.[66] Two years later, the old station was still to be demolished, leaving the project incomplete. The station was discretely inaugurated in 1864, the work completed in 1866.[67] Company headquarters were on the left side of the departure court, expanding beyond the Rue de Maubeuge and joined by an arched passageway.[68] Both the head building and the shed are believed to be the work of Hittorff, who, unlike most contemporary architects, had the engineering knowledge to handle shed design[69] (Figure 5.3).

As evidenced by the May 1861 final design for the façade, Hittorff was aware that this façade could only be seen in full from an oblique angle. Meeks comments that the façade elevation cannot be seen frontally but is nonetheless impressive.[70] As cited above, Haussmann blamed Hittorff for changing the station configuration after the street layout had been agreed upon.[71] Correspondence in the company archives dated between May and September 1863, after work had actually begun, documents the prefect's request to move back the building and the company's protest against the prefect's alterations of the original street and plaza design. The company refused to demolish recent construction. The resulting street layout had reduced the Place de Roubaix (now Napoleon III) to a mere widening of the Rue de Dunkerque, a fact Haussmann does not mention. Extant documents do not enable us to re-create an exact sequence of events, but the resulting layout no longer had the Rue de Compiègne lead to the departure pavilion on the left and the Rue de Saint-Quentin to the arrival pavilion on the right. The aesthetically motivated axial approaches to the side pavilions have been replaced by a functional access to the departure and arrival courts. Given Haussmann's preference for baroque axial perspectives, and his propensity to give his aesthetic notions priority over traffic requirements, this would have been an irritating development, which he would not have condoned had he been party to the decision.[72] In the original configuration of the station as it was built, only commuters entered the station by the central pavilions, approaching by the 30-meter Boulevard de Denain. Commuters, familiar with Haussmann's boulevards and their visual foci, approached the central pavilion axially. The façades of the Boulevard de Denain frame the central pavilion. As they open up obliquely at the boulevard's northern end, they gradually reveal the side arches, and then, upon reaching the Place de Roubaix, the full symmetrical façade.[73] The combination of temple pediment and triumphal arch framed by pilastered pylons on the central pavilion provides a stately gateway to the station's main concourse and to the central, loftier train shed. This alone constituted a powerful statement of company prestige integrated into the accidents of the Parisian urban fabric. The international or long-distance traveler, riding up the Rue de Compiègne, would gradually see more of the departure pavilion on the way to the departure court and, upon reaching the corner of the Place de Roubaix, get an oblique view of the whole station façade before proceeding further toward the archway at the end of the court.[74] The strong verticals of the pylons enhanced by statues and the horizontals of the entablatures would also create a strong visual impression on the traveler. It would actually present him with the view of the station adopted by most photographers, the view by which the station was likely to be known from guidebooks and travel literature, the view that adopted the angle of Hittorff's own drawing of the façade. The arriving passenger, if choosing to look back, would get a similar, although less characteristic, sweeping view. For the observer lingering on the Place de Roubaix, another element of the station façade animates the "compressed and dynamic" space of the station square.[75] The pronounced entablatures of the horizontal wings between the pavilions echo the mansard lines of the Haussmannian façades of the *place* (square) and visible

Figure 5.3 J. I. Hittorff, Gare du Nord, Paris. Façade from the west, 1878. Photograph, The Snite Museum of Art, University of Notre Dame (accession number: 1982.006.2s).

nearby streets, integrating the station, not only in the awkward footprint of the station area, but also in its visual space. This articulated and subtle mode of assertive integration was the architect's ultimate response to the prefect.

The replacement of the first Gare du Nord by a larger facility fits into a Northern Railway pattern of expansion in Paris, reflected in the annual shareholders' reports. The storage facility built at La Chapelle in 1853–54 and connected to both the station and the road to Saint-Denis had become insufficient, and additional land was purchased to build a new coal station facility. Adjustments to facilitate operations were made in and around the first station prior to and during the construction of the new station.[76] Further modifications were made in 1875, 1884, 1889, and 1891.[77] As the annual reports to shareholders indicate, the station represented only a small fraction of the railway real-estate concern, which expanded each year, most notably in the area of La Chapelle. The land around the station was acquired gradually by the company until only a sliver of real estate remained in private hands west of the Rue du Faubourg Saint-Denis between the Boulevard de la Chapelle and the Rue de Dunkerque.[78] The systematic expansion strategy of the company is illustrated in the acquisition in 1876 of the Vacassy property at 185 Rue du Faubourg Saint-Denis, justified like all other projects by the requirements of the operations. Delivery of vital staples such as milk and fish as well as required shunting operations were invoked by the company to justify acquisition by eminent domain of the Vacassy house, which "cut into the station like a hatchet"[79] (Figure 5.4). The records suggest that this was a deliberate, pointed campaign to acquire this and some neighboring properties, not massive expropriations of a large number of properties.[80] This relentless development would continue until the first decades of the twentieth century, when the automobile and motorized freight began to give the railways serious competition.

Gare de l'Est

If Haussmann played a role in the configuration of the Gare du Nord area, he inherited the Gare de l'Est street network. Before work on the station for the Chemin de Strasbourg started in 1847, on the Saint-Laurent fair grounds, the question of its location had been under study by the Ponts et Chaussées between 1832 and 1845. The general direction of the line was prescribed by the Law of 11 June 1842. Considered of strategic importance, the infrastructure for the Paris-Strasbourg line was to be executed by the state, as mandated by the Law of 2 August 1844. Several routes were proposed: along the Marne Valley (the shortest), along the line to Belgium, or with the line to Lyon. The options included

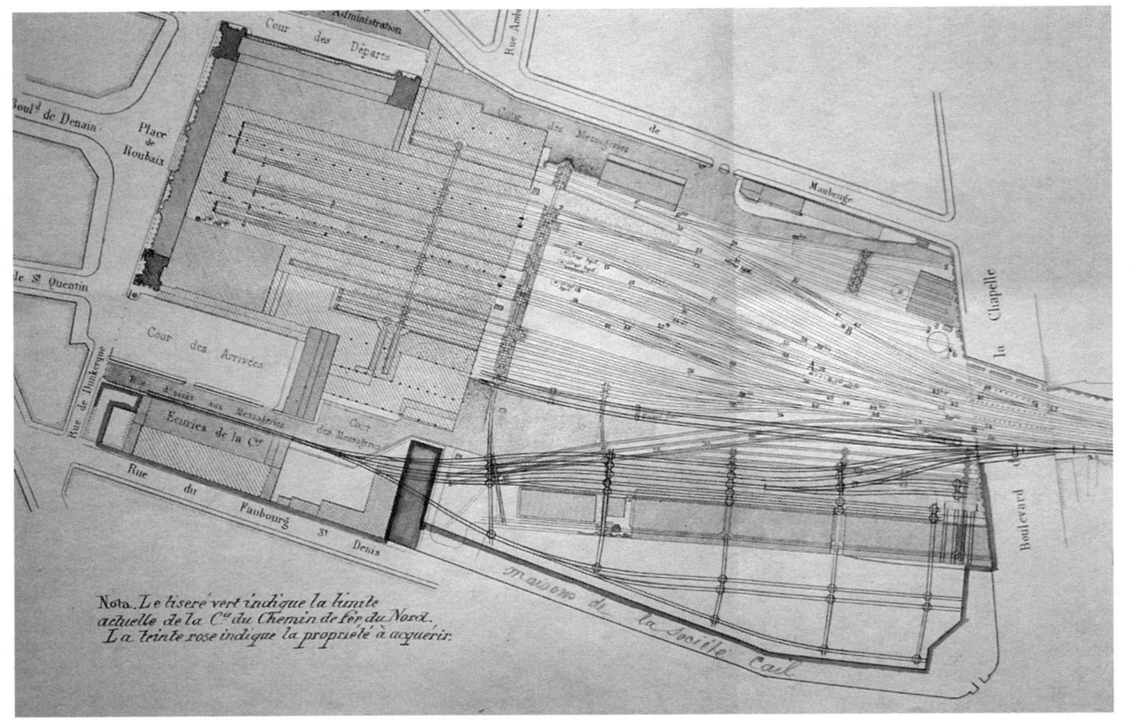

Figure 5.4 Plan of Gare du Nord and Vacassy property. Archives de Paris, Chemin de Fer du Nord, D6S9/4.

a direct, strategic, plateau line toward Strasbourg or a line following the Marne Valley up to Meaux, which eventually prevailed. The Ponts et Chaussées engineer Pierre-Sophie Cabanel de Sermet (1801–75) was put in charge of the first segment between Paris and Meaux. He favored a line along the Marne River up to Lagny and Meaux, which did not interfere with the transport activity of the Canal de l'Ourcq, going from La Villette to Claye.[81]

In his recommendation for a terminal location, contained in a February 1845 report, Cabanel de Sermet took into account the local economy of the areas in the north and east of the city, as well as the interrelated nature of line configuration and station implantation site.[82] In 1844, the municipal council had suggested several sites in the eastern Faubourg Saint-Antoine, which reflected a concern to counter the effect of population displacement toward the northwest. Two options remained in contention: the Faubourg Saint-Antoine and the Rue Neuve-Chabrol in the Faubourg Saint-Martin, to be reached by a northern approach. The Faubourg Saint-Antoine was supported by the municipal council but discouraged by military authorities because it involved going through the Bois de Vincennes. Studies showed that the Faubourg Saint-Antoine option would be shorter and more cost-effective. The possibility of a common station with the northern line had been eliminated, based on anticipated operational needs. Cabanel de Sermet recommended the northern site because of its proximity to the growing canal transport activity at La Villette and to the storage facilities in the Marais. He proposed the Marché Saint-Laurent site on Rue Neuve-Chabrol, with viaducts to cross the lines on the Rue La Fayette and on the peripheral aqueduct. His recommendation for the Faubourg Saint-Martin site was based on the need to facilitate transit between the Atlantic and Germany while consolidating local transport facilities. The selected site also asserted the independence of the railway from municipal pressure and from military constraints.[83] The site was among those considered by Vallée in 1837 for the Gare du Nord. Vallée had indicated that the Rue Neuve-Chabrol site involved only open land and one unimportant building, which should be easy to acquire. In 1844, opposition from neighboring owners was stronger than it had been in the Clos Saint-Lazare for the Gare du Nord.[84] Cabanel de Sermet's recommendations were nonetheless adopted a year later.[85]

The precise location of the terminal was also debated: a more remote and less costly site on the wide Rue La Fayette, designed for heavy traffic, was considered preferable to the "Enclos Saint-Laurent," where the Rues des Faubourgs Saint-Denis and Saint-Martin remained subject to overcrowding. Local owners met (on 16 November 1845) to protest the proposed location on the narrow Rue Neuve-Chabrol, which did not provide enough room for traffic in an area already encumbered by market activity. Also, recent improvement efforts by owners on the upper Rue du Faubourg Saint-Martin would be eradicated by the Rue Neuve-Chabrol terminal. The institution of the Quarantaine Brothers would be threatened and so would their adult education program, as well as the cultural activity of street spectacles congregating around the market. On the other hand, residents of the lower Rues des Faubourgs Saint-Denis and Saint-Martin were in favor of the Rue Neuve-Chabrol location. They anticipated that the Rue La Fayette station activity would be deflected westward by the wide, oblique artery either to the third *arrondissement* (now also tenth), which already enjoyed the activity of the Gare du Nord, or beyond to the more affluent western part of the city. They were eager to retain the benefits of the station business in their *arrondissement*. By 13 December, the administration had settled on the Rue Neuve-Chabrol site.[86]

The 1846 company report gives some details of the implantation process. State engineers had proposed a station of two and a half hectares. The company board provided a counterproposal, which resulted in the design of a 5.2-hectare site, including the new lateral access streets, and a proportional increase of all facilities. New access streets were approved by the government at the company's expense, and it was expected that the street perpendicular to the front of the station would be lengthened as far as the boulevard, but the company was not prepared to assume the cost. The station would penetrate deeper than any other station toward Paris' commercial areas. Freight facilities, located outside the toll collection area, were increased from six hectares in the original project to 18 hectares, not including adjoining access roads.[87]

The Gare de l'Est, called Gare de Strasbourg until 1855, was begun in 1847 and put in service on 5 July 1849.[88] Auguste Perdonnet commented on the successful design of the structure with its 160-meter glass shed, which covered five tracks (Figure 5.5). He regretted that the architect, François Duquesney (1790–1849), did not live to see the completion of what he considered the best specimen of the building type.[89] Writing in 1956, Carroll Meeks concurred: "In its prime and long after, it was acclaimed as the finest station in the world, and there seem to be no reason even now to quarrel with this judgment."[90] About the site, Perdonnet remarked that carriages did not have access to the colonnade to deposit and pick up passengers. The opening of the Boulevard de Strasbourg required the construction of a perron, which eliminated this convenience. Although the Boulevard de Strasbourg would not be opened for several years after the completion of the station in 1849, the architect took into account the potential vista the boulevard would create for the station. The vault of the train shed appears on the façade. Originally unglazed, it was later closed by semicircular glass-and-iron tracery, cloaking the technological innovation of the shed under the traditional elements of a cathedral rose window.[91] The architect did not, however, anticipate the opening of the Boulevard de Sébastopol, which dwarfed the Gare de l'Est as a visual focal point, a fact that caused Haussmann great disappointment.[92]

Like the Compagnie du Nord, the Compagnie du Chemin de Fer de l'Est expanded onto adjacent areas. The narrow configuration of the station had to be modified as early as 1855 to accommodate the new concession of a line to Mulhouse, south of Strasbourg. After transfer of toll collecting to the external fortifications in 1860, additional freight facilities were developed outside the new toll area. The passenger waiting and arrival areas were reconfigured in 1885 and 1900. During this last campaign, neighboring streets such as the Rue de Metz and Rue de Nancy were incorporated into the station premises. The Gare de l'Est was duplicated to the east of the original Duquesney building in 1931, which allowed significant elements of the original, 1849 structure to remain extant today while increasing track capacity from 16 to 30.[93] The station facilities now occupy the entire area between the Rues La Fayette, du Faubourg Saint-Martin, de Strasbourg, and d'Alsace.

At the edge of the area Le Corbusier envisioned demolishing in his 1925 Voisin plan, the station remains a recognizable landmark in today's Paris. Currently, plans are under consideration to cover part of the rail tracks and to create a cantilevered park area along the Rue d'Alsace, possibly related to a pedestrian connection between the two stations. In this *quartier des deux gares* at the heart of the tenth *arrondissement*, the station tracks are the only space convertible to "green space" in this area of the capital most deprived of park facilities.[94]

Urban Reconfiguration near Stations

Once the location of the first stations had been determined and the stations put in service by the late 1840s, communication needs became imperative.[95] The 12,000 vehicles that, every day, used the Rue Neuve-Chabrol, the only, narrow access to the Gare de Strasbourg, caused daily accidents. Concerned as he was to facilitate traffic, Napoleon III supported the construction of a wide avenue from the station to the Grands Boulevards, the Boulevard de Strasbourg, and, on a diagonal, the Boulevard Magenta, which would provide a connection between the Gare du Nord and the Gare de l'Est. This proposal also included the Boulevard Mazas (now Diderot) for the Gare de Lyon, the Boulevards Saint-Marcel and Arago for the Gare d'Orleans, the Boulevards du Port-Royal and Raspail, and the Rue de Rennes for the Gare Montparnasse.[96] In 1860,

Figure 5.5   F.-A. Duquesney, Gare de l'Est, Paris, façade. Photograph by François Auguste Renard, "Gare de Strasbourg," ca. 1852. The Snite Museum of Art, University of Notre Dame (accession number: 1987.015.016).

when Napoleon III and Haussmann integrated the territories between the two lines of fortifications, the stations had developed along the edge of a tight urban fabric. By then, the railway companies were experiencing steady growth and laying claim to additional real estate to expand their facilities.

In the immediate vicinity of the stations, railway facilities and hotels were built, usually in a traditional style, which did not emulate the stations' innovative architectural solutions.[97] Despite their distance from the center, the railway stations radiated development in peripheral areas. Usually slow outside of the main axes, such development could happen at a rapid pace. For instance, change in the Rochechouart area, two blocks west of the Gare du Nord, was such that it warranted a special mention in the 1863–64 cadastral update. From a working-class district where rents were kept low by two gas factories and by slaughterhouses, the area acquired higher status within ten years.[98] In the nearby Faubourg Poissonnière, unscathed by Second Empire projects, the station and ensuing reconfigurations created a knot of perpetual congestion at the crossing of the Rue La Fayette and the Boulevard Magenta. In 1854, irate neighborhood residents addressed a communication to the prefect of the Seine, deploring the conditions of the area and demanding action. They also credited the Compagnie du Nord with commissioning studies for the expansion of the station[99] (Appendix A).

The development of the street pattern in the Gare du Nord area occurred at the margin of the Nouveau Quartier Poissonnière, between the Rues du Faubourg Poissonnière and du Faubourg Saint-Denis. It established as its main axis the Rue d'Hauteville, the church, and Rue Saint-Vincent-de-Paul, interrupted by Place de Roubaix, into the hospital, contiguous with the peripheral boulevard at its northern end (see Figure 5.2). Within the development, the street hierarchy included some arteries that were to expand beyond its limits and connect to a city-wide communication network. The Rue La Fayette (Charles X), authorized in 1822, would later connect the Rue du Faubourg Poissonnière to the *barrière* (toll) of La Villette. The second diagonal, the Rue du Nord, later widened into the Boulevard Magenta, perpendicular to the Rue La Fayette would reach from Montmartre to the Place de la République. By 1830, the crossing of the Rue La Fayette and Boulevard Magenta had been established, as well as a number of other residential streets around the Saint-Vincent-de-Paul church.[100]

As mentioned earlier, in the context of the Rothschild real-estate activity, the subdivision of the area and the development of its street network had left much buildable land vacant toward the end of the July Monarchy. This would change under the Second Empire when the area was modified to accommodate traffic from the Gares du Nord and de l'Est and as part of the regime's street reconfigurations. Included in this campaign were the opening of the Rue La Fayette as far as the Rue du Faubourg Montmartre and the opening of the Rue de Maubeuge to the Rue de Dunkerque near the Gare du Nord. Haussmann commented in his *Memoirs:*

> I cannot leave the rue La Fayette, which leads to the Chemin de Fer du Nord without making a note of the enormous expense (about 32 and a half million) which the City had to assume, alone, to open streets for the new station and for the Rue de Maubeuge, which runs from the Faubourg Montmartre to the Boulevard de La Chapelle, crossing Boulevard Magenta, symmetrically where they meet the Rue Saint-Vincent-de-Paul, in alignment with the Hôpital de La Riboisière.[101]

The expansion of the station diverted the Rue de Maubeuge northward along the western edge of the terminal. Haussmann appeared to begrudge the Chemin de Fer du Nord the large amount of funds expended on the Rue de Maubeuge (and on the lengthening of the Rue La Fayette to the Porte de Pantin done at the same time).[102] At stake here was an understanding of the status of access roads to stations. As noted earlier, the status of streets in developments and near stations was not defined precisely, and questions were further fueled by the hybrid nature of railway companies. Did the streets lead to private or state facilities? The city was reluctant to commit funds, but the Ministry of Transport remained mindful of the limited terms of railway concessions, which would eventually return the companies' physical plant to the state. In 1859, the area around the Gare du Nord was rebuilt, with the expense shared by the city and the company.[103]

Close to a dozen projects were conceived between 1838 and 1856 for the street configuration near the site of the Gare du Nord[104] (Appendix A). All aimed at improving access to the station and reflected two approaches. One used the spine of the Poissonnière development as organizing axis, the other gave the new station organizing power on the surrounding area (the first station had been inserted into the existing street configuration). Few of the solutions contained in these urban configuration projects were implemented, and the Gare du Nord had to make do with the short, widened Rue de Denain, perpendicular to the Rue de Dunkerque. One aspect of these projects is significant. As mentioned in Chapter 4, the Commission des Embellissements, also known as Commission Siméon, was appointed by Napoleon III in August 1853 and silenced by Haussmann shortly afterward, but nonetheless submitted a report in December 1853. The commission recommended the construction of a boulevard from the chevet of Saint-Germain l'Auxerrois (i.e., along the Seine) to the Gare du Nord. It was part of a number of north-south arteries intended to bring greater cohesion between the two banks of the river.[105] Another proposal by the architect Brouty, designed in 1852, and a subsequent reworking would have continued the Rue de Denain, in front of the Gare du Nord, to the Boulevard Bonne-Nouvelles (or the Porte Saint-Denis in a variant included on the same project) by opening a Boulevard Impérial parallel to the Boulevard de Strasbourg. The plan for the Boulevard Impérial was subsequently published in the *Revue Municipale* of 16 November 1855, and Napoleon III awarded Brouty a gold medal for this project. Brouty's 1857 revision, published by Louis Lazare, would have connected the Gare du Nord and the Gare Montparnasse. Such a project would have been devastating for the quartier du Faubourg Poissonnière but was considered favorably by the railway company, which had also produced alternate designs for a Boulevard Impérial. The project was mentioned again as Boulevard du Nord in 1863 by A. Portret, writing for the *Gazette des Architectes et du Bâtiment,* as an expected and desirable development.[106] The reason for the abandonment of the direct link from the Gare du Nord to the Seine or the Grand Boulevards has not surfaced explicitly; it was one of a number of projects abandoned between 1853 and 1864. Haussmann is usually credited with this decision, which is in keeping with his apparent displeasure at the accommodations required at the city's expense for the Gare du Nord.[107] The absence of a direct boulevard connection had an impact for the station's stature on the urban landscape.

The footprint of the Gare du Nord on any Paris map appears awkward. Hittorff complained about the lack of monumental access and, as we have noted, adjusted his design accordingly. The station has not been integrated in Haussmann's boulevard system, and the "suffocatingly small square" of the Gare du Nord contrasts with the boulevards creating the perspectives to the Péreire-controlled stations, the Boulevard de Strasbourg to the Gare de l'Est and the Rue de Rennes to the Gare de Montparnasse.[108]

Another variation from the Siméon Commission plan recommendations is the replacement of the artery that was to connect the Gare Saint-Lazare to the Gare du Nord and the Gare de l'Est by the Boulevard Haussmann further south.[109] This privileged the west of the city and relegated the communication between the three stations to the narrower Rue de Chateaudun before reaching the Rue La Fayette. The resulting configuration did not provide a dedicated communication artery between the three main-line terminals north of the boulevards and forced the traveler going from one area of northern France to another to negotiate the complex street pattern of the capital.

Conclusion

The railways remained understated in Haussmann's projects, and they did not have the same configuring or social urban impact as in other cities, in part because of the magnitude of the various public works undertaken during the Second Empire. No large population displacement can be attributed directly to the railways in Paris, as in London, because most of the demolitions performed were not for railway projects. Nor can the railways be faulted for bisecting the city, as they would in Brussels, or dividing the center from its surroundings, as they did in Berlin. They did, however, create barriers to communications in the areas they crossed, especially in the annexed suburbs. Passenger and freight stations, with their ancillary works and storage and maintenance facilities, redirected traffic and demanded reconfiguration of access routes.[110] The city was unprepared for the importance the stations would acquire and was not yet disposed to treat them with the deferential distance of monuments. In the Gare du Nord and Gare de l'Est areas, Rothschild real-estate and railway involvement may have been a factor in the disparity between the access to the two stations, but extant documents provide no evidence that the Compagnie de l'Est was deliberately given preferential treatment under the Second Empire.[111] Actually, the Gare de l'Est's impressive siting is unusual among stations in Paris and elsewhere.[112]

Railway stations were implicated in strategic planning for the capital, and their ability to channel troop reinforcements to quell insurrections in sensitive areas was invoked to fund Haussmann's first and second networks.[113] However, the railways were not given the radiating and penetrating power of the two strategic rond-points, the Etoile (now Place Charles de Gaulle) in the west and the Place de la Nation in the east (Figure 5.6). It is the connection between these two poles that Haussmann's boulevards privileged, most notably by the artery that bears his name, instead of a connection between stations. Haussmann's third network privileged the west of the city. A differentiation between east and west had become noticeable since the Restoration. The aristocracy, the rising bourgeoisie, and the increasing numbers of professionals and politicians favored the west. Artisans, laborers, and the poor settled in the industrializing east.[114] The Commission des Embellissements recognized this fact, and in the area outside of the *Fermiers généraux* walls, it recommended more axes of communication in the north and in the east than in the west.[115] Beyond the semicircular line created by the Gare du Nord, Gare de l'Est, Canal Saint-Martin, and Boulevard Richard Lenoir (built to cover the canal between 1861 and 1863), the east of the city remained proletarian. It would be the stronghold of the Communards in May 1871 and waited for more than a century to be targeted for development by the city, between 1983 and 2002. Projects realized under Haussmann would be more numerous in the west, creating what the urban historian Pierre Lavedan termed a "West End."[116] The imbalance between east and west was not part of Napoleon III's plan and nor was it included in the recommendations of the 1853 Commission des Embellissements.[117] Despite his claims to have maintained balance in his projects, Haussmann encouraged the continuation of western displacement by giving greater priority to the west.[118] Possibly only priority, rather than emphasis, because Haussmann's work was interrupted by exposure of his financial practices, his failure to consolidate support, and the decline of the empire.

Haussmann's shaping of Parisian space also influenced its social configuration with, beyond the marked distinction between the well-to-do west and the working-class east, a strong gradation between center and periphery. This differentiation process was subtle, there being no marked difference in the scale and mode of planning or street building between the east and the west. The uniformity enforced by codes and building agreements in the whole city even drew complaints for being dull, but the abundant spaces for the bourgeoisie in the west made it harder to attract the middle class in areas where speculative housing for the lower class was more dominant.[119] The historian Jeanne Gaillard blames Haussmann for placing side by side "two cities, that of the rich, and that of the others."[120] This segregation, which was spontaneous rather than enforced, had as corollary

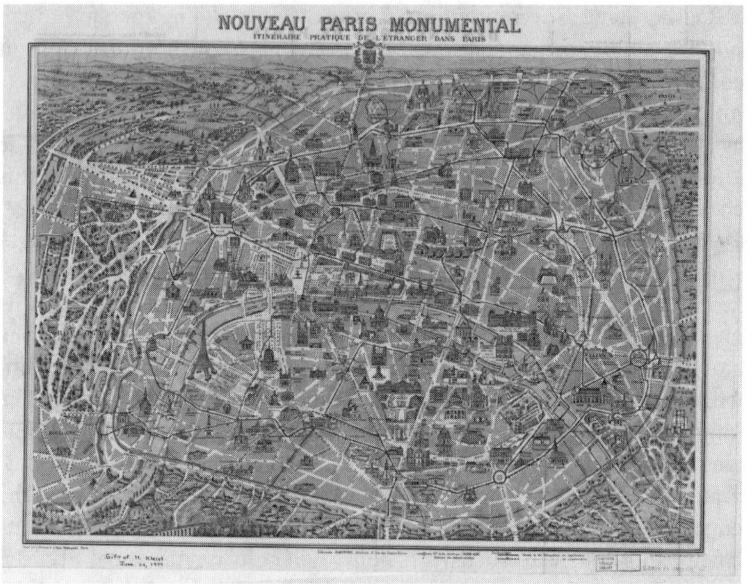

Figure 5.6   Paris, ca. 1900. From L. Poulmaire, *Nouveau Paris monumental: Itinéraire pratique de l'étranger dans Paris* (Paris: Garnier Frères, imp. Dufrénoy [ca. 1900?]), recto. With permission of the Harvard Map Collection, Harvard College Library.

a significant loss of social control: the working class' manners, circumstances, and readiness to political action were no longer tempered by the daily contacts with the bourgeoisie, which occurred when they shared the same streets or houses.[121]

Beyond the demolition of working-class housing in the center, the removal of industry toward the periphery, justified on aesthetic grounds, encouraged the working class (and, as Harvey argues, their political power) to settle at the periphery, where employment had been relegated.[122] Between 1861 and 1870, the population of the ten central *arrondissements* decreased by 33,000, whereas that of the peripheral ones grew by 200,000. The areas of Les Batignolles, Montmartre, La Chapelle, La Villette, and Belleville, between the toll wall and the fortifications, which the working classes had frequented for their cheaper enentertainment before annexation, attracted the displaced and immigrants.[123] The uneven terrain of the northeast (Montmartre, Ménilmontant, the Buttes-Chaumont hills, and the valley of La Villette) had influenced communications and the social configuration of the area. The valley that communicated with the north and the northeast, regions of coal, industry, and agriculture, also attracted the establishment of canals, cattle markets, slaughterhouses, gas works, as well as the workshops, and coal and freight stations of the Companies du Nord and de l'Est. These facilities, requiring large acreage, were not conducive to residential settlement. After 1850, however, moving to this area no longer meant social demotion, for the railway yards, repair shops, and freight stations provided steady employment and training in industries such as metallurgy. In other words, the location of the railway stations and their satellite facilities reinforced the centrifugal population migration.[124]

To a certain extent, the railways also played a part in the east-west disparity. Initially, only the companies operating from the Gare Saint-Lazare, in the west, developed suburban lines. Most of the other stations serviced long-distance traffic. Geography also compounded this trend toward displacement, for the western suburbs included more numerous important and affluent centers (Versailles, Saint-Cloud, Saint-Germain, Maison-Laffite, Argenteuil). The east, with its fragmented relief, had no communities that provided incentive for suburban development. Napoleon III appears to have been sensitive to this as he requested that, when it opened in 1859, the line from the Bastille to Vincennes include third-class carriages, specifically to enable workers to commute to the east and work in Paris. Nonetheless, the western terminal, with the city's main suburban railways, became the right-bank hub of suburban and leisure travel.[125]

As for development inside the city, Rothschild, unlike the other bankers, who lived and speculated in the west, invested in the Gare du Nord area. If there ever was evidence that Haussmann deliberately supported Péreire operations or marginalized those of the Rothschild, it may have gone up in smoke on 24 May 1871. It can be demonstrated that the Rothschild investments in the Gare du Nord area, profitable as they might have been, slowly developed but did not gentrify the area. Unlike the Péreire-sponsored developments around the Parc Monceau, which remained upscale, the Gare du Nord real estate remained tainted by the proletarian nature of the east.[126] This did not prevent the real-estate company Haussmann formed in 1879 with his son-in-law, Camille Dollfus, from turning its attention from the Opera area to that of the Gare du Nord. This was one of many schemes at which Haussmann tried his hand, with little success, to generate much-needed personal income and as outlet for his yet undiminished energy.[127] Today, the *quartier des deux gares* remains tainted by the presence of the railway: it is one of the areas of the capital with the least "green" space and with the highest incidence of substandard education.[128]

The lower priority of Haussmann's plans for the east left them incomplete when he left office in 1870. After 1871, Parliament had greater control over the city and supported carrying out some of Haussmann's schemes. This was encouraged by the international reception of the Second Empire transformations and the perceived need to carry out the work where expropriations had already been authorized. Haussmann's priorities were adopted again, and most projects focused on the west and the center. The east of the *classes laborieuses* (working classes) was unable to stimulate attention to its public health and housing needs when the initiated projects in the west were considered to be of national interest.[129] Today, the railways bracket the east of the city with two lines at each end, the Nord and Est on the north, the PLM and the Vincennes line (converted into a park) on the south, the ceinture line connecting the two arms.[130] The urban grid of this area (and also in the east, south of the Seine) is much looser than in the rest of the city. Haussmann had planned his arteries as a framework for further subdivision, but the Third Republic did not continue the second stage of this process.[131] Haussmann's priorities thus remain imprinted on the configuration of the city. Louis Lazare wrote in 1853: "The creation of our great trunk railway lines must change the map of Paris."[132] Despite his cultivated image as an innovator, Haussmann did not choose to harness the urban potential of railway development. By his arbitrary, inconsistent, and sometimes petty handling of stations, he prevented the emperor's new gateways from becoming dynamic, powerful catalysts of change on the map of the city.

6

The Strategic Role of Railways

The defeat of Austria by Prussia in 1866 revealed that the railways would become a major military asset in Europe. By that time, the American railroads had already played a significant role in the Civil War. The Franco-Prussian War of 1870 was the first European armed conflict where the railways played a decisive role.[1] During the preceding decades, the rhetoric on the advent of peace through the development of improved communications was often accompanied by arguments stressing the strategic potential of the railways on the domestic and foreign fronts. Both peace- and wartime capability of railways were used to justify their development, often in the same speech or document. The role and performance of the railways in time of war has been woven into the history of Europe since the Franco-Prussian War.[2] Noteworthy is also the fact that military features were integral to railway development. Initial railway construction, organization, and discipline relied on military models, and the military authorities exerted some direct or indirect influence during the implantation process. Private initiative or state projects, railways were gradually incorporated in the military arsenal during the second half of the nineteenth century. The civilizing promise they held in the second quarter of that century was further compromised by the breakdown of civilizations, which shook the European continent during the two world wars of the next century.[3] Trains carried the wounded back from the front in the first. They carried Jews, gypsies, homosexuals, and Communists to concentration camps in the second. The events of this grim legacy are coeval with the advent of the automobile and the airplane as common modes of transport, which have considerably reduced the economic, strategic, and configuring power of the railways. As strategic implications transcend national borders, this chapter examines the assimilation of the railways in national arsenals from an international perspective before turning to their role in some of the independent states that would become Germany in 1870.

Railways in Peace and War

The military undertones of railway installations are perceptible in an 1839 report to the Belgian parliament by M. Nothomb, then minister of public works:

> The main stations are not exclusively points of departure and arrival for travelers and freight; they are at the same time arsenals for the equipment and storage for supplies . . . they must have multiple tracks for parking and organizing cars, sheds for locomotives, supply tanks, hangars for cars and finally repair shops; that is a consequence of the exploitation of transport.[4]

This statement is revealing both in its use of the military terminology, equating the stations to arsenals, and in its list of all ancillary facilities required by the railways. All the early manuals, such as those of Nicholas Wood, Auguste Perdonnet, or Dyonisius Lardner, stress the necessity to lay out the operations to accommodate traffic. Their descriptions of the required facilities resemble army manuals, laying claim to vast installations with an authority similar in tone to that of the military. The four countries considered in this book reflect this commanding authority in their railway literature. The language of the British railway managers borrowed terminology from diplomacy and military strategy. Terms such as territorial boundaries, alliances, truces, détente, and treaty reflected the agonistic strategies of the companies.[5] In Germany, foreign terminology was avoided for the railways, and the word *Zug* (train) carried the military connotation of file or column, reinforced by the primarily military acceptance of the word *Feldzug* (campaign).[6] The term *Bahnhof* (station), on the other hand, connotes the court or noble square, possibly evoking the military authority of the ruler. In France, the railway theoretician Auguste Perdonnet introduced a section on railway statistics as an account of the "pacific conquest" of the means of transport.[7] The connection between French railways and the military was also seen in the public works nature of the projects, which would have justified enlisting the army for railway construction as early as 1836.[8] In 1838, the Saint-Simonian writer Michel Chevalier advocated taking army recruits away from unproductive time in the military and employing them on public works such as the railways.[9]

As railways were being built, military authorities soon developed theories on the logistical implications of rail-line construction. They advocated appropriate locations for lines, such as within reach of fire from fortifications, at strategic distance from borders, or on the side of waterways away from enemy territory. Perdonnet made a distinction between rail lines parallel or perpendicular to borders, with parallel lines requiring protection by a natural obstacle such as a wide river or a mountain range.[10] Specific lines with little economic prospects were built because of their strategic location. Other lines were prevented or diverted because of military considerations. For instance, in Paris, military authorities refused to allow the Chemin de Fer de Strasbourg to run through the park at Vincennes, which was considered military grounds. The company engineer, Cabanel de Sermet, was unable to convince the military authorities of the strategic advantages of a direct line toward the east of the country.[11] Civil authorities also expressed their view on the military importance of railways, and these comments were scrutinized abroad. The French statesman Napoléon Daru's 1843 writings on the railways, *Ouvrage des chemins de fer*, was commented upon in the German *Eisenbahn Zeitung* of the same year, where the author suggested adaptation of Daru's position on military use of railways to the German context.[12] Recognition of the strategic implications of the railways happened gradually. By 1862, war was viewed as "a sort of surprise move as in chess, [which] no longer needed to be waged."[13] That the context in which war would be waged had been drastically altered was expressed succinctly by François Jacqmin, director of the Chemin de Fer de l'Est after 1872: "With the railways, all the generals can become Bonapartes."[14]

Once war broke out and the railways were enlisted in military operations, the dreams of peacetime prosperity continued to be evoked:

> War has broken out at once in Saxony, Silesia, Hanover, Frankfurt, on the Mincio, . . . This dreaded plague is reaching all over Germany and upper Italy. . . . The feverish agitation of war succeeds to the fecund works of peace.
>
> Was that the end one was to reach after covering Europe, for the past thirty years, with a vast network of iron lines, doing away with customs barriers and raising international commerce to an unprecedented level of prosperity. It seemed that the old hatreds of the past were dying down and that we were only dreaming of contest in the glorious arena of universal Expositions. The popular masses were to benefit most from our progress which ensured their welfare and cheap necessities. The antique European right was losing ground under the peaceful effort of a new generation.[15]

Despite widely held expectations for the railways' peaceful potential, their strategic applications were codified. The first entry in a Belgian officers' manual published in 1888 is titled *chemins de fer* (railways). It outlines the strategic importance of the railways in its opening lines:

> From the military point of view, the railways are now an essential instrument of mobilization, concentration and supply of armies during war time . . . the importance of the railways is such that they can provide a marked advantage over an adversary . . . and as a result of a few days' head

start gained during mobilization, give victory in the first battles, which are, most of the time, decisive for the final outcome of the war.[16]

This statement is followed by a concise treatise on the railways, with detailed illustrations. It covers their physical plant, equipment and machinery, a brief historical survey, and specific guidelines for use and repair of railway facilities during armed conflicts. This manual reflects the lessons from the Franco-Prussian War, where Germany's superior use of rail transportation won its victory.[17] The impact of military readiness on the configuration of stations was also examined during these postwar years, when Berlin was rebuilding some of its major terminals.[18]

The recognition of such explicitly stated strategic implications of the railways had taken several decades. More characteristic of the early conception of the railways' role is Nothomb's concluding statement in his parliamentary address of 1839, wherein he highlights rail communication as a means to foster national unity and European alliance.[19]

From the onset of its network development, the first on the Continent, Belgium's particular circumstances encouraged this understanding of the railways' potential to reach beyond its recently defined and still fragile political borders.[20]

This spirit was echoed in other countries, which did not have Belgium's international handicap. A Prussian pamphlet protesting the negative impact of the 1844 stock market regulations on railway development refers to the "great idea of connecting the civilized world by railways, bringing its central points closer together, and through these iron veins, pumping a harmonious heartbeat throughout Europe."[21] In France as well, it was hoped that prosperity would breed solidarity and war would be paralyzed by industry and commerce:

> In the past the true sign of a people's power was to be seen in the brilliance of its victories and the vastness of its conquests . . . war was the supreme arbiter of peoples' destiny; everything was submitted to its absolute empire. Times have changed, modern generations have a different idea of the greatness and decadence of nations . . . the development of agriculture and industry are from now on the only solid basis on which nations and governments must base their power.[22]

Speaking to the Chamber of Deputies in 1838, the statesman and poet Alphonse de Lamartine advocated using rail lines to connect populations, not abstract points on a map. For this purpose, a line in the north, which does not have a natural river, would become the Seine of the northern territories. Lamartine also saw an imperious need to take advantage of the "magnificent" lines built within Belgium and to connect to them. He admonished his colleagues for tarrying, thereby encouraging Belgium to develop its rail connections with Germany and to participate in its customs agreement. He accused these colleagues of having "handed [Belgium] over to Prussia."[23]

In the introduction to his 1845 outline of German railway legislation, Friedrich von Reden presented both peace and war arguments in support of railway construction: "Railways are the weapons of peace and the armies which clash against each other today are only industrial armies."[24] Victory would be won by intelligence and understanding of market forces, not by strength. He considered that war had become a mere accident and the normal condition between people would be peace, which fostered the development of human intelligence, arts and sciences, commerce, and industry. War had been encouraged by economists, who saw it as a means to cope with famine, but middle-class participation in the government was profoundly altering the condition of nations. However, "the hour of battle [could] still come. At that time, the railways must come to the help of strategy. The weapons of peace [could] become terrible weapons of war."[25] Whatever role railways might be called upon to perform during armed conflicts, they must be built to reach where the neighbor's lines came to the borders. Von Reden thus advocated an active state railway-building policy for economic and strategic reasons. Over the following decades, Von Reden's position was echoed by other German writers, who also pointed out Germany's need to be armed on two fronts, although France was perceived as the most likely direct threat.[26] The tension between states aiming to control and railway companies seeking to maintain a liberal exploitation climate was further complicated in Germany by the potential of the railways to unite the German fatherland into a national state.[27]

In France, development of the railways was driven primarily by economics in a climate of liberalism operating in consort with the centralizing programs and divergent policies of a succession of national governments. Saint-Simonian writings exalted the transformation of the means of locomotion to the "ark of alliance of humanity," but they did not anticipate the railways' antihumanitarian potential.[28] The pacifist views of the Saint-Simonians were unusual at a time when peace was seen only as an interruption in military campaign, but their views gradually gained currency. Also, the labor of railway construction could provide some relief on the social front. In his 1838 report to the Chamber of Deputies, the scientist and politician François Arago expressed skepticism over the economic importance of the railways. He also expressed great reservations on their strategic value: troops transported by train would become effeminate and lose their marching endurance, and tracks were vulnerable to small groups of enemy scouts.[29] On the other hand, the strategic potential of the railways militated for their construction by the state.[30]

The minister of commerce and public works at the time of the initial railway debates, Aldophe Thiers, did not support development of the railways by the state, but he did see their joint economic and strategic potential. He envisaged a direct north-south line from Le Havre to Algiers, which would deflect trade from Germany and enable the transfer of troops from North Africa to the Belgian border.[31] Von Reden's position, advocating both peace and war roles for the railways in Prussia, was echoed five years later in France by Amédée Lacombe in his 1850 treatise on railways. Lacombe considered the railways as an essential complement to Paris' new fortifications to safeguard national security and territorial integrity.[32] The rhetoric surrounding the drafting of the 1842 railway legislation reinforced the centrality of Paris and advocated both creating contacts with the neighboring countries and enhancing the ability to concentrate troops. Paris as heart of the railway star met political, strategic, and economic needs.[33]

In the early years of railway development, French military authorities, who had several channels at their disposal for input in decision-making, were focusing on defensive strategies in case of occupation rather than considering offensive tactics.[34] Trunk lines were to be laid out to serve as many cities and people as possible, but secondary lines had to be mindful of territorial defense.[35] Companies were pressured into building strategic lines that had poor economic prospects, but they managed to retain some control. For instance, the top administrator of the Compagnie de l'Est after 1872, François Jacqmin, insisted on retaining the power to approve or reject every facility or service required from the company by the Ministry of War. When military expenses were incurred by the company, which was the most strategically sensitive of the country, Jacqmin provided detailed accounting and demanded prompt payment.[36] In France, as well as in Germany, the railways were hailed as an instrument of nationalism, which would reinforce central control, modernize the country to ensure a prosperous future, and give it an edge in the technological and industrial contest with Britain. In this new world, "France [wa]s the brain, the railways the arteries, and the electric wires the fibers."[37] The country saw itself undergoing a transition from a military to an industrial model of civilization.[38]

Britain's insular position and the strength of its navy made invasion appear unlikely during the nineteenth century. Nonetheless, awareness of the railways' international implications did surface early. For instance, Francis Whishaw, writing on the South Eastern Railway in 1842, stated: "There can be little doubt but that, when this line is completed throughout, it will form the great highway from the British metropolis towards that of France, and indeed to the whole of southern Europe."[39]

Emphasized, however, was the railways' potential for moving troops rapidly to calm domestic unrest or to be shipped abroad.[40] In 1842, the government dispatched troops to Manchester to intervene in the Chartist protests. To this end, a battalion of a 1,000 men could be transported from London to Manchester in 9 hours instead of 17 days.[41] The railways consolidated the strength of the government from London over the entire island. After the Franco-Prussian War, British strategists were in agreement about the need for any commander undertaking operations abroad to have under his orders an "efficient railway corps able to move with an army, to construct or repair railways in advancing, and to dismantle and break them down when necessary to cover a retreat."[42]

As in Britain, the role of the railways in maintaining domestic order was considered in Second Empire Paris. Facility of movement within the city motivated urban adjustments that dovetailed with the railways, although in a less-than-optimal manner. The new urban street system could be enlisted in crowd control by linking railway stations and barracks by broad thoroughfares. Troops could be brought back quickly from their border stations and directed to areas where order was threatened within the capital. The main new barracks built during Haussmann's tenure were located at the Place de la République, northeast of the center and in close proximity of the Gares du Nord and de l'Est (north and east stations), which could channel troops to or from the German front.[43] The plan prepared with the 1853 report by the Commission des Embellissements de Paris represents existing streets in green, those to be opened in blue, and stations and barracks in red. Although the strategic intent of Napoleon III's agenda was removed from the final draft of the commission's report, the connection between stations and barracks is implied by their graphic treatment on the map.[44]

The revolution of 1848 also gave Prussia the opportunity to test military theories on the deployment of troops by train for quelling domestic unrest. The railways were thus integrated into each country's domestic, defensive, and offensive arsenal, laying the groundwork for a new form of warfare, where transport technology was to play a decisive role.[45]

Organizational Similarity between Railways and Military

From the points of view of discipline, hierarchy, expected level of dedication, and dress codes, the railways bore a resemblance to the military. Staff regulations assumed a military tone: "Every person receiving a uniform must appear on duty clean and neat."[46] The regulation specified that the staff be clean in their persons and clothes, shaved, and with their shoes brushed. Beard and hair length were also regulated.[47] In Prussia, where most early railway employees did not work for the state, uniforms were prominent, extending to the railways the state's model of military discipline and decorum.[48] Belgium and Germany standardized uniforms for the whole country. In France, a uniform or distinctive insignia was mandated by the regulations of 1846, but each company retained its own distinct uniform until nationalization. These uniforms resembled those of the armed forces, and even included a sword.[49] In Belgium, the 1831 regulation for the Ponts et Chaussées (Public Works) uniform was extended to the railways and revised in 1838. It included stipulations for the regulation of frock coat, trousers, hat, and sword (although the latter was not mandatory during service). Insignia reflected the company hierarchy, and office personnel were also required to wear a uniform. All employees were required to salute their superiors, who were to salute back.[50] The practice of saluting was also extended to railway operations. Victor Hugo's often-quoted passage describing his first railway journey in 1837 concludes with the mention of "a standing spectral form appearing and disappearing as lightning next to the door; it is a road warden, who, as is the custom, gives the convoy a military salute."[51]

The militaristic and authoritarian demeanor of railway company staff led to complaints that the companies were concerned more about their profits than about the welfare of their passengers.[52] This could be attributed to the fact that the engineering challenge of the early railways was matched by an unprecedented need for personnel. Industry could not be tapped nor could it offer a model to provide the manpower needed to build, repair, and operate the trains. Only the military, and especially the navy, which already operated a transport system, could be emulated for its tradition of training and discipline. The railway management was composed of a majority of engineers who, in France, were often graduates from schools where a uniform was customary. This management readily adopted a military model of a hierarchical structure reflected in uniforms and characterized by authoritarian discipline. The uniform reflected the responsibility, authority, and police enforcement function of the railway staff, who had to channel and contain the chaotic, undisciplined, and potentially unruly masses on the premises of the railway companies and on their trains.[53]

This military structure was also reflected in a spirit of solidarity, pride, dedication, heroism, and sacrifice expected from committed staff rather than hourly employees. The shifts were long, the discipline harsh, but the security of employment discouraged strikes and unions until the last decades of the century.[54] In his 1848 treatise on railway exploitation, the French railway manager Albert Schillings equated the discipline required to operate a railway to that expected from the military during wartime.[55] Also, railway companies agreed to give employment priority to men who had served in the military, as they offered better guarantees of orderly conduct, discipline, good behavior, and vigilance. As of 1859, the *cahiers des charges* (schedules of conditions) for the French companies would stipulate that half of the positions should be reserved for former military personnel, but the companies had anticipated this regulation and hired at least a quarter of their staff from the ranks of former soldiers. These included drafted soldiers who had served seven years, or career personnel who had renewed their commission. Staff with prior military experience could be expected to be disciplined, but they were not always polite enough to the public and might have developed the unfortunate habit of spending too much time in cafés. Those who had had two tours of duty and were as old as 34 were less trainable than those who had only had one (and were only 27 or younger).[56] In Belgium, the treaty by which the allied powers had established the country's independence had declared her territory neutral. The ensuing mandated reduction in military forces provided manpower for the railways.[57] In Prussia, an 1851 operations manual stressed the reliability, determination, thoughtfulness, and prudence required from railway personnel, and former military men proved quite adaptable to these requirements.[58] Thus, beyond gradual insertion into the four countries' arsenal, there was a close connection between the military and the railways in their personnel practices.

Military Impact on Cities

Integrated into military strategy and emulating the hierarchy and regimen of armed forces, the railways' urban implantation would bring them in contact with military authorities. Military factors had exerted impact on the configuration of cities before the advent of the railways: most European cities were shaped by military forces. The primary manifestation of the presence of military was a fortress or a fortification wall around the core of a city. Except for London, which had not retained a fortified wall, the cities considered here had fortifications. If the fortified walls had been superseded as effective defenses, they retained their function as toll demarcation up to the second half of the nineteenth century.[59]

In 1860, Paris' toll walls were moved outward to the Thiers fortifications built in the 1840s. This new wall encircled the railway terminals built during the same decade as the fortifications. The presence of this new wall suggested to a journalist writing for *La Démocratie Pacifique* in 1844 that strategic considerations for the configuration of rail lines ranked third, behind political or social and economic considerations.[60] If in the past, the peacetime work of civil engineering, such as roads and canals, had been severely hampered by the intervention of military engineering, the new carapace of fortifications now guaranteed freedom of movement within, and defensive strategy did not depend on the configuration of rail lines. The journalist's confidence in the Thiers wall and forts was not matched by the authorities. The new fortifications interrupted countless rural paths and were penetrable through 17 doors, 26 gates, and 8 posterns in addition to the penetration points of rivers, canals, and railways. Until the end of the nineteenth century, the latter were the object of long negotiations between civilian and military authorities.[61] As pointed out by Félix Tourneux in his 1844 railway encyclopedia, the "zone" adjacent to sea and land borders or fortifications was submitted to specific regulations, and no construction or demolition was permitted without approval from the war ministry, which also established the exact configuration of the restricted area.[62] At issue was also the fact that military land was inalienable, making it impossible for the railway companies to expropriate parcels to run their lines if they were located on the grounds of fortifications.[63] This did not necessarily prevent construction of a line; it simply determined the status of the land on which it would be built, land that was only conceded to companies and would eventually be returned to the state. After the main trunk lines had been constructed and the state had put in place legislation for a second network of lines with lesser economic potential, and in some cases strategic implications, regulations for "mixed works," or portions of lines on border or fortification grounds, were further elaborated.[64] After the Franco-Prussian War, strategic imperatives encouraged building lines toward the border, and means were devised to curtail the delays caused by the "military conferences" required for these "mixed works."[65]

Practical and influential, Auguste Perdonnnet recommended that, in the vicinity of forts and walls, railways should be on ground level as far as possible, thus advocating that rail line construction take into account military needs.[66] On the other hand, when military imperatives no longer obtained, the companies were eager to save the additional expense caused by special requirements.[67] In Prussia as well, the emphasis placed by military engineers on a carefully designed set of fortresses led military authorities to fear that the railways would upset a finely tuned defensive system. Tracks had to be kept away from defensive works or custom-built for the military with no regard for cost, which drew protests from proprietors and municipal authorities.[68]

The fortifications were also a consideration in the location of the *petite ceinture* (belt line) around Paris, a line recognized to have both economic and strategic implications. A rail line outside of the forts encircling the wall would be preferable in peacetime. A line between the forts and the wall would impair the action of the batteries located on the wall and cause obstructions between the forts. Inside the wall, a rail line could interfere with traffic but means could be devised to alleviate this impact, and this was the solution selected.[69] The belt line's strategic implications included the ability to triple troop transfer capacity. Troop transport capacity had already been a factor in the decision to build multiple terminals in Paris, a decision supported by the war ministry.[70] When built, the belt line was in close proximity to a road with heavy horse and carriage traffic in the upscale western area of the city. The impact of locomotives on horses was considered to be of even greater concern because that road was used daily by cavalry detachments.[71]

Railways were driven into cities as fortifications were losing their strategic importance, but the military authorities were reluctant to give up the territorial prerogatives to which they were accustomed. Also, as the role of the railways in armed conflict remained to be tested, private railway companies were submitted to stringent conditions to satisfy military demands rather than integrated in the strategic apparatus of the country's armed forces. When private companies failed to meet military requirements, the state might be forced to step in. Berlin provides an example of this process, as discussed in Chapter 7.

Railways in Germany

When England and Belgium were beginning to build their railways, Prussia was not in a financial position to support such extensive projects. The outstanding war debt after 1815 and the conservative political climate did not encourage the bourgeoisie to lend money to the autocratic and bureaucratic state. The state was reluctant to support competition for its newly expanded road network and for the postal service.[72] Private initiative was not encouraged to develop a mode of transport that predicated liberal policies and heralded reforms toward democracy. Military authorities remained skeptical in the early years of the railways and did not acquire confidence in their usefulness until their carrying capacity increased substantially. Had the authorities foreseen the strategic power of the railways, they would have been in a position to convince King Friedrich Wilhelm III of its advantages in a country that had a long tradition of spending a high percentage of its revenues on the military, even during peacetime.[73] Geographically divided and without natural borders, Prussia was eager to accommodate transportation facilities that would improve mobilization and troop mobility in the unstable decades that followed the Napoleonic Wars and the Congress of Vienna. The German states were also not immune to interstate and international competition in railway development. Friedrich List, a railway pioneer in Saxony, stated in 1834: "The French force the Belgians, the Belgians force the Dutch, all of them together force the Germans to build railroads; and the Germans . . . force one another to build railroads."[74]

Gradually, the advantages of the new mode of transport came to be recognized from commercial, political, and military points of view.[75]

Commerce would gain from improved transport, countries would benefit from the improved contact between their citizens, and internal adjustments would improve a country's strategic position. A commission presided over by the army chief of staff was appointed by the king in 1836 to consider the military implications of railway projects and to attempt to coordinate approval of lines on a federal level.[76] The military authorities remained cautious in their evaluation of the railways' potential for transporting troops and supplies.[77] By midcentury, however, Chief of Staff Helmut von Moltke indicated a marked preference for building railways over fortifications.[78]

David Hansemann, industrialist, finance minister after 1848, and author of a number of early influential works on the railways, believed in the railways' political and military utility. He advocated that the state issue good statutory regulations to attract the capital of private initiative to build rail lines.[79] As of 1837, the Prussian Council of Ministers decided to treat applications for railway charters as those for highways and have them reviewed by military authorities. The Law of 3 November 1838, which determined the relationship between the companies and the state, drew protests because it placed the private capital needed for railway construction under state oversight.[80] The ascension to the throne of King Friedrich Wilhelm IV in 1840 brought the promise of a more liberal climate to Berlin. However, the bourgeoisie remained reluctant to invest in projects heavily regulated by the state. The military authorities began to encourage strategic (mostly east-west) lines, but they still remained wary of railways in the vicinity of fortifications. In 1842, year of the French railway law, the Prussian finance minister von Bodelschwingh, convinced of the importance of the railways for national defense, approved lending military engineers to do preliminary surveys for the eastern rail line to Königsberg.[81] After 1842, the statutes of the conceded railway companies began to include clauses covering the use of rail lines for military purposes.[82] The committee of the provincial delegations convened by the monarch, also in 1842, to consider subsidy and interest guarantees for private construction of railways, strongly supported state construction, given the restricting impact of the law of 1838. The state refused to entertain that option, and delegates were only able to vote in favor of state support for private initiative.[83] Further legislation of the stock market by the Law of 24 May 1844 made finance ministry approval mandatory for subscribing railway stocks, thereby hampering railway development. The businessmen who promoted the construction of rail lines were intent on liberalization and industrialization. They nonetheless stressed the military potential of their projects because of the strong political influence of the German Confederation's military authorities and the size of the national budget expended on the military.[84]

Up to the 1848 revolution, most Prussian railways were built by private enterprise but with increasing state assistance after 1842, when France initiated its policy of railway development. Private companies built lines that promised good and quick returns, without concern for a comprehensive network. The state ensured its ascendancy over the railway lines by purchasing railway bonds. Also, with the taxes collected on the lines, according to the provisions of the Law of 3 November 1838, it purchased railway companies' stocks. As stockholder, the state was in a position to exert influence on railway companies and to buy back lines, when it set out to do so.[85] The state also became increasingly involved in constructing lines, including the Berlin beltway line. *Vormärz* Prussia (1815–49) had built no strategic lines, but this changed in the next decade and especially after 1866. By 1850, the state had built three sections of railways, and complete state lines were opened in 1852. A key figure in this development was August von der Heydt. Appointed minister of commerce in December 1848, he remained in office for 13 years and supported both private railway construction and state railways. In 1862, when Bismarck became prime minister, five state companies accounted for a quarter of Prussian lines, whereas 22 were in private hands. Territorial annexations of Hanover, Hesse, Nassau, and Frankfurt increased the state railway network to 12 lines in 1866, but another 27 private companies were approved between 1860 and 1870, benefiting from the more liberal climate of the decade. After 1870–71, the more strategic a line was, the more the state was likely to participate in its construction.[86]

As noted above, the railways assumed a particular significance in Prussia because of their association with the idea of German unity.[87] The Federal Diet of the German *Bund* (Confederation) did not provide a political structure capable of regulating railway development. The *Zollverein* (customs union), which went into effect among the German states on 1 January 1834, resulted in a paradoxically efficient economic and operational railway structure among these independent political entities.[88] The Association of Prussian Railway Administrations (Verband der Preussischen Eisenbahnen) founded in 1846, in part because of dissatisfaction with the law of 1838, expanded into the Association of German Railway Administrations in 1847 (Verein Deutscher Eisenbahnverwaltungen—VDEV) to include 49 German and Austrian railways.[89] This association did not have the power to enforce its resolutions, but it did provide common ground for exploitation without state intervention in politically divided territories. Another association, the Verein für Eisenbahn-Kunde (VfEK, Association for Railway Information) founded in 1842 as state policies shifted toward greater support for the railways, gathered individual members to discuss railway technology and their implementation. VfEK membership included railway engineers, state officials, and some military men. The military was thus present at the ground level of this organization, which provided a forum for discussion but not an agency for working out standards.[90] Despite the Confederation, the customs union, and these two associations, which operated on a voluntary basis, national particularism and competition prevailed.[91]

The lack of a unified railway structure in Germany was highlighted by the events of 1848 when Prussian troops were unable to reach Baden promptly to quell insurrection because the state had a broader rail gauge. The Prussian campaign of 1849–51 in Schleswig-Holstein relied heavily on the railways to transport troops.[92] Prussia elaborated the first regulations for the conveyance of troops on state railways in 1856, but these were of limited import because most railways were in private hands.[93] Prussia was the first state to make provisions during peacetime to grant its military officers the authority to assume control of the railways in case of armed conflict.[94]

As mentioned earlier, Count Helmut von Moltke, appointed to the Prussian General Staff in 1857, was convinced of the strategic significance of railways. Also, atypical for the military, he did not balk at close collaboration with civilian authorities and concerns. He created a deployment division in the General Staff and enlisted the collaboration of the ministries of war; of the interior; and of commerce, industry, and public works. This division oversaw railway affairs and had the responsibility to devise an organizational structure for the military use of railways. Von Moltke assumed a more prominent role when the General Staff was expanded and reorganized in 1864 and a special railway office was organized in Berlin. Gradually, von Moltke came to limit restrictions for lines near fortifications to the frontier areas and along rivers, recognizing that the existence of a line was more crucial than its exact configuration.[95] After the campaign against Denmark in 1864 and the civil war of 1866, in which the railways began to play an increasing role, the Prussian government adopted a strong statist policy, which was consolidated after the founding of the German Empire in 1871. Von Moltke also organized a committee of civil and military officials to coordinate military operations, and to operate rail lines across state borders in case of war. This resulted in faster transport of troops toward the French border in 1870 but fell short of a fullfledged German railway organization in what remained a war between France and Prussia.[96]

The imperial constitution of 1871 did not provide for a national railway administration, but it subordinated all German railway administration to the empire for matters of national defense. The constitution also authorized the government to build national defense lines through federal states and to modify fortifications even if the states were opposed to it.[97] The Law of 27 June 1873 placed the railways under the oversight of the Reichseisenbahnamt (Imperial Railway Office, REA).[98] Bismarck's attempts to centralize the railway encountered strong opposition from stockholders, railway administrators, and state authorities, especially because of their military implications. After several legislative attempts, the Law of 24 May 1876 finally gave the chancellor the authority to consolidate the imperial rail system. Disappointed with the performance of the REA, Bismarck did not press for implementation of the 1876 law. He focused his efforts on Prussia, where the state resorted to buying up major railways between 1878 and 1885, with the support of the Law of 12 December 1879.[99]

This did not prevent the empire from developing a network where strategic imperatives had the upper hand over economic concerns. An instance of this trend in Prussia was the construction by the state of the *Ostbahn*, the long line from Berlin to Königsberg with limited prospect of profitability. This was at a time when private construction prevailed, as a concession to the military authorities, who were always mindful of the need to contend with an eastern front.[100] Another manifestation of this pressure was Berlin's insistence through the REA that tracks be doubled and signals made consistent primarily for military reasons, a need particularly acute in the independent-minded southern states.[101] The pursuit of an imperial rail network encountered the resistance of state particularism into the twentieth century, and repeated attempts at an imperial railway policy succeeded only in bringing about an agreement on freight wagon exchange in 1908, followed by one on locomotives and passenger cars in 1914.[102] Attempts to reach parity or advantage vis-a-vis Prussia had been a frequent theme in the reports of the French railway press since the Second Empire.[103] In Germany, as the empire was attempting to achieve defensive parity and offensive advantage over France on the eve of the First World War, the individual states continued to resist the REA's requests for additional lines and bridges toward the western front. Most rail lines in all states of the empire had, however, gradually been brought under state control and were thereby easily transferable to military authorities with the assistance of the REA.[104]

As a result of the role played by the railways in the American Civil War, beginning in 1862, Prussia organized field military units during its war with Austria in 1866, but they were disbanded shortly thereafter. As intended by King Wilhelm I since 1869, permanent railway units were integrated into the standing army after the Franco-Prussian War. The Cabinet Order of 19 May 1871 established a 500-man railway battalion by October 1871. First housed in the Berlin Moabit barracks, the four companies, increased by a fifth in 1873, were moved to their own barracks in Schöneberg, between the Kolonnenstraße and Monumentenstraße, east of the Anhalt and Dresden line. The letter "E" on their shoulder epaulettes earned them the nickname of *Schöneberger Engel* (Schöneberg Angels).[105] As it became apparent that other railway operations could only provide temporary and limited training grounds, the railway troops were entrusted with constructing a military line where they would train specifically in all aspects of railway construction, repair, and operations.[106]

Britain, France, and Belgium

As already alluded to above, the railways also acquired a strategic dimension in the other three countries examined here. Railway building was an integral part of Britain's colonial campaigns, and the British built the first field railway to support military operations in 1855–56 at Balaclava in the Crimea.[107] On the domestic front, railway advocates clearly saw its strategic potential as early as 1838.[108] As noted earlier, Britain's insular position and the strength of its naval forces made many consider an invasion unlikely, and the railways were viewed primarily as an extension of domestic forces. In 1842, the government had imposed on railway companies the requirement to convey troops as needed, and the impact of the fast transfer of armed forces had been decisive in the Manchester Chartist upheaval of 1842.[109] The understanding of a potential strategic role for the railways tended to stress their ability to support navy operations. A bill for a line along the southern coast between Dover and Plymouth was passed, but companies could not be persuaded to put up the funding, and the line was never built.[110]

The contingency of territorial invasion appeared unlikely to most, but military leadership was aware of the discussions on the military use of railways in France and Germany since 1833.[111] The government had therefore felt it prudent to take steps to prepare for the use of railways as a means of defense. The Regulations of the Forces Act of 1871 empowered the government to take possession of railways and their facilities upon declaration of a state of emergency. The Cheap Trains Act of 1883 included provisions for the transport of the armed forces by the railways. The 1888 National Defense Act granted, under state of emergency, precedence to military and naval traffic over any other.[112] Besides legislation, an army engineering force was created to build, operate, repair, or destroy railways at home or abroad, and in 1896, the War Railway Council was instituted to ensure readiness for military use of railways in case of invasion.[113] Thus, although Britain took measures to organize rail transport during hostilities later than on the Continent, these measures did not differ substantially from those taken elsewhere. The railways were incorporated in military strategy for troop movement to control domestic unrest, resist invasion, or send troops abroad. Also, as early as the 1846 Royal Commission on Railway Termini in London, the construction of a belt line around the city had been suggested to facilitate the movement of troops and to avoid the "populous part of the Metropolis."[114] As will be examined briefly in Chapter 8, although not fully implemented as a belt line, the rail connections established within and around London in order to convey freight and passengers through the capital provided for the movement of troops during hostilities.

British territorial integrity was also maintained by the failure of a controversial Channel Tunnel project. In the mid-1870s, French promoters had obtained a concession for a Channel Tunnel, with financial backing from the Chemin de Fer du Nord and the Rothschilds. They were, however, unable to come to terms with an English company authorized to build the British end of the tunnel.[115] The tunnel would not be completed until the last decade of the next century.

In France, the role of the military authorities during the first decades of railway development was restricted to designating lines of strategic interest, having some of them doubled, and ensuring that the network would be equipped to perform during armed conflict. Railway development remained independent from military authorities and was driven by economic imperatives, which did not include standardization of line equipment and rolling stock. Strategic considerations advocated by the military Génie (engineering department) did not always have the upper hand in construction decisions for railway lines, where the state Ponts et Chaussées could overrule the minister of war. As Germany was considered the most likely enemy, the Eastern Railway was the most scrutinized and contested. Strategic concerns for Paris tended to find a more receptive ear, as, for instance, the beltway line to connect Paris' stations and a line to the arsenal at Vincennes.[116]

During the Second Empire, railways were put to use for strategic purposes: to send troops to the Crimean War (1854–56) through Marseille and to support the Italian forces against Austria in 1859. Regulations for military transport by the state-controlled private companies were elaborated during the 1850s and renewed in 1861. The companies found it necessary to designate a member of their administration to be in charge of the complex arrangements with the military. Until 1873, the military obligations of railways were included in the *cahiers des charges* under Article 54, which stipulated that companies make all their means of transport available to the government to transport troops and military equipment. Although some attempts were made to coordinate railway military efforts prior to the Franco-Prussian War of 1870–71, that conflict acted as a catalyst for the government to put in place a state organizational structure to manage the railways during military hostilities.[117]

Legislative measures culminated in the Law of 1888, which placed the entire rail service under the military authorities in case of war. The Law of 1875 on military personnel also included provisions for dedicated railway troops.[118] These were less numerous than the corresponding German units, but could be reinforced in wartime by field railway units made up of conscripted railway employees.[119] In the financial climate of an enormous post-1870 national debt, funding for strategic railways was limited, and the railway companies resisted being enlisted in strategic development at their own expense. In border areas, the Ministry of War had been granted the right to be consulted for the construction of every line as of 1872.[120] A mixed committee of military and civilian officials would review contended projects to try to reach a solution, which frequently exhibited a pro-military bias. Such projects included the *grande ceinture* (large beltway) around Paris as the war had highlighted the shortcomings of the existing small beltway inside the Thiers fortifications.[121]

During the early years of the Third Republic, the respective responsibilities of the executive branch of government and the Ministry of War in matters of military decision-making were not clearly defined. A more rational organization of the military hierarchy was put in place by Charles de Freycinet as minister of war as of 1888. His understanding of the importance of the railways for strategic planning led to revised mobilization procedures for the railways and a comprehensive plan for their use in case of military conflict. The level of control exerted by the national Ponts et Chaussées over the private companies in matters of line construction, and the prevalence of double lines on most French territory offset some of the overwhelming economic and industrial advantages of the German adversary. The "transportation plan" of 1888 was amended and elaborated six times before World War I. When war broke out in 1914, each railway company was placed under the control of a *commission du réseau* (network commission), which reported to the military authorities and consisted of an officer from General Staff, a regional army commander, the director of the rail company, and his technical advisor.[122]

In Belgium, the military potential of the railways was acknowledged as of 1833 before the first line was inaugurated in 1835, when the country was still vulnerable to Dutch incursions and retaliation. Troops, munitions, and equipment were to be given priority on the rail lines over passengers and commercial freight during wartime.[123] The initial rail lines were, however, designed to extend past the territorial borders into the neighboring countries, which privileged communication over strategy. As for the Junction between the north and south stations, which is examined in Chapter 8, its strategic role was not highlighted as a priority during the protracted debate before, during, and after its construction. This was in part due to the neutrality imposed on Belgium by the treaty that sanctioned its legitimacy as a country in 1831.[124] It should, however, be noted that the unfinished tunnel of the Junction was used during World War II by the Germans as housing, storage, and shelter and was used for similar purposes by the allied forces, after they regained control of Brussels.

Conclusion

The relationship between the military and the railways in the four countries examined in this book reveals different modes of integrating the railways into the national arsenal. Specific characteristics of the individual countries are reflected in these modalities: geography and liberal economic practices in Britain, and political context for France, Germany, and Belgium. Each country recognized the railways' strategic potential and attempted to integrate them into a structure of military preparedness, which reflected the relationship between the railway companies and the state. How the military hierarchy was able to come to terms with private, profit-driven concerns in France and Germany played a crucial part in how the railways could be developed, or how they could be adapted to military ends and run during armed conflicts. In France, a private-public collaboration prevailed until World War I. In Prussia, and after 1871 in the German Empire, nationalization was gradually set in motion, but local state autonomy and the private railway companies offered strong resistance. The extent of military influence over the political process was also reflected in railway matters and at the local scale. As will be examined more closely in Chapter 7, in Berlin, where the military was pervasive and powerful, it could dictate terms for railway implantation, as in the case of the Anhalt Railway, or provide the impetus for inner city lines. In Paris, the long-established, centralized military and civilian institutions of territorial management, the Génie and the Ponts et Chaussées, both had input in the process of deciding on local lines, such as Paris' beltways. The results depended more on the accident of circumstances than on the weight of one form of authority over another. In Britain, the private railway companies were reined in to operate but not to design or build their lines for military purpose. For Belgium, the early and rapid development of state rail lines constituted a defensive strategy to counter the country's political and economic vulnerability. The political neutrality imposed on the country by the allied powers in 1831 prevented actual strategic railway development. This did not prevent strategic use of the Belgian rail lines by the German forces to bypass the French border defense lines in both world wars. In all four countries, the configuring strategic impact of the railways on capital cities was important but remained circumscribed. The impact of their strategic presence during armed conflicts, however, was pervasive, and changed the nature of warfare.

7

Berlin and Its Railways: Strategy First

This chapter considers the military presence within Berlin, including a closer look at the relationship between the Anhalter Bahnhof and the Tempelhof military grounds. The military implications of Berlin's connecting and belt lines, which have given the map of the city its characteristic outline, are also explored briefly.

Railways and Military Presence in Berlin

During the second half of the nineteenth century, Berlin was morphologically reconfigured by a dominant network of connecting rail lines with strategic application, if not always impetus. It must be added, however, that the impact of rail presence in Berlin is diluted by the sheer size of the city (891 square kilometers compared to Paris' 105 square kilometers). An 1896 map of Berlin illustrates the extent of rail incursion into the city (Figure 7.1). Published in *Berlin und seine Eisenbahnen,* an 1896 publication for the fiftieth anniversary of the Association of German Railway Administrations, the project set out to examine "to what extent the evolution of Berlin was influenced by the railways."[1] The visual evidence of this map is telling, and the evolution of the city over the first 50 years of railway construction is intimately connected with the development of its railways.

In 1734, King Friedrich Wilhelm I (1688–1740) began construction of a toll wall around the territory of the city known as "Old Berlin," doubling its original 6.26 square kilometer surface to 13.3. This wall was gradually replaced by boulevards and squares during the nineteenth century, but it remained the city limit and toll delineation until 1868. As the built area gradually crept up to the edge of the city, the wall also constituted the limit of penetration for railway termini when they were first constructed.[2]

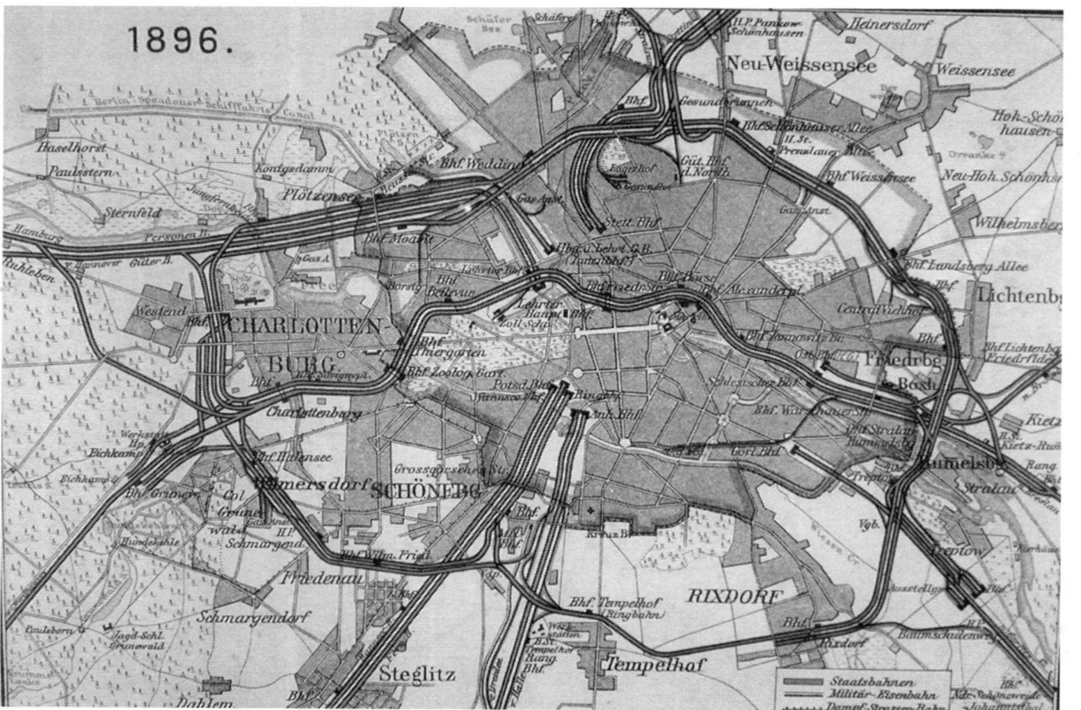

Figure 7.1   Map of Berlin rail network in 1896. From Ministerium der Öffentlichen Arbeiten and A. F. Leyen, *Berlin und seine Eisenbahnen, 1846–1896* (Berlin: Springer, 1896), vol. 1, pl. 8, bottom right, after p. 134.

The Berlin-Potsdam Railway, inaugurated in 1838, was the first rail line in the city. It was followed in 1841 by the Berlin-Anhalt, in 1842 by the Berlin-Stettin, later that year by the Berlin-Frankfurt-on-the-Oder, and in 1846 by the Berlin-Hamburg railways. With lines to the four cardinal points, Berlin was a hub in the German rail network. By 1870, the railways had assumed a dominant presence, dissecting the urban landscape and adjoining residential blocks, which often comprised the infamous *Mietskasernen* (rental housing units or barracks).[3] Besides the 14 lines implanted by 1882, the railways' presence was manifested by a beltway, the archways of the interurban rail lines, the enormous rail yards, and, as of 1902, the subway viaducts.[4] North of the city, population settlement followed the railway lines. After 1865, industry also followed the rail lines northward.[5] The rail network was so dominant that it interfered with attempts to implement a comprehensive plan, thereby challenging the ability of planning to become effective as a discipline before it was formally established.[6]

Historical developments in the twentieth century have encouraged the association of Berlin with military presence and authority. This is not without due cause; already at the time of Friedrich Wilhelm I and later in the eighteenth century, Prussia was jokingly referred to as an army with a country rather than a country with an army.[7] Lewis Mumford observed that, in 1740, the military population in Berlin reached 21,309, close to a quarter of its 90,000 inhabitants.[8] The urbanist Erwin Gutkind considered Berlin a prime example for the extent of physical and economic impact the military presence can exert on a city. By 1833, Berlin had extensive military facilities: barracks, military schools, army hospitals, workshops, arsenals, and drill grounds.[9] Mumford considers that the presence of this "mass of mechanized and obedience-conditioned human beings" colored the fabric of city life and provided a model of discipline and means of coercion, which would extend to industry and later to the railways.[10]

The 1845 plan for Berlin by Peter Josef Lenné, its royal director of gardens, included several military facilities: the Powder Mill grounds and Mars Field to the north and military drill grounds to the south of the Spree River on the land that would become Königsplatz, the site of the Reichstag.[11] By the time Hobrecht's plan was published in 1861, large barrack facilities had become necessary for the sizeable military contingents in the city.[12]

The military grounds at Tempelhof were established in the eighteenth century. This was relatively early in the development of a city founded in the thirteenth century and with an earliest known plan dating back to 1685.[13] Tempelhof was one of two large military maneuver grounds in Berlin. It had been in use since the reign of King Friedrich Wilhelm I as a large parade ground and as drill grounds for the Berlin garrison.[14] Other military facilities in the area included the rifle range located in the nearby Hasenheide, the exercise ground for the Garde-Pionier Battalion near Kreuzberg, and

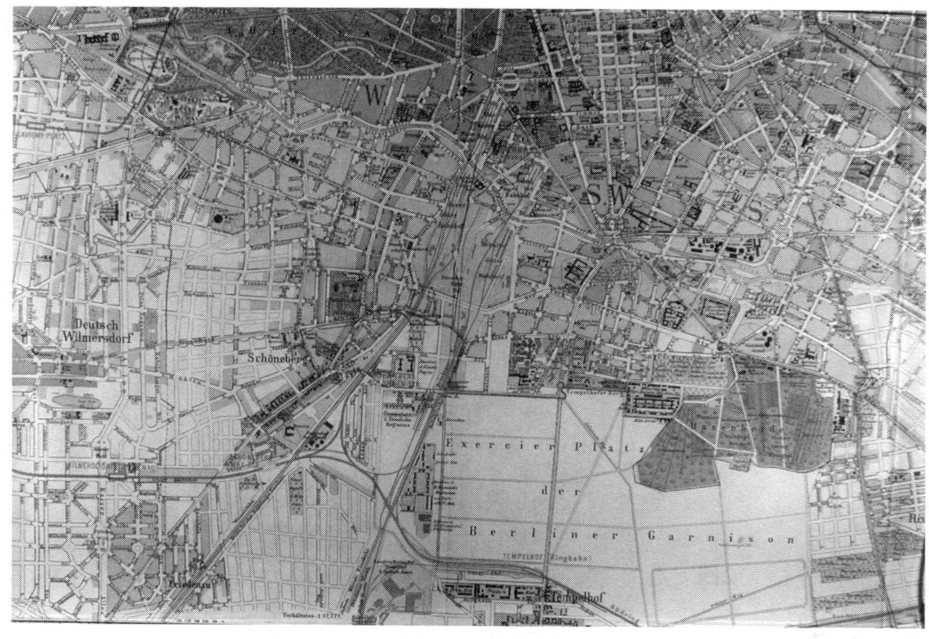

Figure 7.2   Map of Berlin rail network in 1896, detail of SSW section. From Ministerium der Öffentlichen Arbeiten and A. F. Leyen, *Berlin und seine Eisenbahnen, 1846–1896* (Berlin: Springer, 1896), vol. 1, insert 4, bottom center.

the exercise ground for the Railway Battalion near Schöneberg on the Kolonnenstraße (Figure 7.2). This latter facility was connected to the station for the military railway's dedicated Berlin-Sperenberg line, completed in 1875, which was used for training the Railway Battalion and transporting troops and equipment to the new artillery ground transferred from Tegel to the Kummersdorf Forest near Zossen. This new facility was acquired with 1870–71 war damage funds, in order to accommodate the longer range of upgraded artillery.[15]

Military authorities had the upper hand in negotiating arrangements where civilian and military rail facilities intersected. A contract between the Railway Regiment and the Niederschlesiche-Märkischen Railway, dated Berlin, 25 November 1878, shortly after completion of the dedicated military line, exemplifies this. The contract concerned the erection of a connecting line between the Berlin-Potsdam Station and the Berlin *Ringbahn* toward Wilmersdorf. As the line cut along the exercise grounds of the Railway Regiment, the railway company was responsible for taking over the severed, and unusable, part of the grounds and providing compensation (for an estimated value of 60,000 Marks - $252,000). The overpass above the military rail line must leave room for three tracks (two was crossed out on the document), with a width of four meters from center. A new hut for the military station signal on military rail line was to be located at such a height that it will be visible both from the platform of the military station and from the curve south of the belt line. The direct connection between the military station and Tempelhof was to be replaced by a direct connection toward the Berlin-Potsdam Station. Freight price guarantees for transfer of rail cars beyond the military line were to be provided. A substitute exercise ground at the maneuver facility outside of Berlin (20 hectares for an amount not to exceed 45,000 thalers ($567,000) was to be supplied by the company and 15,000 thalers ($189,000) paid to make it fit for use.[16] Obviously, the cost of brushing up against military facilities was quite high for the railway company. This vulnerable position of the railway companies in their relationship to the state, and especially the military, had been made explicit in the Prussian railway legislation of 1838: companies were entitled to no compensation for war damages, whether caused by the enemy or incurred for defensive purposes.[17]

Anhalter Bahnhof

The relationship between the railways and military authorities is also exemplified by the Berlin-Anhalt Railway's implantation in Berlin. This second line into Berlin led to the small, independent state of Anhalt, centered around Dessau, on the Elbe River, northwest of Leipzig. The first segment of this line, Köthen-Dessau, southeast of Dessau, was opened in September 1840, and the line reached Berlin in July 1841.[18] It was the city's first long-distance line, initially conceived as one of six to fan out of Berlin by the economist and railway advocate Friedrich List (1789–1846). List, an influential early advocate of railway development in Germany, had been involved with the planning of the Leipzig-Dresden Railway in Saxony. The initial proposal for the Berlin-Saxony Railway (Berlin-Sächsischen Eisenbahn), which superseded the initial plan of a rail connection to Saxony by the Berlin-Potsdam Railway, was approved by the king in 1837 on condition that the Leipzig-Dresden Railway agree to connect with the new line on the Saxon border near Riesa, halfway between Leipzig and Dresden.[19] The Berlin-Saxony Company was approved by the Cabinet Decree of 25 April 1838.[20] Granted status as a Society on 3 April 1839, the railway was later renamed Berlin-Anhalt Railway Company (Berlin-Anhaltische Eisenbahn-Gesellschaft) at the request of the Anhalt government. The line would eventually branch out toward Halle, Leipzig, and Dresden, with further connections to Nuremberg, Munich, Prague, and Vienna. It was purchased by the state in 1882.[21]

The committee for the Berlin-Saxony Railway acquired the land needed for the line's Berlin terminal, which was to be located right outside of the city walls, then reduced to a toll wall, between the Potsdam and Halle gates in the area of the Prince Albrecht Palace.[22] In order to gain direct access to the city, the company was responsible for building, at its own cost, a new gate and connecting this gate to the Wilhelmstraße by a new street, later called Anhaltstraße.[23] Improved communication between the military exercise facilities in Schöneberg and Tempelhof was considered part of the new urban configuration necessitated by the station.[24]

The location and plans for the station were approved by the king on 8 October 1838.[25] South of the station, the line required extensive negotiations, as its intended layout would cross a large military drill ground in Kreuzberg, which the king had categorically refused to accept. The possibility of combining the line with the Potsdam Railway was explored, but this solution would have created unsafe curves, and the land along the first rail line had increased in value to become prohibitively expensive. The cost for the direct line, approved after protracted negotiations, was not much lower. The company would have to provide and set up a parade ground of 19 acres on the western edge of Kreuzberg; build a wide military road (today's Möckernstraße), including two bridges over the Landwehrkanal, which crossed the rail line about 250 meters south of the station; and connect the new city gate near the terminal with the parade ground on Schönebergerstraße. The company would also have to provide a 33.3-meter bridge for troops and artillery equipment above the rail line in prolongation of the Kolonnenweg (today Kolonnenbrücke).[26]

Land parcels provided by military authorities would have to be compensated by equivalent acreage or purchased at the rate of 450 thalers per acre. In addition, a sum of 15,000 thalers ($189,000) would be paid by the company to the Ministry of War as compensation for the land tenants and for the construction of a hippodrome. Most of the line was built before the issue of this initial strip out of Berlin was resolved, between October 1839 and October 1840.[27]

The station also had a shaping impact on the southwestern area of the city between the Potsdam and Halle gates. The new street leading to the station was later lengthened westward by the construction of the Puttkamerstraße and Besselstraße between the north-south arteries of the Wilhelmstraße and Lindenstraße. The Anhalt Company enjoyed healthy expansion during the 1850s, and by 1857 its line led to uninterrupted tracks to Vienna and to Trieste on the Adriatic Sea. A suburban station was built at Lichterfeld in the vicinity of the Cadets barracks, and special conditions were provided for military personnel. By 1875, the closure of the belt line circumscribed new housing, garage station, and workshops near Tempelhof.[28] As the station became insufficient to handle traffic, the presence of the canal and military facilities encouraged the division of the station between the passenger terminal, north of the canal, and all other ancillary facilities south of the canal. This necessitated the deviation of Yorkstraße southward and other adjustments. These were agreed upon between the company and the relevant authorities in July 1870. The shareholders approved the construction of a new station in the spring of 1871, a project that took nine years to complete. Underpasses along the canal banks and on Yorkstraße, and broad overpasses over the southern Monumentstraße and Kolonnenstraße were constructed, and all station facilities north of the canal were raised 4.5 meters above street level. Freight traffic was further divided into local and long distance, the latter handled at a new facility located where the Anhalt tracks crossed the belt line and where the new workshops were also set up. When the new passenger terminal was completed in 1880, the station facilities stretched southward more than five kilometers from the Askanischer Platz to the connection of the rail tracks with the military and Dresden lines.[29]

The passenger terminal, built in 1876–80 by the Berlin-Anhalt Railway Company based on the design of the architect Franz Schwechten (1841–1924) and the shed engineer Heinrich Seidel, was damaged during World War II, closed in 1952, and demolished between 1959 and 1961 (Figure 7.3).[30] In 1969 it was decided to retain the portico on the Askanischer Platz, described by the architectural historian Ulrich Krings as the largest, most beautiful, and most popular of Berlin's stations, as a last vestige of Berlin's gateway to the south.[31] When the station was demolished in 1961, it had become expendable, partly

Figure 7.3   Portico of Anhalter Bahnhof, Berlin. July 2005. Photograph by author.

because it could not be rebuilt after war damage, but also as a result of the post–World War II division of the country. Located in the west, the tracks leaving the station could no longer reach their destination in the east. Gutted by bombs, the station was paralyzed and asphyxiated as a result of military conflict and ensuing political division.

Berlin Ringbahn and Stadtbahn

Ringbahn (Belt Line)

Military authorities had impact on the site and configuration of the Anhalt railway station. They also influenced the rail links between Berlin's main stations. The connection between Berlin's four rail termini was first discussed in 1844 as a strategic and commercial necessity. When, on 22 March 1845, the finance minister submitted to the king a proposal dated 16 February, he presented the project as not yet urgent but highlighted its advantages from a military point of view.[32] The project was recognized to be of public utility on 28 March 1845, and the king recommended that the private companies collaborate on a connection between their rail lines without issuing additional shares. But the companies were not prepared to do so. Although it was anticipated that the city fortifications on the left bank of the Spree would be dismantled, the wall in the area of the Potsdam gate could not be demolished, as the gate had been built by King Friedrich Wilhelm III (1770–1840) as a monument to beautify the city. The toll authorities also placed costly conditions for crossing the toll wall. The war minister required that the company provide another military hospital as a replacement for the one to be displaced in the Brandenburg gate area.[33]

The revolution of 1848 broke out in Paris as the latest proposal for the project had been approved by the king (4 February) and a Ministerial Order (dated 29 February) outlining the conditions for the concession was ready for release. Given the international political situation, a private concession for the project was no longer appropriate. After the March events in Prussia, the Auerswald-Hansemann ministry supported the execution of the project by the state. Again, the ministers highlighted the commercial and strategic implications of a rail connection between the original four stations for the Potsdam, Anhalt, Stettin, and Frankfurt-on-the-Oder lines and by then a fifth, the Berlin-Hamburg line. This connection would also provide access to the Spree River and the canal. As the project wound its way through bureaucratic channels, the war minister placed the condition that the stations and stops be equipped with secure fencing and that any opening in the fortification wall be equipped with a secure gate. The mobilization of 1850 brought to light the inadequacy of the rail connections in the capital, and the king ordered, as an emergency measure, the construction of a temporary horse-drawn belt line between the three western stations at state expense.[34] The project was begun in December 1850 and its operations regulated by the Law of 12 May 1851, which restated the military applicability of the line.[35] The single-track, street-level, nine-kilometer connecting line was put in service in October 1851 and included the eastern station as well, its company administrators having protested against the unfair advantage the project provided for its competitors. From the onset, horse traction was replaced by locomotives. The line soon proved insufficient to accommodate freight traffic. Special military transport trains were operated on the belt line during the war years 1864, 1866, and 1870, and the line generated steadily increasing profits.[36]

During the 1850s, Prussia's minister of commerce August von der Heydt, who advocated direct state involvement in building rail lines, sponsored projects for the construction of a second belt line in Berlin. Plans were deferred for lack of funds during the late 1850s and because the *Ostbahn* (eastern line), also a strategically motivated project, took precedence in the early 1860s.[37] During the planning for war with Austria in the early 1860s, there was concern about Berlin's vulnerability to attacks by the Austrians across the Bohemian mountains. This reflected the fact that Berlin now acted as a hub of communication between the east and the west and that the unfortified city's capture would paralyze the Prussian forces.[38] In January 1865, the ministries and concerned authorities were asked to express their requirements for a new belt line. War Minister Von Roon requested that in order to allow unencumbered use of the parade and exercise grounds of the Berlin garrison, the line be deviated south of the Tempelhof Field and Hasenheide shooting range and that it be laid out in close proximity to the village of Tempelhof. The Berlin authorities put forth that such a line had the potential to facilitate the commuting of the working class to cheaper developments.[39] Submitted in a bill of 17 December 1866, and approved by the Law of 9 March 1867, this 36.9-kilometer double-track line was put in service in stages between 1871 and 1877, crossing still scarcely populated peripheral areas[40] (see Figure 7.1). Construction of the connection for the Anhalt and Potsdam lines with the Temphelhof station had been accelerated to provide transport, as of August 1870, to the military hospital erected in Tempelhof. The configuration of the Potsdam line connection was arranged to facilitate conveying trains directly from the court at Potsdam to the Tempelhof military grounds.[41]

The first segment of the second ring line from Moabit to Schöneberg through Stralau was 25.42 kilometers long, 22.87 kilometers of it on double tracks. By 1871 it connected the Potsdam, Anhalt, Görlitz, Frankfurt, Ost, Stettin, and Hamburg stations, as well as the most recent addition, the Lehrter Station. Also, it opened the possibility of a complete ring line, avoided railway crossings, and provided for passenger service, which began on 1 January 1872. On 24 August 1871, a project study for the western section of the ring line had been authorized, taking into account the new *Westend* (west end) constructions west of Charlottenburg. Approval and funding followed on 11 June 1873. The potential of the portion of this line between Schöneberg and Charlottenburg to contribute to the development of low-income housing in the area southwest of the city encouraged the acquisition of land for four-track service. It became necessary to separate freight and passenger services on the entire ring line, which was opened on 15 November 1877. Additional work on tracks and stations continued until 1882.

In the large urban area where development did not follow a regular pattern, and where the old fortifications were demolished between 1866 and 1869, the *Ringbahn* replaced the toll wall as the outer delineation of modern Berlin from its suburbs.[42] Nicknamed Dog's Head, with its maw facing the west, the *Ringbahn* connected the eight major stations and enclosed a tightly built area, where only the Tiergarten Park and the Tempelhof airport would remain as open space. The belt rail line, crossed by a limited number of bridges, discouraged construction outside of the 87-square-kilometer area it enclosed. The popular phrase that described the city as divided between Berlin of stone inside the line and green Berlin outside of it testifies to the demarcating and configuring power of this belt line.[43] In 1920, the area inside the ring accounted for one-tenth of the surface area of Greater Berlin but housed 60 percent of its population (2.5 million).[44] The *Ringbahn* encouraged development of the area on the outskirts of Berlin that it serviced, thus contributing to healthy traffic statistics on the line.[45] When the urbanist Herman Josef Stübben wrote his city planning treatise, *Der Städtebau,* in 1890, he considered the primary function of belt lines to be for freight and military transport, with little impact on local or suburban traffic until the city expanded beyond the line. In Berlin, however, the western portion of the line, between Schöneberg and Charlottenburg, brought closure to the ring and the added incentive of cheaper homes outside of the city limits.[46]

Stadtbahn

In addition to the *Ringbahn,* an east-west junction through the central area of the city, or *Stadtbahn,* was added to the Berlin rail configuration. This line was originally connected with the 1872 plan for construction of a long-distance line that would originate in the eastern part of Berlin and run westward through the city, in order to shorten access to southwestern Germany and the newly acquired territories of Alsace and Lorraine. The Berlin component of the line remained on the table after the private company that proposed the southwestern line failed to gather the necessary capital for the whole project.[47] The initiation of planning for this line is usually attributed to strategic considerations that arose right after the Franco-Prussian War began in 1870. The military authorities highlighted the fact that mobilization and troop transport had been severely hampered by the lack of communication between the rail lines in Berlin. The need to administer the conquered territories on the French border also militated for a direct line from the capital.[48]

However, in 1871, civilian authorities, and especially the architect and member of municipal building services August Orth, played a prominent part in conceiving and encouraging the Berlin component of the project.[49] Orth proposed a viaduct rail line following the course of the Spree River to cross Berlin from east to west, which would connect peripheral stations linked to the *Ringbahn* with the inner city and be equipped with local stations for passenger and freight services. The nine stations along the *Stadtbahn* would act as a central station for long-distance transit and improve communication between the city and its growing suburbs. Orth also stressed the need to remedy a severe housing shortage, which would be alleviated by enabling working-class settlement in areas serviced by fast and convenient transit services.[50]

In 1874, the project was reconfigured to include only the portion of the line inside of Berlin.[51] The private company was again unable to raise the funds. The state, which was a participant in the second project, took it over by a convention dated 23 February 1878, and approval was granted by the Landtag (Parliament) on 26 June 1878.[52] The project was not entrusted to its original proponent, Emil Hartwich (1801–79), but to the government-affiliated engineer Ernst Dircksens (1830–99). Dircksens had participated in the construction of the *Ringbahn* in the 1860s and distinguished himself as field railway engineer during the 1870–71 war.[53] The nine-kilometer distance between the end points of the line was connected by an undulating 12.145-kilometer elevated line built between 3.6 and 4.4 meters above the ground, servicing important city points through nine (later 11) inner-city stations: the Charlottenburg, Zoologischer Garten, Bellevue, Lehrter Bahnhof, Friedrichstrasse, Börse, Alexanderplatz, Jannowitzbrücke, and Schlesicher Bahnhof stations, with later addition of Tiergarten and Stralau-Rümmelsburg. The course of the *Stadtbahn* followed the northern edge of the original city, which was delimited by the Spree on the south and fortifications on the north.[54] After long negotiations, a fortification trench that was no longer in use (Königsgraben) was filled in to accommodate part of the line.

The four-track railway viaduct, the first in Europe, was divided between local traffic (on the northern tracks) and long-distance traffic (on the southern tracks). As the *Ringbahn* had reached completion while the *Stadtbahn* was under construction, the city authority created to oversee the project (Eisenbahndirektion Berlin) proposed that the four-track line across the city be integrated into a single city network connecting central and peripheral stations (see Figure 7.1). The line was opened for the nine stations of local traffic on 7 February 1882 and for long-distance traffic on 14 May 1882. Freight services were integrated during the night in 1886. The line was used by 16 million passengers in 1884, 33 million in 1891.[55] In the built-up areas of the city, it was elevated on 731 brick viaduct arches, wooden truss bridges on rivers, and riveted steel girders at road crossings. As Berlin's largest contiguous urban structure, with 597 arches occupied by businesses, the *Stadtbahn* was as commanding an urban presence as the unbuilt central railway station it was designed to make unnecessary.[56]

Conclusion

If strategic considerations provided an impetus for the *Ringbahn* and *Stadtbahn*, economic imperatives were equally powerful. The pace of

Berlin's growth increased dramatically after the completion of this system of urban communication lines, which was hailed as a source of pride for the capital and contributed to its rapid industrial development.[57] When a competition for the planning of Greater Berlin was held in 1907, the reconfiguration of the railway system with its eight terminals was an essential aspect of the program.[58] The precise contribution of military authorities to the overall development of Berlin's rail configuration remains to be examined in greater detail, but the two world wars may have erased some of the archival evidence needed to make a full assessment of this question. The military held considerable power and had a shaping impact on the development of Prussian private lines and state projects. Although military authorities were initially reactionary in railway matters, the railways had advocates among their ranks. When mobilization in 1850 highlighted the shortcomings of the rail network, emergency rail building measures taken by the state brought about radical development. In the three projects examined here—the Berlin-Anhalt Railway, the *Ringbahn,* and the *Stadtbahn*—the military were present at their initiation and placed high demands, both at construction and for the potential strategic use of the completed projects. The powerful military presence in Berlin dovetailed with its equally dominant railway development.

8

Brussels' "Jonction Nord-Midi," the Scar in the Body of the City

It took a 115 years to build the Junction between Brussels' Gare du Nord and Gare du Midi (north and south stations). The project was to connect the Belgian capital's two main stations by an underground rail line. Its protracted labor left an urban scar still blamed today for Brussels' failure to rival other European capitals. From 110,000 in 1830, year of the country's foundation, the metropolitan area population has grown to just above 1 million today. The Junction, bisecting the original core of the city, the pentagon delineated by fourteenth-century fortifications, is blamed for the capital's poor self-image (Figure 8.1). Today, the Junction is qualified as a "deep scar at the heart of the urban fabric."[1] The historian Thierry Demey's phrases "anarchic, useless destruction" and "the worst constructions to which modern architecture has given birth" retain currency.[2] The examination of this long-drawn project and its urban implications deviates from this book's pattern of general exploration of a facet followed by a more focused case study. Instead, the Brussels chapters examine first the Junction as a painfully long and arduous project to connect two terminal stations with its social and urban consequences. The following, final chapter will place the Junction within its national context and suggest its role in Belgium's current political configuration.

Countless speakers and writers have commented on the long parturition and the aftermath of this much-debated project. Surgical metaphors are pervasive in the postmortem assessments of the Junction, testifying to the extent the scar is deeply felt by those who care or reflect about Brussels. Organic analogies were used in early debates on the Junction, but surgical metaphors did not appear until the Junction was nearing completion. Only when the damage could be assessed was the Junction described as a

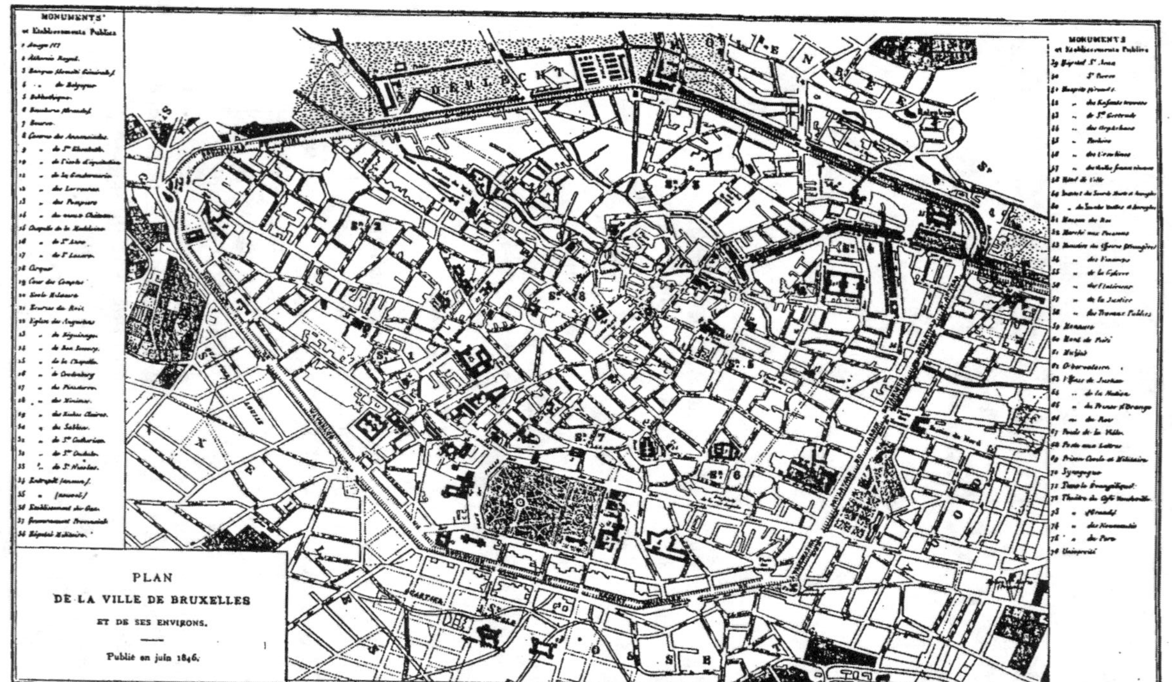

Figure 8.1 Plan of Brussels and Environs, 1846. From Patrick Abercrombie, "Brussels: A Study in Development and Planning," *Town Planning Review* 3, no. 3 (October 1912): pl. 85.

wound in the body of the city. In his 1959 book on the Junction, Fernand Brunfaut (1886–1972), the most prominent administrator among those who brought the project to completion, attempted to address the criticism against the project. He referred to the Junction's Gare Centrale (central station) as the "lung of life for the city" and its boulevards as "quivering arteries," countering negative assessments by a continued use of organic metaphors.[3] As Alain Corbin has pointed out, hygienist policies were a driving factor in nineteenth-century urban reconfiguration and social control of the laboring classes. The connection between hygiene and epidemics, fostered by crowded, insanitary living conditions, encouraged state and municipal authorities to assume more and more control over the handling or processing of biological and industrial waste and remove the lower classes from sight of the voting public. Because it affected the upper as well as the lower classes, the need for olfactory and hygienist control superseded the social concerns for the consequences of urban reconfigurations. The recurrence of organic metaphors in the rhetoric on Brussels' nineteenth-century projects reveals the pervasive top-down hygienist approach of the elite responsible for the railway Junction.[4]

The Railways in Brussels

The short distance between Brussels' two main termini was a genuine gap, characterized by the urbanist Patrick Abercrombie as "a failure of contact in an electric circuit."[5] Trains from Antwerp (and the Netherlands), Liège (and Germany), or Namur (and Luxemburg, Switzerland, or Italy) reached Brussels by the Gare du Nord, on the territory of the Commune of Saint-Josse-ten-Noode, whereas those from Ghent and Ostend (and London) or from Charleroi, Mons (and Paris, hub to the rest of France), rode into the Gare du Midi on the territory of the Commune of Saint-Gilles. Brussels did not have a station in its central area, commonly referred to as the "pentagon." The political segregation of this central area of the city, delineated by pentagonal fortifications, had been imposed by Napoleon I. This created a tactical choke hold, which isolated the fortified portion of a potentially too powerful provincial capital. The severed administrative and economic connections between the capital and its surrounding *communes* (boroughs) remains a situation that local authorities have, up to the present day, been unable to rectify. The rupture between the two poles of railway activity at the periphery of Brussels' core hampered the development of a national network. This was considered a serious handicap because the international scope of this network was an integral part of the original concept for railway development in Belgium. Leopold I, Belgium's first king, encouraged the national development of a state-owned railway system. The pioneering railway development efforts were intended to protect and promote, at home and abroad, the economy and commerce of the newly independent and politically neutral country. Given Brussels' history as a crossroads, a stop on the medieval trade routes, and its intended role as the hub of an international rail network, the absence of a connection between the city's major stations appears grievous indeed.[6]

The first steam train on the Continent left Brussels on 5 May 1835, from the Allée Verte (Green Lane) Station just outside the city limits along a tree-lined promenade heading north from the northwestern angle of the pentagon. Located just east of the Charleroi Canal, inaugurated three years earlier, this area had great economic potential.[7] The Allée Verte facility, however, became inadequate very quickly because of its size and its location outside of the pentagon. It was too remote for urban passenger traffic, which was rapidly outpacing freight in importance. The decision to move this first station to the center of the pentagon's northern edge was reached in 1839. The new facility, the first Gare du Nord (north station), located in Saint-Josse-ten-Noode, outside of the city limits, was inaugurated on 26 September 1841 and completed in 1862.[8] As examined elsewhere, railway stations were routinely located outside of urban areas to reduce the cost of real estate. In Brussels, this also helped to avoid local taxes and city tolls (in effect until 1860, despite the removal of the pentagonal walls during the first half of the century). However, as Brussels' surrounding communes remained autonomous political entities, asserting the long-standing principle of Belgian municipal freedom, the issue of stations established outside of the pentagon became increasingly sensitive.[9]

The southern station, or the Gare des Bogards, was inaugurated on 18 May 1840. It was named after the Franciscan Brothers, whose convent had been established in the area from the thirteenth century until 1796. Located on the Place Rouppe, the station fronted on one of two squares laid out on former religious property, in the thinly developed southwestern section of the city. The city administration, eager to attract business, agreed to grant the station exemption from toll tax. This station was replaced by a larger facility, the Gare du Midi (south station), in 1869. The new station retracted the rail lines behind the southwestern pentagon boulevard onto 13 hectares in the Commune of Saint-Gilles, again, outside city limits.[10]

Both the Nord and Midi stations acted as catalysts for the rapid development of their surrounding areas into commercial districts and residential *quartiers* (neighborhoods). Besides construction, stations also prompted the creation of new streets and the redirection of existing ones. The ad hoc communication developing through the street network also caused a shift from residential to commercial use or increase in commercial activity, supplanting established commercial streets with those in closer proximity of the stations. The activity generated by stations tended to have a positive economic impact. However, by the second half of the century, the addition of a belt line turned the rails into obstacles to communication between the center and the new peripheral suburban neighborhoods. Pedestrian footbridges or underground tunnels only provided awkward connections across the rails.[11]

Unlike the state-sponsored national network, which the king and his engineers had conceived as a whole, Brussels' railway system underwent piecemeal developments responding to unplanned or unexpected factors. The role of Brussels as hub of the network generated problems, which were solved slowly, with difficulty and at great cost. The location of the city's two main stations resulted from accidental circumstances. Each station was located in areas that differed considerably from aesthetic, economic, and social points of view. The visitor disembarking at the north station would be at the heart of the upscale commercial district; at the south station, he would have to negotiate the dense street network in the populous neighborhoods of the lower city. In addition, communication between the Nord and Midi terminals strained the existing street pattern along the Senne River.[12]

The "Jonction Nord-Midi"

A Necessary Link

The need for a connection between the Nord and Midi stations became apparent very early and prompted the city authorities to investigate the matter in 1837, as the second station was in the planning stage.[13] Land was expropriated in 1839, and on 24 March 1840 the city authorized the government to build a connecting rail line. Between 1841 and 1871, a single-track, street-level freight service connected the Allée Verte and the Bogards stations along the pentagon boulevards. This rail line amidst boulevard traffic caused difficulties and discouraged development of the western suburbs.[14] Building an external belt line was then adopted as a solution to connect the two stations. The western ring line was inaugurated in 1871 and replaced the boulevard Junction. It was used for some passenger traffic but considered inconvenient as it required trains to change direction at either station and ran more than 11 kilometers to connect points less than 3 kilometers apart.[15]

As of 1845, the idea of a direct connection between the two stations had gained favor among the city's business and engineering community. Five years after the opening of the second station, the lack of connection between the terminals was bringing the matter to the foreground. A commission was appointed by the city council in 1855 and charged with examining strategies to retain station activity within the pentagon. Plans to move the Bogards/Midi station out of the city were already under discussion by the state. The commission recommended a junction between the stations and the construction of a central station. This triggered a number of proposals to the city authorities from concession seekers, engineers, artists, and other interested individuals. The commission examined in detail four among the requests for concessions submitted in 1855 but was unable to make recommendations (see Appendix B). It was divided between those in favor of an internal rail line and those supporting an external connection. It became further polarized on the issue of moving the south station to Saint-Gilles versus creating a central station. The city council requested such a station in 1856 and informed the king of this desideratum but remained unable to recommend a single solution. Meanwhile, in February 1860, the state reached the decision to move the south station.[16]

In the absence of a rail connection, the limited passenger service provided between the two stations by local transport companies was considered inadequate. For the railways, a direct connection offered a number of advantages: transformation of the Nord and Midi stations from terminals to through stations, direct connection between the two districts of the national rail network, cost savings with reduction of shunting operations in the stations, and the possibility of building a central station. A junction would also allow building connections between outlying communities separated by the "Chinese Wall" of the railway tracks. For the city, a central station was seen as a means to attract business and passenger travel to the center, thereby retaining control of its economic development while relegating to the ring-line stations the freight traffic for which it had less of a financial stake. A central station would also compensate for the loss of economic activity to the Commune of Saint-Gilles as plans to move the outgrown Bogards/Midi station outside of the pentagon were reaching implementation.[17] Ancillary to the building of a station, the renovation of neglected neighborhoods and new buildings would attract the bourgeoisie, who had been fleeing the city for upscale suburbs. As commercial and housing real estate constituted the fiscal base of the city, cultivating property owners reflected sound municipal management.

From the early planning stages for a junction, urban sanitizing was part of the agenda. Hygienist arguments became prevalent because they made unpopular and difficult expropriations more acceptable. In a country where private property was inviolable, the laws of 1858 and 1867 made it easier to carry out expropriations, but only for urban sanitation projects. The medical imagery used at the preliminary stages of the project reflects concern for purifying the city. Making the body of the city wholesome would promote the physical and moral health of its inhabitants, especially those in disadvantaged neighborhoods. Hygiene, health, and morality went hand in hand. Healthy body functions for the city, such as circulation and elimination (including that of populous neighborhoods), were to be entrusted to engineers. Surgeons would be invoked later. Even King Leopold II indicated as early as 1861 that improving working-class housing and general welfare were key factors in his agenda to put Brussels on the international map and attract the prosperity foreign visitors would bring.[18]

Many projects were put forward for a junction and a station between the 1840s and the last decade of the century (see Appendix B). They fell into three main categories: a dedicated rail line through the city, a viaduct, or an underground line. They were proposed in four waves: in the 1840s, around 1855, around 1865, and in the last decade of the nineteenth century. The 1840s projects were prompted by the opening of the second station, the Gare des Bogards. The 1855 projects were encouraged by the appointment of a city commission. The 1865 group was triggered by the election of a new mayor in 1863, and the 1890s projects responded to the increasingly intolerable traffic congestion at the Nord and Midi stations. Each proposal was rich in rhetoric, aimed at convincing the authorities of its superiority. Counter projects and detractions, backed by lengthy arguments, financial or statistical data, and maps, yielded an abundant and colorful pamphlet literature. The primary arguments of this rhetoric were heavy reliance on technical factors, hygienist ideology, functionalism, speculation on expected increase in land value, creating opportunities for commerce, and concern for the capital's image abroad.[19]

The Senne River Vaulting

The proposed routing of the mid-1850s Junction projects coincided with the boulevards created by the vaulting of the Senne River a decade later. The Senne River, which ran northward through Brussels, drained poorly, meandered around low islands, and encouraged swamps (see Figure 8.1). The shortest line between the Nord and Midi stations ran along the Senne in the lower, western part of the city, but the river hampered street development. The Senne, as the Seine in Paris and the Thames in London, had become polluted from industrial refuse and untreated sewage. Periodic flooding also caused property damage and contributed to making the lower city the unhealthy refuge of the poorest inhabitants, where cholera epidemics broke out in 1852 and 1866. By the 1860s, these conditions encouraged those who could afford it to move to the suburbs.[20]

Solving the problem of the insanitary river was a priority for the newly elected, dynamic, young burgomaster, Jules Anspach (1863–79). He opened a competition, which resulted in the submission of more than 40 river improvement projects to the city administration between 1863 and 1865. The project adopted by the city council in October 1865 included filling in the river's secondary arm, straightening its main course, and covering its canal with boulevards over the two-kilometer distance between the Boulevard du Midi and the Boulevard d'Anvers. Two collecting sewers were to flank the underground river. Containment of the river was inaugurated in 1871. Eleven hundred houses had been demolished in the lower city. Sale of land for rebuilding began in 1872, but development lagged as bankruptcy plagued the French builder who, between 1874 and 1877, held a concession to build Paris-inspired apartment buildings along the boulevards.[21]

The Senne project is frequently described in surgical terms as "the first large scale urban surgery operation."[22] The historian Yvon Leblicq qualifies it as "horse's medicine: bloodletting," invoking Pierre Lavedan's phrase "surgical urbanism."[23] The surgical metaphors evoke both the invasive nature of the procedure and the restored functionality it provided. As things settled after this major upheaval, the boulevards atop the Senne vaulting, built slightly higher than the neighboring streets, created a new and much-needed north-south axis.[24] These boulevards connected the two main stations (Nord and Midi), supplanting in importance the medieval market trade route or *steenweg* (road, literally "stone way") running in the east-west direction. The new axis was expected to attract the kind of commerce that had tended to develop near stations, and retain well-to-do taxpayers in new *quartiers* within the pentagon.[25]

One of the mid-1860s projects ingeniously combined the Senne vaulting and the Junction, which would have reduced considerably the destruction of the original urban fabric eventually caused by both projects. The Keller brothers, contractors from Antwerp, proposed in 1864 the diversion of the river into a culvert, with collecting sewers on the sides, and an underground railway track between the Nord and Midi stations. The project, which would have required lowering both stations to connect with the underground tracks, gained considerable support from various constituencies, including the press, but failed to gain government approval. The Anspach municipal administration decided to treat the vaulting of the Senne, and the creation of the boulevards, as an independent project, unconnected to the building of a central station. This exhibited pragmatism in responding to urgent sanitation needs and reflected the expectations of the liberal middle class, which had put Anspach in office. The Junction and central station were thus put on the back burner. In 1872, year of the inauguration of the tramways on the new boulevards, Anspach spoke favorably of the central station project, but he did not initiate any action to revive it before the end of his administration in 1879.[26]

Mont des Arts and Bruneel Project

During the last two decades of the nineteenth century, the project for a Junction (and a central station) was integrated into plans for a connection between the lower and upper city in the former St. Roch neighborhood. Called *Montagne de la Cour* (Mount of the Court) and later *Mont des Arts* (Mount of the Arts), the project attracted several proposals that earmarked part of the site for a central station. The *Montagne de la Cour* would eventually pit King Leopold II and his architect, Balat, against the popular antiquarian burgomaster of Brussels, Charles Buls (1880–99), who resigned in protest against this project. Communication between the lower western populous city and the upper eastern aristocratic district had occurred through steep, narrow, and tortuous streets extending from the lower city, which retained its irregular medieval fabric until the nineteenth century. In the upper city, the area between the Royal Palace and Parliament had been redesigned in the late eighteenth century to conform to the geometric plan aesthetic inspired by Versailles. The north-south axis of newly laid-out streets and park alleys reinforced the demarcation between upper and lower city. Also, the Quartier Leopold area had been annexed to the east of the pentagon in 1853 to comply with the demands of the war ministry for a permanent military drill field. A new railway station for the privately built train line to the southeast of the country was put in service in the annexed area in 1855. The early-nineteenth-century eastward expansion of the eighteenth-century grid and subsequent annexation caused increased activity, which made the inadequate communication between the two parts of the city more conspicuous. During the second half of the nineteenth century, more than 200 projects were proposed to establish more direct communication between the lower and upper city. Among them, 162 projects were submitted to a city commission appointed in 1881 to investigate this problem. The Balat project, supported by the king, was partially realized, and Burgomaster Buls resigned as the even grander project of Balat's successor, Maquet, for what he now called the *Mont des Arts*, appeared to have gained favor.[27]

The urban sanitation component of the Balat/Maquet project was accomplished with the demolition of the St. Roch neighborhood. As the 1910 international exposition was approaching, the French landscape architect Vacherot was enlisted in 1909 to create a temporary park masking the ruins. This park was enjoyed for 50 years before further revisions of the Balat/Maquet plan led to the current layout with the Royal Library, museums, and convention center.[28] At issue in the conflict between Leopold II and Buls were two approaches to urbanism. Leopold II, inspired by Haussmann, imposed monumental concepts on live urban fabric. Buls, on the other hand, strongly influenced by the work of Camillo Sitte, advocated a more conservative form of urbanism, respectful of the city's vernacular heritage, especially where it was still enjoying healthy activity.[29] A pawn between these two approaches to urbanism and a liminal space between two distinct areas of the pentagon, the *Mont des Arts* projects also included proposals for a central station. The plans devised by Henri Maquet, Leopold II's architect, proposed alternate sites for a station either at the current location, in what was formerly known as the "Putterie" area, or further east toward the foot of the hill in the Rue Isabelle. Burgomaster Buls and his successor, Emile De Mot (1899–1909), were in favor of such a station, Buls because it would bring business to its surroundings, De Mot and the city council because it would replace insalubrious alleys and rookeries with new buildings.[30] Leopold II also appeared to have been supportive of the idea. As the station was proposed in close proximity to the royal residence, some suggested, however, that the king's wishes for direct train access from his palace bedroom was too expensive for the state.[31]

The Junction project remained on the agenda of commissions appointed by the railway administration in 1895, 1897, and 1901 to remedy the strain caused by increased activity on the Brussels railway facilities. Options included expansion of the terminal stations, but this was considered impractical because of expropriation costs and impact on street layout. A second option suggested moving the Nord station north to Schaerbeek and the Midi station south to Forest, where expansion would be easier and cheaper, but this would make the stations too remote. The third option was to transform the Nord and Midi stations into through stations and connect them with a line similar to the Berlin *Stadtbahn,* put in service in 1882.[32] The carefully thought-out solution proposed in 1893 by the state railway engineer Frédéric Bruneel was recommended by the three commissions. Bruneel's proposal had been presented to an alumni reunion of the Gent Engineering School after an 1892 fatal accident at the Gare du Nord. The accident was attributed primarily to the increased traffic the facility was unable to handle. Bruneel acknowledged his debt to the work he had seen in Germany and especially in Berlin. His project, which ran over 3.6 kilometers, consisted in an underground line between the northern boulevards and Notre-Dame de la Chapelle (1,928 meters), reached by viaduct sections between the stations and the tunnel (Figure 8.2). Both the Nord and Midi stations would be moved back (300 and 150 meters, respectively) and raised to be transformed into through stations. The central station would be located in the Putterie area. The mixed underground/viaduct solution was to safeguard most of the central areas and use viaducts only in the less critical neighborhoods, where land was cheaper, aesthetics was a minor issue, and foreign visitors were unlikely to go.[33]

The project was submitted to the Chamber of Representatives on 28 March 1899 and funding allocated by May 1900. The project submitted in 1899 included four tracks (Bruneel's only had two underground lines) and a two-hectare station in the Putterie area with ten tracks and platforms. Access roadways to the station would have required 14,000 additional square meters of expropriations, which would have resulted in considerable loss of taxable real estate for the city. The city's protests led to the reconfiguration of the station into an eight-track underground facility of smaller proportions. An agreement was signed on 7 April 1903, between the city and the state, defining both the specifications of the Junction and the city's responsibility in the reconfiguration of the neighboring areas, including the Putterie, Terarken, Isabelle, and *Mont des Arts* neighborhoods. The agreement would make the city a European capital at the expense of the state. Under the terms of the 1858 and 1867 laws, the city assumed responsibility for all required expropriations, a process the state was not legally authorized to carry out. The agreement bore Leopold II's imprimatur with a clause stipulating height limitations below the Royal Palace sight lines.[34]

Progress and Interruptions

The components of the project that were under the city's full responsibility were carried out in a timely manner: expropriations were essentially completed by 1913. Progress was slower where state collaboration was required. The Putterie area was not demolished until 1911, and by the start of World War I some clearing and draining projects had been carried out, but no building had begun. Between Notre-Dame de la Chapelle and the Midi station, that is, the southern third of the project area, demolitions had begun in 1911 and work was almost completed by 1914. Early in 1914, demolitions and some clearing also took place near the Nord station, but in August, all work was interrupted until 1919.[35] After a brief resumption, the project was shut down in December 1920 to allow the new minister for railways, Xavier Neujean, to perform another study of the Junction project. This led to the introduction of a bill to authorize the cessation of the project in 1922. Neujean had full support of the Brussels city administration, with the burgomaster and an almost unanimous city council now aligned against the Junction. After 42 changes of position in Parliament, a subsequent version of the Neujean Bill was approved by the House of Representatives on 2 March 1927, but rejected by the Senate on 24 July 1928. Unlike most issues in Belgium, the highly contested project for the Junction did not rely on partisan support, and changes of position were not uncommon. Feelings on the issue ran high, but they stemmed from individual convictions that did not fall into regional (Flemish against Walloon) or party line (Catholic versus Liberal or Socialist).[36]

The possibility of cessation had been anticipated. As early as 1915, while he was a war prisoner in Germany, Adolphe Max, burgomaster of Brussels

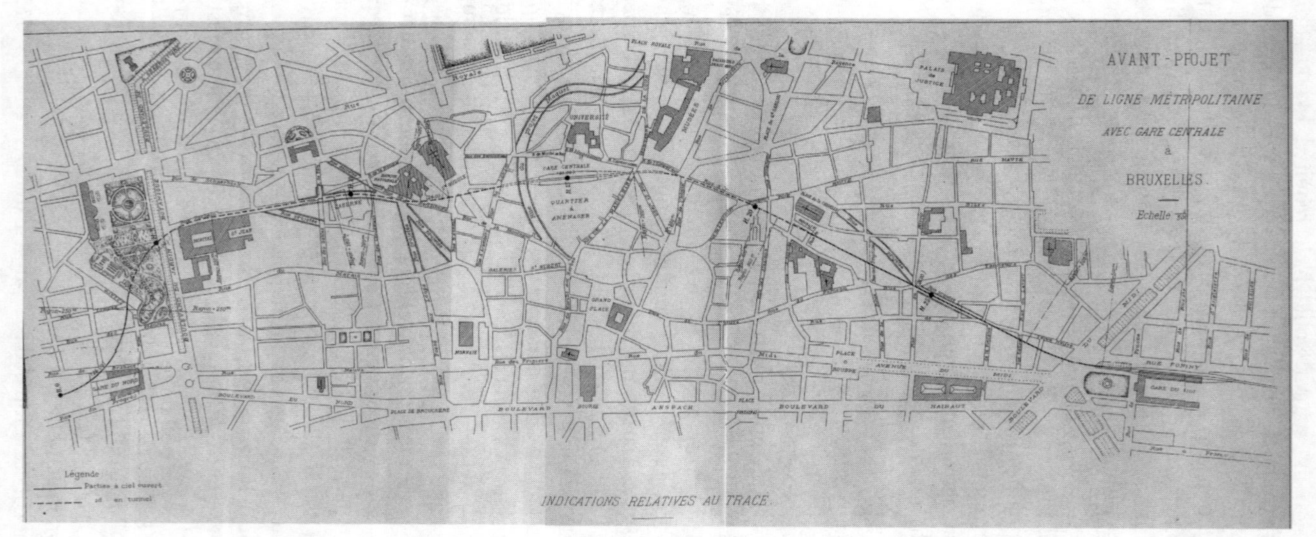

Figure 8.2   Frédéric Bruneel. Project for the Brussels Junction, 1893. From Bruneel, "Avant-projet de chemin de fer métropolitain avec Gare Centrale à Bruxelles," *Annales de l'Association des Ingénieurs sortis des Ecoles Spéciales de Gand* 16, no. 4 (1893), map.

(1909–39), had sent instructions to the chief city engineer to devise a plan for use of the expropriated properties, should the railways abandon the Junction project. The city was eager to put back on the tax rolls ten out of its 234 hectares of taxable land. After the Representatives' vote the city resumed work to carry out street improvements. These eventually received temporary government approval on 31 October 1928 in an agreement that modified the 1903 Junction plan. The 1928 document reflects eagerness to clean up the capital for the upcoming universal exposition of 1935. As the country was hovering in the aftermath of opposing votes on the Junction by the House and the Senate, the construction site suggested to foreign visitors that the "devastated areas" resulted from war damage, not domestic procrastination.[37] Concern about the project's image abroad remained a recurrent thread of Junction rhetoric: as stated by Paul Segers during the 18 February 1931 Senate debate, "Abandoning the project would make the country the laughing stock of the world."[38]

Meanwhile, supporters of the project continued their lobbying efforts.[39] In 1935, both Houses of Parliament voted to resume work on the Junction, and the Office National pour l'Achèvement de la Jonction Nord-Midi (National Office for the Completion of the North-South Junction, ONJ) was constituted by the Law of 11 July 1935. This office, chaired by the minister of transport, operated independently from the railways with a substantial budget intended in part as a public works project, addressing the unemployment caused by the 1930s international economic crisis. Bruneel's route was maintained but engineering specifications were updated, including the addition of electric traction. The station was designed to fit within the street network as it had just been reconfigured by the city in the triangular site between the Cantersteen, Boulevard de l'Impératrice, and the Rue de la Putterie. The major modification in the ONJ plans was the switch from tunnel to cut-and-cover construction of the underground line, which involved unroofing the whole length of the tunnel. This necessitated further expropriations and increased the urban impact of the project. Like the Putterie area, the new expropriation zone was deemed to contain only expendable real estate, which did not meet modern hygiene and circulation criteria.[40]

Work resumed in December 1936 and continued, at a slower pace, during the German occupation until 1943. Material and manpower shortages plagued the resumed project between 1944 and 1950, when normalized conditions, and some Marshall Plan assistance, allowed progress toward inauguration of the Junction on 4 October 1952. The Junction's opening enabled a quick reconfiguration of services on the entire network into an integrated rail system. Fifty years after its inauguration, the Junction remains a vital cog of the Belgian rail network. It has performed beyond expectations and has reached maximum capacity. Initially intended to accommodate 600 to 800 trains daily, with 50,000 passengers using the central station, the Junction would be used by 734 trains daily (48 of them international trains) and 24,000 passengers right after inauguration. In 2000, the Junction serviced 1,200 trains and more than 140,000 (occasionally up to 180,000) passengers daily, with peak activity of 85 trains per hour, or a train every 40 seconds.[41]

Engineering Challenge

As urban historian Yvon Leblicq has pointed out, most of the publications on the Junction focus on its technical aspect.[42] Among decision-makers, those with technical training tended to support the project, which was presented primarily as an engineering challenge and a financial operation. Numerical data and technical argumentation were enlisted on both sides of the polemical debates. The technical difficulty of driving a cut-and-cover tunnel in Brussels' unstable sandy subsoil, which had been used as an argument against the project, fascinated the engineering- and progress-minded politicians and audiences. The technical reports made it possible to present the project in a positive light as a remarkable accomplishment, and they justified pride. Accurate historical accounts could not skirt the sluggishness of the decision, approval, or financing processes and the controversy over the urban impact of the project, an issue still reverberating in the city.[43]

Despite updating by the ONJ, one might question whether a project designed before 1900 still provided the most appropriate solution and reflected available technology after 1935. Technical reasons were invoked to justify abandoning the project. Most prominent among them were difficult terrain, ventilation, and the danger of transforming the churches adjoining the line (SS. Michel and Gudule and Notre-Dame de la Chapelle) into leaning towers of Pisa. Ventilation, which had been successfully handled in London's Metropolitan Railway since 1863, became less compelling with the development of electrification, proven technology abroad, in the initial stages of implementation on the Brussels-Antwerp line by 1935. The monuments endangered by the proximity to the trench, 35 to 66 meters wide and 8 to 18 meters deep, would be monitored by seismographs and other precision instruments to protect them from structural damage. The primary hurdle of the unstable subsoil was approached with greater confidence as the recently completed tunnel under the Schelde in Antwerp testified to mastery of underground construction technology.[44]

Central Station: Horta's Last Project

The Central Station, a prominent component of the Junction, was designed to accommodate heavy traffic. Intended as a train stop rather than a full service station, it had no luggage service. A flat-roofed triangular structure with regular pilasters and understated art deco ornamentation, the building remains carefully below the sight lines from the upper city. Victor Horta's program for a triangular site with strong declivity between the Boulevard de l'Impératrice and the Rues de la Putterie and Cantersteen needed to accommodate the six curved tracks separated by three 8 × 300 meter platforms of the underground level, which the building would not entirely overlap. Initial plans, begun around 1910, relied heavily on metal, but Horta shifted to concrete after his 1919 visit to the United States. Further revisions were necessary as the street configuration was modified between 1928 and 1933. At the location of the station, the tunnel was widened from 35 to 60 meters. The station has three levels: the tracks, an intermediary concourse, and a street entrance, with an additional mezzanine at the level of the Rue Cantersteen, 2.25 meters above the main floor. Designed to house railway offices in one–third, and income-producing administrative and commercial facilities in the remaining two-thirds, this mixed-use building discreetly incorporates two additional levels in the peripheral spaces.

The main feature of the passenger hall is the majestic staircase descending toward the intermediary concourse, which provides access to the separate platforms. Several underground pedestrian access tunnels and an additional train line to the national airport were added by the architect Maxime Brunfaut, who completed the project after Horta's death in 1947. Innovative features to accommodate high-volume traffic included the suppression of doors, which were replaced by circulating air curtains countering exterior temperature variations. Facing materials included marble, blue or gray stone, and bronze with copper roofing. The Royal Salon, at the disposal of the monarch for his private use and to welcome state visitors, put an end to Brussels' embarrassment at not having had a proper station on its territory.[45]

As the last step in the progression from the Parc de Bruxelles to the Putterie, the building looks to the architecture of the park area and the Palais des Beaux-Arts (1895, also by Horta), rather than to the picturesque vernacular of the lower city, tactfully avoiding allusion to the devastated areas below. Rather than assuming the assertive stance of a monument, the station exhibits the tendency to insert a structure within its context, which the architect adopted in his later years. Inside the building, Horta also negotiates complex geometric relationships between the rectangular staircase within the irregular triangle of the building.[46] Despite the project's sensitivity to surrounding terrain and structures, the station, as it was realized, did not generate the neighborhood development its promoters expected. Local residents considered it a greater asset for those who resided elsewhere than for themselves. Marked by the questionable urban legacy of the Junction, the station's design did not receive the understanding it deserved.[47]

Slum Clearing. and Urban Exodus

The Junction's slum-clearing agenda was included repeatedly in the early proposals and expressed in the 1893 Bruneel project:

> The portions of the lines near the Nord and Midi Stations cut across properties of average value and the above ground portion between Rues de la Prévote and des Tanneurs is to be built on land of the lowest value within the territory of the City of Brussels.
>
> The Central Station, planned for a totally disinherited neighborhood in need of reconfiguration, also occupies land of low value. The passenger facilities could be installed most economically above the trench of the station, within an interior courtyard bordered by private constructions. Costly buildings would be avoided while street frontage real estate would acquire great value.[48]

Although Bruneel focuses primarily on the technical and operational aspects of the project, this passage reveals his awareness of land values as well as of the potential impact the railway and the station could have on them. The area earmarked for the central station was disinherited, and it demanded intervention. Land could be had cheaply and developed into valuable real estate. Bruneel seemed to make a geographical assessment of the area, not a political one. However, his statement was intended to appeal to his audience and reflects the propensity to justify projects by their urban sanitizing component. As mentioned above, Emile De Mot, Brussels' burgomaster when the Bruneel project was originally approved and funded in 1900, was in favor of the slum-clearing agenda. The issue, linked to the project from the onset, became integral to the planning process from then on, as evidenced by the influential and comprehensive Helleputte report for the 1922–23 parliamentary session. As Fernand Brunfaut would point out in a House debate, the issue was used repeatedly, with divergent motives, by both those in favor and those against the Junction and by the press. Bruneel's project attempted to minimize impact by confining demolitions to the Putterie neighborhood and to peripheral areas. The revised ONJ cut-and-cover construction claimed the older quarters of Notre-Dame de la Chapelle, Putterie, Douze-Apôtres, Ter Arken, Isabelle, Saint-Roch, Sainte-Gudule, Sainte-Elisabeth, Bas-fonds, and Pachéco. Marcel Mathieu described the Putterie area as "one of the oldest neighborhoods in the city, . . . insalubrious and overpopulated," whereas some urban historians claim it as the oldest but also the most beautiful area of the city.[49]

The area affected by the Junction covered 17 hectares; the area needed for construction was only 7 hectares. Ten additional hectares were expropriated, some to give elbow room for construction, no doubt, but some to clear older neighborhoods.[50] Mathieu, who performed the most detailed study of the Junction's urban impact in 1961, stated that the expropriation zone was deliberately expanded for urban renewal. He estimated cautiously, in the absence of accurate statistics, that 1,195 buildings were demolished and 9,095 inhabitants displaced.[51] More recent sources list 1,626 buildings and 13,600 people.[52] Even the lower figures account for greater impact on the city than that caused by the two world wars.

In 1903, when demolition plans for the Putterie and other areas became public, Charles Buls and like-minded advocates of retaining the city fabric founded the Comité d'Etude du Vieux Bruxelles (Committee for the Study of Old Brussels). As Marville and others did in Paris, the committee photographed the areas earmarked for demolition. Even if, as suggested in a recent publication, the committee omitted to photograph some of the back alleys to focus on the more distinguished façades, the area contained a lot more than slums—aristocratic hotels, businesses, and houses, a good number of them owner-occupied—in other words, monuments and vernacular fabric, some of which dated back to the Middle Ages.[53] The urban historian Victor-Gaston Martiny took stock of the architectural losses in these populous areas, which also included the Hospital Saint-Jean; the Sainte-Elisabeth barracks and hospital; the remains of the ancient Clutinc Castle; the Montagne-des-Aveugles; the former Cardinal Granvelle Palace, on the Rue des Sols, then home of the Université Libre de Bruselles; the fifteenth-century Salazar Chapel; and many houses with stepped gables and vaulted cellars. Martiny also underlined the profound morphological change on the hillside because the demolitions isolated from their surroundings such buildings as SS. Michel and Gudule, Notre-Dame de la Chapelle, and the Brigittines Chapel, none intended to stand alone, out of context.[54] As in Agar Town, the documentation from Buls' committee as well as other numerous extant sources, including the documents prepared for expropriations, would make it possible to reconstruct some of the city's fabric beyond the monuments outlined by Martiny. Such a study would reveal and people a lively and active fabric where different social classes interacted. Support networks and attachment to place were integral components of these *quartiers,* which had their own distinctive dialects.

It is therefore clear that the rhetoric of slum clearance for the common good, which the ONJ readily adopted when it took over the project, rests on shaky ground. Implicit in the slum clearance process is the conversion of real estate of dubious value into buildings with higher tax returns. As mentioned earlier, slum clearance was, however, the only ground that could be invoked for large-scale expropriation, according to the laws of

1858 and 1867. The impact of this process was not unknown to the authorities. As Charles Buls indicated in 1891, when he reported to the city council on an investigation of workers' housing, displaced people, who usually received no assistance with rehousing, tended to attempt to resettle in the immediate area. His evaluation of the problem was that "demolitions are good business for slum owners," who can raise the rent on remaining housing.[55] Crowding more inhabitants into residual housing aggravated hygiene conditions. It also increased lack of privacy and promiscuity, especially between generations, which could lead to immoral behaviors and even incest.

There is no precise documentation of the impact on population exodus from the city caused by the demolition of entire streets and alleys. These demolitions were also accompanied by destruction of social and economic networks within these neighborhoods.[56] Despite close scrutiny, Mathieu did not see a consistent increase in the areas near the expropriation zones, but where increase did occur, it was followed by a decrease. He attributed this to the centrifugal population movement, which became more intense after 1890. Between 1890 and 1947, 75,530 inhabitants or 47 percent left the city. The 1910 census commented on this decrease and made a distinction between accidental and permanent causes. Accidental causes reflected work being performed in several areas of the city; permanent causes were attributable to social and economic changes noticeable in all large cities. Mathieu indicated that, between 1900 and 1947, the pentagon lost 70,888 inhabitants, 8,841 due to the Junction, 9,554 due to other projects (or 18,395 due to accidental causes), and 52,493 due to permanent causes.[57] As suggested more recently, the Junction may have fostered a climate where expropriations and demolitions caused deterioration of living conditions in the city, which encouraged emigration.[58] Also, the protracted nature of the project encouraged neglect and speculation, which contributed to further deterioration. Increase in land value also played a part in this process as owners attempted to maximize revenue from former residential land. Given these factors in a context where social conditions were improving with better hygiene, assistance for home ownership, and more efficient transportation, the Junction appears to have been an aggravating, not a causative, factor for urban exodus.[59]

Conclusion: Urban Legacy

The ONJ's additional demolitions, required by the shift from underground to cut-and-cover tunnel construction, further deteriorated the project's social image. Except for two housing projects, below Notre-Dame de la Chapelle near the Midi station, the area of the Junction shifted to business or administrative use.[60] However, two of the ONJ's directors, Waucquez and Brunfaut, were also socialist members of the Brussels city council, both extremely concerned with working-class housing. Brunfaut's career as an architect greatly benefited from the early-twentieth-century socialist projects of facilities and housing for the lower classes, some of which were financed by special funding bearing his name. When taken to task about the urban exodus attributed to the Junction, Brunfaut pointed to the state and its large-scale projects such as the Cité Administrative along the northern edge of the pentagon, characterized recently by a local scholar as "catastrophic urban chaos."[61]

Once the Junction trench was filled in, the underground facility was aptly managed by the Société Nationale des Chemins de fer Belges (National Society of Belgian Railways, SNCB), but the surface area was not taken in hand. As Martiny and Demey point out, a new urban landscape emerged without urban planning.[62] After completion of the Junction, the legacy of outsized, modern, mostly administrative or business buildings continues to be seen as a painful scar, and the memory of the protracted work site has not entirely faded. The surgical metaphors, already applied to the Senne vaulting, resurfaced to reflect the traumatic impact of the Junction. Powerfully evocative phrases such as "a second bloodletting" or, more recently, "bloodletting, the most deplorable case of self-mutilation [worthy] of Ceausescu's Budapest [sic]" or "amputation of 17 hectares sustained over 50 years" alternate with lengthier clinical descriptions: "The last project, barely passed by the 1901 Parlement, will only be completed in 1952, after leaving the heart of Brussels eviscerated for half a century."[63] A 1951 article in the leftist paper *Germinal* bemoans Brussels' ubiquitous work sites, mixing religious and surgical metaphors: "Brussels is a martyr to urbanistic surgery. Will her Calvary end one day? No doubt, the scar of the most serious operation, named "Junction" is slowly healing. But the operation Albertine is already being talked about, and it too will require deep scalpel cuts."[64] The rhetoric contemporary to the construction of the Junction did not include urbanistic considerations beyond the stated expectations of creating wide boulevards and a modern city. During the years of the Junction's gestation, urbanism was emerging as a discipline in the works of Camillo Sitte, Herman Stübben, Ebenezer Howard, Ildefons Cerdá, Tony Garnier, and Le Corbusier. Haussmann's Paris was familiar to Brussels' educated and influential elite. Leopold II occasionally enlisted Stübben as advisor. Charles Buls knew and corresponded with Sitte and Stübben, whose work he studied closely. World War I had exiled a number of Belgian architects, who then came in contact with British or Dutch colleagues, and Belgians were active in the Congrès Internationaux d'Architecture Moderne (CIAM).[65] Belgium was therefore not without exposure to urbanism, and although most urban theorists attempted to propose ideal cities in tabula rasa settings, some were negotiating solutions in response to existing urban fabrics such as that of Brussels.

The absence of deliberate urban discourse in tandem with the Junction may have played a large part in its failure as a city project. The project's protracted gestation over generations when urbanism shifted in its espousal of symbolic, functionalist, or social agendas may have prevented the emergence of a vision for a project that did not transcend engineering and highway requirements. The agreement between the city and the state provided for the creation of an administrative structure to deal with reconstruction after completion of the tunnel. This Advisory Commission included members from the Junction office staff and from the city. Since the creation of an Office for Urbanism in 1945, a delegate from this administration had been added to the group. When, in 1953, it debated the issue of rebuilding after completion of the Junction, the city council expected reports from this commission to provide plans for a city with a brand-new look, hallmark of the twentieth century, and new circulation patterns that combined buildings and open spaces.[66] The municipal administration would soon be in a position to decide on future development, which would nonetheless be expected to require special effort, given the size and high cost of the real estate involved. Neighboring areas also needed attention, as evidenced by the city council's discussion of lighting in adjacent "commercial streets which have suffered from the works of the Junctions and whose inhabitants are making superhuman efforts to attempt to regain former prosperity."[67] Projects were publicized in June 1954 to begin in October of that year, with an expected completion date of 1958, year of the Brussels international exposition.[68]

Until the 1990s, large administrative or bank buildings alternated with empty lots or structures still awaiting demolition. The new structures included, to name just a few, the Cité Administrative (1958–80) at the northern end; the Banque Nationale facilities on both sides of the Boulevard de Berlaimont (1958–77); the Westbury Hotel (1962–63) and the Sabena headquarters (1952–54), both in close proximity of the Gare Centrale. Further south, the Royal Library (1955–69) and the Palais des Congrès on the Boulevard de l'Empereur completed the *Mont des Arts* project.[69] The architecturally undistinguished large-scale constructions were staggered over four phases of architectural development—brick and stone, glass and steel, modular prefabricated concrete architectonic surfaces, and a recent return to vernacular brick—but no attempt was made to connect them with the remaining adjacent urban fabric. With the shift to administrative and official land use along the entire length of the new boulevards, the only returning residents were the superintendents for the office buildings. Martini writes of "a dead zone after office hours, . . . from the Botanical Garden to Notre-Dame de la Chapelle, which literally severs the city in two with a dark no man's land."[70] Phrases such as "desert," "wasteland," and "wall of silence" are used to characterize the area. Office buildings were attracted by the proximity to the Gare Centrale, but this administrative and business implantation impaired the development of the expected commercial and travel amenities characteristic of the other stations.[71]

The protracted maturation of the project caused the gap or fault created between the lower and upper city to remain unbridged for decades.[72] Like the Senne vaulting, the Junction was to create another wide north-south communication artery from Notre-Dame de la Chapelle to the Botanical Garden. Like the boulevards covering the Senne, those created by the Junction were raised above original street level but considerably higher, thus creating greater disjunction between new boulevards and old street patterns. The new north-south axis of the Junction cuts business connections between the lower and upper city and slices though the city between Schaerbeek and Saint-Gilles along boulevards, awkwardly truncated in the Notre-Dame de la Chapelle area, which renders them useless as effective communication channels. Indeed, the undulating sequence of the Boulevards Pacheco, de Berlaimont, de l'Impératrice, and de l'Empereur is divided into the Rue des Ursulines and the Rue des Brigitines on either side of the emerging tracks at the Chapelle station. This dissolves the wide boulevard into an older, irregular street pattern, forcing vehicular traffic to make 90-degree turns into awkwardly narrow streets to proceed toward parallel circulation arteries.[73]

The aftermath of the Junction is generally blamed for Brussels' second-rank status as an international capital. No urban historian of post–World War II Brussels has refrained from qualifying the Junction as an urban failure. The narrow tortuous streets with gable-fronted houses, which Charles Buls had attempted to save, have been replaced by monolithic office buildings on wide arteries. The old city has been confined to some showcase blocks barely guaranteed survival as a foil to modernity. The readiness to sacrifice what the urban historian Chloé Deligne calls the "disparate colorful heritage from the past" for progress and modernity made the Junction possible.[74] As politicians and urbanists strove to emulate the conceptual models of new cities influenced by the leading proponents of the Athens Charta, they failed to take into account the "spatial and temporal complexity of the city" and the "affective relations between humans and the space where they live."[75] Like the demolished populous neighborhoods, the canyon walls of the Junction's new buildings, already dated by their dull, stripped functionalism, will demand "reconfiguration." The ubiquitous presence of uninspired and uninspiring modernism will render these buildings as expendable as the slums, alleys, and vernacular heritage of the old city.

More recently, an emerging architectural firm, V+, named after the slogan for the Junction, "Vers plus de bien être" (toward greater well-being), worked on the Junction as a thesis project at the Architecture School of La Cambre in 1997. Born in a city where the Junction had always been present, the young architects wanted to consider the Junction as a potential rather than as a stigma. In their attempt to transcend the negative aura of the Junction, they envisioned it operating on three scales: local in the Chapelle area in the south, urban in the Cité Administrative at the northern end, and as world metropolis in the Quartier de l'Europe and Gare Centrale in between. They proposed discrete projects for each of these areas, aimed at maximizing the multivalent potential of the space. For instance, in the case of the Cité Administrative, which suffers from reduced occupancy with the removal of many administrative functions to the regional rather than state level, V+ advocated recycling the space into 24-hour use with residential, day care, and other activities. A small publication/manifesto produced by the group outlines a concrete program. Along the margins, it also includes a surreal and satirical timeline of the fictitious events taking place as a wall is built around the Junction area and the space taken away from the city. This invented account of administrative and popular reactions reveals a cunning understanding of the political context and underlines the fact that the Junction has become an integral part of the city.[76] Unfortunately, the young firm, which continues to be invited to participate in urban debates, is becoming discouraged by the glacial pace of change.[77]

As was stated in 1948, much was expected from the Junction: "By contributing to its economic revival, the Junction Nord-Midi will prove to be an inexhaustible mine of material and intellectual benefits for the country."[78] At its inauguration, the project was credited with the progress of science and construction technology, slum clearing, preservation of historic buildings, making Brussels a European city, cementing the unity of the country with a direct link between Wallonia and Flanders, and "reaching toward all the European capitals."[79] Abercrombie's contact had been made.

Connecting Stations in London, Paris, and Berlin

The problem of connecting stations presented itself by the second quarter of the nineteenth century in all countries developing a rail network around a central city with terminals on its outskirts. Some of the projects assumed utopian dimensions. In Paris, for example, a viaduct on the Seine from the Jardin des Plantes to the Champs-Elysées was proposed in March 1842.[80] In London, Joseph Paxton, designer of the Crystal Palace for the 1851 exhibition, proposed the Great Victorian Way in 1855. He envisaged an enclosed glass gallery with pedestrian lanes and railways, as well as shops and other public spaces. According to the 1855 Parliamentary Report on Communications, this ambitious and highly innovative project connected all the railway lines reaching London. The £34,000,000 price tag, which Paxton considered an appropriate government expense, discouraged construction.[81]

Such projects, and many others, appealed to the imagination, but actual connections between stations followed a predictable pattern, described by the Belgian minister Liebart as "a general law, a law of progress we would be wrong to resist. The first railways near large cities were created with terminal stations, then came the connections with beltways around the cities, so-called ring lines, then, because of the multiple maneuvers required to operate those beltway lines with dead-end stations, we are now resorting to direct connections."[82]

Each capital city interpreted this "law" differently and reached a different stage of its implementation by the end of railway expansion at the beginning of the twentieth century.

Versatile Connections in London

In London, the complexity of the railway configuration is to be attributed to British reliance on private initiative to develop railway lines. The first London line to Greenwich opened in 1833, that of the London and Birmingham reached Euston in 1838. The last London station, Marylebone, would be inaugurated in 1899. In the meantime, 15 stations were constructed in the London metropolitan area, whereas Paris only built eight.

The French engineer de Bassompièrre-Sewrin described the London terminals in an article published in 1854 in the *Journal des Chemins de Fer,* where he indicated that the companies were unable to penetrate toward the City and established their terminals at the limit of developed squares and neighborhoods.[83] Stations were unable to penetrate further into the metropolitan area because an exclusion zone for rail lines had been decreed in 1846 by the Royal Metropolitan Railway Commission, charged with examining all the railway projects submitted in London that year. These had proved too numerous and too complex for the usual concession approval procedures. The commission recommended an exclusion zone for rail lines and a more comprehensive approach in the evaluation of London railway projects.[84] Enforcement for this exclusion of concessions from the center was gradually eroded, but the rule nonetheless had a shaping effect on the configuration of London railways. Out of the 15 London stations, most were built at the periphery of the exclusion area, forming a circle around the City. The only station with a central position was Charing Cross (1864), near Trafalgar Square.[85]

The proliferation of stations contributed to severe congestion on London streets, especially in the City. In 1851, Charles Pearson, solicitor for the City of London, proposed building a central station. This proposal would be repeated many times, by Pearson and, among others, *The Builder,* an architectural journal with a social conscience edited by George Godwin. Railway companies were reluctant to raise necessary funds, and Parliament did not approve the project because of the expected concentration of traffic in a single area and the cost of land acquisition.[86] Pearson also proposed an underground train service that would provide reduced-fare tickets for workers at hours convenient for their commute to work. His recommendations led to the approval in 1853 for a cut-and-cover line under Euston Road from Paddington to King's Cross and on to the Farringdon Street terminus. Inaugurated with much success on 10 January 1863, the Metropolitan Railway, initially operated by the Great Western, was installed with double-gauge tracks. This line was extended to Moorgate in 1865. The Great Northern and Midland companies had connected their lines to the underground line, which gave them access to the City and necessitated the installation of four instead of two tracks between King's Cross and Moorgate. The western arm of the line, as far as Kensington, was authorized in 1864 and completed four years later. Another company, the Metropolitan District Company, began work on the southern half of the circle, from Kensington to Westminster, which opened in 1868. Along the Thames, the project was incorporated into the Thames Embankment. Progress was slow and left a one-mile gap between Mansion House and Aldgate. This last stretch was completed in 1884 by a joint effort of both companies. The expense caused by this last cut-and-cover section made it a public service rather than a profitable venture, and this method was not used again in London. Instead, the underground lines of the "tube" were built between 1898 and 1907. This nickname reflects the configuration of a rail line in a steel tube dug through the clay layer of London's subsoil, deeper than cellars and sewers. Enabled by electric traction, this method did not require large-scale expropriations, which made it more affordable.[87]

In addition to the Metropolitan Railway's circular line, the London, Chatham and Dover Railway received permission in 1861 to build an extension from Herne Hill to Blackfriars and to connect with the Metropolitan Railway near Farringdon Street, which would give access to the south of the Thames for northern companies and vice versa as of 1866. Discontinued in 1916 for passengers and in 1969 for freight, this line was put back in service with great success in 1988, under the name of Thameslink. Beyond the central circle and its diameter, there were other ring lines. For instance, in the northeast, the North London Railway, put into service between 1850 and 1852, circled at the edge of the built area of the metropolis. On the west, the West London Extension Railway connected the trunk lines reaching London from the north and east with those from the south and southeast as of 1862. This line carried freight, suburban trains, and a few direct trains from the north toward the south coast. The London, Tilbury and Southend Railway, inaugurated in 1854 and bought by the Midland Railway in 1912, is another example of a ring line, in this case, on the eastern side.[88]

Huet, a French Ponts et Chaussées engineer responsible for municipal railways, reporting on an 1876 mission to London, expressed his admiration for the versatility of communications there, which he considered superior to those of Paris.[89] As of 1842, the Railway Clearing House redistributed revenues among the different companies that constituted these complex and versatile connections.[90]

"Ceintures" in Paris

In Paris, railway stations were built outside of Philippe Auguste's thirteenth-century fortifications and its later additions, but inside of those erected by the *Fermiers généraux* as of 1784 and, therefore, also inside the walls built by Thiers between 1840 and 1845.[91] If some of the French railway companies, for instance, the Compagnie du Nord, proposed a number of projects to reach the heart of the city, these were not built because the city and the government did not approve them.[92] Railway omnibuses and later tramways brought passengers to the stations on the periphery of the city and provided connections between terminals.

The need to connect stations for freight transfer without going through the city was recognized as early as the 1840s. The *Journal des Chemins de Fer* already mentioned the issue in 1842.[93] Plans for a ring line along the strategic route inside the fortifications were designed and approved in December 1851.[94] This circle line was to connect the Ouest and Rouen, Nord, Strasbourg, Lyon, and Orleans stations and would be built by a syndicate of these companies under the leadership of state engineers. The line would carry passengers, but its main objectives were commercial and strategic. The ring line was first built on the right bank, from Auteuil to Bercy, then in 1865 on the left bank to reach a total of 38 kilometers. Passenger service was first provided on 14 July 1862, but it remained slow and inconvenient for more than 20 years. The whole line was not put in service until 1867, in time for the exposition. It connected the main freight stations: Les Batignolles, La Chapelle, La Villette, and Bercy.[95]

In 1875, a decree approved a convention between the same companies, except the Ouest, to build a larger circle line (*grande ceinture*), which began in 1876 and took freight transport out of the initial ring line (*petite ceinture*).[96] The latter was converted into passenger service in 1889, with trains every five minutes at peak hours for the daily commute to and from working-class and professional districts. Plans for a north-south rail line were abandoned in 1913, leaving Paris as the only city in France without a direct rail connection.[97] For passenger traffic, the *Métropolitain* (underground) would supplant the railways. It was already being considered in 1865, and the first projects date back to 1872, but it was not declared as a local project of public interest until 30 March 1898, just in time for the 1900 exposition. Its stations, designed by the architect Hector Guimard, dot the Paris landscape with Art Nouveau landmarks.

Berlin

As examined in Chapter 7, Berlin combined belt and junction lines. The *Ringbahn* retained delimiting power for the urban area until the twentieth century. The *Stadtbahn* provided a direct east-west connection linked to the belt line. It substituted to a central station the inner-city distributive versatility of its initial nine stations.[98] The nineteenth-century rail configuration in Berlin did not include a north-south axis. Such an axis was the backbone of Albert Speer's 1936–41 plan for the city. A modified version of the railway component for this plan has been implemented by the Lehrter Bahnhof inaugurated as Berlin's Hauptbahnhof on 28 May 2006.

9

Brussels' "Jonction" as the Heart Valve of a Commuting Workforce

The Junction Nord-Midi (north-south) has repeatedly taken the blame for Brussels' poor self-image. Brussels did not develop into a metropolis as large as London, Paris, or Berlin. Rather, the limited geographical expanse of the country combined with the densest rail and tramway networks in the world, workers' rail passes, and policies encouraging working-class home ownership stemmed the growth of the capital.[1] As soon as it was put in service, the Junction became an essential link in a national pattern of commuting, which contributed to the shift from predominantly blue- to white-collar work in the capital. Today, the Junction does not get mentioned without reference to those who use it daily. The 80,000 commuters who come through the station every day have become part of the Junction's identity.

Train commuting began early in Brussels. As soon as the Bogards (later Midi) station opened in 1840, night trains were put in service to bring workmen daily from the Hainaut Province.[2] By the turn of the century, one out of five workers was commuting by train.[3] After inauguration of the Junction and of the Gare Centrale (central station) located on its route in 1952, urban redevelopment catered to administrative and business activity, attracted by convenient rail access. For Junction advocates, the rail link that closed the gap between the two parts of the country's network was expected to offer greater commuting flexibility for a national labor market and reinforce the unity between the two linguistically and ethnically distinct parts of Belgium. Primed by a long-established national pattern of commuting, which allowed workers to remain rural residents while working in the cities, commuters came to the Junction by the thousands. They streamed through the underground passages, propelled by the arrival of a train every 40 seconds at peak hours, flowing into nearby offices for the day, to be funneled again through the monumental staircase of the station, draining life and animation from the streets of the capital into the provincial towns and villages for the night.[4] Their swift motion in rapid waves through the arteries of underground corridors animated the station by the pulsating echo of their feet and voices. But this heart has ceased to beat as one: the attachment to local communities nurtured by commuting has encouraged linguistic, ethnic, and regional particularism, which has led to the country's revisions of its constitution into a federal state. As mentioned at the beginning of Chapter 8, this last chapter argues that the Junction has further encouraged a long-established pattern of commuting and played a contributing role in the federal reconfiguration of Belgium.

The 1831 constitution, which established the country as a constitutional monarchy, had been revised only three times, in 1893, 1899, and 1921. Between 1969 and 1995, four consecutive constitutional reforms have made the country a federal monarchy.[5] The ensuing successive waves of political restructuring have turned the country's government into an increasingly complex bureaucracy that reflects the ethnic divisions of the country into three cultural communities (French, Dutch, and German) and into three regions (Wallonia, Flanders, and Brussels). The federal government has been reduced in size and responsibility. This gradual but radical shift in the country's political underpinnings is not free from growing pains. Indeed, one can wonder if, propelled along their own autonomous trajectories, the regions will retain enough reasons to remain together. A divorce may be in the cards. In this political context, convenient and inexpensive access to commuting within a small national territory has reinforced the ethnic division that is undermining the viability of the country as a political unit.

A Commuting Workforce

One of the recurring arguments of Junction rhetoric was the ease of access to various parts of the city it would provide for travelers and, most particularly, for workers to reach their place of employment.[6] Already present in the 1893 Bruneel project, the need for workers to reach their workplace was taken to heart by Fernand Brunfaut, the socialist administrator of the Office National pour l'Achèvement de la Jonction Nord-Midi (National Office for the Completion of the North-South Junction, ONJ), after resumption of the project in 1935. On this matter he was in lively opposition to the city's burgomaster, Adolphe Max, who had remained a staunch antagonist to the project since 1915.[7] For Brunfaut, the Junction was to have more lasting influence on employment than as a public works project during the 1930s: the connection between the two halves of the country's rail network would increase workers' mobility and their ability to respond to available employment.[8] Brunfaut's emphasis on the Junction's expected impact on commuting was motivated by the unique history of commuting in Belgium.

Commuting in Belgium

The sociologist Ernest Mahaim published his findings on the influence of reduced-fare workers' passes on commuting in a 1910 monograph. He set out to document what already then "had become a social phenomenon of prime importance."[9] Based on data collected between 1906 and 1910, his study also examined the social implications of reduced fares for workers in Belgium. Mahaim credited the state management of the railways for this unique social service: by 1909, 41 percent of journeys on state lines were made with workers' passes.[10] Quoting B. Seebohm Rowntree, he exhibited justified national pride: "Transit facilities in Belgium are better than in any other country in the world. . . . Not only has she a wonderful system of railways, but the fares charged for workmen's passes are the cheapest in the world."[11] Mahaim's comparative examination of England, France, and Germany, although hampered by the absence of similar statistical measurements, shows that workers' passes are more prevalent and fares cheaper in Belgium.[12]

Reduced fares for workers were proposed in April 1869 by the Catholic representative Kervyn de Lettenhove; approved by Alexandre Jamar, Liberal minister of public works; decreed in September 1869; and first used in February 1870. This revolutionary policy apparently stemmed from humanitarian concern for the prejudicial moral, hygienic, material, and social effects of urban housing conditions and was intended to facilitate continued family life in the country. Catholic factions were in favor of such a policy as they considered that family and rural communities provided better moral and social support systems than the city. Mahaim's examination of the approval process does not support the commonly held notion that the policy was promoted by a Liberal government intent on supporting industrial development and providing management with cheaper manpower. Such consensus between Catholics and Liberals was unusual in the political climate of the time, possibly reflecting the fact that the solution, enabled by an exiguous national territory, met a genuine social need. On the other hand, Mahaim pointed out that the railways were dealing with low returns and experimenting with fare reforms, informed by recent experience of reduced tariffs causing increased ridership. Made possible by a state-run railway system, where financial gain could take a backseat to social welfare, workers' passes gradually permeated the country's economic system. According to the Belgian socialist politician Emile

Vandervelde, they were to lead 20 years later to "possibly the deepest revolution in the regime of labor in Belgium."[13]

Unlike dedicated workers' trains operated in other countries, provisions in Belgium were more extensive right from the start. Workers' passes were granted to individuals who met specific conditions (usually performing manual labor, employees being excluded at first) and for specified numbers of journeys on regular trains. Initially restricted to special trains and the first and last daily regular trains, passes became valid on all trains' third-class carriages as of 1890. The practice was gradually adopted by the largest private rail company of the country, the Nord-Belge, between 1872 and 1897. The cost of six return fares, the common weekly quota, was cheaper than a one-way fare at regular tariff. Gradually, more flexibility was introduced among available options such as single fares or one weekly return fare and other formulas designed to meet employers' needs. From 14,233 tickets issued in 1870, a peak of 6,693,036 was reached in 1907, accounting for 42.85 percent of travelers that year, between one-fourth and one-fifth of the working population.[14]

Although industry was primarily localized in the provinces of Liège, Hainaut, and Antwerp, the lion's share of workers' passes was gradually issued for Brussels and the surrounding Brabant Province, where workers came from every area of the country. This pattern remains prevalent today. Mahaim's findings revealed a blue-collar working population with shifting patterns, closely reflecting annual industry statistics.[15] He described the activity of this population and its ties to the native soil:

> It is the humming hive where our workers, bees in constant motion, go to and fro, arriving and departing in tight ranks. They are peasants, or former peasants, whom the earth—though as rich as one could wish—refuses to feed, as there are too many of them. They rush to the public works, to the workshops, to the stores in the big city, they crowd into the factories of heavy industry, or into the coal mines. All of these are within close proximity and exert an irresistible attraction. But they come back, every evening or every Saturday, to the village where the family hearth is huddled.[16]

According to Mahaim, the impact of commuting was twofold. It enabled workers to remain rural dwellers, but it also opened the door to emigration by acquainting the workers with the opportunity to leave the rural setting. According to him, commuting was not a frivolous choice and usually reflected some initial difficult situation, which drove to the decision to commute. He also attributed a number of social consequences to the state-supported commuting phenomenon, which he considered unique to Belgium in its intensity. Commuting as a mode of daily migration as opposed to seasonal or permanent emigration enabled pass holders to leave their residences without abandoning them. However, as surfaced from Mahaim's analysis of season ticket travel, regular commuting to steady employment was on the whole relatively limited compared to the large number of occasional commuters. Women accounted for 20 percent of commuters around the turn of the century.[17]

Commuting workers were not exclusively dependent on the railways. In Brussels, horse-drawn omnibuses had been put in service in 1840, and tramways were installed along the major ancient access roads to the city, which eventually became the densest light rail network in the world. This light railway network also issued workers' passes as of 1884 under the same conditions as the railways. Bicycles, introduced in 1891, were becoming widespread and were increasing the catchment area of stations as well as reducing travel time and fatigue for workers. On the other hand, the railways' importance for commuters lasted longer in Brussels than in most Western cities: Brussels' Metro was not inaugurated until 1976, at least 75 years later than in most other capitals.[18]

Related Factors

Mahaim was wary of comparing demographic statistics from different European countries, but he sees a possible connection between access to reduced-fare commuters' passes and the 25 percent of the population residing in towns of 5,000 to 20,000 inhabitants in Belgium, as opposed to 11 percent in France and 13 percent in Germany. Although he cannot back this up with numerical data, he is convinced that the reduced-fare passes have slowed down the migration out of rural areas and into cities. They have reduced the dangers of rapid urban overpopulation.[19] It must be added here that Mahaim's cautious examination of demographics during the period when workers' passes were available does not account for the fact that substantial migration did take place. Between 1846 and 1900, the population of the country grew by 54 percent (from 4,337,196 to 6,679,282). During that time, communities with under 2,000 inhabitants lost population; all others gained from 29 percent (for communities with between 2,000 and 5,000 inhabitants) to 240 percent (for those with more than 100,000 inhabitants), gains increasing progressively with the size of the communities.[20] However, the percentage of the country's population in towns with more than 100,000 inhabitants grew less in Belgium that in other western European countries.[21] This data does not put in question Mahaim's position, which credits the density of the rail network, short distances, and the workers' passes with the impressive but comparatively limited growth of cities in Belgium. Also, this restrained urban expansion coexisted with continued growth of the rural population.[22]

Workers' passes made Belgium a single labor market and left no area of the country immune to their influence. Agricultural workers were lured toward industry by higher wages. Between 1866 and 1910, the proportion of workers employed in agriculture and industry shifted from 32.35 percent and 22.57 percent to 16.97 percent and 35.14 percent, respectively.[23] The flexibility afforded commuting workers placed them in a stronger position with management, although workers' passes also enabled some factory managers to hire rural workers unexposed to labor unions rather than urban union members. As regulators of supply and demand, the workers' passes reduced unemployment and the impact of industrial crises on employment. When work was truly hard to come by, the dissemination of unemployed populations in rural areas reduced the danger of collective action. Availability of manpower kept wages relatively low in Belgian industry and hampered laborers' efforts to organize effectively, although trains could provide fertile ground for union recruiting or socialist propaganda. The Catholic government in power between 1884 and 1914 instituted policies encouraging commuting and rural residence, which resulted in a large group of workers harder to recruit by the left and organized labor. Besides retaining closeness to the rural lifestyle, within earshot of the village church bells, workers' passes enabled families to cultivate a garden and benefit from fresh produce, livestock, and poultry. Such additions to the diet were commonplace in the rural setting but expensive and exceptional for the urban dweller. They made lower salaries more tolerable. Even residents of very modest housing enjoyed healthier surroundings in the country, which benefited the worker's family.[24]

Overcrowded urban conditions, aggravated by public works (rather than railways in nineteenth-century Brussels), were rendered more visible by the 1852 and 1866 cholera epidemics as well as labor unrest in 1847 and 1886.[25] After a general labor strike in 1886, a Labor Commission was constituted to study working-class conditions. The commission's recommendations led to the Housing Law of 9 August 1889, which included provisions enabling workers to own their own homes by making low-interest loans accessible to them and by reducing real-estate fees and taxes.[26] Between 1890 and 1910, probably more than 100,000 houses were built to be owned by workers.[27] Single-family housing, whether urban or rural, was credited with safeguarding independence and being more effective at fostering morality than multiple-unit dwellings, usually branded as "barracks." The preference for single-family dwellings with gardens became even more prominent in the first decades of the twentieth century.[28] This housing legislation benefited the working class with steady employment and some savings. Rented housing remained predominant for workers in more precarious conditions. The leveling effect of workers' passes also had impact on the cost of rental housing, which usually remained below 15 percent of the worker's income.[29] Except for two small-scale projects, Brussels'*communes* (administrative units) did not assume responsibility for social housing, which remained in private hands, as a conservative but secure investment with a 4 to 12 percent return.[30]

The Junction and Commuting

Mahaim's work provides a detailed picture of commuting at the beginning of the twentieth century. Much of the data was collected at his request, in collaboration with the railways and industrial concerns. No such data was collected for the Junction. The Société Nationale des Chemins de fer Belges (National Society of Belgian Railways, SNCB) claims to have no statistics that could be used to examine the connection between the Junction and the commuting pattern.[31] However, the SNCB annual reports do not leave us entirely in the dark on commuting figures because data on workers' passes was included each year. The Society began running at a deficit before World War II, and the railway administration had a stake in documenting the number of tickets it was mandated to issue at a reduced rate. The figures listed in the annual reports indicate that workers' passes accounted for between 32.5 percent (1938) and 38 percent (1932 and 1934) of passenger kilometers on the network before World War II. After the war, these figures were between 33 percent and 34 percent from 1945 to 1948, jumping to 41.3 percent in 1949 and hovering between 42.5 percent and 46.6 percent from 1950 to 1960.[32] Another category of these figures includes the percentage of passenger kilometers accounted for by reduced fares. Here, we witness a steady progression from 55.5 percent in 1933 to 65 percent in 1960, with a dip to 50 percent in 1940, which can be attributed to the war. Also, the exposition year 1958 exhibits a justifiable 2.5 percent increase of nonseason ticket activity. If we look at the total number of passengers, we see an unequivocal increase in numbers from 190 million (in 1932 and 1938) to 260 million by 1960, or an increase of 37 percent in activity. The combined increase in the number of passengers and proportion of workers' passes indicates that the number of commuters conveyed by rail was increasing. In 2001, commuter pass holders accounted for 45 percent of passenger kilometers on the domestic rail network, 50 percent of them originating or ending in Brussels.[33]

Another source, based on the 1961 census, also supports this reading of the SNCB statistics. Commuters increased from 40 percent of the employed population in 1947 to 48 percent in 1961.[34] Between these years, the working population in Brussels grew from 555,000 to 582,500, and commuters to Brussels from 133,000 to 190,300 or from one-fifth (22 percent) to one-third (32 percent) of the working population of the capital. In 1990, commuters still accounted for one-third of Brussels' working population.[35] A characteristic of the Brussels workforce was and remains its high percentage of white-collar workers. By 1931, the white-collar workforce needed by the capital's ministries and administrative offices, which were in close proximity to the intended site for the central station, was already invoked as an additional argument in favor of the Junction.[36] The 42 percent (57,300) growth in the number of commuters between 1947 and 1961, which occurred as the country's working population decreased by 14,000, consisted primarily of white-collar workers.[37] This substantial growth in the percentage of commuters among the workforce in Brussels between 1947 and 1961 (22 percent to 32 percent) is attributable to a number of factors, among them, improved transportation, which includes the opening of the Junction in 1952.[38]

In his study of the Junction and its impact on the urban geography of Brussels, the geographer Marcel Mathieu established a more direct connection between the inauguration of the Junction and the commuting patterns. The coupling of lines from the north and south railway networks made possible by the Junction encouraged commuters to modify their routes and destinations, most frequently to the Midi and central stations. Mathieu compared the number of tickets and passes obtained in 1949 and 1954 in a number of stations that would have been directly affected by the Junction. His figures show a sudden growth of up to 100 percent on lines such as Antwerp-Charleroi, which had been reconfigured at the opening of the Junction. Parallel *vicinaux* (light railway) lines did not indicate significant fluctuations over the same period. His comparison of itineraries between railways and light railways revealed time savings of up to one hour each way for train commuters on lines affected by the Junction. In 1952, passenger traffic through Brussels' stations was 185,000; in 1959, it had grown to 275,000, which represents a 48.6 percent increase with 85 percent of these passengers holding work passes. More specifically, the Gare Centrale became the most heavily used passenger station in the country between 1952 and 1960, with an increase from 18,000 to 102,000 daily users. In March 1960, Mathieu documented peak activity between 7:30 and 8:30 a.m. and between 5:00 and 6:00 p.m. for a passenger count of 102,589, 90 percent of them pass holders. He further documented the direction taken by these commuters out of the station in 1958: 70 percent of them headed for the banking and government offices of the upper city (a pattern that would gradually change as the Junction boulevards' real estate was developed into administrative and business facilities). Mathieu thus documents both a connection between the Junction and increased commuting activity and a primacy of white-collar activity in the Junction area.[39]

Conclusion

A long-standing practice of reduced-fare workers' passes in a small country with a dense rail network, incentives for individual home ownership in rural or small-town settings, and growth of the administrative and business sectors in the capital have led to a large commuting workforce in Brussels. This stemmed the development of Brussels as an outsized metropolis such as Paris or London. The "tens of thousands of commuters" who come daily through the central station are "redistributed over the national territory at night."[40] The question of Belgian commuting has received little historical attention since the publication of Ernest Mahaim's monograph in 1910. As pointed out by the American scholar Janet Polasky, commuting is too common in Belgium to attract scholarly examination: "[It] has become such a part of everyday life that it goes unnoticed."[41] Among a small number of geographical studies on commuting in Brussels, Mathieu's work has connected commuting specifically to the Junction. The area serviced by the Junction's central station is dependent on the armies of commuters brought in by rail, which becomes evident when SNCB service is interrupted by social actions or strikes.[42] Inasmuch as the Junction and the central station fostered the growth of the administrative and business activity in their immediate vicinity, they contributed to the urban reconfiguration of the capital.[43] Their impact on commuting patterns had implications for settlement and demographics in the entire country, one of the most densely populated in the world. By fostering the ability to reside and retain allegiance to an ethnically and linguistically divided landscape of small communities, the hundreds of commuters' trains that pass through the Junction every day have foiled social and, most importantly, ethnic integration. Commuting has further accentuated the ethnic polarization of the country.[44] By countering the nation-building work of generations of politicians and historians, the commuters, including those of the Junction, have written a different history for the country. They have contributed to subverting its nationalism.[45]

Conclusion

The examination of the railways' urban presence in four European capitals reveals the problematic interaction of rail lines with the urban fabric. Among the models that can be invoked for considering railway impact, biology informed the thinkers, planners, and politicians at the time of implantation.[1] As a discipline where momentous discoveries were being made during the years of railway implantation and expansion, it offers a paradigm for the city that was frequently invoked at the time.[2] As pointed out, most explicitly about Brussels, circulation, respiration, alimentation, and evacuation were metaphorically applied to an urban organism perceived as diseased. Nineteenth-century planners such as Haussmann or Cerdá saw their own intervention as making the city healthy by bringing air, light, and ease of circulation. H. J. Dyos built on this metaphoric context when he described rail lines acting as tourniquets on areas where gangrene could set in.[3] The descriptions of the Senne vaulting or the Junction in Brussels as surgical intrusions into the body of the city rely on a biomorphic notion of the urban configuration. Powerfully evocative, this model tends to conflate railways and city into one organism.

Another model, more recent and more useful, attributes the problematic nature of a station to its role both as node of a network and as a place in the city. The station is thus imbued with the dynamics of both the land-use and transport domains.[4] This translates into a need for stations to operate at different levels: at the level of neighborhood residents and landowners, within a city's transport network, and at national and international scale. This polyvalence has been implicit in this examination of the implantation process. Engineers establishing the *tracé* (configuration) of a line responded to national, regional, and local factors in addition to the constraints or challenges of their discipline. Local landowners were pitted against the requirements of the companies, a tension that acquired greater complexity if the needs of the land users were also factored into the equation. As railway companies expanded within cities, the operational demands of growing traffic were at odds with the rising costs of urban real estate, attributable in part to the presence of railway facilities. The need to reconfigure access routes to stations and create connections between stations attempted to reconcile their role as urban points of convergence and points on the trajectory of passengers' journey or freight transit. This polyvalent model allows for a reading of the role played by a station in the contemporary urban context. The transport node must relate to its local context as well as its function in the transportation network. It also enables a reading of the problematic implantation process. Initial railway building focused on the transportation function of the line. The nodal role emerged gradually as the transportation networks acquired complexity with the proliferation of terminals, especially in capital cities. The role of stations as place in the city came to the fore as a response to the impact caused by dispositions taken to meet the other two imperatives of transportation and communication. Inconsequential to the railway companies, this impact and response at the urban scale of the station site has been the primary focus of this study.

London enabled examination of the local impact of railway construction on densely populated areas and, through the social cost of demolitions, to tie railway implantation to urban living conditions, housing shortages, and adjustments in settlement patterns within and on the outskirts of the metropolitan area. In the light of available documentation and research, the rhetoric of beneficial railway slum clearance must be questioned. The area examined here, north of Euston Road, is acquiring a more prominent scholarly presence since the British Library has replaced the Midland Railway's Somers Town goods depot. Its new distinction has begun and will continue to encourage closer historical scrutiny. If the area was a slum, it was not London's worst, but it is representative of areas where railways were built in London. The chronological sequence of construction for three stations located in close proximity to each other, Euston, King's Cross, and St. Pancras, revealed a progression in the nature and intensity of social impact at the implantation sites.

Paris encouraged focus on the relationship between the railways and their context at the urban scale. The advent of the railways in Paris had been met with more public debate, and more deliberate planning, than in the other capitals. The municipal council's decision, supported by the military authorities, to select six large station sites showed foresight in anticipating the urban impact of the railways. Large tracts where development had been nonexistent or unsuccessful were available because of the historical circumstances of the Revolution. By the end of the July Monarchy, the railway terminals generated enough traffic to warrant street reconfiguration. Despite Napoleon III's eagerness to create better access to railway stations, Haussmann did not provide dedicated, functional connections between Paris' terminals. The failure to integrate these stations as foci in a comprehensive urban reconfiguration project highlights the limited configuring power of the railways at the metropolitan scale as much as the lesser priority attributed to them by Haussmann. The prefect's projects had, however, not yet been examined specifically from the point of view of their relationship to the railways.

Berlin provided evidence for the strategic implications of railway development within the Prussian capital and within the political entity that would become a major power in western Europe. Understanding the military role of the railways in Berlin required shifting from the microcosm of station areas to national rail policies in the context of strategic railway development and deployment. At every level of this examination—in the vicinity of the Anhalter Bahnhof, at the urban scale of the *Ringbahn* and *Stadtbahn,* and at the national or federal level—the military authorities exerted influence on development or operations. The incorporation of the railways into the national arsenals occurred slowly, over several decades, and required legal and political adjustments. This process invited examination of similar developments in the other countries included in this study.

Brussels was scarred by the building of a direct rail connection between its two main stations, a project under consideration since 1837 though completed only in 1952. The Brussels Junction, inspired by the Berlin *Stadtbahn,* exhibits similarities with London and Paris. As in London, the rail Junction caused two successive and progressively more invasive demolition campaigns in poor neighborhoods. Also, albeit under different conditions and with different social consequences, commuting became a prevalent remedy for lower-class housing problems. As in Paris, the Junction occasioned substantial urban reconfiguration, which, in Brussels, failed to meet the expectation of creating a beautiful, modern city. The dovetailing of this invasive railway project with a national strategy of dispersed home ownership, facilitated by the widespread practice of commuting within a small country, revealed unique social and political consequences. If much ink has been spilled about the Brussels Junction, and, from Mahaim to Polasky, some attention devoted to commuting in Belgium, no connection had been made between the Junction, its urban aftermath, and recent federal developments in the fragile Belgian national context.[5]

In the four cities examined here, the impact of rail implantation on housing, social conditions, commuting, urban growth, urbanism, strategy, or rail-line connections was, of course, not limited to the case under study. The imprint left by these factors on the other cities was considered briefly, as concluding remarks in the relevant chapters.

The "facets" or focused investigations included in Chapters 2–9 provide a richer texture for the fabric woven from the common threads outlined in Chapter 1. Roads, waterways, and postal delivery systems already performed the tasks that would be assumed by the railways in the second quarter of the nineteenth century. These established modes of transport had received attention and been expanded in the generations preceding railway construction. Whether they were viewed as complement or competition to existing networks and institutions, the railways would change the relationship between transport and its environment. The railways created a new environment, discrete from the urban and rural landscape. With its smoke and machinery in urban spaces designed with the rationality of engineering and industry but faced with the thin cloak of an ambivalent architectural statement, stations exerted their industrial influence "upstream" and their urban impact "downstream."

Private citizens, politicians, company engineers, contractors, or legal experts were driven to express firmly held opinions on various aspects of railways, giving rise to an abundant, spirited, and frequently polemic pamphlet literature. From configuration of a line to its mode of operation, legislation, financing, and occasionally urban impact, railway issues were hotly contested. Railway development intersected with such other concerns as sanitation, urban reconfiguration, social legislation, and strategic considerations. Some projects, such as Paxton's Great Victorian Way and viaducts in the middle of the Thames or Seine rivers, revealed visionary imagination, but their outlandish nature aborted their full development. Other projects forecast developments that would not take place until decades later, as, for instance, Thameslink in London, or the Channel Tunnel.

The engineering of early railway development generated enthusiasm and pride, often tainted with nationalism. Engineering reports also displayed a keen understanding of social factors connected to proposed line implantation sites. As early as 1831, Stephenson revealed his awareness of the social and political implications of line configuration by advocating keeping railways out of parks and gentlemen's estates. In the urban context, engineers' reports, such as those of Cabanel de Sermet in Paris and Bruneel in Brussels, often exhibited remarkable sensitivity to the context where the line and terminal were to be built. The decisions based on these documents did not reflect the reports' ability to assess and articulate complex situations.

After initial protests subsided, the presence of a station was coveted by towns and metropolitan neighborhoods. The recommended station sites, on the outskirts of cities, offered similarities in their remoteness, for instance as former treatment or confinement sites for communicable diseases in two cities, leprosy in Paris and smallpox in London. This distance from the urban center is a factor that prevailed in all four cities for the initial main-line terminals. This peripheral location of terminals was also tied to the continued existence of toll collection by the cities and the gradual disappearance of that practice in the four capitals during the course of the nineteenth century. Real estate would increase in value near stations, and this would affect railway development as well, when additional acreage was needed for expansion or for additional lines. By the 1860s, the detrimental effect of traffic, smoke, and noise stigmatized station areas. Residential neighborhoods were replaced by businesses catering to the needs of travelers. Areas severed or adjoined by rail lines would be tainted by their presence. The three terminals north of Euston Road in London showed progression from implantation into market garden acreage to a progressively more densely populated metropolitan periphery, with increasingly severe social and economic consequences. This pattern was also perceptible in Paris, where less than five years later the acquisition of the Gare de l'Est site caused more local resistance than for the Gare du Nord. Implanted as multiple sperms through the outer membrane of an egg, the terminals did not shed their tails in their drive toward the central nucleus, but they would stimulate a stem-cell pace of growth in metropolitan areas.

As outlined in Chapter 1, and mentioned in the next eight, legislation in all four countries required adjustments, both to determine the legal footing on which railways would be built and operated and to enable them to acquire the real estate necessary to build lines, terminals, and other facilities. The legal status of railways, when they were first established, varied from privately owned or joint-stock companies to state-owned operations.[6] This did not have significant impact on urban implantation because recognition of public utility for railway projects enabled expropriations regardless of status. Expropriation legislation was revised, more than once in France and Britain, to enable the railways to obtain by eminent domain the land they needed and settle compensation procedures for dispossessed owners. Legislation aimed at facilitating the clearing of insalubrious housing was also introduced in Britain, France, and Belgium during the second half of the nineteenth century and further refined to allow more effective urban clearing by permitting expropriation of buildings in good condition in designated areas earmarked for reconfiguration. Although initially not directly tied to railway construction, this legislation was used for railway building or expansion projects. This was the case in London, where the Great Northern and Midland railways claimed developed lower-class neighborhoods, and in Brussels, where the Junction sanitized the Putterie and adjacent populous districts.

Railway construction relied on detailed surveying. In the decades following early implantation, the need to come to terms with growth and rapid change in the capitals prompted early attempts at urban planning. These attempts were concretized in comprehensive plans, such as those of Lenné (1845) and Hobrecht (1861) in Berlin, Besme (1863) in Brussels, and the work performed by Eugène Deschamps under Haussmann in Paris. In Britain, the requirement to include detailed plans with railway bills submitted to Parliament reinforced the existing practice of extensive surveying and mapping of the country. The Ordnance Survey of London provided a skeletal map of a 12-mile radius circular area with St Paul's Cathedral at the center. Completed in three years, the project's maps were available for sale to the public by the 1851 Great Exhibition.[7]

This comprehensive mapping as early planning strategy did not encompass railway development. The reconfigurations of the area north of Euston

Road for the Great Northern and the Midland railways were not checked by city plans and were allowed to proceed in spite of Parliament's attempts to curb railway development in the capital. On Euston Road (a mid-eighteenth-century road project), the reconfiguration of Euston Square would claim adjacent streets, which were incorporated into Euston Station. In Paris, the Gare de l'Est commands a vista at the end of the city's *cardo* (north-south axis), but the Gare du Nord adjusts to an awkward street configuration. The Gares Saint-Lazare, de Lyon, and d'Austerliz, also built on peripheral, undeveloped sites, are equally poorly sited. The Gare Montparnasse faces the Rue de Rennes, which loses its axial power as it narrows near the river. Also, the large expanse claimed by railway yards and workshops at La Chapelle and La Villette/Pantin north and northeast of the Gares du Nord and de l'Est exhibits the characteristic randomness of "upstream" facilities rather than evidence of planned urban development. In Berlin, the five-kilometer track area of the Anthalter Bahnhof was hemmed in by military facilities, which prevented further spreading but did not inflict urban order on the terrain. The *Ringbahn,* diverted southward to accommodate military drill grounds, encircled the city in an iron collar before the discipline of city planning could assume normative power. The belt line retained its configuring and demarcating power into the first decades of the twentieth century and until Albert Speer's plan for Third Reich Berlin. Also, the fragmented Germanic context resulted in Berlin's limited influence in urban theory. Equally influential abroad were Sitte, active in Vienna or eastern Austro-Hungary, and Stübben, in Cologne and other German cities (Dresden, Munich, Darmstadt). Brussels, duly informed of the work of Haussmann, Sitte, and Stübben, and of the Congrès International d'Architecture Moderne (International Congress of Modern Architecture, CIAM), a generation later, disregarded the teachings of urbanism in coming to terms with the aftermath of the Junction.

As urbanism was developing theoretical footing during the last decades of the nineteenth century, cities were also attempting to respond to unprecedented growth, facilitated in part by the railways. Railway implantation occurred simultaneously with and contributed to a process of more spatially distributed social segregation. In London, commuters settled in socially differentiated suburbs. In Paris, east and west gradually assumed distinct social characteristics, a process shaped in part by the presence of railway facilities and commuting patterns. Berlin's belt rail lines were laid out to encourage development of working-class housing in outlying districts, and the industrial facilities that gravitated toward the rail lines also attracted workers' settlements. In Brussels, however, commuters retained ties to rural communities or small cities where social conformity and religious influence encouraged ethnic rather than economic segregation.

Each country voiced high expectations for the peace the railways would foster but soon began to integrate the new technology into war preparations.

This also required legal and political adjustments in the four countries. The strategic impact of railways remained circumscribed in cities. It included belt and connecting lines, negotiating an acceptable configuration around fortifications, or constructing specific lines to military facilities, such as the arsenal at Vincennes or the Schöneberg barracks and Zossen drill grounds near Berlin. The details of such arrangements usually resulted from power struggles between the state, the railway companies, and the military authorities. The association of the railways with the grim reality and the heroic tales of war changed the nature of warfare. Soldiers no longer marched to the front, they left by train; and the ability to mobilize rail support effectively had decisive impact on the front lines. During armed conflict, the need to repair or rebuild rail facilities continued to rely on an engineering tradition of problem-solving, prompt, and efficient response to challenge.

Coeval with the disenchantment caused by a protracted armed conflict; more stringent social legislation, with its related costs for the railway companies; and the rise of alternate modes of transport, the railways experienced a downward slide. Despite periodic attempts to revitalize rail service as metropolitan transit, as rapid interurban national or international passenger service, today's railways cannot be complacent about their share of transportation statistics. More recently, a carbon-footprint-conscious mind-set is making the railways more competitive. Nonetheless, the loss of economic influence has been accompanied by a loss of configuring and integrating power in the railways' urban physical plant. Combination with other modes of transport such as local transit, air travel, and private passenger car, both within and outside metropolitan areas, has created new spatial needs. Rail operations have become more versatile, relying on outlying facilities for preparation and maintenance of trains. Railways no longer need to command the same urban space as they did in the past. Large terminal stations have outlived their usefulness or become available for conversion as monuments to a disappearing industrial past.[8] Corollary to these diminished spatial needs for rail operations is the expendability of its architecture. If, as we have seen in London, Brussels, and Paris, much urban fabric was sacrificed to the railways, some early railway architecture has also been demolished or become vulnerable. The demolition of the Euston portico in 1961 was a catalyst for a more preservation-conscious approach to the architectural heritage of the railways and industry.

From Euston Station to Horta's Gare Centrale, the stations considered here trace the evolution of a building form. The janiform configuration of Euston with its "downstream" monumental portico and its "upstream" ad hoc industrial sheds and outbuildings would give way to more integrated solutions. King's Cross and the Gare de l'Est both reflected the structural component of their sheds on their façades. This presence of the functional engineering element remains in the façades of the Anhalter Bahnhof and of the central pavilion at Paris' Gare du Nord. St. Pancras Station, fronting one of the most ingeniously designed sheds, opted to discard this feature in its Euston Road building, which combined hotel and railway terminal. The innovative architectural solutions of the stations were widely disseminated in architectural publications, which assessed their aesthetic value, and analyzed in railway journals or manuals, which discussed the opportune nature of configuration or design features for operations. The influence of railway station design was more prevalent on other stations in different locations than it was at their implantation site, where surrounding buildings remained more conventional. The corporate prestige and power displayed by some stations such as the Gare du Nord and St. Pancras provided evidence that the states' ability to fund large sumptuary projects had been outpaced by the railways. The attribution of a stylistic label, "Picturesque Eclecticism," for nineteenth-century stations, a style characterized by variety, movement, irregularity, intricacy, and roughness, according to Meeks, was acknowledged by Karen Bowie in her doctoral dissertation.[9] It is significant that her subsequent publications have discarded this nomenclature and that her more recent work has turned to implantation and urban issues as more germane to railway impact.[10] As for Horta's Gare Centrale, chronologically the last station examined here, it retained few features of nineteenth-century stations. It does exhibit some of Meeks' characteristics of the modern style: planarity, transparency, and simplicity. It was no longer entirely dedicated to railway functions but incorporated income-generating retail and business facilities (possibly thereby earning Meeks' other modern attribute of "interpenetration").[11] It emulated the underground stations by providing inconspicuous access to below-surface rails. It did, however, continue a tradition of noble construction materials and of technological innovations. It also exhibited a concern for integrating with adjacent structures and into the declivity of the terrain rather than asserting a discordant presence on an urban landscape the architect could not anticipate and did not live to influence.

That the impact of railway implantation was significant in the four cities examined here cannot be denied. The attempt to assess this impact must take into account the energetic impetus of railway construction and the equally dynamic response of the urban context where implantation occurred. The railways did not constitute a single major force, but they encompassed more than transport and radiated through the complex web of nineteenth-century political, economic, social, and cultural forces. Their implantation touched most major aspects of society and urban development: geography, politics, economics, demographics, culture, sociology, industry, and technology, as well as urban planning and architecture. The railways changed how we see, and from the site of their urban implantation their lines redrew the maps, and the landscapes, of cities with the pencil of evolutionary forces.

Paris: Plans for the Gare du Nord

1. "Plan général de la station des chemins de fer de la Belgique dans Paris, projet présenté pour être exécuté par la compagnie John Cockerill. A. Bourla et Ed. Renaud Architectes Ingénieurs," ca. 1838 (Archives Nationales).

2. "Plan du nouveau quartier Poissonnière et des abords des chemins de fer du Nord et de Strasbourg, dressé par Jacinthe Leclère, ingénieur-géomètre," 1 February 1847 (Archives SNCF).

3. "Plan de la gare du chemin de fer du Nord et de ses abords." Minor reconfiguration of Nr 2 in 1852 (Archives SNCF).

4. "Projet de C. Brouty," 1852.

5. "Plan d'ensemble du quartier Poissonnière. Prolongement de la rue La Fayette et rue de Maubeuge projetée. Dégagement des abords de l'église Saint-Vincent-de-Paul, de l'Hôpital du Nord et de la gare du Nord," C. Brouty, architecte (*Revue Municipale,* no. 128 [1 August 1853]), listed in René Clozier, *La Gare du Nord* (Paris: J.-B. Baillière et Fils, 1940), 43.

6. "IIIe arrondissement, quartier du faubourg Poissonnière, Projet de reconstruction de la gare du Nord. Création d'un boulevard partant de cette gare pour aboutir au boulevard de Bonne Nouvelle," C. Brouty, architecte (Musée Carnavalet, Cabinet des Estampes, from *Revue Municipale,* 16 November 1855, 1582–83), listed in Thomas von Joest, "Hittorff et la nouvelle gare du Nord," in *Hittorff, un architecte du XIXème siècle* (Paris: Musées de la Ville de Paris, 1986), 271, top; and Karen Bowie, *Les Grandes gares parisiennes: Historique, les grandes gares parisiennes au XIXe siècle* (Paris: Délégation à l'Action Artistique de la Ville de Paris, 1987), 101.

7. "Plan général de la gare du Nord et des abords, Paris, 24 mars 18??" (Archives SNCF).

8. "Plan des échanges de terrains entre le baron James de Rothschild et la ville de Paris, 1856, dressé par Moutry, géomètre" (Archives SNCF).

9. "Projet d'un boulevard rattachant l'embarcadère du Nord à celui de l'Ouest," M. Brouty, architecte (*Revue Municipale,* 228 [1 August 1857]).

10. "Chemin de Fer du Nord, gare de Paris, projet définitif" (Archives de la SNCF).

This list is based on the work of Pierre Pinon, with some elaboration from other sources. Compiled in the unpublished report Pierre Pinon, "L'Inscription de la gare du Nord dans le réseau viaire des quartiers Nord de Paris entre les faubourgs Poissonnière et Saint-Martin," in "Polarisation du territoire et développement urbain: Les Gares du Nord et de l'Est et la transformation de Paris au XIXe siècle," ed. Karen Bowie (Paris: Plan Urbain, PREDIT, SNCF, and RATP, 1999), 61–70 (now accessible at http://urbamet.documentation.equipement.gouv.fr/documents/EQU-TEX00005329/EQUTEX00005329.pdf) and published in abbreviated form in Pierre Pinon, "L'Inscription de la gare du Nord dans le réseau viaire des quartiers Nord de Paris entre les faubourgs Poissonnière et Saint-Martin," *La Gare: Dedans, dehors* (Paris: Plan Urbain, DRAST, RATP, and SNCF, 1996), 1:166–69.

Appendix B

Brussels: List of Junction Projects

The entries are presented in chronological order.

1840

Convention du 24 Mars 1840. Arrêté qui approuve la convention relative à la jonction des chemins de fer du Nord et du Midi à Bruxelles. Archives de la Ville de Bruxelles (AVB), Travaux Publics, 18860.

AVB PP 863, Vifquain, Arrêté Royal du 30 mars 1840. Fait et dressé par l'inspecteur des Ponts et Chaussées. Bruxelles, le 25 avril 1841, signed Vifquain (includes plan & section).

1841

AVB PP 864 1-3/3, 1841, 3 plans, Jonction Nord-Midi.

Projet de Jonction des Stations du Nord et du Midi à Bruxelles, perspective, #2; Victor Besme, Architecte, Imp. Simonau & Toovey, Canelle Lithograph.

Projet de Jonction Directe des Stations du Midi et du Nord, elevation, #3; Victor Besme, Architecte, Imp. Simonau & Toovey, J. Vandendaelen, Graveur.

Echelle de 0.0075 m par 1.00 m (1841 is date of map, project should be later).

1855

For a more detailed account of the Junction projects between 1855 and 1865, see Marguerite Silvestre, "Les Premiers projets de jonction Nord-Midi (1855–1865)," in *Bruxelles et la jonction Nord-Midi,* ed. Serge Jaumain and Chloé Deligne (Bruxelles: Archives de la Ville de Bruxelles, 2004), 53–68.

1855, Groetaers.

Listed in (Gustave Abeels, "Les Communications dans et vers la ville aux XIXe et XXe siècles," in *La Région de Bruxelles. Des Villages d'autrefois à la ville d'aujourd'hui,* ed. Arlette Smolar-Meynart and Jean Stengers [Bruxelles: Crédit Communal, 1989], 238).

1855, Le Hardy de Beaulieu (Membre de la Chambre des Représentants et ingénieur).

Chemin de fer de la jonction directe des railways de l'Etat à Bruxelles, avec station centrale dans l'intérieur de la ville pour le service des voyageurs, des postes et des télégraphes (Bruxelles: Ch. Vanderauwera, 1855). AVB PP 427 1-2/2, 2 pl.

Station centrale à Bruxelles: Quelques considérations nouvelles et examen de divers projets proposés (Bruxelles: Ch. Vanderauwera, 1855).

Jonction centrale des chemins de fer de Belgique. Demandeurs en concession MM. Waring frères, 19 Fludyer street, Westminster à Londres, représentant MM. A. Le Hardy de Beaulieu et A. Vifquain, demandeurs primitifs (Bruxelles: E. Devroye, 1855).

Jonction centrale des chemins de fer de Belgique. Développements nouveaux. Demandeurs en concession MM. Waring frères, 19 Fludyer street, Westminster à Londres. Ingénieurs en chef MM. PP. Baly à Londres, A Dandelin à Bruxelles (Bruxelles: E. Devroye, Mars 1855). 55p (Bibliothèque Royale II 18590 A II, 28) with map: "Jonction centrale des chemins de fer de Belgique. Tracé à travers la ville de Bruxelles." Carte annexée au mémoire du 27 mars 1855; Echelle 1 à 10,000, Etablissement Géographique de Bxl de Ph. Vandermaelen 593. AVB 2376/111.

Jonction centrale des chemins de fer de Belgique, Waring etc [1855], Bibliothèque Royale—CP VDM I 425 (elevated viaduct and central station).

1855, Dubois-Nihoul.

Jonction générale des chemins de fer à Bruxelles. Demande en concession adressée par M. Dubois-Nihoul, Entrepreneur de Travaux publics, le 14 Avril 1855.

Etablissements de L. Mois, Rue de l'Evêque.

Mémoire à l'appui du projet et devis estimatif (Bruxelles: Imp. Hayes, 1856).

Dubois-Nihoul, *Projet de jonction souterraine* (Bruxelles: Imp. Bols-Withouck, 1856).

AVB PP 2730, Bibliothèque Royale: 0.156. (Underground line in eastern pentagon, three tracks and cul de sac behind Theater de la Monnaie, with two branches on either side of Ste. Gudule.)

1855, A. C. Gérard.

Aperçu d'un projet de raccordement des lignes du Nord et du Midi avec station centrale au Marché aux Grains, à Bruxelles, Demande en concession par A. C. Gérard, Ingénieur civil (Bruxelles: E. Devroye, 1855). AVB 2376/110 & 4 plans PP 431 [428 A] (viaduct, from Allée Verte to Midi, curved line avoids built area).

1855, Alexandre Goupy de Quabeck.

Projet de jonction de la station du Nord à celle du Midi par un chemin de fer du système Loubat, à établir sur la Senne voutée et rectifiée (Bruxelles: Poloack, 1855)

(combines Junction and Senne vaulting, single-track, horse-drawn project).

1855–56, Goffaux, Deneef, Evrard.

G. Helleputte, Ministre d'Etat et ancien Ministre des Chemins de fer, "Projet de Loi concernant l'abandon des travaux de la jonction des gares de Bruxelles-Nord et Bruxelles-Midi, Note de la Minorité" (Chambre des Représentants, Document No. 266 [annexe], Session de 1923–24 [2e supplément], 1923–24), 14.

1856

1856, Adrien Carton de Wiart, Avocat.

Avant-projet d'une rue de fer entre la station du Nord et la station du Midi, à Bruxelles (Bruxelles: E. Devroye, 1856). AVB, Bibl. 44155 (dedicated above ground line, iron street with four tracks and central station as simple stop, includes urban sanitation).

1858

1858, F. Wellens.

"Projet de chemin de fer de jonction des deux stations du Nord et du Midi, à Bruxelles," *Annales des Travaux Publics de Belgique* (Bruxelles: B. J. Van Domen, 1858), tome XVI.

Gare du Midi (nouvelle), projet 1858, 4 plans.

Projet de jonction directe des stations du Nord et du Midi à Bruxelles, Plan d'ensemble de la station du Midi. Echelles de 0,002 m. pour 1 mètre, Place Rouppe (i.e., on location of original Midi Station). Proposé par l'ingénieur en chef soussigné. Bruxelles, le 26 mars 1858, signed Wellens. Donné pour le soussigné le 22 mars 1858, signed Victor Besme. AVB PP 864 & Bibliothèque 449036, AVB PP 446 1–4. (Wellens was Ingénieur en chef des Ponts et Chaussées. New boulevard on vaulted Senne with stop. Proposed after law of 1858, which allows expropriation for clearing unsanitary neighborhoods.)

1864

1864, Formanoir de la Cazerie.

Listed in Gustave Abeels, "Les Communications dans et vers la ville aux XIXe et XXe siècles," in *La Région de Bruxelles: Des Villages d'autrefois à la ville d'aujourd'hui* (Bruxelles: Crédit Communal, 1989), 238.

1864, Pierre Keller.

Chemin de fer souterrain à Bruxelles, jonction directe des stations de l'Etat. Demande de concession par P. Keller et Cie, Bruxelles, 1865. AVB PP 866.

(This project, submitted by Keller, a contractor from Antwerp, was one among 40 proposed after Anspach became burgomaster and undertook the Senne cleaning project. The proposal combined Senne vaulting and Junction. Promoted by Keller as one project for the price of two, it included a central stop near the Marché aux Poulets and would have required lowering the Nord and Midi stations to connect with the underground tracks.)

1866

1866, J. B. Pauwels.

Solution de plusieurs questions de travaux publics qui intéressent la capitale. Raccordement souterrain des trois gares du Nord, du Midi, du Luxembourg. Création d'une gare centrale. Communication entre le haut et le bas de la ville (Bruxelles: Imprimerie E. Devraye, 1866).

1866, Demasy-Lacroix.

G. Helleputte, Ministre d'Etat et ancien Ministre des Chemins de fer, "Projet de Loi concernant l'abandon des travaux de la jonction des gares de Bruxelles-Nord et Bruxelles-Midi: Note de la Minorité" (Chambre des Représentants, Document No. 266 [annexe], Session de 1923–24 [2e supplément], 1923–24), 15.

1893

1893, Frédéric Bruneel.

"Avant-projet de chemin de fer métropolitain avec gare centrale à Bruxelles," *Annales de l'Association des Ingénieurs Sortis des Ecoles Spéciales de Gand* 16 (1892–93): 339–45. AVB PP 2732.

(Engineer for the Belgian railways, project adopted 1901, convention-loi between city and state signed 7 April 1903.)

1893, Prosper Hanrez.
(Viaduct in canal zone, central station at location of Marché aux Grains. Similar to earlier projects, discarded by 1895 commission.)

1899

1899, V. Dumortier (principal architect of the province of Brabant).
"Projet de suppression des gares à rebroussement de Bruxelles-Nord et de Bruxelles-Midi ainsi que de leurs nombreux passages à niveau et d'établissement d'une ligne souterraine desservant l'agglomération bruxelloise," *L'Emulation* 6 (1899): 6, cols. 86–88. (Two additional external stations 3 km from Nord and Midi. Central station in Rue Isabelle area. Too costly.)

1900

1900 and 1901, M. D. Motte.
(Underground direct junction through lower city. Second project replaced Junction by surface electric tramway from inside both Nord and Midi stations.)

1901

1901, L. Vanderswaelmen.
Projet de jonction par voie souterraine entre les gares du Nord et du Midi. Notice descriptive annexée au plan, Louvain, typo. F. Ickx, 1901. (Tunnel between Nord and Midi with central station at location of Palais des Beaux-Arts Quartier Isabelle with underground tunnel between station, Royal Palace, and Parliament with additional branch to Bruxelles-Luxembourg.)

1903

1903, M. le duc d'Ursel.
(Maintains both Nord and Midi stations, central station on peripheral boulevard at the level of the Hotel de Ville.)

1903, M. le sénateur Montefiore Levi.

(Removes Nord station entirely, places new station at the Allée Verte location.)

1903, M. Müllender.

(Two single-track underground electric rail lines between Nord and Midi, no central station.)

1903, M. Maréchal.

(Primarily modification of ring lines.)

1903, MM. Rau and Zwicker.

(Similar to Müllender project with different layout for the rail line.)

1903, M. Foetinger.

(Puts back Allée Verte station in service and spreads the additional traffic between three stations.)

1918

1918, Prosper Hanrez, Senator.
Faut-il continuer les travaux de la jonction Nord-Midi ? Avec plan de la Jonction (Bruxelles: M. Weissenbruch, 1918).

1936

1936, Fer. Regnier, Ch. Van Hoeg, and Ed. Wester.
Création d'une nouvelle gare du Nord sur le territoire de la ville de Bruxelles: Dégagement et expansion de la capitale vers le Nord. Ce que l'opinion publique devrait savoir au sujet de la jonction Nord-Midi (Bruxelles: Imprimerie des Travaux Publics, 1936).

Notes

All translations from the original French, German, and Dutch are by the author.

Introduction

1. Henri Vincenot, *La Vie quotidienne dans les chemins de fer au XIXe siècle* (Paris: Hachette, 1975), 7, quoting his grandfather, a railway man.
2. "For them, the railways meant technology. Today, we are fascinated by computers." Anonymous visitor to a companion, in front of Monet's 1877 Gare Saint-Lazare at the Musée d'Orsay, Paris, 14 June 2001.
3. Victor Hugo, "Anvers à Bruxelles," letter to Adèle, 22 August 1837, in *Oeuvres complètes: Voyages,* ed. Jacques Seebacher (Paris: Laffont, 1985), 13:611.
4. National Gallery, London.
5. Tate Gallery, London.
6. Carroll L. V. Meeks, *The Railroad Station: An Architectural History* (New Haven, CT: Yale University Press, 1956), 4–8.
7. H. J. Dyos, "Railways and Housing in Victorian London: I, Attila in London; II, Rustic Townsmen," *Journal of Transport History* 2 (1955): 11–21, 90–100.
8. John Reginald Kellett, *The Impact of Railways on Victorian Cities* (London: Routledge & Kegan Paul, 1969).
9. Karen Bowie, " 'L'Eclectisme pittoresque' et l'architecture des gares parisiennes au XIXe siècle" (PhD diss., Université de Paris I, 1985); Bowie, *Les Grandes gares parisiennes* (Paris: Délégation à l'Action Artistique de la Ville de Paris, 1987).
10. Karen Bowie, "L'Implantation des gares du Nord et de l'Est dans Paris, 1830–1870: Premiers résultats d'une recherche," in *La Gare: Dedans, dehors* (Paris: Plan Urbain, DRAST, RATP, and SNCF, 1996), 135–42; Bowie et al., "Polarisation du territoire et développement urbain: Les Gares du Nord et de l'Est et la transformation de Paris au XIXe siècle" (Paris: Plan Urbain, PREDIT, SNCF, and RATP, 1999).
11. Exceptions to this are Allan Mitchell, *The Great Train Race: Railways and the Franco-German Rivalry* (New York: Berghahn Books, 2000) and the collection of essays edited by Marie-Noëlle Polino and Ralf Roth, *The City and the Railway in Europe* (Aldershot: Ashgate, 2003).
12. Nancy Stieber, "Microhistory of the Modern City: Urban Space, Its Use and Representation," *Journal of the Society of Architectural Historians* 58, no. 3 (December 1999): 383.
13. Michel de Certeau, "L'Opération historique," in *Faire de l'histoire,* ed. Jacques Le Goff and Pierre Nora (Paris: Gallimard, 1974), 1:11.

Chapter 1

1. Cited in François Caron, *Histoire des chemins de fer en France,* vol. 1, *1740–1883* (Paris: Fayard, 1997), 99.

2. Ibid., 98; Allan Mitchell, *The Great Train Race: Railways and the Franco-German Rivalry* (New York: Berghahn Books, 2000), 68. See also chap. 4.

3. For an examination of railways and cities in other countries, see Marie-Noëlle Polino and Ralf Roth, eds., *The City and the Railway in Europe* (Aldershot: Ashgate, 2003).

4. Caron, *Histoire des chemins,* 100–101; Simon P. Ville, *Transport and the Development of the European Economy, 1750–1918* (New York: St. Martin's Press, 1990), 118.

5. *The Times,* 1835; quoted in Great Western Railway Company of England, *Great Western Progress, 1835–1935* (reprint of the Great Western Railway Centenary Number of *The Times,* 1935), 46.

6. Ibid., 45.

7. James Watson, *A Paper on the Present Railway Crisis* (Glasgow: William Lang, 1846). The employment potential of railway building was frequently invoked to marshal support for line projects.

8. Richard Zachariah Mudge, *Observations on Railways, with Reference to Utility, Profit and the Obvious Necessity for a National System* (London: James Gardner, 1837), 10.

9. *Great Western Progress,* 45.

10. Ibid.; Auguste Perdonnet, *Les Chemins de fer. Conférences populaires faites à l'Asile Impérial de Vincennes sous le patronage de S.M. l'Impératrice* (Paris: Hachette, 1866), 11.

11. An extensive collection of early railway pamphlets is at the London School of Economics library (originally part of the Acworth Collection). Copies of most pamphlets listed in *Gladstone Library, National Library Club, Early Railway Pamphlets, 1825–1900* (London: National Liberal Club, 1938) are at the British Library. Other libraries also have such collections.

12. Records of the Dartford and Strood Turnpike Trust, Kent Record Office, Maidstone (AG 54); cited by Jack Simmons, "Railway History in English Local Records," *Journal of Transport History* 1 (1953–54): 161.

13. United Kingdom, Parliament, London and Birmingham Railway, Copy Preamble [of the Bill], 2 July 1832 (London, 1832), 2.

14. Perdonnet, *Vincennes,* 11.

15. London and Birmingham Railway [Bill], 2.

16. Public Records Office, RAIL-384-27, 1830–31, Survey Committee Book, 21 October 1830–29 August 1831, and app. #10. Extract of letter from M. George Stephenson & Son, 23 September 1831, responding to instructions in the minutes of July 29.

17. Caron, *Histoire des chemins,* 100–101. Tunnels provoked enough concern to cause the establishment of a Committee of the House of Commons on the London and Brighton Railways on the subject of Tunnels during the 1837 session.

18. John Cooke Bourne and John Britton, *Drawings of the London and Birmingham Railway* (London: J. C. Bourne, 1839).

19. Auguste Perdonnet, *Notions générales sur les chemins de fer* (Paris: Lacroix et Baudry, 1859), 42; Lamartine quoted in Caron, *Histoire des chemins,* 100–101.

20. The introduction of canals in England took place between 1750 and 1830, later than in France, but more extensively. See W. T. Jackman, *The Development of Transportation in Modern England,* 2nd ed. (London: Frank Cass, 1962), 355–451.

21. Jack Simmons, *The Victorian Railway* (London: Thames and Hudson, 1991), 14–15, 155.

22. Quoted in F. R. Conder, *The Men Who Built Railways,* ed. Jack Simmons (London: Thomas Telford, 1983), 9.

23. Ibid.

24. Herbert Stanley Morrison, *Socialisation and Transport: The Organisation of Socialised Industries with Particular Reference to the London Passenger Transport Bill* (London: Constable, 1933), 243.

25. Records Office of the Corporation of London, Common Council Minutes, 3 March 1836; cited in Simmons, "Railway History," 163–64.

26. John Reginald Kellett, *The Impact of Railways on Victorian Cities* (London: Routledge & Kegan Paul, 1969), 16.

27. *What Will Parliament Do with the Railways?* (London: Henry Renshaw, 1836), 4.

28. *A Practical Treatise on Railways, Explaining Their Construction and Management . . . being the article "Railways" in the seventh edition of the Encyclopedia Britannica* (Edinburgh: A. & C. Black, 1839), 13.

29. David Turnock, *A Historical Geography of Railways in Great Britain and Ireland* (Brookfield, VT: Ashgate, 1998), 190.

30. Victor Hugo, "Le Rhin," letter 8, in *Oeuvres complètes: Voyages,* ed. Jacques Seebacher (Paris: Laffont, 1985), 13:57.

31. Gary Richard Hawke, *Railways and Economic Growth in England and Wales, 1840–1970* (Oxford: Clarendon Press, 1970); R. W. Ambler, *The History and Practice of Britain's Railways* (Aldershot: Ashgate, 1999), 9–10.

32. Beginning in 1855, the French *Journal des Chemins de Fer* covered in its weekly columns the incorporation and progress of the Sociétés Immobilières in Paris, such as the Société de l'Hôtel et des Immeubles (de Rivoli). This indicates that calls for railway and real-estate investments were targeted at the same audience.

33. A. Saussay, *Les Gares des grandes lignes de chemin de fer par rapport aux grandes villes qu'elles desservent* (Paris: Maulde et Renou, 1845), 3–5.

34. Kellett, *Impact of Railways,* 31–32, 101.

35. René Clozier, *La Gare du Nord* (Paris: J.-B. Baillière, 1940), 241; David Owen, Donald Olsen, and Roy MacLeod, eds., *The Government of Victorian London, 1855–1889: The Metropolitan Board of Works, the Vestries and the City Corporation* (London: Belknap Press of Harvard University Press, 1982), 102.

36. Kellett, *Impact of Railways,* 2, 320–21; Anthony Sutcliffe, *The Autumn of Central Paris: The Defeat of Town Planning, 1850–1970* (London: Edward Arnold, 1970), 147; Mitchell, *Great Train Race,* 30, 57; Robert Herbert, *Impressionism, Art, Leisure and Parisian Society* (New Haven, CT: Yale University Press, 1988), 261; Mudge, *Observations on Railways,* 15; Léon Say, "Les Chemins de fer," in *Parisguide par les principaux écrivains et artistes de la France,* ed. Charles Yriarte, pt. 2, *La Vie,* vol. 2 (Paris: Librairie Internationale, 1867), 1663; Max Maria von Weber and Richard Hoch, *Schule des Eisenbahnwesens,* 4th ed. (Leipzig: J. J. Weber, 1885), 29; Ministerium der Öffentlichen Arbeiten and A. F. Leyen, *Berlin und seine Eisenbahnen, 1846–1896* (Berlin: Julius Springer, 1896), 2:317, 336, 338, 341.

37. Pierre-Charles Laurent de Villedeuil, *Bibliographie des chemins de fer: Index chronologique, 1771–1846* (Paris: Librairie Générale, 1906), 26.

38. "Transport de céréales," *Journal des Chemins de Fer,* 6 October 1855, 835; Johannes Willms, *Paris, Capital of Europe: From the Revolution to the Belle Epoque* (New York: Holmes & Meier, 1997), 287; Alfred Picard, *Les Chemins de fer français: Etude historique sur la constitution et le régime du réseau* (Paris: J. Rothschild, 1884–85), 2:74; "Un décret du 2 septembre [B.L., 2e sem., 1853, no. 89, p. 427], autorisant les compagnies concessionnaires des chemins de fer, qui abaisseraient leurs tarifs pour le transport des grains et farines et de pommes de terre, avant le 31 décembre 1853, à les relever ensuite dans les limites du maximum prévu par les cahiers des charges."

39. Clozier, *Gare du Nord,* 251.

40. Jean Bastié, *La Croissance de la banlieue parisienne* (Paris: Presses Universitaires de France, 1964), 105; Jeanne Gaillard, *Paris: La Ville, 1852–1870* (Paris: L'Harmattan, 1976), 180.

41. Gaillard, *Paris,* 181.

42. Timothée, *Funeste influence des chemins de fer en France sur le bien-être du peuple* (Meulan: Nicolaï, 1850), 16.

43. Nikolaus Pevsner and Bridget Cherry, *London 4: North,* The Buildings of England (Harmondsworth, UK: Penguin, 1998), 35; Mudge, *Observations on Railways,* 11.

44. Anthony Sutcliffe, *Paris: An Architectural History* (New Haven, CT: Yale University Press, 1993), 81, 87.

45. Hartwig Schmidt, "Architecture and Urban Planning, 1850–1914," in *Berlin-New York, Like and Unlike: Essays on Architecture and Art from 1870 to the Present,* ed. Josef Paul Kleihues and Christina Rathgeber (New York: Rizzoli, 1993), 129–43.

46. William Denton, *Observations on the Displacement of the Poor, by Metropolitan Railways and by Other Public Improvements* (London: Bell & Dalby, 1861).

47. Auguste Perdonnet, *Traité élémentaire des chemins de fer,* 3rd ed. (Paris: Garnier Frères, 1865), 3:7.

48. Isabelle Guérin Brot and Jean Pierre Babelon, *Les Débuts du chemin de fer en France, 1831–1870* (Paris: Ministère de la Culture et de l'Environnement and SNCF, 1977), 35; Jeffrey Richards and John M. MacKenzie, *The Railway Station* (Oxford: Oxford University Press, 1986), 224–84 passim.

49. Charles Booth, *Life and Labour of the People in London,* 2nd ser. (1892; repr., New York: AMS Press, 1970), 3:336–49.

50. Prosper de Pietra Santa, *Chemins de fer et santé publique: Hygiène des voyageurs et des employés* (Paris: Hachette, 1861), 3.

51. Wolfgang Schivelbusch, *The Railway Journey: Trains and Travel in the 19th Century* (New York: Urizen Books, 1979), 71, 118–60.

52. Allan Mitchell, "Private Enterprise or Public Service? The Eastern Railway Company and the French State in the Nineteenth Century," *Journal of Modern History* 69, no. 1 (March 1997): 33–38.

53. See the 125-plate atlas of Auguste Perdonnet, Camille Polonceau, and Eugène Flachat, *Nouveau portefeuille de l'ingénieur des chemins de fer,* vol. 3 (Paris: E. Lacroix, 1866). The French photographer Baldus was commissioned to record the works of the French railway companies. See Malcolm R. Daniel, "Edouard-Denis Baldus and the Chemin de fer du Nord Albums," *Image* 35, no. 3–4 (1992): 2–37.

54. Turnock, *Historical Geography*, 187–89; Barrie M. Ratcliffe, "Urban Space and the Siting of the Parisian Railway Station, 1830–1847," *Proceedings of the Western Society for French History* 15 (1988): 224; Kellett, *Impact of Railways*, 290, 318, 327.

55. Herman Josef Stübben, *Der Städtebau, Handbuch der Architektur*, 2nd ed. (Stuttgart: A. Kröner, 1907), 4:241–43; Thomas Nipperdey, *Germany from Napoleon to Bismarck, 1800–1866* (Princeton, NJ: Princeton University Press, 1996), 115; Kellett, *Impact of Railways*, 299–300.

56. Turnock, *Historical Geography*, 192.

57. Marc Baroli, *Le Train dans la littérature française* (Paris: La Vie du Rail, 1964), 3.

58. Laura Hollengreen, "Medieval Sacred Place to Modern Secular Space: Changing Perspectives on the Cathedral and Town of Chartres" (paper presented at the annual meeting of the Society of Architectural Historian, Richmond, VA, 18 April 2002).

59. Clozier, *Gare du Nord*, 246–47; Booth, *Life and Labour*, 3rd ser., 2:174 and 186; Manfred Berger, *Historische Bahnhofsbauten Sachsens, Preussens, Meckleburgs und Thüringen* (Berlin: Transpress, 1980), 22; Schivelbusch, *Railway Journey*, 171–73, 180; David Blackbourn and Goeff Eley, *The Peculiarities of German History: Bourgeois Society and Politics in Nineteenth-Century Germany* (Oxford: Oxford University Press, 1984), 215–16. See also Kellett, *Impact of Railways*, 289, 297, 318–19.

60. Ad. Le Hardy de Beaulieu, *Station centrale à Bruxelles: Quelques considérations nouvelles et examen des divers projets proposés* (Brussels: Ch. Vanderauwera, 1855), 6–7; Clozier, *Gare du Nord*, 247.

61. Elihu Burritt, *A Walk from London to John O'Groats*, 2nd ed. (London: S. Low, Son & Marston, 1864), 2; quoted in Jack Simmons, "The Power of the Railway," in *The Victorian City: Images and Realities*, ed. H. J. Dyos and Michael Wolff (London: Routledge & Kegan Paul, 1973), 300.

62. Adrien Dumont, "Les Etablissements insalubres et les chemins de fer," *Annales des Chemins de Fer, des Travaux Publics et des Mines*, 6 October 1850, 540.

63. Auguste Perdonnet, *Traité élémentaire des chemins de fer*, 1st ed. (Paris: Langlois et Leclercq, 1855–56), 75–78; Perdonnet, *Traité*, 3rd ed., 2:30 and 4:401–2. The difference between the two editions of Perdonnet is also noted in Schivelbusch, *Railway Journey*, 172, n. 1; see also Kellett, *Impact of Railways*, 303.

64. *Punch*, 10 October 1863, 146; cited in Simmons, *Victorian Railway*, 10, 167, n. 60.

65. O. Blum, "Bahnhofvorplatz," in *Enzyklopädie des Eisenbahnwesens*, ed. Victor von Röll, 2nd ed. (Berlin: Urban & Schwarzenberg, 1912–23), 1:410–12. See also Bob Martens, *Der Bahnhofsvorplatz in der Großstadt im 19. und 20. Jahrhundert*, Dissertation der Technischen Universität Wien, no. 46 (Wien: VWGÖ, 1988).

66. Blum, "Bahnhofvorplatz," 1:410–12; Clozier, *Gare du Nord*, 274; Mitchell, "Private Enterprise," 18, where he refers to Theodore Zeldin, *France, 1848–1945* (Oxford: Oxford University Press, 1973–77), 1:637–38; Mitchell, *Great Train Race*, 58; Röll, ed., *Enzyklopädie des Eisenbahnwesens*, 4:302–3.

67. Lewis Mumford, *The Culture of Cities* (New York: Harcourt, Brace, 1938), 150.

68. Simmons, *Victorian Railway*, 20 indicates that some owners required embankments to be covered with plantings as a condition for sale.

69. Joseph Moreau, *Abris et plantations pour les chemins de fer et moyens de prévenir les amoncellements de neige* (Brussels: Auguste Decq, 1865), 10–16.

70. Belgian laws of 15 April 1843 and 25 July 1891. French law of 15 July 1845.

71. From personal conversation with John Dixon Hunt, University of Pennsylvania, 21 February 2002. Station grounds were and still are frequently decorated with flowers and other ornamental plantings cultivated by station staff. This practice was encouraged by competitions between stations and continues today in some communities with civic pride, adequate funds, and low incidence of vandalism (Simmons, *Victorian Railway,* 260).

72. Karen Bowie et al., "Polarisation du territoire et développement urbain: Les Gares du Nord et de l'Est et la transformation de Paris au XIXe siècle" (Paris: Plan Urbain, PREDIT, SNCF, and RATP, 1999), 5–38; Karen Bowie, "Introduction au rapport de l'ingénieur en chef des Ponts et Chaussées Cabanel de Sermet sur les tracés étudiés et sur celui à adopter pour la première section du chemin de fer de Paris à Strasbourg," *Revue d'Histoire des Chemins de Fer* 23 (Fall 2000): 79–137. See also E. F. Clark, *George Parker Bidder: The Calculating Boy* (Bedford, UK: KSL Publications, 1983), 292–93; Jack Simmons, *The Railways of Britain: An Historical Introduction,* 2nd ed. (London: Macmillan, 1968), 52–85.

73. Auguste Perdonnet and Camille Polonceau, *Portefeuille de l'ingénieur des chemins de fer,* 2nd ed. (Paris: E. Lacroix, 1861), 1:3, and chap. 1: "De l'Espace occupé par les différentes parties d'un chemin de fer."

74. Perdonnet and Polonceau, *Portefeuille,* 424–27.

75. M. Jacqmin, *De l'Exploitation des chemins de fer: Leçons faites en 1867 à l'Ecole Impériale des Ponts et Chaussées* (Paris: Garnier Frères, 1868), 1:39.

76. Perdonnet, *Traité,* 2nd ed., 1:2; Röll, ed., *Enzyklopädie des Eisenbahnwesens,* 4:300–302.

77. Félix Tourneux, *Encyclopédie des chemins de fer et des machines à vapeur* (Paris: J. Renouard et cie, 1844), 471–73.

78. Camille Polonceau and Victor Bois, "De la Disposition et du service des gares et stations sur les chemins de fer," *Revue Générale de l'Architecture* 1 (1840): cols. 513–43, 733–45.

79. Auguste Perdonnet and Camille Polonceau, *Nouveau portefeuille de l'ingénieur des chemins de fer* (Paris: Lacroix-Comon, 1857); Perdonnet, *Traité,* 1st ed., 2:30; Schivelbusch, *Railway Journey,* 176.

80. C. Bricka, *Cours de chemins de fer, professé à l'Ecole Nationale des Ponts et Chaussées* (Paris: Gauthier-Villars et Fils, 1894), 225.

81. Kellett, *Impact of Railways,* 5; Perdonnet and Polonceau, *Portefeuille,* 430–33. Already in the first edition of the *Traité,* Perdonnet only recommends shared stations in areas of lesser activity, not in Paris (p. 79).

82. "Circulaire du 25 janvier 1854 du Ministre des Travaux Publics réglant les formes de l'enquête sur le nombre, l'étendue et l'emplacement des stations," in Picard, *Chemins de fer français,* 4:75–76.

83. Ulrich Krings, *Bahnhofsarchitektur: Deutsche Grossstadtbahnhöfe des Historismus* (Munich: Prestel, 1985), 85; Kellett, *Impact of Railways,* 324.

84. Saussay, *Gares des grandes lignes,* 2, 7.

85. S. E. Hoffmann, after Storch. Facilities for the Berlin-Saxony Railway (*Anlage für die Berlin-Sächsischen Eisenbahn*), lithographs, 1842. Staatsbibliothek zu Berlin, Preußischer Kulturbesitz, Kartenabteilung, Unter den Linden, 44780 and 44783.

86. Schivelbusch, *Railway Journey*, 174.

87. Bowie et al., "Polarisation," 5; Henri Lefebvre, *The Production of Space* (Cambridge, MA: Blackwell, 1991), 361.

88. Perdonnet and Polonceau, *Portefeuille*, 428–29; Perdonnet, *Traité*, 1st ed., 2:75; Perdonnet, *Traité*, 3rd ed., 1:125–29.

89. Saussay, *Gares des grandes lignes*, 6.

90. Ibid., 2, 3, 7. This had also been advocated in the review of *De la Politique des chemins de fer*, by Pierre-Edmond Teisserenc–de-Bort, in *Journal des Chemins de Fer*, 5 September 1842, 196–97.

91. Tourneux, *Encyclopédie*, 471–73.

92. Bassompièrre-Sewrin, "De la Pénétration des chemins de fer dans les villes," *Journal des Chemins de Fer*, 25 November 1854, 831.

93. Simmons, *Victorian Railway*, 159. According to Simmons, penetration within city walls began in the 1840s, some instances being respectful, others termed "callous" by Pevsner (Nikolaus Pevsner, *Shropshire*, The Buildings of England [Harmondsworth, UK: Penguin, 1958], 249, 270).

94. Kellett, *Impact of Railways*, 4–5, 8–9; Schivelbusch, *Railway Journey*, 179.

95. Bassompièrre, "Pénétration des chemins," 831.

96. Perdonnet, *Traité*, 3rd ed., 1:128–29. See also Barrie M. Ratcliffe, "The Building of the Paris-Saint-Germain Railway: Some Entrepreneurial and Financial Problems of the Launching of Railways in France in the 1830s and 1840s," *Journal of Transport History* 2 (February 1973): 29.

97. Bowie et al., "Polarisation," 61; Le Hardy de Beaulieu, "*Considérations nouvelles*," 3.

98. For a chronology of railway and expropriation legislation, see Micheline Nilsen, "The 'Other Side of the Tracks': The Implantation of the Railways in Western European Capitals" (PhD diss., University of Delaware, 2003), app. A-1. For references on this topic see the separate legislation section in the bibliography.

99. O. Cyprian Williams, *The Historical Development of Private Bill Procedure and Standing Orders in the House of Commons* (London: HMSO, 1948), 1:61–63.

100. See Nilsen, "Implantation," app. B-5 for a list of Acts of Parliament and other official documents related to the railways in Britain. For an overview of legislation pertaining to railway development, see Volker Then, *Eisenbahnen und Eisenbahnunternehmer in der Industriellen Revolution: Ein Preussisch/deutsch-englischer Vergleich* (Göttingen: Vandenhoeck & Ruprecht, 1997), 112–16.

101. Kellett, *Impact of Railways*, 26–27; Charles E. Lee, "Railways and the mid-Victorian Growth of London" (manuscript ca. 1979), 6. The Act of 14 July 1856 (19 & 20 Vict., cap. 47) defined the nature of a limited liability company.

102. Kellett, *Impact of Railways*, 25.

103. HC, 1846 (687), XIV, SC, on Railway Acts and Enactments; HC, 1847–48, XVI, SC, on Railway Bills; both quoted in Kellett, *Impact of Railways*, 30.

104. Dominique Audet-Perrier, *Les Premiers pas des chemins de fer en Charente: Mythes et réalités, 1836–1883* (Paris: Le Croit-vif, 1997), 20; Caron, *Histoire des chemins*; Jean-Paul Adam, *Instauration de la politique des chemins de fer en France* (Paris: Presses Universitaires de France, 1972); Pierre-Edmond Teisserenc-de-Bort, *Les Travaux publics en Belgique et les chemins de fer en France: Rapport adressé à M. le Ministre des Travaux Publics* (Paris: Mathias, 1839), 144.

105. Bowie et al., "Polarisation," 6, 31; E. Vigouroux, *Législation et jurisprudence des chemins de fer et des tramways* (Paris: E. Thorin, 1886), 117–21.

106. Isabelle Brot, "Le Financement," in Isabelle Guérin Brot and Jean Pierre Babelon, *Les Débuts du chemin de fer en France, 1831–1870* (Paris: Ministère de la Culture et de l'Environnement and SNCF, 1977), 29.

107. Caron, *Histoire des chemins,* 194; Mitchell, "Private Enterprise," 18–19, 40–41.

108. Colleen Dunlavy, *Politics and Industrialization: Early Railroads in the United States and Prussia* (Princeton, NJ: Princeton University Press, 1994), 69–70. For a summary of Prussian legislation, see Volker Then, *Eisenbahnen und Eisenbahnunternehmer,* 103–12.

109. Dunlavy, *Politics and Industrialization,* 51, 56, 63, 133, 157, 159.

110. Friedrich Wilhelm von Reden, *Législation des chemins de fer en Allemagne* (Paris: L. Mathias, 1845), 9; J. A. Schrötter, *Das Preussische Eisenbahnrecht in seiner heutigen Gestalt umfassend das Gesetz über die Eisenbahn-Unternehmungen, vom 3. November 1838* (Berlin: H. W. Müller, 1883).

111. The limited stock company law of 9 November 1843, a cabinet decree of 22 December 1843, and the Stock Market Decree of 24 May 1844. *Preussens Eisenbahngesetzgebung: Eine Zusammenstellung der bisher erschienen, die Eisenbahn-Unternehmungen betreffenden Gesetze und Ministerial-Rescripte* (Glogau: Karl Flemming, 1844), 32.

112. Dunlavy, *Politics and Industrialization,* 162–66.

113. François Bartholony, *Quelques idées sur les encouragements à accorder aux compagnies concessionnaires des grandes lignes de chemin de fer et autres travaux d'utilité publique* (Paris: Firmin Didot Frères, 1836), 28–29; Alexis Godin, *Observations sur le projet de loi d'expropriation des chemins de fer* (Paris: Imprimerie de Bonaventure et Ducessois, 1848); T. H. Hovenden, *New Railways and New Streets: A Few Hints to Those Affected by Proposed Public Improvements* (London: Effingham Wilson, 1872); Max Haushofer, ed., *Grundzüge des Eisenbahnwesens in seinen ökonomischen, politischen und rechtlichen Beziehungen* (Stuttgart: Verlag von Julius Maier, 1874), 99–108. For a detailed comparative examination of expropriation legislation and procedures in western and central European countries, consult von Röll, ed., *Enzyklopädie des Eisenbahnwesens,* 4:342–61 (with bibliography on p. 361).

114. 1845 (8 Vict., cap. 18; HC, 1845, 420) and (8 Vict., cap. 20; HC, 1845, 420); Kellett, *Impact of Railways,* 28; A. W. Nicholls, *Compensation for the Compulsory Acquisition of Land* (Hadleigh, Essex: Thames Bank, 1952), 31–121.

115. Edwin Course, *London's Railways* (London: B. T. Batsford, 1962), 217.

116. E. Dresser Rogers, *Report on the Projected Railway Schemes Affecting the Ward of Aldgate, of Session 1864* (London: Roxbrough, 1864), 12; Metropolitan Railway Commission, Parliamentary Papers, HC,1846, xvii (719), & 21, Q. 2185 (also listed as Royal Commission on Metropolis Railway Termini).

117. Metropolitan Railway Commission, 6–7.

118. Villedeuil, *Bibliographie des chemins de fer,* 23–29.

119. Article 545 of the Code Civil promulgated on 6 February 1804. Pierre Lavedan, *Histoire de l'urbanisme à Paris,* 2nd ed., ed. Jean Bastié (Paris: Hachette, 1993), 422; Pierre Pinon, *Atlas du Paris haussmannien* (Paris: Parigramme, 2002), 17.

120. Picard, *Chemins de fer français,* 1:23.

121. Ratcliffe, "Building Paris-Saint-Germain," 27; Adam, *Instauration de la politique*, 101–28, 151–68; Lavedan, *Histoire de l'urbanisme*, 422. A Senatus Consultum of 21 December 1852 would return the power of declaration of public utility to the emperor. Picard, *Chemins de fer français*, 4:3–18; Pinon, *Atlas*, 17–19.

122. The so-called Armand de Melun Law (Lavedan, *Histoire de l'urbanisme*, 422). A Council of State decree of 27 December 1858 returned unused land with betterment value to previous owners. In 1860, the Court of Cassation enforced tenant compensation even when eviction did not take place. David H. Pinkney, *Napoleon III and the Rebuilding of Paris* (Princeton, NJ: Princeton University Press, 1958), 185; Vigouroux, *Législation et jurisprudence*, 113–21.

123. Bartholony, *Quelques idées sur les encouragements*, 28–29, vol. 4, "De la prise de possession des terrains nécessaires à l'établissement des chemins de fer."

124. Villedeuil, *Bibliographie des chemins de fer*, 23–29; Pinkney, *Napoleon III*, 185; Onfroy de Bréville, "Ministère des travaux publics: Chemin de fer de Paris en Belgique, 11 novembre 1843," Archives Nationales F/14/9376; Karen Bowie, "Gares et villes au XIXe siècle: Deux ingénieurs des Ponts et Chaussées et l'implantation des gares du Nord et de l'Est à Paris," *Annales des Ponts et Chaussées* 89 (April 1999): 5, 7–8; Bowie et al., "Polarisation," 33–34.

125. Amédée Brun, *Des Dommages causés par l'exécution de travaux publics de chemins de fer* (Paris: A. Pedone, 1898).

126. Conditions for land purchase by the state for highway construction had been stipulated by an edict of 18 April 1792 and modified by a Royal Ordnance of 8 August 1832. Von Reden, *Législation des chemins de fer en Allemagne*, 58–61; Heinrich Siegfried, *Das Gesetz über die Enteignung von Grundeigenthum: Erläutert unter Benutzung des amtlichen Motive sowie der Kommissionsberichte und Verhandlungen der beiden Häuser des Landtages* (Berlin: Gustav Hempel, 1874); Friedrich Seydel, *Das Gesetz über die Enteignung von Grundeigenthum vom 11. Juni 1874* (Berlin: Carl Heymanns Verlag, 1882).

127. von Reden, *Législation des chemins de fer en Allemagne*, 56. Article 48 of the Law of 3 November 1848.

128. Pierre-Edmond Teisserenc-de-Bort, *Les Travaux publics en Belgique et les chemins de fer en France: Rapport adressé à M. le Ministre des Travaux Publics* (Paris: L. Mathias, 1839), 140–41; von Reden, *Législation des chemins de fer en Allemagne*, 7–8, 15.

129. von Reden, *Législation des chemins de fer en Allemagne*, 7, 61–67.

130. N. Bullock, "The Origins of English Planning and the Example of Germany," in *Villes en mutation, XIXe-XXe siècles* (Brussels: Crédit Communal, 1982), 53–59. Emil Koffka, *Kommentar zum Gesetz über die Enteignung von Grundeigenthum vom 11. Juni 1874*, 2nd ed. (Berlin: Franz Vahlen, 1913), 149; "Zum preussichen Expropriationsrechte," *Deutsche Bauzeitung* 9 (1875): 352.131. P. Godding, "L'Evolution de la législation en matière d'urbanisme en Belgique au XIXe siècle," in *Villes en mutation*, 14; Thierry Demey, *Bruxelles: Chronique d'une capitale en chantier* (Brussels: Paul Legrain, 1990–92), 1:27.

132. Teisserenc-de-Bort, "Travaux publics," 495; Jules Gendebien, *Législation et jurisprudence des chemins de fer en Belgique, 1834–1858* (Brussels: Bruylant, 1858), 32–40. Godding, "Evolution," 11–35 also includes survey of legislation related to social conditions.

133. M. Nothomb, *Travaux publics en Belgique, 1830–1839: Chemins de fer et routes ordinaires*, Rapport Présenté aux Chambres Législatives, 12 November 1839 (2nd ed. 1840), 123; Louis Verniers, "Les Transformations de Bruxelles et l'ur-

banisation de sa banlieue depuis 1795," *Annales de la Société Royale Archéologique de Bruxelles* 37 (1934): 132–35.

134. Godding, "Evolution," 22–23; Le Hardy de Beaulieu, *Chemin de fer de la jonction directe des railways de l'Etat à Bruxelles avec station centrale dans l'intérieur de la ville pour le service des voyageurs, des postes et des télégraphes* (Brussels: Ch. Vanderauwera, 1855), 21.

135. Godding, "Evolution," 26–27. The cholera epidemic of 1866 brought the issue of urban sanitation to the foreground.

136. Godding, "Evolution," 35. The expropriation legislation was further amended by the Laws of 27 May 1870 and 9 September 1907 (Röll, ed., *Enzyklopädie des Eisenbahnwesens*, 4:343).

137. Jean Bastié, "Supplément," in Lavedan, *Histoire de l'urbanisme*, 661, 663.

138. Michel Chevalier, *Des Chemins de fer en France* (Paris: H. Fournier, 1838), 3–5; Marc Baroli, "Le Train dans la littérature Française," in *Ecritures du chemin de fer: Actes de la journée scientifique organisée en Sorbonne, le 11 mai 1996*, ed. François Moureau and Marie Noëlle Polino, 11–23 (Paris: Klincksieck, 1997).

139. M. Henry, *Considérations générales sur l'établissement des chemins de fer* (Boulogne, France: Imprimerie de Le Roy-Mabile, 1836), 6. The map included in this pamphlet is titled "From London to Calcutta."

140. Herbert, *Impressionism*, 270; David S. Landes, *The Unbound Prometheus: Technological Change and Industrial Development in Western Europe from 1750 to the Present* (London: Cambridge University Press, 1969), 158.

141. Mudge, *Observations on Railways*, 10. For Belgium, see Depouhon, *Du Mode d' exécution du système des chemins de fer en Belgique* (Brussels: Pelcot et Boissaux, 1833), art. 12. "Chemins de fer," in *Sciences appliquées à l'art militaire: Chemins de fer, télégraphe électrique et optique, téléphone, pigeons voyageurs, aérostation, ponts militaires, routes militaires* (Brussels: Spinieux, 1888), 1.

142. As documented by the essays in Polino and Roth, *City and Railway*.

Chapter 2

1. George Manville Fenn, "Where Are They to Go?" *The Working Man*, 8 September 1866, 109.

2. Charles Dickens, "Attila in London," *All the Year Round* 15, no. 370 (26 May 1866): 466–69; H. J. Dyos, *Victorian Suburb: A Study of the Growth of Camberwell* (Leicester, UK: Leicester University Press, 1961), 75; Dyos, "Railways and Housing in Victorian London: I, Attila in London," *Journal of Transport History* 2 (1955): 11–12. See also John R. Kellett, *The Impact of Railways on Victorian Cities* (London: Routledge & Kegan Paul, 1969), 337–46; Jack Simmons, *The Railway in Town and Country, 1830–1914* (Newton Abbot, UK: David & Charles, 1986), 32–35.

3. Dyos, *Victorian Suburb*, 75; Dyos, "Attila," 11–12. See also Kellett, *Impact of Railways*, 337–46; Simmons, *Railway in Town and Country*, 32–35.

4. Jack Simmons, *The Victorian Railway* (London: Thames and Hudson, 1991), 20, 80, 155.

5. Kellett, *Impact of Railways*, 2, 11.

6. Jack Simmons, "The Power of the Railway," in *The Victorian City: Images and Realities*, ed. H. J. Dyos and Michael Wolff (London: Routledge & Kegan Paul,

1973), 297; H. J. Dyos, "Some Social Costs of Railway Building in London," *Journal of Transport History* 3 (1957–58): 23–25.

7. H. J. Dyos, "Railways and Housing in Victorian London: II, Rustic Townsmen," *Journal of Transport History* 2 (1955): 95; Kellett, *Impact of Railways,* 8.

8. Kellett, *Impact of Railways,* 18.

9. Simmons, *Victorian Railway,* 156, 164.

10. Metropolitan Railway Commission, Parliamentary Papers, HC, 1846 (719) XVII, 21, also listed as Royal Commission on Metropolis Railway Termini; Kellett, *Impact of Railways,* 10, 35–43.

11. HC, 1846, XVII, Q. 2355; quoted in Kellett, *Impact of Railways,* 37.

12. HC, 1846 (719) XVII, 7, Q. 2185; also noted in Kellett, *Impact of Railways,* 37.

13. On the map of the Metropolitan Railway Commission, this central zone was bordered by Edgeware Road, Park Lane, Grosvenor Place, Vauxhall Road and Bridge, Kennington Lane, Walcot Lane, Lambeth Road, Blacksmith Street, Borough High Street, Wellington Street, London Bridge, Bishopsgate, Sun Street, Crown Street, Finsbury Square, City Road, Euston Road, and Marylebone Road. HC, 1846 (719) XVII. All existing terminals were outside of these limits in 1846.

14. Dyos, "Attila," 14.

15. H. J. Dyos, "The Slums of Victorian London," *Victorian Studies* 11 (September 1967): 37–38; see also H. J. Dyos and D. A. Reeder, "Slums and Suburbs," in Dyos and Wolff, *Victorian City,* 1:366; Kellett, *Impact of Railways,* 8–9, 331.

16. Royal Commission on Housing of the Working Classes, Q. 10771 (Clerk of the Public Bills, Lords); Q. 10687 (Denton); 3 Hansard, CLXI (1861), 67.

17. Dyos, "Rustic Townsmen," 95–96.

18. Dyos, "Slums," 9; Dyos and Reeder, "Slums and Suburbs," 1:359–88; E. Gwynn, "The Jerry Builder Considered in Relation to the Housing of the Poor," *Public Health* 13, no. 4 (January 1901): 246.

19. Dyos and Reeder, "Slums and Suburbs," 1:363–64; Benjamin Francis C. Costelloe, *The Housing Problem* (London: John Heywood, 1899), 44–47; David Cannadine and David Reeder, eds., *Exploring the Urban Past: Essays in Urban History by H. J. Dyos* (Cambridge: Cambridge University Press, 1982), 141.

20. Dyos, "Slums," 25.

21. Ibid., 27.

22. Charles Booth, *Life and Labour of the People in London,* 3rd ser., Religious Influences (London: 1902–4; repr., New York: AMS Press, 1970), 2:67. Booth frequently refers to the railway as a division or barrier in his notebooks.

23. In such diverse publications as *Punch* (1841–), *The Illustrated London News* (1842–), and others; Thomas Wright, *Some Habits and Customs of the Working Classes* (London: Tinsley Brothers, 1867); Wright, *The Great Unwashed* (London: Tinsley Brothers, 1868). Dickens in fiction such as *Dombey and Son* (1846) and the periodicals *All the Year Round* and *Household Words.*

24. Dyos, "Slums," 11.

25. Ibid., 6.

26. Dyos, "Attila," 13.

27. Charles Pearson, *City Improvements and Railroad Termini* (London: Effingham Wilson & J. Ridgway, 1851), 5.

28. W. Blanchard Jerrold, "Observations on Some of the Plans Adopted for the Relief of the Poor of Paris," *Transactions of the National Association for the Promotion of Social Science,* 1864, 631; "Government and the Evicted

Poor," *The Builder* 25, no. 1250 (1867): 37–38; Kellett, *Impact of Railways*, 327–30.

29. By such contemporaries as William Denton (*Observations on the Displacement of the Poor, by Metropolitan Railways and by Other Public Improvements* [London: Bell & Dalby, 1861]). See also Dyos, "Rustic Townsmen," 94, 98–99; Dyos, "Social Costs," 23–24.

30. Charles Booth, *Life and Labour of the People in London* (London: Macmillan, 1892); Booth, *Life and Labour*, 3rd ser.; Booth, "Descriptive Map of London Poverty" (London: Stanford's Geographical Establishment, 1889). In some areas, the maps document worsening of conditions between the first and second editions of the book.

31. Dickens, "Attila," 466.

32. Charles Dickens, *The Works of Charles Dickens*, vol. 14, *Dombey and Son* (London, 1846–48; New York: Books, n.d.), 60–61.

33. Wright, *The Great Unwashed*, 125–50.

34. For example, Henry D. Davies, *"The Way Out," A letter addressed (by permission) to the Earl of Derby, K. G., in which the evils of the overcrowded Town Hovel, and the advantages of the Suburban Cottage, are contrasted* (London: Longman, Green, Longman & Roberts, 1861); J. Stevenson, *New Railways in London: How and where they should be constructed so as to avoid the destruction of house property. . . .* (Hounslow, UK: J. Gotelee, 1866).

35. George Godwin, *An Appeal to the Public on the Subject of Railways* (London: J. Weale, 1837); Godwin, "Architecture for the Poor," *The Builder* 3 (8 February 1845): 61; quoted in H. J. Dyos, "Workmen's Fares in South London, 1860–1914," *Journal of Transport History* 1, no. 1 (1953): 4.

36. George Godwin, *London Shadows* (London: Routledge, 1854), 71; Godwin, *Another Blow for Life* (London: Allen, 1864), 30.

37. 44 Hansard, 3rd ser., 161 (1861), 64; Dyos, "Workmen's Fares," 4.

38. Dyos, "Attila," 16.

39. Parliamentary Papers, 1887, XV, Tabulation of the Statements made by Men living in Certain Selected Districts of London in March 1887 (C. 5228), covering the areas of St. George's-in-the-East, Battersea, Hackney, and Deptford; quoted in Dyos and Reeder, "Slums and Suburbs," 1:367–68.

40. *Punch* 40 (1861): 98, and 44 (1863): 128, 146; quoted in Dyos, "Attila," 17.

41. Dyos, "Slums," 1:366.

42. *Times* (London), 2 March 1861; quoted in Dyos, "Attila," 14.

43. A. S. Wohl, "The Housing of the Working Classes in London, 1815–1914," in *The History of Working-Class Housing: A Symposium*, ed. Stanley D. Chapman (Totowa, NJ: Rowman and Littlefield, 1971), 18.

44. Editorials, *Times* (London), 12 and 23 March 1861; quoted in Dyos, "Rustic Townsmen," 97.

45. See note 42.

46. As illustrated by Thomas Wright in *The Great Unwashed*, 125–50.

47. Costelloe, *Housing Problem*, 47; Patricia E. Malcolmson, "Getting a Living in the Slums of Victorian Kensington," *London Journal* 1 (May 1975): 28–55.

48. John Hollingshead, *Ragged London in 1861* (London: Smith, Elder, 1861); HC, 1884–85, xxx, 22–23.

49. PP, 7, 1882, Minutes of Evidence, Select Committee on Artizans' and Labourers' Dwellings, 128; quoted by Wohl, "Housing of the Working Classes," 16–17.

50. McCullagh Torrens: Hansard, 3rd ser., 181 (1866), 821; quoted in Dyos, "Attila," 15.

51. Corporation of London, *The City of London: A Record of Destruction and Survivals* (London: The Corporation, 1951), 165; quoted in Dyos and Reeder, "Slums and Suburbs," 1:365–67; and Dyos, "Workmen's Fares," 4–5. See also Wohl, "Housing of the Working Classes," 27–28; Kellett, *Impact of Railways*, 309–10, 321–23.

52. Denton, *Observations*, 23; brought to my attention by Dyos, "Attila," 14.

53. Wohl, "Housing of the Working Classes," 18. Farringdon Street, Southwark Street, New Cannon Street, New Oxford Street, Commercial Street, Bethnal Green Road, Wapping High Street, Clerkenwell Road, Holborn, and Queen Victoria Street were built through slum areas.

54. Malcolmson, "Slums of Victorian Kensington," 31.

55. The Metropolitan Board of Works (MBW) started work in 1857 and did not begin to rehouse until 1870. It rehoused only 10,340 out of the people displaced to create 3,000 new streets (Wohl, "Housing of the Working Classes," 19).

56. "Evicted Tenants' Aid Association," *The Builder* 25, no. 1249 (1867): 33; cited in Dyos, "Attila," 15; E. Dresser Rogers, *Report on the Projected Railway Schemes affecting the Ward of Aldgate, of session 1864: and remarks on the unjust state of the Law of Compensation* (London: Roxbrough, 1864); Kellett, *Impact of Railways*, 332–36.

57. *Times* (London), 7 January 1867; quoted in Dyos, "Attila," 15.

58. House of Lords Journals, 85 (1853): 140; quoted in Kellett, *Impact of Railways*, 54.

59. Lord Shaftesbury: 3 Hansard, 125 (1853): 1292; LJ, 85 (1853), 244, SO 191; quoted in Dyos, "Attila," 13.

60. 3 Hansard, 126 (1853): 402. See also Simmons, "Power," 297; Dyos, "Social Costs," 23; Kellett, *Impact of Railways*, 325–36.

61. Kellett, *Impact of Railways*, 54, who refers to O. Cyprian Williams, *The Historical Development of Private Bill Procedure and Standing Orders in the House of Commons* (London: HMSO, 1948), 2:65.

62. Dyos, "Social Costs," 23–24.

63. Dyos, "Attila," 14. The total number of persons listed to be displaced on demolition statements for bills passed between 1854 and 1900 is approximately 69,000. The total is approximate because some figures have alternates. Dyos, "Social Costs," 25–29. A recent publication gives the total figure of displaced persons as 100,000. See Peter Ackroyd, *London: The Biography* (London: Chatto & Windus, 2000), 592.

64. The London, Chatham & Dover and South Eastern (Kennington, Clapham, and Brixton) Railway Bill of 1866, if approved, would have displaced 3,743 persons; noted in Dyos, "Attila," 18–20.

65. House of Commons Journals, 129 (1874): 351; quoted in Dyos, "Attila," 18.

66. Dyos, "Attila," 18; Dyos, "Rustic Townsmen," 95. See also Jack Simmons, *St. Pancras Station* (London: George Allen & Unwin, 1968), 24–25 and Wohl, "Housing of the Working Classes," 18, who both mention a rare instance of an actual court case on behalf of tenants.

67. Dyos, "Attila," 18 refers to PP, 1884–85, xxx, Q. 8838–39, 8386–88, 9984, 9987, 10,412; Q. 10,676 (Denton); Q. 9,940 (Surveyor to MBW); Q. 10,777–78 (Clerk of Public Bills).

68. Kellett, *Impact of Railways*, 54–55; and Dyos, "Attila," 18, who refers to PP, 1882, vii, 216–18.

69. 61 & 62 Vict., c, ccliii; Rep. Joint Select Committee on Housing of the Working Classes, Report, PP, 1902, v. 147, in Dyos, "Attila," 19. The Great Central Railway nonetheless takes credit for having provided for those displaced in northwest London by its London extension (G. Dow, *Great Central* [London: Locomotive Publications, 1959–65], 2:244, 279, 287; quoted in Simmons, "Power," 297). See also Kellett, *Impact of Railways,* 335.

70. Gwynn, "Jerry Builder," 247.

71. PP, 1905, vii, Rep. vii; quoted in Dyos, "Rustic Townsmen," 93.

72. Charles Booth, *Improved Means of Locomotion as a First Step Towards the Cure of the Housing Difficulties of London* (London: Macmillan, 1901), 12.

73. Author of *Report on the Sanitary Condition of the Labouring Population of Great Britain* (Edinburgh: University Press, 1842).

74. Lost through the parliamentary process, the Torrens bill did not become law until 1868 (31 & 32 Vict., c. 130); Dyos, "Rustic Townmen," 94, 100. The Artizans' and Labourers' Dwellings Improvement Act is generally known as the first Cross Act of 1875. The 1879 Torrens Act Amendment further elaborated the terms for compensation and rehousing of persons displaced by improvement schemes.

75. Wohl, "Housing of the Working Classes," 19–20, 23; Costelloe, *Housing Problem,* 46. See also London Metropolitan Archives, MA-MBW-1838-26, a letter of 1877 from Thomas Stevenson, medical officer of health for the Parish of St. Pancras; Charles Booth, "Improved Means," 12.

76. Dyos, "Slums," 22 and n. 63; Gwynn, "Jerry Builder," 241–58.

77. Booth, *Life and Labour,* 3rd ser., 2:190.

78. Joseph Corbett, "On the Re-housing of the Poorer Classes of Central London," in *Essays on the Street Re-alignment, Reconstruction and Sanitation of Central London* (London: George Bell, 1886), 242.

79. Wohl, "Housing of the Working Classes," 21–22. LCC London Statistics, 12 (1901–2), x; quoted in Wohl, "Housing of the Working Classes," 24.

80. Kellett, *Impact of Railways,* 54.

81. Dyos, *Victorian Suburb,* 22.

82. Donald J. Olsen, "House upon House: Estate Development in London and Sheffield," in Dyos and Wolff, *Victorian City,* 339.

83. H. J. Dyos, "The Growth of a Pre-Victorian Suburb: South London, 1580–1836," *Town Planning Review* 25, no. 1 (1954): 59–78. Parish registers also offer evidence of this process (Dyos, *Victorian Suburb,* 31).

84. Olsen, "House upon House," 338; Gwynn, "Jerry Builder," 241–58.

85. *Times,* 2 March 1861; quoted in Dyos, "Attila," 14 and Wohl, "Housing of the Working Classes," 29. For commuting to be viable, the cost of housing and transport had to be equal or inferior to what could be rented in London for the same price. Booth reported on this fact, but it was not until the Draft Reports of the Select Committee on Workmen's Trains of 1905 that officials considered the workman's weekly arithmetic of rent, transit, travel time, and meal expenses as factors to be figured into fare pricing. Booth, *Life and Labour,* 1:263; and Report of the 1903–5 Royal Commission on London Traffic, HC, 1905, XXX, 605–11.

86. Edwin Course, "Transport and Communications in London," in *The Geography of Greater London,* ed. Robert Clayton (London: G. Philip, 1964), 94.

87. The Midland Company managed to keep workmen's trains clauses out of the acts authorizing its London extension in 1863–64 because its lines ran just out-

side of the defined metropolitan area (Simmons, "Power," 298; Kellett, *Impact of Railways*, 342).

88. See PRO, RAIL-410-1242.
89. Janet Polasky, "Transplanting and Rooting Workers in London and Brussels: A Comparative History," *Journal of Modern History* 73, no. 3 (2001): 529; and 1905 Royal Commission, 15.
90. H. P. White, *A Regional History of the Railways of Great Britain*, vol. 3, *Greater London* (London: Phoenix House, 1971), 3:15; Edwin Course, *London's Railways* (London: B. T. Batsford, 1962), 198.
91. Kellett, *Impact of Railways*, 94.
92. 1905 Royal Commission, 2.
93. Booth, "Improved Means," 9–10.
94. Jeanne Pronteau, "Construction et aménagement des nouveaux quartiers de Paris," *Histoire des Entreprises* 2 (November 1958): 8–32.
95. Maxime du Camp, *Paris, ses organes, ses fonctions, sa vie dans la seconde moitié du XIXe siècle* (Paris: Hachette, 1875), 5:333.
96. Anthony Sutcliffe, *The Autumn of Central Paris: The Defeat of Town Planning, 1850–1970* (London: Edward Arnold, 1970), 29; "Halles de Paris, from Journal des Débats," *Journal des Chemins de Fer*, 1849, 487.
97. "Chemin de fer de l'Est: Ligne de Paris à Vincennes," *Journal des Chemins de Fer*, 24 September 1859, 810.
98. Ministerium der Öffentlichen Arbeiten and A. F. Leyen, *Berlin und seine Eisenbahnen, 1846–1896* (Berlin: Julius Springer, 1896), 1:253, 309.
99. Arthur Cawston, *A Comprehensive Scheme for Street Improvements in London* (London: Edward Stanford, 1893), 22.
100. Johann Friedrich Geist and Klaus Kürvers, *Das Berliner Miethaus, 1740–1862* (Munich: Prestel, 1980).
101. Victor-Gaston Martiny, "Le Développement urbain," in *La Région de Bruxelles: Des Villages d'autrefois à la ville d'aujourd'hui*, ed. Arlette - Smolar-Meynart and Jean Stengers (Brussels: Crédit Communal, 1989), 176.
102. Charles Buls, "Rapport sur le logement ouvrier," *Bulletin Communal de la Ville de Bruxelles* (1891), 2: 650–69.

Chapter 3

1. John R. Kellett, *The Impact of Railways on Victorian Cities* (London: Routledge & Kegan Paul, 1969), 292.
2. Ben Weinreb and Christopher Hibbert, eds., *The London Encyclopaedia* (London: Macmillan, 1983), 7, 774, 776.
3. Kellett, *Impact of Railways*, 245; Donald J. Olsen, *Town Planning in London: The Eighteenth and Nineteenth Centuries* (New Haven, CT: Yale University Press, 1964), 40–69, 103–51.
4. Kellett, *Impact of Railways*, 244–62; see also Hermione Hobhouse, *Thomas Cubitt, Master Builder* (London: Macmillan, 1971), 72, 189, 253, 359–60.
5. Kellett, *Impact of Railways*, 252; Olsen, *Town Planning*, 145; see also Peter Atkins, "Freeing the Streets of Victorian London," *History Today* 43 (March 1993): 5–8.
6. Charles E. Lee, "Railways and the Mid-Victorian Growth of London," unpublished article (Camden Local Studies and Archives Centre), ca. 1979, 2–3.

7. *London Encyclopaedia*, 272.

8. Nikolaus Pevsner and Bridget Cherry, *London 4: North*, The Buildings of England (Harmondsworth, UK: Penguin, 1998), 34–35.

9. Francis Sheppard, *London: A History* (Oxford: Oxford University Press, 1998), 14–17; C.E.N. Bromehead, "The Influence of Its Geography on the Growth of London," *Geographical Journal* 60, no. (1922): 125–35; M. Emily Cooke, *A Geographical Study of a London Borough: St. Pancras* (London: University of London Press, 1932), 58–60.

10. Edwin Course, "Transport and Communications in London," in *The Geography of Greater London*, ed. Robert Clayton (London: G. Philip, 1964), 82–86.

11. John C. Bourne and John Britton, *Drawings of the London and Birmingham Railway* (London: J. C. Bourne, 1839), 12.

12. M. de Bassompièrre-Sewrin, "De la Pénétration des chemins de fer dans les villes," *Journal des Chemins de Fer*, 3 December 1854, 847–49.

13. George Manville Fenn, "Where Are They to Go?" *The Working Man* 2 (8 September 1866): 109–10.

14. Charles Dickens, *The Works of Charles Dickens*, vol. 14, *Dombey and Son* (New York: Books, n.d.), 210.

15. Charles Booth, *Life and Labour of the People in London* (London: Macmillan, 1892); Booth, *Life and Labour of the People in London*, 3rd ser., Religious Influences (London: 1902–4; repr., New York: AMS Press, 1970), 2:169, 174, 181, 183, 187–89, quoting Rev. Arthur Woods, *Twenty-five Years in Somers Town*.

16. Booth, *Life and Labour*, 3rd ser., 2:174.

17. Charles Booth, *Descriptive Map of London Poverty* (London: Stanford's Geographical Establishment, 1889).

18. Booth divided people into eight groups, H–A, ranging from "wealthy" to the "lowest class," but colored in his maps in seven colors, as follows:

yellow: H, upper-middle class, wealthy (three or more servants)
red: G, well-to-do, middle class (one or two servants)
pink: F, fairly comfortable (good ordinary earnings)
purple: E, better-paid laborers and artisans, small shopkeepers (enjoying regular, standard earnings, consistently above the poverty line)
light blue: C&D, poor but not in want (intermittent employment or small regular earnings, insufficient means for a decent life)
dark blue: B, incapable of looking after themselves (very poor, casual: chronic want)
black: A, lowest class (vicious, semicriminal)
white: nonresidential.

19. Booth, *Life and Labour*, 3rd ser.

20. Booth indicated that the area had been "blackened." See also Jack Whitehead, *The Growth of Camden Town, AD 1800–2000* (London: Jack Whitehead, 1999), 70.

21. Whitehead, *Growth of Camden*, 72. For a detailed study of the development and housing stock of Somers Town, see Linda Clarke, *Building Capitalism: Historical Change and the Labour Process in the Production of the Built Environment* (London: Routledge, 1992).

22. Nikolaus Pevsner, *London, except the Cities of London and Westminster*, The Buildings of England (Harmondsworth, UK: Penguin, 1952), 356.

23. PRO, RAIL-410-1510.

24. "British Rail Put Profit before People, Councillor Says," press release from Press & Public Relations Office, London Borough of Camden, 23 January 1991 (4182) and appended British Rail letter dated 1 November 1990.

25. Stephen P. Duckworth and Barry V. Jones, *King's Cross Development Site: An Inventory of Architectural and Industrial Features* (London: English Heritage, Historic Buildings and Monuments Commission for England, 1988), with abbreviated version in Michael Hunter and Robert Thorne, eds., *Change at King's Cross: From 1800 to the Present* (London: Historical Publications, 1990), 140–56.

26. Such as *The King's Cross Guide,* 2nd ed. (London: King's Cross Partnership, March 2001); and *Four Kings Cross Walks,* 2nd ed. (London: King's Cross Partnership, December 2000).

27. Thomas Roscoe and Peter Lecount, *The London and Birmingham Railway, with the Home and Country Scenes on Each Side of the Line, including Sketches of Kenilworth, Learnington, Warwick, Grey's Cliff, Stratford, &c. . . .* (London: C. Tilt, 1839), 1–2.

28. Arthur Freeling, *The Railway Companion, from London to Birmingham, Liverpool, and Manchester. . . .* (London: Whittaker, 1838), 19.

29. Wolfgang Schivelbusch, *The Railway Journey: Trains and Travel in the 19th Century* (New York: Urizen Books, 1979), 175.

30. 44 feet 2 inches, according to the *London Encyclopaedia,* 273; Walter H. Godfrey and J. R. Howard Roberts, eds., *Survey of London,* vol. 21, *Tottenham Court Road and Neighborhood: The Parish of St. Pancras, Part III* (London: London County Council, 1949), 111.

31. *London Encyclopaedia,* 273.

32. J. D. Billington, "Mr. Dombey Travels by Rail," *Dickensian* 28 (1932): 205.

33. See published descriptions of the three Euston Road terminals in the bibliography.

34. *London Encyclopaedia,* 273.

35. F. R. Conder, *The Men Who Built Railways: A Reprint of F. R. Conder's Personal Recollections of English Engineers,* ed. Jack Simmons (London: Thomas Telford, 1983), 18–26.

36. Bourne and Britton, *London and Birmingham,* 16.

37. Conder, *Men Who Built Railways,* 18–26.

38. Pevsner and Cherry, *London 4: North,* 361.

39. Jack Simmons, *The Victorian Railway* (London: Thames and Hudson, 1991), 171.

40. Pevsner and Cherry, *London 4: North,* 361.

41. The London and Birmingham and the London and North Western railways submitted bills for expansions almost annually. For a listing of bills related to the Euston Road terminals, see Micheline Nilsen, "The 'Other Side of the Tracks': The Implantation of the Railways in Western European Capitals" (PhD diss., University of Delaware, 2003), app. B-4.

42. R. L. Moorcroft, "Station Reconstruction at Euston, London," *Architect's Journal* 148, no. 51 (18–25 December 1968): 1455.

43. *London Encyclopaedia,* 447.

44. Pevsner and Cherry, *London 4: North,* 362.

45. PRO, RAIL-236-538 (former #GN3/92), 1890–1905, Buildings in Front of Station: Four Different Proposals.

46. *London Encyclopaedia,* 448.
47. Jack Simmons, "Suburban Traffic at King's Cross, 1852–1914," *Journal of Transport History,* ser. 3, 6, no. 1 (March 1985): 71.
48. Charles Mackie, *Itinerary of the Great Northern Railway from London to York comprising historical and descriptive accounts . . . ,* new ed. (London: W. H. Smith, 1854), 1–3.
49. John Weale, ed., *London and Its Vicinity Exhibited in 1851* (London: J. Weale, 1851), 811; quoted in Jack Simmons, "The Power of the Railway," in *The Victorian City,* ed. H. J. Dyos and Michael Wolff (London: Routledge, 1973), 297.
50. Medcalf, GNR outdoor goods manager; quoted in Chris Hawkins, *The Great British Railway Station: Kings Cross* (Pinner, Middlesex: Irwell Press, 1990), ii.
51. PRO, RAIL-236/545, plan and section, signed by Joseph Cubitt; listed in Hawkins, *Kings Cross,* 1.
52. PRO, RAIL-796/9, Great Northern Railway, working plans and sections, London terminus King's Cross, dated ca. 1846 in the record but containing no annotation earlier than 1869, thus probably later.
53. Hawkins, *Kings Cross,* 3; citing "Notable Railway Stations No. 6," *Railway Magazine,* 1900.
54. Medcalf, GNR Outdoor goods manager; quoted in Hawkins, *Kings Cross,* 3.
55. Oswald Stevens Nock, *The Great Northern Railway* (London: Ian Allan, 1958), 63.
56. Simmons, "Power of the Railway," 299.
57. Kellett, *Impact of Railways,* 95–96, 251, including quotation from Charles Herbert Grinling, *The History of the Great Northern Railway, 1845–1922* (London: George Allen & Unwin, 1966), 373.
58. Simmons, "Suburban Traffic at King's Cross," 76; also Alan Jackson, "Suburbs and Railways," in *The Oxford Companion to British Railway History from 1603 to the 1990s,* ed. Gordon Biddle and Jack Simmons (Oxford: Oxford University Press, 1997), 485.
59. *London Encyclopaedia,* 776.
60. W. M. Acworth, "The Midland Railway," *Murray's Magazine,* March 1888, 306. The original access for the Midland Railway to London had been through connection to the London and Birmingham Railway at Rugby.
61. Acworth, "Midland Railway," 309; see also Kellett, *Impact of Railways,* 277.
62. E. G. Barnes, *The Rise of the Midland Railway, 1844–1874* (London: George Allen & Unwin, 1966), 193.
63. Report from the Select Committee Appointed to Join with a Committee of the House of Lords on Railway Schemes (Metropolis); together with the Proceedings of the Committee, Minutes of Evidence, and an Appendix, PP 1864, Report Committee, 87 (XI), p. 241, iv.
64. Ibid., v; Midland Railway (Extension to London) Local and Personal Act, 26 & 27 Vict., cap. lxxxiv.
65. Frederick S. Williams, *The Midland Railway: Its Rise and Progress, A Narrative of Modern Enterprise* (London: Bemrose, 1877), 334.
66. The widest until Jersey City's Pennsylvania Station reached 252 feet in 1888, quickly outshined by the 383 feet of the Halle des Machines at the 1889 Paris exhibition. Carroll L. V. Meeks, *The Railroad Station: An Architectural History* (New Haven, CT: Yale University Press, 1956), 170.
67. John Summerson, "Red Elephant in Euston Road," *Illustrated London News,* 7 October 1967, 17–18.

68. Jack Simmons, *St. Pancras Station* (London: George Allen & Unwin, 1968), 11.

69. Purchased for £20,000 out of a total land acquisition for £35,000 (Barnes, *Rise of the Midland Railway*, 205).

70. Barnes, *Rise of the Midland Railway*, 211, 229.

71. Now partially occupied by the new British Library.

72. Dated 29 March 1870, it was published in the *Institution of Civil Engineers, Proceedings* 30, no. 1253 (1869–70): 79.73. A. S. Wohl, "The Housing of the Working Classes in London, 1815–1914," in *The History of Working Class Housing: A Symposium*, ed. Stanley D. Chapman (Totowa, NJ: Rowman and Littlefield, 1971), 18.

74. *Working Man* 1 (13 January 1866): 30, and 2 (8 September 1866): 110–11; see also 3 Hansard, 181 (1866): 1025. Both quoted in Wohl, "Housing of the Working Classes," 18.

75. Barnes, *Rise of the Midland Railway*, 233–35.

76. Ibid., 239.

77. Ibid.

78. Pevsner and Cherry, *London 4: North*, 252.

79. Simmons, *St. Pancras Station*, 21, 23; *London Encyclopaedia*, 774.

80. Cuthbert Hamilton Ellis, *The Midland Railway* (London: Ian Allan, 1953), 35-36ff.; Barnes, *Rise of the Midland Railway*, 233, 241–42; Williams, *Midland Railway*, 352.

81. 27 & 28 Vict., cap. cxxxi, 25 July 1864; cited by Barnes, *Rise of the Midland Railway*, 239.

82. Simmons, *St. Pancras Station*, 23.

83. Ibid., 24.

84. It was not uncommon for the church to own areas developed with lower-class housing. Kellett suggests that the church found it "inappropriate" to exclude lower-class tenants from its lands by granting exclusive covenants. Kellett, *Impact of Railways*, 248–49, 257–58.

85. Simmons, *St. Pancras Station*, 21.

86. Jack Simmons and Robert Thorne, *St Pancras Station, Revised and with a New Chapter by Robert Thorne* (London: Historical Publications, 2003), 159; H. J. Dyos, "Railways and Housing in Victorian London: I, Attila in London," *Journal of Transport History* 2 (1955): 11–21; Dyos, "Railways and Housing in Victorian London: II, Rustic Townsmen," *Journal of Transport History* 2 (1955): 90–100. Simmons, *St. Pancras Station*, 24, n. 5 refers to the Dyos articles in a complementary footnote. Simmons' *The Victorian Railway* (London: Thames and Hudson, 1993), written almost 25 years later, gives more nuanced consideration to the impact of the railways (especially, pp. 153–73).

87. As, for example, the account of a court case on behalf of tenants (Simmons, *St. Pancras Station*, 24–25, n. 199).

88. Moy Thomas, "A Suburban Connemara," printed in Dickens' *Household Words* (1851), 564–65.

89. *Survey of London*, 19:60–61 and pls. 115–17; London Topographical Society, *The Kentish Town Panorama, drawn by James Frederick King, with a Commentary by John Richardson* (London: London Topographical Society, 1986).

90. *Survey of London*, 60.

91. J. F. King (ca. 1850), quoted in *Survey of London*, 19:61; also quoted in Simmons, *St. Pancras Station*, 23–24.

92. Steven L. J. Denford, *Agar Town: The Life and Death of a Victorian Slum*, Occasional Paper of the Camden History Society (London: Camden History Society, 1995), 14.

93. Middlesex Register 1860/6/996, listed in Denford, *Agar Town*, 14.

94. Ibid., 16.

95. Ibid., 21.

96. Ibid., 25.

97. David Cannadine and David Reeder, eds., *Exploring the Urban Past: Essays in Urban History by H. J. Dyos* (Cambridge: Cambridge University Press, 1982), 141.

98. A compilation of articles written for *The Morning Post* (Denford, *Agar Town*, 26); Hollingshead, *Ragged London*, 131–33, 138. The railway men, who, according to Booth, usually enjoyed steady employment and reasonable wages, must have been primarily Great Northern Railway (GNR) employees, and were therefore no deterrent for the Midland Railway Company. For railway labor conditions, see Booth, *Life and Labour*, 2nd ser., 3:332–49.

99. Hollingshead, *Ragged London*, 134.

100. Ibid., 137.

101. Ibid., 134–42.

102. Steven L. J. Denford, "Agar Town: Working Class Response to Housing Need in Early Victorian London" (MA thesis, Birbeck College, University of London, 1994); Denford, *Agar Town*, 2.

103. Denford, *Agar Town*, 3.

104. The only other work devoted to Agar Town, written in 1935 by the Reverend R. Conyers Morrell, dealt with the antiquarian and ecclesiastical aspect of the locality. Morrell, *The Story of Agar Town: The Ecclesiastical Parish of St. Thomas, Camden Town, N.W.1* (London: Premo Press, 1935).

105. For a similar assessment of a working-class area as an autonomous and supportive community, see François Bédarida, on east London's Poplar ("Urban Growth and Social Structure in Nineteenth-Century Poplar," *London Journal* 1, no. 2 [1975]: 159–88).

106. H. J. Dyos, "The Slums of Victorian London," *Victorian Studies* 11 (September 1967): 6.

107. Ibid., 40. Although the work of Linda Clarke for Sommers Town demonstrates that an extensive investigation can be carried out (Clarke, *Building Capitalism*).

108. E. Gwynn, "The Jerry Builder Considered in Relation to the Housing of the Poor," *Public Health* 13, no. 4 (January 1901): 241–58.

109. Gwynn, "Jerry Builder," 247; Donald J. Olsen, *The City as a Work of Art: London, Paris, Vienna* (New Haven, CT: Yale University Press, 1986), 182.

110. Patricia E. Malcolmson, "Getting a Living in the Slums of Victorian Kensington," *London Journal* 1 (May 1975): 28–55.

111. H. J. Dyos, *Victorian Suburb: A Study of the Growth of Camberwell* (Leicester, UK: Leicester University Press, 1961), 7.

Chapter 4

1. Michel Carmona, *Haussmann* (Paris: Fayard, 2000), 9.

2. The emperor's plans for Paris continued work begun during the July Monarchy. For a list, see Pierre Casselle, "Les Travaux de la Commission des

Embellissements de Paris en 1853: Pouvait-on transformer la capitale sans Haussmann?" *Bibliothèque de l'Ecole des Chartes* 55 (1997): 649, n. 11. Also, Casselle, *Commission des Embellissements de Paris: Rapport à l'empereur Napoléon III rédigé par le comte Henri Siméon* (Paris: Commission du Vieux Paris, Rotonde de la Villette, 2000).

3. Merruau reports, "in blue, red, yellow and green, according to their degree of importance." Charles Merruau, *Souvenir de l'Hôtel de Ville de Paris, 1848–1852* (Paris: Plon, 1875), 364–65; also quoted in Jean Des Cars and Pierre Pinon, *Paris-Haussmann: "Le pari d'Haussmann"* (Paris: Edition du Pavillon de l'Arsenal, 1991), 54.

4. The 24 May 1871 fire during the Commune in the Paris Hôtel de Ville destroyed the map along with most other municipal records. A copy had been given to the king of Prussia, Wilhelm I, during the 1867 exposition. It was found by A. Morizet in 1930 at the Schloss-Bibliothek in Berlin. David Van Zanten, "Mais quand Haussmann est-il devenu moderne?" in *La Modernité avant Haussmann: Formes de l'espace urbain à Paris, 1801–1853,* ed. Karen Bowie (Paris: Editions Recherches, 2001), 154–55. For an examination of the various versions of Napoleon III's maps and the elusiveness of a definitive state, see Pierre Pinon, *Atlas du Paris haussmannien* (Paris: Parigramme, 2002), 33–39.

5. Louis Girard, *La Politique des travaux publics sous le Second Empire* (Paris: Armand Colin, 1952), 111; quoted in David Harvey, "Paris, 1850–1870," in *Consciousness and the Urban Experience: Studies in the History and Theory of Capitalist Urbanization,* ed. David Harvey (Baltimore: Johns Hopkins University Press, 1985), 70. The railways grew from 1,931 kilometers in 1850 to 17,400 kilometers in 1870 (Harvey, "Paris," 70).

6. Merruau, *Souvenir,* 364.

7. The program was included with a letter dated 2 August 1853, from the minister of the interior to Siméon, confirming the appointment of the commission (Casselle, "Travaux de la Commission des Embellissements," 650).

8. The study of the streets connecting with the railway stations was entrusted to Louis Pécourt (1791–1864), but Siméon was responsible for the report given to the emperor on 27 December 1853 (Casselle, "Travaux de la Commission des Embellissements," 652–53). See also Nicholas Papayanis, *Planning Paris before Haussmann* (Baltimore: Johns Hopkins University Press, 2004), 226–46.

9. Casselle, "Travaux de la Commission des Embellissements," 647 refers to Françoise Choay, ed., *Baron Haussmann: Mémoires* (Paris: Seuil, 2000), 470–71; orig. ed., 2:55, 57–58.

10. "Discours de l'empereur à l'ouverture de la session législative de 1858," *Journal des Chemins de Fer,* 23 January 1858, 58.

11. Léon Say, "Les Chemins de fer," in *Paris guide par les principaux écrivains et artistes de la France,* pt. 2, *La Vie* (Paris: Librairie Internationale, 1867), 2:1657–71.

12. Not until the Gare d'Orsay opened in 1899 (Casselle, "Travaux de la Commission des Embellissements," 654). The Law of 11 June 1842 determined that railway termini should remain at the edges of the city. For reference to projects attempting to drive rail lines into Paris, see Karen Bowie et al., "Polarisation du territoire et développement urbain: Les Gares du Nord et de l'Est et la transformation de Paris au XIXe siècle" (Paris: Plan Urbain, PREDIT, SNCF, and RATP, 1999), 20, n. 2; Papayanis, *Planning Paris,* 201–25.

13. Jeanne Gaillard, *Paris: La Ville, 1852–1870* (Paris: Editions Honoré Champion, 1997), 35–36, 75; Bernard Rouleau, *Le Tracé des rues de Paris: Formation, typologie, fonctions* (Paris: CNRS, 1975), 104.

14. This line was approved on 10 December 1851 and constructed in segments between 1851 and 1867. It would stimulate suburban growth before being replaced by the *grande ceinture* for freight in 1875 and the Métro for passenger traffic at the turn of the century. Harvey, "Paris," 75; Jean Bastié, *La Croissance de la banlieue parisienne* (Paris: Presses Universitaires de France, 1964), 122.

15. Karen Bowie, "The Rothschilds, the Railways, and the Urban Form of 19th Century Paris," in *Die Rothschilds: Eine europäische Familie [The Rothschilds: Essays on the History of a European Family]*, ed. Georg Heuberger (Frankfurt: Thorbecke/Boydell & Brewer and Jüdisches Museum, 1994), 2:90.

16. Pierre Lavedan, "L'Influence de Haussmann: L'Haussmanisation dans l'urbanisme et habitation," *La Vie Urbaine,* n.s. (July-December 1953): 302–17; Harvey, "Paris," 75; David Van Zanten, *Building Paris: Architectural Institutions and the Transformation of the French Capital, 1830–1870* (Cambridge: Cambridge University Press, 1994), 198–99; Priscilla Parkhurst Ferguson, *Paris as Revolution: Writing the 19th Century City* (Berkeley: University of California Press, 1994), 119; Karen Bowie, ed., *La Modernité avant Haussmann: Formes de l'espace urbain à Paris, 1801–1853* (Paris: Editions Recherches, 2001); Pinon, *Atlas,* 24–25; Papayanis, *Planning Paris,* 2004.

17. Pinon, *Atlas,* 6–9 also points out that the detailed nature of Haussmann's *Memoirs* influenced scholarship for decades.

18. Sigfried Giedion, *Space, Time and Architecture* (Cambridge, MA: Harvard University Press, 1941), 648–49.

19. The commission's report would place the railways as the first item, following the order of the emperor's agenda (Casselle, "Travaux de la Commission des Embellissements," 655). This order was maintained in a statement by Merruau on the transformation of Paris, which reflected the emperor's and the commission's order of priority. The change of emphasis would be Haussmann's (Des Cars and Pinon, *Paris-Haussmann,* 74).

20. Casselle, "Travaux de la Commission des Embellissements," 648, 661, 673–74.

21. Haussmann did develop some autonomy (Carmona, *Haussmann,* 408); Casselle, "Travaux de la Commission des Embellissements," 674.

22. Brian Chapman, "Baron Haussmann and the Planning of Paris," *Town Planning Review* 24, no. 3 (1953): 185.

23. Anthony Sutcliffe, *Paris: An Architectural History* (New Haven, CT: Yale University Press, 1993), 84; Haussmann, *Memoirs,* introduction by Françoise Choay, 36 refers to Viollet-le-Duc, *Entretiens sur l'architecture* (Paris: Morel, 1863–72), 2:111–12 (12th entretien); Harvey, "Paris," 74.

24. Des Cars and Pinon, *Paris-Haussmann,* 56; Casselle, "Travaux de la Commission des Embellissements," 664–66.

25. On political issues at stake, see François Caron, *Histoire des chemins de fer en France,* vol. 1, *1740–1883* (Paris: Fayard, 1997), 113, 122–23, 148–49.

26. Theodore Zeldin, *France, 1848–1945* (Oxford: Oxford University Press, 1973–77), 2:1050–51. As of 1 January 1938, the SNCF operated with 51 percent state capital and 49 percent from the former private companies.

27. Karen Bowie, *Les Grandes gares parisiennes: Historique, les grandes gares parisiennes au XIXe siècle* (Paris: Délégation à l'Action Artistique de la Ville de Paris,

1987), 11; in fact, the private companies participated more and more actively in the design and construction of their stations; Bowie, *Modernité,* 261.

28. The Ponts et Chaussées (Public Works) engineers were the elite corps responsible for road design and construction in France since Louis XV. Dependence on state services as opposed to private enterprise to build railways continued to be a concern after the Law of 11 June 1842. In 1859, Auguste Perdonnet (1801–67), France's first railway theoretician, contrasted the work of the companies (adaptable, incentive- and interest-driven) to that of the state (encumbered by administrative bureaucracy, political favoritism, and unproductive personnel habits). Perdonnet, *Notions générales sur les chemins de fer* (Paris: Lacroix et Baudry, 1859), 127. See also Caron, *Histoire des chemins,* 79–80ff.

29. The Legrand star was named after its designer, Alexis Victor Legrand, general director of the Ponts et Chaussées between 1832 and 1847. Alfred Picard, *Les Chemins de fer français: Etude historique sur la constitution et le régime du réseau* (Paris: J. Rothschild, 1884–85), 1:96, citing "Discussion générale sur les chemins de fer à la Chambre des députés, 1838, exposé par M. Legrand, directeur général des Ponts et Chaussees et des Mines," *Moniteur Universel,* 16 February 1838. By 1852, the companies were consolidated into six: Nord, Orléans, Paris-Lyon-Mediterrannée (PLM), Est, Ouest, and Midi.

30. The Grands Boulevards replaced the fortifications under Louis XIV, who did not anticipate needing them again. The toll wall of the *Fermiers généraux* (begun in 1784 with interruption of enforcement between the Revolution and 1799) remained in operation until 31 December 1859, when the toll barrier was transferred to the nineteenth-century fortifications built between 1841 and 1844. Anthony Sutcliffe, *The Autumn of Central Paris: The Defeat of Town Planning, 1850–1970* (London: Edward Arnold, 1970), 147.

31. Compelled to maintain their stations at the fringe of the city, and serviced by railway omnibuses, the railways contributed little to metropolitan transport (Sutcliffe, *Autumn,* 28).

32. Established thoroughfares such as the Rue Saint-Martin (the ancient Roman road), which were no wider than 10 meters, were proving insufficient to handle the vehicular and pedestrian traffic.

33. Sutcliffe, *Autumn,* 21–22.

34. Pierre Lavedan, *Histoire de l'urbanisme à Paris* (Paris: Hachette, 1993), 414.

35. The Rue de Rivoli project had been initiated under Napoleon I. The reference to a Gallo-Roman set of axes crossing at the center of the city is apocryphal. The *cardo* (north-south axis) of the Rues Saint-Jacques and Saint-Martin was parallel to the Second Empire north-south axis, but traces of the Roman settlement, mostly south of the Seine, and its *decumanus* (east-west axis) had been eradicated. On the *croisée* (crossing), see Des Cars and Pinon, *Paris-Haussmann,* 62–69.

36. Haussmann, *Memoirs,* 666. Harvey, "Paris," 74–75 indicates 135 kilometers.

37. Haussmann, *Memoirs,* 112–14, 122–23, 305, 457, 556, 623, 716, and 1030; orig. ed., 1:67–71, 84–85, 391; 2:34, 201, 313, 469; and 3:406. Haussmann also mentions interest in tunnel construction projects and providing state oversight for PLM accounts during his tenure in the Yonne department (308; orig. ed., 1:395–96).

38. Wolfgang Schivelbusch, *The Railway Journey: Trains and Travel in the 19th Century* (New York: Urizen Books, 1979), 182.

39. The Paris cemeteries were Montmartre, Père Lachaise, and Montparnasse. This plan was actually well thought-out but presented late in Haussmann's tenure at the Hôtel de Ville. Connected in public opinion to the Montmartre cemetery displacement of sepulchers, the plan was never examined on its own merits (Georges Valance, *Haussmann, le grand* [Paris: Flammarion, 2000], 270–73). See also Karen Bowie and Simon Texier, eds., *Paris et ses chemins de fer* (Paris: Action Artistique de la Ville de Paris, 2003), 103–11.

40. David Van Zanten, "Mais quand Haussmann est-il devenu moderne?" in Bowie, *Modernité,* 162–63; Nicholas Papayanis, "Urbanisme du Paris souterrain: Premiers projets de chemin de fer urbain et naissance de l'urbanisme des cités modernes," *Histoire, Economie, Sociétés* 17, no. 4 (1998): 745–70; Allan Mitchell, "La Gare centrale: Un rêve avorté," in Bowie and Texier, *Paris et ses chemins de fer,* 95–101. Flachat and Armand were responsible for the Péreire-sponsored Gare Saint-Lazare design.

41. This is illustrated by the organization charts of Haussmann's services. Haussmann, *Memoirs,* 1137–47.

42. Schivelbusch, *Railway Journey,* 182.

43. In the preface to her edition of Haussmann's *Memoirs,* Françoise Choay comments on Haussman's belief in the superiority of training at the Ponts et Chaussées over the Beaux-Arts (Haussmann, *Memoirs,* 25); Haussman's statement, 68, orig. ed., 1:x-xi. After progressive reconfigurations, Haussmann's staff, which he termed "instruments of his plans," was headed by two engineers from the Ponts et Chaussées, Adolphe Alphand (1817–91) and Eugène Belgrand (1810–78), and two Beaux-Arts-trained architects, Victor Baltard (1805–74) and Eugène Deschamps (in charge of mapping services) (Casselle, "Travaux de la Commission des Embellissements," 668–69).

44. These include Hittorff at the Gare du Nord, Armand at the Gare Saint-Lazare, and Duquesney at the Gare de l'Est, as well as Labrouste (Carmona, *Haussmann,* 543).

45. Haussmann, *Memoirs,* 17.

46. Giedion, *Space, Time,* 660.

47. François Prosper Jacqmin, *De l'Exploitation des chemins de fer: Leçons faites en 1867 à l'Ecole Impériale des Ponts et Chaussées* (Paris: Garnier Frères, 1868), 1:74.

48. This was limited to large cities (Van Zanten, *Building Paris,* 179–81).

49. The first Gare du Nord and Gare de l'Est were entrusted to Ponts et Chaussées engineers (Bowie, *Grandes gares,* 11; Sutcliffe, *Paris,* 95, 96, 103).

50. Papayanis, *Planning Paris,* 10.

51. Lavedan, *Histoire de l'urbanisme,* 420.

52. Jean Castex, *Formes urbaines: De l'Îlot à la barre* (Paris: Bordas, 1977), 26; Erwin Gutkind, *International History of City Development,* vol. 5, *France and Belgium* (New York: Free Press, 1970), 261.

53. Haussmann, *Memoirs,* 2:185; quoted in Lavedan, *Histoire de l'urbanisme,* 420.

54. Haussmann, *Memoirs,* 728, 828–29, 1101; orig. ed., 2:488; 3:60–61, 530–31.

55. Gutkind, *International History,* 5:261.

56. Maurice Agulhon, Françoise Choay, and Maurice Crubellier, *La Ville de l'âge industriel: Le Cycle haussmannien,* in *Histoire de la France urbaine,* ed. G. Duby (Paris: Seuil, 1998), 4:106–14. For a list of alignment and expropriation legislation, see Rouleau, *Tracé,* 112–13.

57. Archives de la Ville de Paris, D6S9/4 and Calepins du Cadastre, Archives de la Ville de Paris, D1P4-Carton 1056.

58. Maxime du Camp, *Paris, ses organes, ses fonctions, sa vie dans la seconde moitié du XIXe siècle,* 2nd ed. (Paris: Hachette, 1875), 6:255; Maurice Halbwachs, *Les Expropriations et le prix des terrains à Paris (1860–1900)* (Paris: Cornély, 1909), 29–35; Harvey, "Paris," 87–88.

59. Haussmann, *Memoirs,* 617, 666–67; orig. ed., 2:303–4, 385–88.

60. The first network covered 9,467 meters and was inaugurated on 5 April 1858.

61. Declared of public utility between 1854 and 1859 (Pinon, *Atlas,* 60), the second network included 21 new streets or 26 kilometers (26,294 meters) to be laid within ten years outside of the city center. David H. Pinkney, *Napoleon III and the Rebuilding of Paris* (Princeton, NJ: Princeton University Press, 1958), 183; Lavedan, *Histoire de l'urbanisme,* 424; Johannes Willms, *Paris, Capital of Europe: From the Revolution to the Belle Epoque* (New York: Holmes & Meier, 1997), 264.

62. Van Zanten, *Building Paris,* 213 implies that the connections to the annexed areas were more significant than the links to and between the stations.

63. The third network reached 28,000 meters. It was declared of public utility between 1859 and 1866. Pinkney, *Rebuilding,* 169–73.

64. Willms, *Paris,* 265; Pinon, *Atlas,* 69–70ff.

65. The publication of Jules Ferry's "Les Comptes d'Haussmann" in 1867–68 in *Le Temps* gave the prefect's operations much adverse publicity. A Rothschild protégé, Léon Say, had first drawn public attention to the city's finances in the January and February issues of the *Journal des Débats* (Harvey, "Paris," 107; Pinkney, *Rebuilding,* 196). Pinkney, *Rebuilding,* 174–209 contains a clear account of Haussmann's financial practices. See also Geneviève Massa-Gille, *Histoire des emprunts de la Ville de Paris, 1814–1875* (Paris: Commission des Travaux Historiques de la Ville de Paris, 1973), 279–306.

66. Persigny's lack of success in encouraging Berger, Haussmann's predecessor, to adopt this concept had led to the cautious prefect's replacement by Haussmann, who agreed with such financing.

67. The largest road transport company operated with a capital of 6 million; the railway companies averaged 50 to 80 million. Jocelyne George, *Paris province de la révolution à la mondialisation* (Paris: Librairie Arthème Fayard, 1998), 77.

68. For a narrative on the Rothschild-Péreire rivalry, see Jean Bouvier, *Les Rothschild* (Brussels: Editions Complexe, 1983), 151–96; Bowie, "Rothschilds," 97.

69. The Rothschild French assets were derived from the loans they made to the state after Waterloo (Zeldin, *France,* 1:78). Rondo E. Cameron, *France and the Economic Development of Europe, 1800–1914: Conquests of Peace and Seeds of War* (Princeton, NJ: Princeton University Press, 1961), 107; Harvey, "Paris," 76–77.

70. Cameron, *Economic Development,* 114–17.

71. Emile (1800–1875) and Isaac (1806–80) Péreire.

72. The Société Générale du Crédit Mobilier was founded with the support of the Fould Bank and Napoleon III. Others included the Crédit Foncier, the Crédit Lyonnais (1863), the Crédit Agricole, and in 1864 the Société Générale (Zeldin, *France,* 1:82, 84); Harvey, "Paris," 76–77, 100.

73. The Rothschilds had strong influence on the emperor (Harvey, "Paris," 207); Bowie, "Polarisation," 7, n. 9; Bowie, "Rothschilds," 92.

74. Lavedan, *Histoire de l'urbanisme,* 369. Rothschild had predicted this failure in a letter to the emperor and may have been instrumental in it. Zeldin, *France,* 1:83; Harvey, "Paris," 107, 116.

75. Harvey, "Paris," 78–80; Bouvier, *Rothschild,* 145–50. To the state-backed Crédit Mobilier, founded by the Péreires in 1852, it responded by establishing the Réunion Financière in 1855 with a Rothschild controlling interest and foreign banking connections, which gave the consortium international scope (Bowie, "Rothschilds," 92).

76. Pinon, *Atlas,* 41; Harvey, "Paris," 79. The Péreires were also associated with Haussmann's works, especially in the Parc Monceau area.

77. Harvey, "Paris," 87.

78. Zeldin, *France,* 1:554.

79. H. J. Dyos, "Railways and Housing in Victorian London: I, Attila in London," *Journal of Transport History* 2 (1955): 16.

80. Lynda Nead, *Victorian Babylon: People, Streets and Images in Nineteenth-Century London* (New Haven, CT: Yale University Press, 2000), 29; *Illustrated London News,* 30 July 1864, 114.

81. John R. Kellett, *The Impact of Railways on Victorian Cities* (London: Routledge & Kegan Paul, 1969), 287.

82. A. S. Wohl, "The Housing of the Working Classes in London, 1815–1914," in *The History of Working Class Housing, A Symposium,* ed. Stanley D. Chapman (Totowa, NJ: Rowman and Littlefield, 1971), 18; Patricia E. Malcolmson, "Getting a Living in the Slums of Victorian Kensington," *London Journal* 1 (May 1975): 31.

83. Arthur Cawston, *A Comprehensive Scheme for Street Improvements in London* (London: Edward Stanford, 1893), 1, 49, 62.

Chapter 5

1. *Quartier,* or ward, literally quarter, or one-fourth of one of the city's 20 administrative subdivisions or *arrondissements.* The annexation of the area between the *octroi* (toll) wall of the *Fermiers généraux* (tax administrators) and the 1840 fortifications in 1860 was accompanied by redistricting from 12 to the 20 *arrondissements* still in effect today. As Karen Bowie indicates, current usage of the term *quartier* is ambiguous, referring either to the administrative subdivision or to the neighborhood, with its affective and social connotations. Karen Bowie, "Les Gares du Nord et de l'Est au siècle dernier," in *Villes en gares,* ed. Isaac Joseph (La Tour d'Aigues: Editions de l'Aube, 1999), 35, 39.

2. Carole Saturno, "La Gare de l'Est et les guides de Paris, un siècle de modes d'emploi," in *Villes en gares,* ed. Isaac Joseph (La Tour d'Aigues: Editions de l'Aube, 1999), 104.

3. Karen Bowie and Simon Texier, eds. *Paris et ses chemins de fer* (Paris: Action Artistique de la Ville de Paris, 2003), 26, 246.

4. The difficult relationship between Napoleon III and the baron James de Rothschild, director of the Compagnie du Nord (Northern Railway), was common knowledge (Karen Bowie et al., "Polarisation du territoire et développement urbain: Les Gares du Nord et de l'Est et la transformation de Paris au XIXe siècle" [Paris: Plan Urbain, PREDIT, SNCF, and RATP, 1999], 7).

5. Pierre Lavedan, *Histoire de l'urbanisme à Paris* (Paris: Hachette, 1993), 369.

6. As, for example, Andrézieux-Roanne, Andrézieux-Saint-Etienne, and Saint-Etienne-Lyon.

7. Isabelle Guérin Brot and Jean Pierre Babelon, *Les Débuts du chemin de fer en France, 1831–1870* (Paris: Ministère de la Culture et de l'Environnement and

SNCF, 1977), 38. The London and Greenwich Railway, first partially opened in 1836, was a similar project.

8. On Saint-Simonianism, see Theodore Zeldin, *France, 1848–1945* (Oxford: Oxford University Press, 1973–77), 1:437–38; Guérin, *Débuts du chemin de fer*, 12; Lavedan, *Histoire de l'urbanisme*, 372; Barrie M. Ratcliffe, "The Origins of the Paris-Saint-Germain Railway: Some Entrepreneurial and Financial Problems in the Launching of Railways in France in the 1830s," *Journal of Transport History* 1, no. 4 (1972): 197–219. On James de Rothschild and railways, see François Caron, *Histoire des chemins de fer en France, 1740–1883* (Paris: Fayard, 1997), 112, 120, 121. The Péreire brothers were aware of the problems of mobilizing capital for the railways. Robert Bruce Carlisle, *The Proffered Crown: Saint-Simonianism and the Doctrine of Hope* (Baltimore: Johns Hopkins University Press, 1987), 210.

9. After a temporary station on the Rue de Londres near the Place de l'Europe. Lavedan, *Histoire de l'urbanisme*, 373; Barrie M. Ratcliffe, "The Building of the Paris-Saint-Germain Railway: Some Entrepreneurial and Financial Problems of the Launching of Railways in France in the 1830s and 1840s," *Journal of Transport History*, n.s., 2 (February 1973): 29–32.

10. Lavedan, *Histoire de l'urbanisme*, 369.

11. Karen Bowie, *Les Grandes gares parisiennes: Historique, les grandes gares parisiennes au XIXe siècle* (Paris: Délégation à l'Action Artistique de la Ville de Paris, 1987), 11.

12. These stations were to be as close to the Seine as possible (Johannes Willms, *Paris, Capital of Europe: From the Revolution to the Belle Epoque* [New York: Holmes & Meier, 1997], 226).

13. Forty hectares was the surface area of the first stations in London and Brussels, as well (Bowie, *Grandes gares*, 18). On the evolution of the city council's position toward station implantation between 1832 and 1844, see Barrie M. Ratcliffe, "Urban Space and the Siting of the Parisian Railway Station, 1830–1847," *Proceedings of the Western Society for French History* 15 (1988): 229–31.

14. Léonce Reynaud and Edouard Collignon, eds., *Les Travaux publics de la France* (Paris: J. Rothschild, 1883), 2:8.

15. Ratcliffe, "Urban Space," 227. Concerns for the public good encouraged lines serving cities and their people, as opposed to the roads, which had been designed initially to link noblemen's castles, outside of cities (M. Henry, *Considérations générales sur l'établissement des chemins de fer* [Boulogne, France: Le Roy-Mabile, 1836], 1). Auguste Perdonnet, *Traité élémentaire des chemins de fer* (Paris: Langlois et Leclercq, 1855–56), 2:70–74.

16. Bernard Lepetit, *Les Villes dans la France moderne, 1740–1840* (Paris: Albin Michel, 1988), 379, 380. René Clozier also points out that most early railway engineers had been trained during the canal building years and had more of a track record for building in valleys than on inclines (Clozier, *La Gare du Nord* [Paris: J.-B. Baillière, 1940], 32). Pierre-Edmond Teisserenc-de-Bort, *Des Principes généraux qui doivent présider au choix des tracés des chemins de fer* (Paris: Schneider et Langrand, 1843), 54. Teisserenc also recommended taking strategic considerations into account. On the relationship between the *tracé* and the Law of 11 June 1842, see Caron, *Histoire des chemins*, 130–31, on lobbying efforts, 185–91.

17. David Van Zanten, *Building Paris: Architectural Institutions and the Transformation of the French Capital, 1830–1870* (Cambridge: Cambridge

University Press, 1994), 202; Clozier, *Gare du Nord,* 23–25; Bowie, "Polarisation," 17; Karen Bowie, "Gares et villes au XIXe siècle: Deux ingénieurs des Ponts et Chaussées et l'implantation des gares du Nord et de l'Est à Paris," *Annales des Ponts et Chaussées* 89 (April 1999): 9.

18. Bowie, "Gares du Nord," 41; Ratcliffe, "Urban Space," 227, 230.

19. Promoter for the Paris–Saint-Germain line, Emile Péreire also held the position of administrator for the Nord until 1853. Bowie, *Grandes gares,* 96–98; Bertrand Gille, *Histoire de la maison Rothschild* (Geneva: Droz, 1965–67), 2:174. *Chemin de fer, lignes du Nord et de l'Est, entrée dans Paris: Mémoire adressé aux deux chambres et au ministère par les délégués de la majorité des arrondissements de Paris* (Paris, 1842); *A messieurs les députés: Mémoire adressé par les 3e, 4e, 5e, 7e et 8e arrondissements au conseil général municipal de la Seine* (Paris: E.-B. Delanchy, 1842); Compagnie des Chemins de Fer de l'Est, *La Gare de l'Est* (Paris: Chemin de Fer de l'Est, 1931); Clozier, *Gare du Nord,* 28; Karen Bowie, ed., *La Modernité avant Haussmann: Formes de l'espace urbain à Paris, 1801–1853* (Paris: Editions Recherches, 2001), 259–62.

20. Lavedan, *Histoire de l'urbanisme,* 374, 398; Karen Bowie, "L'Implantation des gares du Nord et de l'Est dans Paris, 1830–1870: Premiers résultats d'une recherche," in *La Gare: Dedans, dehors* (Paris: Plan Urbain, DRAST, RATP, and SNCF, 1996), 141–42; "Des Gares communes," *Journal des Chemins de Fer,* 23 July 1842, 137, and 10 September 1842, 196–97. Pierre Lavedan, *La Question du déplacement de Paris et du transfert des Halles au conseil municipal sous la monarchie de juillet* (Paris: Commission des Travaux Historiques, 1969).

21. Auguste Perdonnet, *Traité élémentaire des chemins de fer* (Paris: Langlois et Leclercq, 1855–56), 2:78; Ibid., 3rd ed. (Paris: Garnier, 1865), 1:129–30; Auguste Perdonnet and Camille Polonceau, *Portefeuille de l'ingénieur des chemins de fer* (Paris: E. Lacroix, 1861), 1:430–33.

22. Clozier, *Gare du Nord,* 29–30. Plans such as those of Delagrive (1728), Verniquet (1791), as well as Vasserot and Bellanger (1827–36), and others.

23. Bernard Rouleau, *Le Tracé des rues de Paris: Formation, typologie, fonctions* (Paris: CNRS, 1975), 95–98. Personalities played a role in these disputes, Haussmann being more forceful than Rambuteau or Berger, his predecessors. Bowie, "Polarisation," 23, 35–37; Patrick Cognasson, *Gare de l'Est: Porte ouverte sur l'Europe* (Paris: La Vie du Rail et des Transports, 1994), 39, 41.

24. Bowie, "Polarisation," summary, 2; Bowie, *Grandes gares,* 23.

25. The expropriation judgment was handed down on 29 March 1843 (Clozier, *Gare du Nord,* 35); the concession was adjudicated on 9 September 1845, sanctioned by royal order on the 10th (Caron, *Histoire des chemins,* 180–83).

26. Caron, *Histoire des chemins,* 121, 150. James de Rothschild was supportive of the early Péreire railway projects and became involved in railways as he recognized his English brother's mistake, who remained uninvolved with British railways and missed out on substantial profits. Carlisle, *Proffered Crown,* 210. See also Jean Bouvier, *Les Rothschild* (Brussels: Editions Complexe, 1983), 123–35. Bertrand Gille, *Histoire de la maison Rothschild* (Geneva: Droz, 1965–67), 2:159, 166. Other members of the Rothschild European banking establishments were involved in railway development projects in other countries. See Marie-Noëlle Polino and Ralf Roth, eds., *The City and the Railway in Europe* (Aldershot: Ashgate, 2003), 21, 157.

27. Rapports aux actionnaires: 1855–62 and 1863–69 (Le Mans, 091C17, 091C18). He was succeeded by his son, Alphonse (1827–1905). "Mort du

Baron James de Rothschild (1792–1868)," *Journal des Chemins de Fer,* 21 November 1868, 755.

28. Louis Léger Vallée, *Exposé général des études faites pour le tracé des chemins de fer de Paris en Belgique et en Angleterre et d'Angleterre en Belgique* (Paris: Ministère des Travaux Publics, de l'Agriculture et du Commerce, Direction Générale des Ponts et Chaussées, Imprimerie Royale, 1837); Clozier, *Gare du Nord,* 25–28, 34; Lavedan, *Histoire de l'urbanisme,* 374; Bowie, *Avant Haussmann,* 254–63.

29. Bowie, *Grandes gares,* 96–99; Gare du Nord, Projet Bourla, Archives Nationales, Série F14 10330-1-54, 56, 57, Plan général, projet à être exécuté par Cockerill, A. Bourla et Ed. Renaud, Architectes Ingénieurs.

30. Bowie, "Polarisation," 23; and Doc. Nord/1&2, Onfroy de Bréville, "Département de la Seine, Ville de Paris, Ministère des Travaux Publics, Ponts et Chaussées, Chemin de fer de Paris en Belgique, Gare de Paris, Légende explicative des dispositions que présentent les plans parcellaires des terrains que cette gare doit occuper, 23 janvier 1843," SNCF Archives des Domaines Région Nord (Gare du Nord); Clozier, *Gare du Nord,* 34, fig. 6.

31. J.-A. Durbec, *Contribution à l'histoire du chemin de fer de Paris à la mer (Paris-Rouen-Le Havre): Les Avant-projets et la réalisation (1825–1843)* (Paris: Imprimerie Nationale, 1956); Clozier, *Gare du Nord,* 32; Bowie, "Implantation," 137–39; Bowie, "Polarisation," 27, 29–31.

32. The real estate, with an area of 65,367 square meters, was acquired in May 1845 for F1.5 million; the concession was granted in September. Pauline Prévost-Marcilhacy, "Lotissements autour de la gare du Nord: Rôle de James de Rothschild," in "Polarisation du territoire et développement urbain," ed. Karen Bowie (Paris: Plan Urbain, PREDIT, SNCF, and RATP, 1999), 39–45.

33. The exchange is documented by a contract and a detailed plan. Rapports aux actionnaires: 1855–62, 091C17 (Le Mans), 28 April 1856, 4; Bowie, "Polarisation," 34, 37; Prévost-Marcilhacy, "Lotissements," 45.

34. Prévost-Marcilhacy, "Lotissements," 39–49. Prévost-Marcilhacy correlated the *calepins du cadastre* (cadastral notebooks—Archives de la Ville de Paris, D1P4) and *sommier foncier* (real-estate register—Archives de la Ville de Paris, DQ18) with the notarial archives of the Rothschild family, especially the inventory after the death of James de Rothschild in 1868 to document real-estate activity.

35. Onfroy de Bréville, "Gare de Paris," SNCF archives. The Saint-Germain station only covered 2.5 hectares. Bowie, "Gares et villes," 4–7.

36. Carroll L. V. Meeks, *The Railroad Station: An Architectural History* (New Haven, CT: Yale University Press, 1956), 61. Reynaud was professor of architecture at the Ecole Polytechnique and also director of the Ecole des Ponts et Chaussées. Design and organization of the station were considered disappointing in the *Journal des Chemins de Fer* (25 October 1845, 796 and 6 December 1845, 916 [Supplement]). For more extensive descriptions, see Bowie, *Grandes gares,* 100–104; Clozier, *Gare du Nord,* 34–37; and Donald David Schneider, *The Work and Doctrine of Jacques Ignace Hittorff, 1792–1867* (New York: Garland, 1977), 1:616–21.

37. *Journal des Chemins de Fer,* 1843, 438; 1844, 374; 1845, 581 and 796.

38. Caron, *Histoire des chemins,* 196.

39. The first Gare du Nord was dismantled and rebuilt in Lille. Clozier, *Gare du Nord,* 39; Schneider, *Hittorff,* 1:619–20. Bowie, *Grandes gares,* 103–4; Allan Mitchell, *The Great Train Race: Railways and the Franco-German Rivalry* (New York: Berghahn Books, 2000), 24.

40. A site near Saint-Philippe-du-Roule, a stone's throw from the Gare Saint-Lazare. Schneider, *Hittorff,* 1:620, 648; Clozier, *Gare du Nord,* 4549.

41. Karl Hammer, *Jakob Ignaz Hittorff: Ein Pariser Baumeister, 1792–1867* (Stuttgart: Anton Hiersemann, 1968), 206, nn. 3–6, citing mainly Paris, Archives Nationales 48AQ; quoted in Schneider, *Hittorff,* 1:620.

42. Karen Bowie, "The Rothschilds, the Railways, and the Urban Form of 19th Century Paris," in *Die Rothschilds: Eine europäische Familie [The Rothschilds: Essays on the History of a European Family],* ed. Georg Heuberger (Frankfurt: Thorbecke/Boydell & Brewer Jüdisches Museum, 1994), 2:92, refers to Schneider, *Hittorff,* 1:620–24.

43. Schneider, *Hittorff,* 1:612; Hammer, *Hittorff,* 207.

44. Bowie, *Grandes gares,* 109.

45. Thomas von Joest, "Hittorff et la nouvelle gare du Nord," in *Hittorff, un architecte du XIXème siècle,* ed. Thomas von Joest and Claudine de Vaulchier (Paris: Musées de la ville de Paris, 1986), 269, 276; Bowie, *Grandes gares,* 112.

46. Letter to Hittorff dated 16 January 1861, Archives Nationales, Archives de la Compagnie des Chemins de fer du Nord, 48AQ2844; cited in Von Joest, "Hittorff," 271.

47. Documents held by the Direction régionale de la SNCF, Paris-Nord, 18 Rue de Dunkerque; cited in Von Joest, "Hittorff," 272.

48. Rapport sur la construction de la gare définitive de Paris, lu par M. Couche, 5 May 1860, Archives Nationales, Archives de la Compagnie des Chemins de fer du Nord, 48AQ13; quoted in Von Joest, "Hittorff," 270.

49. As Karen Bowie points out, by 13 prominent Prix de Rome sculptors (Bowie, *Grandes gares,* 110–12).

50. Rapports aux actionnaires: 1855–62, 091C17 (Le Mans), 28 April 1862, 4.

51. Bowie, "Polarisation," summary, 2, quoting a pun by Bertrand Gille.

52. David Harvey, "Paris, 1850–1870," in *Consciousness and the Urban Experience: Studies in the History and Theory of Capitalist Urbanization,* ed. David Harvey (Baltimore: Johns Hopkins University Press, 1985), 80.

53. Bowie, "Rothschild," 95, 97. Jeanne Gaillard, *Paris: La Ville, 1852–1870* (Paris: Editions Honoré Champion, 1997) has shown that the royalist factions had been excluded from the profits of the Second Empire reconfigurations.

54. Louis Bergeron, *Les Rothschild et les autres. . . . : La Gloire des banquiers* (Paris: Perrin, 1991), 154.

55. Bowie, "Rothschild," 93–95.

56. "Foreign Railway Works," *The Builder,* 18 (3 March 1860): 140; "Edifices de l'industrie privée," *Revue Générale de l'Architecture et des Travaux Publics* 20 (1862): cols. 283–84. Approval was still expected at the 29 April 1861 shareholders' meeting and was granted in May (Rapports aux actionnaires: 1855–62, 091C17 [Le Mans], 29 April 1861, 2; and 28 April 1862, 4).

57. Hammer, *Hittorff,* 211; Schneider, *Hittorff,* 1:624, 647–82ff. and 2:342, n. 27.

58. Schneider, *Hittorff,* 1:641–48; Bowie, *Grandes gares,* 106–7. Haussmann's influence may also be detected in the absence of polychrome decoration in the building. Henry-Russell Hitchcock, *Architecture: Nineteenth and Twentieth Centuries* (Harmondsworth, UK: Penguin Books, 1958), 45, 433, n. 4; Schneider, *Hittorff,* 1:637–38.

59. An ancestry the two men had in common, since Haussmann's family originated from Alsace. Françoise Choay, ed., *Baron Haussmann: Mmémoires*

(Paris: Seuil, 2000), 927, 1078; orig. ed., 3:228, 490. Haussmann favored Baltard, his former Lycée Henri IV Protestant classmate. Lavedan, *Histoire de l'urbanisme*, 421.

60. Schneider, *Hittorff,* 1:342–44, 357–59. The exterior panels were installed in 1846 and 1856 and removed by 1861, if not before.

61. Haussmann, *Memoirs,* 1079; orig. ed., 3:491.

62. Ibid.

63. Ibid., 1085; orig. ed., 3:503. This consultation would have taken place in 1858, prior to Hittorff's involvement with the Gare du Nord project (Clozier, *Gare du Nord,* 42–43). It is likely that Haussmann is making reference to a later modification made in concert with the architect (Bowie, *Grandes gares,* 106). See also Lavedan, *Histoire de l'urbanisme,* 436 and Schneider, *Hittorff,* 1:624.

64. Although there is evidence of Haussmann's differences with Hittorff, there is no documentation of conflict between the Rothschilds and the prefect. Haussmann's position toward Rothschild reflects political allegiance and tensions related to power and financial control, not a personal relationship. See Prévost-Marcilhacy, "Lotissements," 43.

65. The new station covered a surface area three times the first and had eight tracks and ten platforms (Clozier, *Gare du Nord,* 45–50). Clozier, *Gare du Nord,* 46 gives the shed dimensions as 72 meters in width, 38 meters in height, and 200 meters in length for the central nave, with side aisles measuring 30 meters in width and 15 meters in height. Meeks, *Railroad Station,* 168 and the *Revue Générale de l'Architecture et des Travaux Publics* 20 (1862): cols. 283–84 describe the span as 72 meters with 36 meters for the central nave and two 18-meter side aisles, which coincides with a reading of the plan as published by Perdonnet in *Portefeuille de l'ingénieur des chemins de fer* (Paris: E. Lacroix, 1873), pls. 50 & 51.

66. For a list of specific sculptures and their attributions, see Von Joest, "Hittorff," 272, and Bowie, *Grandes gares,* 110–12.

67. Schneider, *Hittorff,* 1:650; Von Joest, "Hittorff," 273. Expenses as of 31 December 1862 had reached F2,459,853. Rapports aux actionnaires: 1863–69, 091C18 (Le Mans), 30 April 1863, 6.

68. Designed by Lejeune (Von Joest, "Hittorff," 270), these were completed and occupied in June 1862. Rapports aux actionnaires: 1863–69, 091C18 (Le Mans), 30 April 1863, 6.

69. Meeks, *Railroad Station,* 58 credits Reynaud with work on the shed but gives no source; Hammer and other sources offer no evidence to support this. See Schneider, *Hittorff,* 1:627–28, 2:343n36; Bowie, *Grandes gares,* 106–7. Hittorff was assisted by his son, Charles-Joseph (1825–98), and by the young H. H. Richardson (1838–86) (Schneider, *Hittorff,* 1:629, 2:344–46n41).

70. Meeks, *Railroad Station,* 67.

71. Haussmann, *Memoirs,* 1085; orig. ed., 3:503.

72. Hammer, *Hittorff,* 211–12 and n. 23. The original plan was for a broad circular *place* (square) at the crossing (Van Zanten, *Building Paris,* 253). Schneider, *Hittorff,* 1:674–79.

73. Schneider, *Hittorff,* 1:678; Van Zanten, *Building Paris,* 250–55. Schneider equates the effect with Perrault's east façade for the Louvre and Gabriel's Place de la Concorde with its view toward the Church of La Madeleine.

74. There were around 400 international travelers leaving or arriving at the Gare du Nord daily in 1868. François Caron, *Histoire de l'exploitation d'un grand*

réseau: La Compagnie du Chemin de Fer du Nord, 1846–1937 (Paris: Mouton, 1973), 145.

75. Van Zanten, *Building Paris,* 254. The most comprehensive description of the station is in Karen Bowie, *Grandes gares,* 104–16. For an attempt at stylistic analysis, see Schneider, *Hittorff,* 1:674–79. For an examination of the place of the station in Hittorff's work, see Van Zanten, *Building Paris,* 250–55. See also, Hammer, *Hittorff,* 206–16, figs. 130–41; Von Joest, "Hittorff," 266–77.

76. Rapports aux actionnaires: 1855–62, 091C17 (Le Mans), 30 April 1855, 5 and 27 April 1860, 2.

77. Clozier, *Gare du Nord,* 54–60, 69–70ff.

78. For examples of successive modification and expansion projects, see Archives de Paris, Chemin de Fer du Nord, D6S9/4, "Gares de Paris et de la Chapelle," 1846–1914.

79. Archives de Paris, Chemin de Fer du Nord, D6S9/4; and Archives de la Ville de Paris, D1P4, Cartons 409, 411, and 413.

80. Maurice Halbwachs, *Les Expropriations et le prix des terrains à Paris (1860–1900)* (Paris: Cornély, 1909), 188–89.

81. For a brief examination of the initial studies, see Bowie, "Polarisation," 74–78. See also "Allocation pour l'exécution par l'Etat de l'infrastructure du chemin de Paris à Strasbourg et des embranchements de Reims et de Metz," in *Les Chemins de fer français: Etude historique sur la constitution et le régime du réseau,* ed. Alfred Picard (Paris: J. Rothschild, 1884–85), 1:439–41; *Journal des Chemins de Fer,* 29 November 1845, 892. Meaux was also connected with Paris by the Canal de l'Ourcq, completed in 1838 (Bowie, "Implantation," 140–41).

82. Pierre-Sophie Cabanel de Sermet, "Rapport de l'ingénieur en chef sur les tracés étudiés et sur celui à adopter pour la première section du chemin de fer de Paris à Strasbourg," Centre des Archives SNCF, Le Mans, Archives Région Est, 1845, 104 pp. mss, Carton VB4. See also Karen Bowie, "Introduction au rapport de l'ingénieur en chef des Ponts et Chaussées Cabanel de Sermet sur les tracés étudiés et sur celui à adopter pour la première section du chemin de fer de Paris à Strasbourg," *Revue d' Histoire des Chemins de fer* 23 (Fall 2000): 79–137.

83. The Faubourg Saint-Antoine option with access through the Bois de Vincennes was vetoed by the military authorities, who were determined to maintain the Bois as military land. Sermet pointed out the strategic potential of the line for communication between the Vincennes military facilities and the fortifications in the east. The *Journal des Chemins de Fer* (29 November 1845, 892) related the competitive struggle between the eleventh (then eighth) and the tenth (then fifth) *arrondissements* (districts) to become the site of the station. The tenth *arrondissement* prevailed for the Gare de l'Est, and the eleventh would become the site of the Gare de Lyon. Bowie, "Implantation," 140–42; Bowie, "Polarisation," 73–90.

84. Karen Bowie, "Polarisation," 19 raises the question whether the engineer had misestimated the situation or if this was the result of rapid urbanization in the area.

85. Bowie, "Polarisation," 85; Louis Maurice Jouffroy, *Une Etape de la construction des grandes lignes de chemin de fer en France: La Ligne de Paris à la frontière d'Allemagne, 1825–1852* (Paris: J. Barreau & Cie, 1932), 2:211–17.

86. Despite recent improvements, such as wide sidewalks. Saussay, *Les Gares des grandes lignes de chemin de fer par rapport aux grandes villes qu'elles desservent*

(Paris: Maulde et Renou, 1845), 10. *Journal des Chemins de Fer*, 29 November 1845, 892 and 13 December 1845, 937; Bowie, "Polarisation," 85–87; Cognasson, *Gare de l'Est*, 19.

87. Compagnie du Chemin de Fer de Paris à Strasbourg, 1846–54, 091B16 (Le Mans), 11 November 1846 (Assemblée extraordinaire), 17–18.

88. It was inaugurated on 2 September 1849. Compagnie des Chemins de Fer de l'Est, *La Gare de l'Est* (Paris: Chemin de Fer de l'Est, 1931), 2.

89. Perdonnet, *Traité*, 1st ed., 2:75–78. More detailed descriptions of the station can be found in 2:112–13; Bowie, *Grandes gares*, 32–38, 43, 117–23; Cognasson, *Gare de l'Est*, 37–42.

90. Meeks, *Railroad Station*, 61.

91. Anthony Sutcliffe, *Paris: An Architectural History* (New Haven, CT: Yale University Press, 1993), 96–97.

92. Anthony Sutcliffe, "Architecture and Civic Design in Nineteenth-Century Paris," in *Growth and Transformation of the Modern City*, ed. Ingrid Hammarström and Thomas Hall (Stockholm: Swedish Council for Building Research, 1979), 94.

93. Some of this station expansion was mandated by the state and resisted by the companies, which were concerned about the financial implications of such projects. Allan Mitchell, "Private Enterprise or Public Service? The Eastern Railway Company and the French State in the Nineteenth Century," *Journal of Modern History* 69, no. 1 (1997): 22. The new façade has a width of 180 meters, same as the Gare du Nord. This project required the expropriation of 48 buildings and the displacement of 1,021 tenants, 500 of whom the company rehoused without official mandate to do so (Cognasson, *Gare de l'Est*, 31–32). See also Perdonnet, *Traité*, 3rd ed., 128; Bowie, *Grandes gares*, 119–20.

94. Lavedan, *Histoire de l'urbanisme*, 488. The park project is similar in concept to the "Jardin Atlantique" at the Gare Montparnasse. Bowie, *Paris et ses chemins de fer*, 242.

95. Jean Bastié, *La Croissance de la banlieue parisienne* (Paris: Presses Universitaires de France, 1964), 107–8.

96. David H. Pinkney, *Napoleon III and the Rebuilding of Paris* (Princeton, NJ: Princeton University Press, 1958), 39.

97. Sutcliffe, *Paris*, 97.

98. Gaillard, *Paris*, 70–71, with reference to AS DP2 37, notice Rochechouart.

99. Grands travaux d'utilité publique. Le quartier Poissonnière. Le clos Saint-Lazare. Les abords de l'Hôpital Lariboisière," *Revue Municipale*, 16 October 1854, 1330–34; cited in Von Joest, "Hittorff," 269.

100. Rouleau, *Tracé*, 95–98; Pierre Pinon, "L'Inscription de la gare du Nord dans le réseau viaire des quartiers Nord de Paris entre les faubourgs Poissonnière et Saint-Martin," in *La Gare: Dedans, dehors* (Paris: Plan Urbain, DRAST, RATP, and SNCF, 1996), 161–86; Pierre Pinon, "L'Inscription de la gare du Nord dans le réseau viaire des quartiers Nord de Paris entre les faubourgs Poissonnière et Saint-Martin," in Bowie, "Polarisation," 51–70; Pierre Pinon, *Atlas du Paris haussmannien* (Paris: Parigramme, 2002), 152–56.

101. Haussmann, *Memoirs*, 845; orig. ed., 3:89.

102. Lavedan, *Histoire de l'urbanisme*, 436; Pinon, *Atlas*, 63. The question of responsibility for Paris streets has a complicated history. Under the Old Regime, Paris streets were under the financial responsibility of the state, but regulations issued in 1821, 1848, and 1856 introduced new dispositions.

Bernard Landau, "La Fabrication des rues de Paris au XIXe siècle," *Annales de la Recherche Urbaine* 57–58 (June 1993): 24–45.

103. Van Zanten, *Building Paris,* 321, n. 19.

104. Pinon, "Polarisation," 61–70.

105. Marked on the plan by Achin, engraved by Andriveau-Goujon in 1853, and submitted with the commission report held in the Bibliothèque Administrative de la Ville de Paris (Pinon, *Atlas,* 37, 50–52). A working document among the commission papers indicates cancellation of this boulevard as redundant, and it is not included in the commission report (Pierre Casselle, "Les Travaux de la Commission des Embellissements de Paris en 1853: Pouvait-on transformer la capitale sans Haussmann?" *Bibliothèque de l'Ecole des Chartes* 55 [1997]: 659–61, 686).

106. Published in "Gazette municipale," *Revue Municipale* 183 (16 November 1855): 1582–83; cited in Pascal Etienne, *Le Faubourg Poissonnière: Architecture, élégance et décor* (Paris: Délégation à l'Action Artistique de la Ville de Paris, 1986), 291–92. Award of medal in *Revue Municipale,* 16 November 1855, cited by Prévost-Marcilhacy, "Lotissements," 44. *Revue Municipale,* 1 August 1857, 228, cited in Bowie, "Gares du Nord," 41–42; A. Portret, "Boulevard du Nord," *Gazette des Architectes et du Bâtiment,* 1863, 135–36.

107. Pinon, *Atlas,* 56 and Haussmann, *Memoirs,* 845; orig. ed., 3:89. Von Joest, "Hittorff," 273 indicates that Haussmann never approved because of the enormous expropriation costs, but gives no evidence.

108. Bowie, "Polarisation," 72.

109. Casselle, "Travaux de la Commission des Embellissements," 662.

110. Ratcliffe, "Urban Space," 225.

111. Bowie, "Polarisation," 8.

112. Jack Simmons, "The Power of the Railway," in *The Victorian City,* ed. H. J. Dyos and Michael Wolff (London: Routledge & Kegan Paul, 1973), 301. In this regard, the Gare du Nord fared respectably with a recognizable façade, several access streets, and the Boulevard de Denain allowing viewers to step back some distance from the central pavilion. This was not provided to the Gare Saint-Lazare, a Péreire station (Pinkney, *Rebuilding,* 216).

113. As the Commune would show, the main danger came no longer from the center but from east of the Bastille (Anthony Sutcliffe, *The Autumn of Central Paris: The Defeat of Town Planning, 1850–1970* [London: Edward Arnold, 1970], 34).

114. Adeline Daumard, "Conditions de logement et position sociale," in *Le Parisien chez lui au XIXe siècle,* ed. Jean Favier (Paris: Archives Nationales, 1976); Ratcliffe, "Urban Space," 226.

115. Florence Bourillon, "A Propos de la Commission des Embellissements: La Rénovation du grand Paris à l'intérieur des fortifications," in *La Modernité avant Haussmann: Formes de l'espace urbain à Paris, 1801–1853,* ed. Karen Bowie (Paris: Editions Recherches, 2001), 143.

116. Lavedan, *Histoire de l'urbanisme,* 482–83.

117. Casselle, "Travaux de la Commission des Embellissements," 661.

118. Haussmann, *Memoirs,* 917; orig. ed., 3:210–13.

119. Donald J. Olsen, *The City as a Work of Art: London, Paris, Vienna* (New Haven, CT: Yale University Press, 1986), 144. Casselle, "Travaux de la Commission des Embellissements," 655, n. 27.

120. Gaillard, *Paris*, 35–36, 67, 75; Olsen, *City as Work of Art*, 143.

121. Gaillard, *Paris*, 74–75; Harvey, "Paris, 1850–1870," 165; Daumard, "Conditions," 1976.

122. Harvey, "Paris, 1850–1870," 119.

123. Pinkney, *Rebuilding*, 165–66.

124. Clozier, *Gare du Nord*, 24; Halbwachs, *Expropriations*, 85; Willms, *Paris, Capital of Europe*, 226, 275; Pinkney, *Rebuilding*, 163; John M. Merriman, ed., *French Cities in the Nineteenth Century* (New York: Holmes & Meier, 1981), 36.

125. "Chemin de fer de l'Est: Ligne de Paris à Vincennes," *Journal des Chemins de Fer*, 24 September 1859, 810; Sutcliffe, *Autumn*, 28, 322; Bastié, *Croissance*, 107. The western suburbs were still serviced by a greater number of suburban trains in 1940 (Clozier, *Gare du Nord*, 253, 275–79).

126. The Péreires also owned real estate in the east, for example, apartment houses on Boulevard Voltaire, but they were mainly invested in the west (Willms, *Paris, Capital of Europe*, 272); Bowie, "Rothschild," 96.

127. Michel Carmona, *Haussmann* (Paris: Fayard, 2000), 376.

128. Célia Mercier, "Un Jardin au-dessus des voies de la gare de l'Est," *Le Figaro*, 13 November 2001, 14. Gilles Duhem, Boris Grésillon, and Dorothée Kohler, eds., *Paris-Berlin. Regards croisés sur deux capitales Européennes* (Paris: Anthropos, 2000), 211.

129. Willms, *Paris, Capital of Europe*, 331; Sutcliffe, *Autumn*, 326.

130. Completed in 1859, the Vincennes line was closed in 1969 and has been converted into a park above the viaduct, the "coulée verte" or "promenade plantée Bastille-Vincennes," begun in 1986 (Bastié in Lavedan, *Histoire de l'urbanisme*, 692).

131. Sutcliffe, *Autumn*, 327.

132. Louis Lazare, *Revue Municipale*, 16 August 1853, 1045.

Chapter 6

1. Allan Mitchell, *The Great Train Race: Railways and the Franco-German Rivalry* (New York: Berghahn Books, 2000), 81.

2. Allan Mitchell, "Les Chemins de fer français et allemands au XIXe siècle," *Revue d'Histoire des Chemins de Fer* 16–17 (1997): 265.

3. Marc Baroli, "Le Train dans la littérature française," in *Ecritures du chemin de fer, Symposium, Sorbonne, 11 May 1996*, ed. François Moureau and Marie Noëlle Polino (Paris: Klincksieck, 1997), 13, 18.

4. M. Nothomb, *Travaux publics en Belgique, 1830–1839: Chemins de fer et routes ordinaires*, Rapport présenté aux Chambres Législatives, 12 November 1839 (2nd ed. 1840), 31.

5. John Reginald Kellett, *The Impact of Railways on Victorian Cities* (London: Routledge & Kegan Paul, 1969), 67.

6. Jack Simmons, *The Victorian Railway* (London: Thames and Hudson, 1991), 179.

7. *Conquête pacifique*. Auguste Perdonnet, *Chemins de fer, extrait de l'annuaire encyclopédique de 1862* (Paris: Encyclopédie du XIXe siècle, 1862), col. 333.

8. François Bartholony, *Quelques idées sur les encouragements à accorder aux compagnies concessionnaires des grandes lignes de chemin de fer* (Paris: Firmin Didot Frères, 1836), 37.

9.   Georges Ribeill, *La Révolution ferroviaire: La Formation des compagnies de chemin de fer en France, 1823–1870* (Paris: Belin, 1993), 336.

10. Auguste Perdonnet, *Traité élémentaire des chemins de fer,* 3rd ed. (Paris: Garnier, 1865), 4:406.

11. Karen Bowie, "L'Implantation des gares du Nord et de l'Est dans Paris, 1830–1870: Premiers résultats d'une recherche," in *La Gare: Dedans, dehors* (Paris: Plan Urbain, DRAST, RATP, and SNCF, 1996), 141–42.

12. Napoléon Daru, *Ouvrage des chemins de fer* (Paris: s.n., 1843); *Eisenbahn Zeitung,* 1843, 35–36.

13. Ludwig Börne, *Gesammelte Schriften* (Hamburg: Hoffmann & Campe, 1862), 9:149; cited in Volker Then, *Eisenbahnen und Eisenbahnunternehmer in der Industriellen Revolution: Ein Preussisch/deutsch-englischer Vergleich* (Göttingen: Vandenhoeck & Ruprecht, 1997), 78.

14. François Jacqmin, *De l'Exploitation des chemins de fer: Leçons faites en 1867 à l'Ecole Impériale des Ponts et Chaussées* (Paris: Garnier Frères, 1868), 2:129.

15. "Bulletin de la Semaine," *Journal des Chemins de Fer,* 23 June 1866, 401.

16. "Chemins de fer," *Sciences appliquées à l'art militaire: Chemins de fer, télégraphe électrique et optique, téléphone, pigeons voyageurs, aérostation, ponts militaires, routes militaires* (Brussels: Spinieux, 1888), 1.

17. Mitchell, *Great Train Race,* 82.

18. Eduard Schmitt, *Vorträge über Bahnhöfe und Hochbauten auf Lokomotiveisenbahnen* (Leipzig: Arthur Felix, 1873–82), 1:56.

19. Nothomb, *Travaux publics en Belgique,* 95.

20. David Salomons, *Railways in England and France: Being Reflections Suggested by Mr. Morrison's Pamphlets and by the Report Drawn Up by Him for the Railway Act's Committee* (London: Pelham Richardson, 1847), 4; Louis Hymans, *Le Chemin de fer* (Brussels: A. N. Lebègue, 1884), 28–29.

21. Von L . . . , *Die Preussischen Eisenbahn-Unternehmungen und die Allerhöchste Verordnung von 24. Mai d.J. [1844]* (Berlin: Enslin, 1844), 4.

22. Pillet-Will, *De la Dépense et du produit des canaux et des chemins de fer: De l'Influence des voies de communication sur la prospérité industrielle de la France* (Paris: Dufart, 1837), 1–3.

23. "Lamartine to the Chambre des Députés, 1838," in *Les Chemins de fer français: Etude historique sur la constitution et le régime du réseau,* ed. Alfred Picard (Paris: J. Rothschild, 1884–85), 1:13.

24. Friedrich Wilhelm von Reden, *Législation des chemins de fer en Allemagne* (Paris: L. Mathias, 1845), vi-viii.

25. Ibid., ix-x.

26. Grote, *Über ein Eisenbahnsystem für Deutschland* (1834), 1–2; Friedrich List, *Andeutung der Vorteile eines Preussischen Eisenbahnsystems und insbesondere einer Eisenbahn zwischen Hamburg, Berlin, Magdeburg und Leipzig* (Leipzig: printed as manuscript, 1835); Friedrich List, *Le Monde marche* (manuscript, Paris, 1837, published Göttingen: Vandenhoeck & Ruprecht, 1983), cited by Mitchell, *Great Train Race,* 38; Carl Eduard Pönitz, *Die Eisenbahnen als militärisch Operationslinien betrachtet und durch Beispiele erläutert* (Adorf: Verlags-Bureau, 1842); Max Maria Freiherr von Weber, *Schule des Eisenbahnwesens,* 4th ed. (Leipzig: J. J. Weber, 1885), 29; Mitchell, *Great Train Race,* 60–61, 168.

27. Mitchell, *Great Train Race,* 38–39.

28. Michel Chevalier, *Des Chemins de fer en France* (Paris: H. Fournier, 1838), 3; Pierre-Charles Laurent de Villedeuil, *Bibliographie des chemins de fer: Index*

chronologique, 1771–1846 (Paris: Librairie française, 1906), 12–13; François Caron, *Histoire des chemins de fer en France,* vol. 1, *1740–1883* (Paris: Fayard, 1997), 98.

29. François Arago, "Raport à la Chambre des Députés rédigé par Arago (professeur à l' Ecole Polytechnique)," *Moniteur Universel,* 26 April 1838; reprinted in Picard, *Chemins de fer français,* 1:106.

30. Robert Bruce Carlisle, "The Saint-Simonians and the Foundation of the Paris-Lyon Railroad, 1832–52" (PhD diss., Cornell University, 1957), 51.

31. Mitchell, *Great Train Race,* 5.

32. Amédée Lacombe, *Projet sur l'organisation générale des chemins de fer dans toute la France* (Bordeaux: Ouvriers-Associés, 1850), 7.

33. David Harvey, "Paris, 1850–1870," in *Consciousness and the Urban Experience: Studies in the History and Theory of Capitalist Urbanization,* ed. David Harvey (Baltimore: Johns Hopkins University Press, 1985), 72.

34. Caron, *Histoire des chemins,* 126.

35. Pierre-Edmond Teisserenc-de-Bort, *Des Principes généraux qui doivent présider au choix des tracés des chemins de fer* (Paris: Schneider et Langrand, 1843), 54.

36. Allan Mitchell, "Private Enterprise or Public Service? The Eastern Railway Company and the French State in the Nineteenth Century," *Journal of Modern History* 69 (March 1997): 24.

37. Victor Hugo, *Napoléon le Petit* (London: Jeffs, 1852); quoted in Caron, *Histoire des chemins,* 98–100.

38. J. Lobet, "Introduction," in *Des Chemins de fer en France et des différents principes appliqués à leur tracé, à leur construction et à leur exploitation* (Paris: Parent-Desbarres, Mathias, 1845).

39. Francis Whishaw, *The Railways of Great Britain and Ireland* (London: John Weale, 1842), cited in Gordon Biddle, *Britain's Historic Railway Buildings* (Oxford: Oxford University Press, 2003), 5.

40. George Findlay, *The Working and Management of an English Railway* (London: Whittaker, 1889), 257, 260–61.

41. Report of quartermaster-general, Sir James Willoughby Gordon, evidence to the Commons Committee on Railways, 1844, PP 1844, xi, 187–93; cited in Simmons, *Victorian Railway,* 365.

42. Findlay, *English Railway,* 260–61.

43. Anthony Sutcliffe, *The Autumn of Central Paris: The Defeat of Town Planning, 1850–1970* (London: Edward Arnold, 1970), 27–32, 34; Pierre Lavedan, *Histoire de l'urbanisme à Paris* (Paris: Hachette, 1993), 421. Harvey, "Paris, 1850–1870," 74, 103; Maurice Halbwachs, *Les Expropriations et le prix des terrains à Paris (1860–1900)* (Paris: Société Cornély, 1909), 7; David Van Zanten, *Building Paris: Architectural Institutions and the Transformation of the French Capital, 1830–1870* (Cambridge: Cambridge University Press, 1994), 214.

44. Pierre Casselle, "Les Travaux de la Commission des Embellissements de Paris en 1853: Pouvait-on transformer la capitale sans Haussmann?" *Bibliothèque de l'Ecole des Chartes* 55 (1997): 653–54.

45. Dennis E. Showalter, *Railroads and Rifles: Soldiers, Technology, and the Unification of Germany* (Hamden, CT: Archon Books, 1975), 35–37, 47.

46. From an 1847 rule book cited in Michael Robbins, *The Railway Age* (Manchester: Manchester University Press, 1998), 62.

47. Robbins, *Railway Age,* 62; Ribeill, *Révolution ferroviaire,* 351.

48. William Taussig, *Some Aspects of Foreign Railway Management and Their Lessons* (St. Louis, MO: Studley, 1896), 2; Mitchell, *Great Train Race*, 75.

49. Ribeill, *Révolution ferroviaire*, 349–51. See also Georges Ribeill, "Les Fondations stratégiques des grandes gares parisiennes," in *Les Grandes gares parisiennes*, ed. Karen Bowie (Paris: Délégation à l'Action Artistique de la Ville de Paris, 1987), 29.

50. *Chemin de fer, exploitation, arrêtés du roi et règlement général du 1er septembre 1838* (Brussels: Imprimerie de Vroom, 1838), 3, 114.

51. Lettre à Adèle du 22 août 1837, Anvers à Bruxelles, in Victor Hugo, *Oeuvres complètes: Voyages* (Paris: Laffont, 1985), 13:611.

52. Léonce Reynaud, ed., *Les Travaux publics de la France*, vol. 2, *Les Chemins de fer*, by Edouard Collignon (Paris: J. Rothschild, 1883), 42.

53. *Les Débuts du chemin de fer en France, 1831–1870* (Paris: Ministère de la Culture et de l'Environnement and SNCF, 1977), 35; Ribeill, "Grandes gares parisiennes," 34; Ribeill, *Révolution ferroviaire*, 343, 349–50.

54. Fines for infractions were deposited in the staff assistance fund. Robbins, *Railway Age*, 63; Mitchell, *Great Train Race*, 183, 185, 187.

55. Albert Schillings, *Traité pratique du service de l'exploitation des chemins de fer* (Paris: Carilian-Goeury, 1848); quoted in Ribeill, *Révolution ferroviaire*, 342.

56. Prosper de Pietra Santa, *Chemins de fer et santé publique: Hygiène des voyageurs et des employés* (Paris: Hachette, 1861), 36; Conseil de Direction de la Compagnie du Nord, 26 December 1845, cited in Ribeill, *Révolution ferroviaire*, 355; see also 345, 360–61.

57. Salomons, *Railways in England and France*, 4.

58. J. Frank, *Der Praktische Eisenbahnbeamte* (Magdeburg: Emil Bänsch, 1851), 15, 85.

59. In Paris and Brussels until 1860, in Berlin until 1868. Tolls also remained in effect in London until 1864. Thomas Nipperdey, *Germany from Napoleon to Bismarck, 1800–1866* (Princeton, NJ: Princeton University Press, 1996), 115, 117.

60. "De la Discussion des tracés de chemins de fer," *La Démocratie Pacifique* 161 (9 June 1844): 2.

61. Antoine Picon, Jean-Paul Robert, and Anna Hartmann, *Le Dessus des cartes: Un Atlas parisien* (Paris: Pavillon de l'Arsenal, Picard, 1999), 228. Archives SNCF, Le Mans, VB 4, Carton 3, Liasse 3, Ligne de Paris à Strasbourg, Tracé 1e section, 30 avril 1846, Chemin de Fer de Paris à Strasbourg, 1ère Section, Pièce n. 12, 1er arrondissement, Département de la Seine, Plan de détails relatifs au passage des fortifications.

62. Félix Tourneux, *Encyclopédie des chemins de fer et des machines à vapeur* (Paris: J. Renouard et cie, 1844), 513–14.

63. In France, this was stipulated by Article 13 of the Law of 10 July 1791, and Articles 537 and 540 of the Civil Code. "Chemin de fer de Lyon, inaliénabilité du domaine militaire," *Journal des Chemins de Fer*, 27 March 1847, 230.

64. Decrees of 16 August 1853, 8 September 1878, 6 December 1884, and 12 December 1884. Circulaire by S. de Herredia, Minister, Archives de Paris, D1S9/1-3.

65. Archives de Paris, D1S9/1-3; document dated 13 January 1880.

66. Perdonnet, *Traité*, 3rd ed., 4:406.

67. In a document dated 1908, the Compagnie du Nord gave notification that since the northern and western fortifications for Paris were about to lose their

strategic status, repairs would not be performed on the railway bridges over the fortifications. Archives de Paris, D6S9-4, unnumbered document dated 1908.

68. Showalter, *Railroads and Rifles*, 32.

69. "Paris, ceinture et fortifications," *Annales des Chemins de Fer, des Travaux Publics et des Mines* 1 (20 October 1850): 566.

70. Karen Bowie, "'L'Eclectisme pittoresque' et l'architecture des gares parisiennes au XIXe siècle," PhD diss., Université de Paris I, 1985, 318; Compagnie des Chemins de Fer de l'Est, *La Gare de l'Est* (Paris: Compagnie du Chemin de Fer de l'Est, 1931), 6–7. This practice of multiple terminals was also advocated by Stübben in his city planning treatise: Herman Josef Stübben, *Der Städtebau, Handbuch der Architektur*, 2nd ed. (Stuttgart: A. Kröner, 1907), 4:243–44, pt. 9.

71. *Journal des Chemins de Fer*, 18 December 1852, 924, and 3 February 1853, 91.

72. Martin Christopher Edmund Lodge, *On Different Tracks: Designing Railway Regulation in Britain and Germany* (Westport, CT: Praeger, 2002), 9–11.

73. Showalter, *Railroads and Rifles*, 18; Wolfgang Klee, *Preussische Eisenbahngeschichte* (Stuttgart: Kohlhammer, 1982), 98, 102, 106. The state's ability to increase the national debt was regulated by the Edict of 18 January 1820. Loans above a specified limit required Landrat approval. *Journal des Chemins de Fer*, 18 September 1868, 613.

74. Cited in Colleen Dunlavy, *Politics and Industrialization: Early Railroads in the United States and Prussia* (Princeton, NJ: Princeton University Press, 1994), 109–10.

75. Victor von Röll, ed., *Enzyklopädie des Eisenbahnwesens*, 2nd ed. (Berlin: Urban & Schwarzenberg, 1912–23), 7:278.

76. Geheime Staatsarchiv, Preußischer Kulturbesitz I HA Rep. 90 Preußisches Staatsministerium, 1674 Bd. I, Doc. 1, Abschrift. St. M. 459, dated Berlin, 26 April 1836, and Allerhöchsten Kabinets Ordre of 17 May 1836.

77. Showalter, *Railroads and Rifles*, 26.

78. Von Moltke was chief of staff from 1857 to 1888. Marcel Peschaud, *Les Chemins de fer allemands et la guerre* (Paris: Charles Lavauzelle, 1927), 351.

79. David Justus Ludwig Hansemann, *Kritik des Preussischen Eisenbahn-Gesetzes vom 3. November 1838* (Aachen: J. A. Mayer, 1841), 24–25; cited by Dunlavy, *Politics and Industrialization*, 133.

80. Klee, *Preussische Eisenbahngeschichte*, 101–3. Paragraphs 7–22 elaborated regulations for land acquisition and construction.

81. The regulations for such a process had been elaborated in 1838. See chap. 1, "Prussia," under "Adjustments to Legislation," in this book. Dunlavy, *Politics and Industrialization*, 64, n. 46; James M. Brophy, *Capitalism, Politics, and Railroads in Prussia, 1830–1870* (Columbus: Ohio State University Press, 1998), 46.

82. For example, the Berlin-Anhalt Eisenbahn and the Berlin-Frankfurt Eisenbahn conceded in 1838 and 1840, respectively, included no such stipulations in their statutes; the Niederschlesich-Märkishe Eisenbahn, conceded in 1843, did (Volker Then, *Eisenbahnen und Eisenbahnunternehmer*, 109).

83. *Journal des Chemins de Fer*, 18 September 1868, 613; Brophy, *Capitalism, Politics*, 40–42.

84. Half of the Prussian budget (Showalter, *Railroads and Rifles*, 18–19).

85. Nipperdey, *Germany from Napoleon to Bismarck*, 116; Klee, *Preussische Eisenbahngeschichte*, 165; Showalter, *Railroads and Rifles*, 31. Although the

state did not levy these taxes in the 1840s to avoid worsening the situation of the failing securities market (Brophy, *Capitalism, Politics,* 44). See also Henry Ferrette, *Etude historique sur l'intervention financière de l'état dans l'établissement des lignes de chemin de fer* (Paris: L. Larose, 1896), 154.

86. Volker Then, *Eisenbahnen und Eisenbahnunternehmer,* 86–87; Showalter, *Railroads and Rifles,* 38; Dunlavy, *Politics and Industrialization,* 105; Mitchell, *Great Train Race,* 50, 52.

87. *Deutsche Bauzeitung* 9 (1875): 76; *Zehn Jahre Preußisch-Deutschen Eisenbahnpolitik* (Leipzig: Veit, 1876), 4; Dunlavy, *Politics and Industrialization,* 105.

88. Von Reden, *Législation des chemins,* xii; Heinrich Bechtel, *Wirtschaftsgeschichte Deutschlands im 19. und 20. Jahrhundert* (Munich: Georg D. W. Callwey, 1956), 57; Ministerium der Öffentlichen Arbeiten and A. F. Leyen, *Berlin und seine Eisenbahnen, 1846–1896* (Berlin: Julius Springer, 1896), 1:5–6.

89. Marcel Peschaud, "Les Chemins de fer français et allemands et la guerre," *La Revue Politique et Parlementaire* 10 (December 1927): 352; Mitchell, "Chemins de fer," 266.

90. Dunlavy, *Politics and Industrialization,* 157–58.

91. Dunlavy, *Politics and Industrialization,* 109; Klee, *Preussische Eisenbahngeschichte,* 167.

92. Mitchell, *Great Train Race,* 62; von Röll, *Enzyklopädie des Eisenbahnwesens,* 4:139.

93. "Reglement für die Beförderung von Truppen auf Staatseisenbahnen," cited in Peter Bley, *Königlich Preußische Militäreisenbahn: 125 Jahre Berlin-Zossen-Jüterborg* (Düsseldorf: Alba, 2000), 7.

94. von Röll, *Enzyklopädie des Eisenbahnwesens,* 4:139; Showalter, *Railroads and Rifles,* 45–46.

95. He had been member of the board of directors for the Berlin-Hamburg Company since 1841 (Bley, *Militäreisenbahn,*7–8). Military officers with good connections served on the boards of railway companies as of 1840, and many invested in them to supplement modest junior officer pay (Showalter, *Railroads and Rifles,* 19, 29, 31, 39–41, 43); Mitchell, *Great Train Race,* 62–63.

96. Mitchell, *Great Train Race,* 64–66; Showalter, *Railroads and Rifles,* 52.

97. Signed on 16 April 1871, the constitution stipulated that the railways (except Bavaria) be placed under imperial control and legislation for matters of territorial defense (von Röll, *Enzyklopädie des Eisenbahnwesens,* 7:280; Klee, *Preussische Eisenbahngeschichte,* 167–68; Peschaud, "Chemins de fer," 353–54. Article 41 of the 1867 constitution already allowed the Confederation to build lines across states despite their objection (Mitchell, *Great Train Race,* 52).

98. Peschaud, "Chemins de fer," 352; Ferrette, *Etude historique,* 156; Mitchell, *Great Train Race,* 123.

99. Klee, *Preussische Eisenbahngeschichte,* 172; Eugen Richter, *Die falsche Eisenbahnpolitik des Fürsten Bismarck dargelegt von E. R. vor dem Preußischen Abgeordnetenhause in drei Reden am 26. April 1876, 12. u. 13. Dezember 1877* (Berlin: C. Barthel, 1878); Ferrette, *Etude historique,* 158–59; Gröner, *Die Eisenbahn als Faktor der Politik: Vortrag gehalten in der Hochschule für Politik, Berlin* (Stuttgart: Ferdinand Enke, 1921), 6–12; Taussig, *Foreign Railway Management,* 20; Dunlavy, *Politics and Industrialization,* 49. By 1896, only 10 percent of Prussian lines remained in private hands, mostly minor lines (Mitchell, *Great Train Race,* 129, 136–37).

100. Built between 1851 and 1879. Peschaud, "Chemins de fer," 354–55; *Berlin und seine Eisenbahnen,* 1:224–36; Mitchell, *Great Train Race,* 42, 80; Klee, *Preussische Eisenbahngeschichte,* 106, 108, 119–21.

101. Geheime Staatsarchiv, Preußischer Kulturbesitz I HA Rep. 90 Preußisches Staatsministerium, 1674 Bd. I, communication from Bundesrat, session 1883–84, dated 27 March 1884, and p. 240, Abschrift, Berlin, 8 March 1888, 505/88; Mitchell, *Great Train Race,* 139–41, 229.

102. Mitchell, *Great Train Race,* 230, 233.

103. *Journal des Chemins de Fer,* 23 June 1866, 406.

104. Mitchell, *Great Train Race,* 234, 242; Peschaud, "Chemins de fer," 352–53.

105. von Röll, *Enzyklopädie des Eisenbahnwesens,* 4:140; Bley, *Militäreisenbahn,* 8; von Weber, *Schule des Eisenbahnwesens,* 27–28; Architekten-Verein zu Berlin, *Berlin und seine Bauten,* 2nd ed. (Berlin: Ernst & Korn, 1896), 1:394–98.

106. *Berlin und seine Eisenbahnen,* 1:131, 288–90; Landesarchiv, Berlin, 080-13398I, 13399, Landesarchiv, Berlin, A Rep. 080 Nr.13400 Bd 2, HaiV 1/11b. For the impact on the Berlin-Anhalt line, see Peter Bley, *150 Jahre Berlin-Anhaltische Eisenbahn* (Düsseldorf: Alba, 1990), 56–57.

107. von Röll, *Enzyklopädie des Eisenbahnwesens,* 4:144; Gordon Biddle and Jack Simmons, eds., *The Oxford Companion to British Railway History from 1603 to the 1990s* (Oxford: Oxford University Press, 1997), 324–25; Simmons, *Victorian Railway,* 367.

108. *The Railway Times,* 22 December 1838, 752.

109. Regulation of Railways Act of 1842, 5 & 6 Vict., cap. 59. This was further regulated in 1844 and 1867 (Biddle and Simmons, *Oxford Companion,* 556); Simmons, *Victorian Railway,* 365; PP 1844 xi, 187–93.

110. Volker Then, *Eisenbahnen und Eisenbahnunternehmer,* 114; Simmons, *Victorian Railway,* 366.

111. Edwin A. Pratt, *The Rise of Rail Power in War and Conquest, 1833–1914* (London: Routledge, 1915), 2–8.

112. Findlay, *English Railway,* 257; Simmons, *Victorian Railway,* 367; von Röll, *Enzyklopädie des Eisenbahnwesens,* 7:285.

113. Pratt, *Rail Power,* 175.

114. Royal Commission, Report on Railway Termini within or in the immediate vicinity of the Metropolis, 1846, Metropolitan Railway Commission, Parliamentary Papers, 1846, xvii, HC, 1846 (719) XVII, 5, 21, 255–57.

115. Horace Courtenay Gammell Forbes, *Shall We Have a Channel Tunnel?* (London: Simpkin, Marshall, 1883).

116. Peschaud, "Chemins de fer," 353; Mitchell, *Great Train Race,* 28, 31, 33–34, 82, 93.

117. Peschaud, "Chemins de fer," 351, 356; Mitchell, *Great Train Race,* 32, 34–36, 80, 112.

118. Peschaud, "Chemins de fer," 356–57; von Röll, *Enzyklopädie des Eisenbahnwesens,* 7:283.

119. Peschaud, "Chemins de fer," 359; von Röll, *Enzyklopädie des Eisenbahnwesens,* 7:289.

120. Mitchell, *Great Train Race,* 113.

121. Ibid., 109–10.

122. Ibid., 114–15, 118–19, 168, 204–5, 263, 265; Mitchell, "Chemins de fer," 266–67.

123. Yvon Leblicq, "L'Evolution de la physionomie de Bruxelles au XIXe siècle," in *Bruxelles, construire et reconstruire,* ed. Crédit Communal de Belgique (Brussels: Crédit Communal, 1979), 23.

124. Depouhon, *Du Mode d'exécution du système des chemins de fer en Belgique* (Brussels: Pelcot et Boissaux, 1833), article 12.

Chapter 7

1. Ministerium der Öffentlichen Arbeiten and A. F. Leyen, *Berlin und seine Eisenbahnen, 1846–1896* (Berlin: Julius Springer, 1896), 1:v.
2. Maurice Halbwachs, " 'Gross Berlin': Grande agglomération ou grande ville?" *Annales d'Histoire Economique et Sociale* 6 (1934): 552; *Berlin und seine Eisenbahnen*, 1:22.
3. Hans Kollhoff, "The Metropolis as a Construction: Engineering Structures in Berlin, 1871–1914," in *Berlin-New York, Like and Unlike: Essays on Architecture and Art from 1870 to the Present,* ed. Josef Paul Kleihues and Christina Rathgeber (New York: Rizzoli, 1993), 48.
4. *Berlin und seine Eisenbahnen,* 1:131; Kollhoff, "Metropolis as a Construction," 49, 51.
5. Halbwachs, "Gross Berlin," 556–57.
6. Kollhoff, "Metropolis as a Construction," 51, 57. Helmut Maier, *Berlin Anhalter Bahnhof* (Berlin: Aesthetik und Kommunikation, 1983), 55.
7. Mary Fulbrook, *A Concise History of Germany* (Cambridge: Cambridge University Press, 1992), 78.
8. Lewis Mumford, *The Culture of Cities* (New York: Harcourt, Brace, 1938), 89.
9. Erwin A. Gutkind, *Urban Development in Western Europe: France and Belgium* (New York: Free Press, 1970), 313.
10. Mumford, *Culture of Cities,* 89.
11. Hartwig Schmidt, "Architecture and Urban Planning, 1850–1914," in Kleihues and Rathgeber, *Berlin-New York, Like and Unlike,* 131.
12. Ibid., 133; Thomas Nipperdey, *Germany from Napoleon to Bismarck, 1800–1866* (Princeton, NJ: Princeton University Press, 1996), 118.
13. Halbwachs, "Gross Berlin," 551–52.
14. Its size was 1600 × 3400 meters.
15. Architekten-Verein zu Berlin, ed., *Berlin und seine Bauten* (Berlin: Ernst & Korn, 1877), 256; ibid., 2nd ed. (Berlin: Ernst & Korn, 1896), 1:287, 2:399.
16. Landesarchiv Berlin, A Rep. 080, Nr. 13400, Bd 2, HaiV 1/11b.
17. *Preussens Eisenbahngesetzgebung: Eine Zusammenstellung der bisher erschienen, die Eisenbahn-Unternehmungen betreffenden Gesetze und Ministerial-Rescripte* (Glogau: Karl Flemming, 1844), p. 31, par. 43, item 28: "Kriegsbeschädigungen."
18. It was opened to traffic on 10 September 1841. Ulrich Krings, *Bahnhofsarchitektur: Deutsche Grossstadtbahnhöfe des Historismus* (Munich: Prestel, 1985), 161.
19. Peter Bley, *150 Jahre Berlin-Anhaltische Eisenbahn* (Düsseldorf: Alba, 1990), 1–9.
20. *Preussens Eisenbahngesetzgebung,* 177 (sec. 5, Law of 15 May 1839), 376 (Codicil of 7 December 1840), 77 (Codicil of 18 February 1842).
21. Treaty of 8 March 1882, and Law of 13 May 1882 (Victor von Röll, ed., *Enzyklopädie des Eisenbahnwesens,* 2nd ed. [Berlin: Urban & Schwarzenberg, 1912–23], 2:231). Operations were transferred to the state on 21 May 1882 (Krings, *Bahnhofsarchitektur,* 161).

22. Comité der Berlin-Sächsischen Eisenbahn-Gesellschaft, *Rundschreiben an die Herren Actien-Zeichner zum Bau der Berlin-Sächsischen Eisenbahn* (Berlin: Weible, 1838), 34–35.

23. Landesarchiv, Berlin, I Rep. 89, 28623, Durch ein Gesuch. der Berlin-Anhaltchen Eisenbahngesellschaft bewirkte Anlage einer neuen von der Wilhelmstraße in Berlin über das Grundstück Nr.108 nach der Stadtmauer hinführende Straße und eines neuen Tores, 1838–1840, signed Berlin, 13 October 1838, responding to document of 17 April 1838.

24. Bley, *Anhalt*, 2–3.

25. *Berlin und seine Eisenbahnen*, 1:163 (Kabinets Ordre of 24 October 1838); Maier, *Berlin Anhalter Bahnhof*, 46–61.

26. *Berlin und seine Eisenbahnen*, 1:163–64.

27. Bley, *Anhalt*, 15–21.

28. *Berlin und seine Eisenbahnen*, 1:167.

29. Ibid., 1:169–72; Maier, *Berlin Anhalter Bahnhof*, 18–61.

30. Krings, *Bahnhofsarchitektur*, 161–62. The shed was 167.79 meters long, 60.72 meters wide, 34.25 meters high. Maier, *Berlin Anhalter Bahnhof*, 12–13.

31. For building plans and description of the station building, see Krings, *Bahnhofsarchitektur*, 162–81; Maier, *Berlin Anhalter Bahnhof*, 18–61, 307–14.

32. Geheime Staatsarchiv, Preußischer Kulturbesitz, I Rep. 89, 29565, Die Verbindung der verschiedenen Eisenbahnen in Berlin unter sich und mit der Spree, Verbindungsbahn. Document dated Berlin, 22 March 1845; *Berlin und seine Eisenbahnen*, 1:238.

33. *Berlin und seine Eisenbahnen*, 1:239.

34. Ibid., 1:241–42; Peter Bley, *Königlich Preußische Militäreisenbahn: 125 Jahre Berlin-Zossen-Jüterborg* (Düsseldorf: Alba, 2000), 7; Wolfgang Klee, *Preussische Eisenbahngeschichte* (Stuttgart: Kohlhammer, 1982), 121.

35. *Berlin und seine Eisenbahnen*, 1:129–32, 244–45. Geheime Staatsarchiv, Preußischer Kulturbesitz, I Rep. 77, 258a, 47, v. 1. Approval document for proposal by the minister of commerce, industry, and public works (von der Heydt) and finance minister (Rabe) was signed by the king on 10 April 1851. The document stresses the importance of a connection between stations and includes detailed description of the project. The military importance of the rail line is again indicated in Report No. 263 by the Commission on Commerce and Industry, signed 14 April 1851.

36. *Berlin und seine Eisenbahnen*, 1:248, 251–52.

37. Ibid., 1:224–36, 252; Klee, *Preussische Eisenbahngeschichte*, 119.

38. Dennis E. Showalter, *Railroads and Rifles: Soldiers, Technology, and the Unification of Germany* (Hamden, CT: Archon Books, 1975), 54–55.

39. *Berlin und seine Eisenbahnen*, 1:252–53.

40. von Röll, *Enzyklopädie des Eisenbahnwesens*, 2:243; Landesarchiv, Berlin, A Rep. 080, 13422, Verbindungsbahn, I-IV; a decree of 6 March 1867 determined the line configuration. Opening of the first segment from Moabit to Schöneberg by Stralau took place on 17 July 1871 (*Berlin und seine Eisenbahnen*, 1:254, 304).

41. *Berlin und seine Eisenbahnen*, 1:304, 307.

42. Ibid., 1:129–32, 2:487; Brian Ladd, *The Ghosts of Berlin: Confronting German History in the Urban Landscape* (Chicago: University of Chicago Press, 1997), 240.

43. Gilles Duhem, Boris Grésillon, and Dorothée Kohler, eds., *Paris-Berlin: Regards croisés sur deux capitales européennes* (Paris: Anthropos, 2000), 42, 138.

44. Halbwachs, "Gross Berlin," 558–59.

45. von Röll, *Enzyklopädie des Eisenbahnwesens*, 2:245.

46. Herman Josef Stübben, *Der Städtebau, Handbuch der Architektur*, 2nd ed. (Stuttgart: A. Kröner, 1907), 4:246, pt. 9; *Berlin und seine Eisenbahnen*, 1:309.

47. Landesarchiv, Berlin, 080 459 13458, Hai V 2/13, Die Anlage der Berliner Stadtbahn, 1872–1925 (8 vols.).

48. G. Helleputte, "Projet de Loi concernant l'abandon des travaux de la jonction des gares de Bruxelles-Nord et Bruxelles-Midi: Note de la Minorité" (Chambre des Représentants, Document No. 266 [annexe], Session de 1923–24 [2e supplément], 1923–24), 63–69.

49. The architect August Friedrich Wilhelm Orth (1828–1901) had been a student at the Bauakademie in Berlin and had designed stations in Berlin before turning his attention to the *Stadtbahn* project as of 1871 (Krings, *Bahnhofsarchitektur*, 470). See also *Berlin und seine Eisenbahnen*, 1:314, 325. August Orth, "Berlin Centralbahn: Eisenbahnproject zur Verbindung der Berliner Bahnhöfe nach der innern Stadt" (Berlin, 1871), mentioned in Orth, *Zur bauliche Reorganisation der Stadt Berlin* (Berlin: Ernst & Korn, 1875), 1.

50. Krings, *Bahnhofsarchitektur*, 261.

51. Berliner Stadt-Eisenbahn-Gesetz of 20 März 1874, Staat, unter der Firma Berliner Stadteisenbahn-Gesellschaft. Geheime Staatsarchiv, Preußischer Kulturbesitz IHA Rep. 77 tit. 258a No. 68 Bb. 2.

52. The bill was submitted on 8 March 1878 (Helleputte, "Bruxelles-Nord et Bruxelles-Midi," 63–64ff.; *Berlin und seine Eisenbahnen*, 1:317).

53. *Berlin und seine Eisenbahnen*, 1:315; Krings, *Bahnhofsarchitektur*, 262.

54. Krings, *Bahnhofsarchitektur*, 263–64.

55. *Berlin und seine Eisenbahnen*, 1:318, 325–26; von Röll, *Enzyklopädie des Eisenbahnwesens*, 2:246–47; Helleputte, "Bruxelles-Nord et Bruxelles-Midi," 63–69.

56. *Berlin und seine Eisenbahnen*, 1:323; Landesarchiv, Berlin, A Rep. 080-13458, Berlin Stadtbahn (8 vols.).

57. Helleputte, "Bruxelles-Nord et Bruxelles-Midi," 63–69; *Berlin und seine Eisenbahnen*, 1:325; Anthony Sutcliffe, "Environmental Control and Planning in European Capitals, 1850–1914: London, Paris and Berlin," in *Growth and Transformation of the Modern City*, ed. Ingrid Hammarström and Thomas Hall (Stockholm: Swedish Council for Building Research, 1979), 83.

58. Albert Hofmann, "Gross-Berlin, sein Verhältnis zur modernen Grosstadtbewegung und der Wettbewerb zur Erlangung eines Grundplanes für die städtebauliche Entwicklung Berlins und seiner Vororte im zwansigsten Jahrhundert," *Deutsche Bauzeitung* 28, Beilage für Wettbewerbe (2 April 1910): 198.

Chapter 8

1. Pierre de Maret, "Ouverture du colloque," paper delivered at the colloquium Bruxelles et la Jonction Nord-Midi: Histoire, Architecture et Mobilité Urbaines, Brussels, 1 October 2002.

2. Thierry Demey, *Bruxelles: Chronique d'une capitale en chantier*, vol. 1, *Du Voûtement de la Senne à la jonction Nord-Midi* (Brussels: Paul Legrain, 1990), 240.

3. Fernand Brunfaut, *La Jonction* (Brussels: Ad. Goemaere, 1959), 185.

4. Alain Corbin, *Le Miasme et la jonquille* (Paris: Aubier, 1982), 267–70.

5. Patrick Abercrombie, "Brussels: A Study in Development and Town Planning," *Town Planning Review* 4 (January 1913): 259.

6. M. Nothomb, *Travaux publics en Belgique, 1830–1839: Chemins de fer et routes ordinaires,* Rapport présenté aux Chambres Législatives, 12 November 1839 (2nd ed. 1840), 95. Michel Laffut, "Belgium" characterizes the Belgian network as the embryo of the European network, in *Railways and the Economic Development of Western Europe, 1830–1914,* ed. Patrick O'Brien (New York: St. Martin's Press, 1983), 223.

7. Connecting the industrial Hainaut Province to the seaport of Antwerp by linking with the Willebroeck Canal (open since 1561), the Charleroi Canal was inaugurated on 25 September 1832. Louis Verniers, *Un Millénaire d'histoire de Bruxelles, depuis les origines jusqu'en 1830* (Brussels: A. de Boeck, 1965), 240.

8. Gustave Abeels, "Les Communications dans et vers la ville aux XIXe et XXe siècles," in *La Région de Bruxelles: Des Villages d'autrefois à la ville d'aujourd'hui,* ed. Arlette Smolar-Meynart and Jean Stengers (Brussels: Crédit Communal, 1989), 236–37.

9. Guillaume Jacquemyns, "Le Problème de la Cuve de Bruxelles de 1795 à 1854," *Revue de l'Université de Bruxelles* 37, no. 3 (1932): 349.

10. Guillaume Jacquemyns, *Histoire contemporaine du grand Bruxelles* (Brussels: Librairie Vanderlinden, 1936), 146.

11. Louis Verniers, "Les Transformations de Bruxelles et l'urbanisation de sa banlieue depuis 1795," *Annales de la Société Royale Archéologique de Bruxelles* 37 (1934): 110–11, 113–14, 131, 205; Abeels, "Communications," 238.

12. Brunfaut, *Jonction,* 95. See also J. E. Horn, *Brüssel nach seiner Vergangenheit und Gegenwart, Brockhaus Reise-Bibliothek für Eisenbahnen und Dampfschiffe* (Leipzig: Brockhaus, 1855); cited in Wilfried Krings, "Perception et aménagement du centre historique des villes: Contributions belges, 1870–1914," *in Villes en mutation, XIXe-XXe siècles* (Brussels: Crédit Communal, 1982), 399–400.

13. Joseph Delmelle, *Histoire des chemins de fer belges* (Brussels: Legrain, 1977), 55.

14. Ulysse Lamalle, *Histoire des chemins de fer belges,* 2nd ed. (Brussels: Lebègue, 1943), 33.

15. Victor Besme, *Faubourgs de Bruxelles: Plan d'ensemble pour l'extension et l'établissement de l'agglomération bruxelloise,* Rapport fait au gouvernement du Brabant (Brussels: E. Guyot, 1863), 15–17.

16. Jacquemyns, *Histoire,* 125–26, 148; Brunfaut, *Jonction,* 29; Marguerite Silvestre, "Les Premiers projets de jonction Nord-Midi (1855–1865)," in *Bruxelles et la jonction Nord-Midi,* ed. Serge Jaumain and Chloé Deligne (Brussels: Archives de la Ville de Bruxelles, 2004), 53–68.

17. Yvon Leblicq, "L'Urbanisation de Bruxelles au XIXe et XXe siècles (1830–1952)," in *Villes en mutation, XIXe-XXe siècles* (Brussels: Crédit Communal, 1982), 364–65; Bart van den Herten, Michelangelo van Meerten, and Greta Verbeugt, *Un Tunnel sous Bruxelles: Les 50 ans de la jonction Nord-Midi* (Brussels: Editions Racine, 2002), 11.

18. Marcel Mathieu, "La Jonction Nord-Midi: Ses conséquences pour la géographie urbaine de Bruxelles," *Bulletin de la Société Royale Belge de Géographie* 84, fasc. 3–4 (1961): 173; Chloé Deligne, "Discours politique et urbanisme: Réflexion à partir du cas de la jonction Nord-Midi Bruxelles, 1900–1960,"

Revue Belge de Géographie 122, n.s. 1, fasc. 63 (1998): 39, 45; G. Stinglehammer and Paul Dresse, *Léopold II au travail* (Brussels: Editions du Sablon, 1945), 223.

19. Demey, *Capitale en chantier,* 1:189–94; Silvestre, "Premiers projets."

20. The mortality rate in Brussels was the highest among European capitals. In 1866 (excluding cholera epidemic statistics), it was 328/10,000 versus 244 in London and 235 in Paris. Gustave Abeels, "Une Opération immobilière de grande envergure: L'Assainissement du bas de la ville," *in Pierres et rues: Bruxelles, croissance urbaine, 1780–1980* (Brussels: Société Générale de Banque & Sint Lukasarchief, 1984), 184–85.

21. In 1866, a cholera epidemic killed 3,467 people as the project was getting underway. Victor-Gaston Martiny, "Une Ville qui se cherche un visage de capitale (XIXe-XXe siècles)," in *Histoire de Bruxelles,* ed. Mina Martens (Toulouse: Editions Universitaires, 1976), 274. The sewer component of this project is similar to those initiated in the preceding decade both in Paris (1857) and in London (1858) (Leblicq, "Urbanisation," 346–49). Anne Van Loo, "L'Haussmannisation de Bruxelles: La Construction des boulevards du centre, 1865–1880," *Revue de l'Art* 106, no. 4 (1994): 42.

22. Martiny, "Une Ville qui se cherche," 274.

23. Leblicq, "Urbanisation," 344.

24. Hence their nickname *bosse d'Anspach* (Anspach's hunchback); Abeels, "Opération immobilière," 170.

25. Leblicq, "Urbanisation," 33, 70.

26. Silvestre, "Premiers projets," 65–67; G. Helleputte, "Projet de Loi concernant l'abandon des travaux de la jonction des gares de Bruxelles-Nord et Bruxelles-Midi, Note de la Minorité," Chambre des Représentants, Document No. 266 (annexe), (Session de 1923–24, 2e supplément 1923–24): 15.

27. Leblicq, "Urbanisation," 354–55, 366; Yvon Leblicq, "L'Evolution de la physionomie de Bruxelles au XIXe siècle," *Bruxelles, construire et reconstruire* (Brussels: Crédit Communal, 1979), 23.

28. Martiny, "Une Ville qui se cherche," 278.

29. Sitte's *Der Städtebau nach seinen künstlerichen Grudsätzen* was published in 1889. Buls had regular contact with Sitte and Stübben. M. Bots, *Het Dagboek van C. Buls* (Ghent: Liberaal Archief, 1987), 93–95.

30. The Putterie *quartier* (neighborhood) was in the area delineated today by the Rues de la Madeleine, de la Montagne, de Loxum, and Cantersteen; the Rue Isabelle was at the current location of the Palais des Beaux-Arts. Leblicq, "Urbanisation," 367.

31. Comte de Smet de Nayer, cited by Demey, *Capitale en chantier,* 1:208–10.

32. Berlin's central rail line and the London, Paris, Vienna, and Budapest underground projects were completed or in progress as the commissions struggled with the situation in Brussels. Brunfaut, *Jonction,* 67–68; Leblicq, "Urbanisation," 367–68.

33. Bruneel was chief engineer for the railway administration. Frédéric Bruneel, *Avant-projet de chemin de fer métropolitain avec gare centrale à Bruxelles* (Ghent: Imprimerie C. Annoot-Braeckman, 1893), 2, 12.

34. Archives de la Ville de Bruxelles, PP 2851.

35. Expropriation litigations stretched between 1905 and 1924. According to Demey, in addition to the war, technical difficulties of tunneling through unstable, waterlogged terrain also caused delay. Bruneel had mistakenly esti-

mated that the tunnel would not reach the second, problematic layer of the Brussels subsoil. Demey, *Capitale en chantier,* 1:202–3, 206.

36. Helleputte, "Bruxelles-Nord et Bruxelles-Midi," 25–30; Brunfaut, *Jonction,* 31, 45–102. Fernand Brunfaut voted against the project in 1923 and 1924 but became one of its staunch defenders and headed the Junction office after 1952. See Valérie Piette, "Les Brunfaut: Une Famille d'architectes socialistes au service de la jonction," in *Bruxelles et la jonction Nord-Midi,* ed. Serge Jaumain and Chloé Deligne (Brussels: Archives de la Ville de Bruxelles, 2004), 180–86. This was also the case for Charles Woeste (Deligne, "Urbanisme," 36–37).

37. Helleputte, "Bruxelles-Nord et Bruxelles-Midi," 25; Brunfaut, *Jonction,* 47, 51–52, 75.

38. Brunfaut, *Jonction,* 88.

39. Particularly Maurice Waucquez, member of Brussels City Council (Deligne, "Urbanisme," 33).

40. ONJ leadership was assumed by the vice president, Waucquez, until 1952 and Fernand Brunfaut afterward. The need for cut-and-cover construction was due to problematic subsoil and the switch from a ground-contact rail to overhead catenaries, which required higher tunnel clearance. Demey, *Capitale en chantier,* 1:217–18, 221, 222, 229, 238; Brunfaut, *Jonction,* 59, 80–81, 95, 211–24.

41. The total number of individuals using the station daily is actually around 80,000; 60,000 commuters use the station twice daily, supplemented by an additional 20,000 passengers in transit, which adds up to 140,000 passengers passing through the station during a business day (van den Herten, van Meerten, and Verbeugt, *Tunnel,* 29); Leblicq, "Urbanisation," 382–83; Demey, *Capitale en chantier,* 1:227–30.42. Leblicq, "Urbanisation," 364, n. 129.

43. Brunfaut, *Jonction,* 48; Deligne, "Urbanisme," 30–31.

44. The subsoil contained fine waterlogged sand deposits over the watertight clay layer in the eastern bank of the Senne River valley. This second, fine sand layer below the surface of coarse sandy soil contained water pockets, which created unstable sandy subsoil treacherously unpredictable as structural support for building foundations (Aimé-Louis Rutot and E. Van den Broeck, *Le Sol de Bruxelles à travers les âges géologiques* [Brussels: Bruylant-Christophe, n.d.]). Sheetpiling technology allowed gradual drying and removing of the soil while progressively shoring up the sides of the tunnel walls. Pierre Gourou, "L'Agglomération bruxelloise, éléments d'une géographie urbaine," *Bulletin de la Société Royale Belge de Géographie* 82, fasc. 1–4 (1958): 80.

45. L. Novgorodsky, "La Jonction Nord-Midi: Liaison ferroviaire à travers la ville de Bruxelles," *La Technique des Travaux* 24, no. 1–2 (1948): 24–33.

46. Jos Vandenbreeden, "Naar een Stedenbouwkundige Architectuur: Victor Horta's Projecten voor het Centraal Station en het Municipal Development-Project," in *Bruxelles et la jonction Nord-Midi,* ed. Serge Jaumain and Chloé Deligne (Brussels: Archives de la Ville de Bruxelles, 2004), 167–75; Francis Strauven, "Art Nouveau to Art Deco: Horta's Later Development from a Historical Perspective," in *Horta: Art Nouveau to Modernism,* ed. Françoise Aubry and Jos Vandenbreeden (Ghent: Ludion Press, 1996), 222.

47. Abeels, "Communications," 240.

48. Bruneel, "Gare centrale à Bruxelles," 12.

49. Helleputte, "Bruxelles-Nord et Bruxelles-Midi," 16; House of Representatives debate on 24 February 1927 (Brunfaut, *Jonction,* 55); Mathieu, "Jonction

Nord-Midi," 173, 190–91; Deligne, "Urbanisme," 32; Abeels, "Comm-unications," 240.

50. The Junction is 35 meters wide and two kilometers long, or an area of 70,000 square meters (or 7 hectares); the area demolished was 17 hectares.

51. Mathieu, "Jonction Nord-Midi," 173, 175, 201.

52. Demey, *Capitale en chantier,* 1:17, 238; Martiny, "Une Ville qui se cherche," 288 lists 1,500 structures and 12,830 displaced inhabitants. Van den Herten, van Meerten, and Verbeugt, *Tunnel,* 23 lists 1,000 buildings in the 1904 registers, plus those expropriated by the ONJ three decades later. See also Brunfaut, *Jonction,* 210.

53. Van den Herten, van Meerten, and Verbeugt, *Tunnel,* 24; Deligne, "Urbanisme," 43.

54. Martiny, "Une Ville qui se cherche," 285.

55. Charles Buls, "Rapport sur le logement ouvrier," *Bulletin Communal de la Ville de Bruxelles (BCB)* (1891), 2: 650–69.

56. Deligne, "Urbanisme," 41–42.

57. Mathieu, "Jonction Nord-Midi," 200–201; Gourou, "Agglomération bruxel-loise," 80, probably Mathieu's source, gives the same figures.

58. Van den Herten, van Meerten, and Verbeugt, *Tunnel,* 24.

59. Leblicq, "Urbanisation," 364, 387, 390.

60. Verniers, "Transformations," 147; Martiny, "Une Ville qui se cherche," 288.

61. Brunfaut Biography. See Musée des Archives d'Architecture Moderne, *Catalogue des collections* (Brussels: Archives d'Architecture Moderne, 1986), 1:122. See also Waucquez Obituary, *BCB* 1 (1952): 84–85; Piette, "Brunfaut," 177–91. Puissant, Junction Colloquium.

62. Martiny, "Une Ville qui se cherche," 288; Demey, *Capitale en chantier,* 232.

63. Abeels, "Communications," 240; Demey, *Capitale en chantier,* 235; *Bruxelles et sa région* (Tournai: La Renaissance du Livre, 2000), 11, cited by Jaumain, in *Bruxelles et la jonction Nord-Midi,* p. 96; Gourou, "Agglomération bruxelloise," 80–81; Liane Ranieri, "Bruxelles au coeur de l'Etat libéral," in *Histoire de Bruxelles,* ed. Mina Martens (Toulouse: Editions Universitaires, 1976), 366.

64. *Germinal,* 28 October 1951, 12. "L'Albertine" is the colloquial name for the Royal Library on the Mont des Arts.

65. Deligne, "Urbanisme," 29–54.

66. *BCB,* 19 Ocober 1953, 2:922. The only restrictions imposed on redevelopment concerned street alignment and building height to retain the panoramic views from the upper city (Demey, *Capitale en chantier,* 1:232).

67. "Modernisation de l'éclairage électrique des rues de la Madeleine, de la Montagne, d'Arenberg, de la Putterie et du Marché-aux-Herbes: Question de M. de Grauw," *BCB,* 23 February 1953, 1:547.

68. "L'Urbanisation des terrains de la jonction: Les Aménagements projetés des quartiers riverains," *Le Soir,* 3 June 1954 reports on statement by Fernand Brunfaut, chair of the ONJ Committee.

69. Mathieu, "Jonction Nord-Midi," 181. For a list of structures erected on the Junction boulevards, see Martiny, "Une Ville qui se cherche," 288, 297; and Demey, *Capitale en chantier,* 1:232–40. The undistinguished nature of these structures is evidenced by their absence from contemporary architecture guidebooks.

70. Victor-Gaston Martiny, "Faut-il construire des tours à Bruxelles?" *Brabant: Revue Bimestrielle de la Fédération Touristique du Brabant* 3 (1966): 39–40.

71. Demey, *Capitale en chantier*, 1:234–36, 239.

72. Leblicq, "Urbanisation," 383–84.

73. Demey, *Capitale en chantier*, 1:35, 231, 240.

74. Deligne, "Urbanisme," 52.

75. Ibid., 52–53.

76. Undated document produced by Jörn-Aram Bihain, Thierry Decuypere, Antoine Warin, and others.

77. Meeting with Jorn Bihain, 30 September 2002.

78. Novgorodsky, "Jonction Nord-Midi," 37.

79. *La Libre Belgique*, 10 October 1952, 2; quoted in Demey, *Capitale en chantier*, 227.

80. "De la Jonction parisienne," *Journal des Chemins de Fer*, 1 March 1842, 17.

81. *Journal des Chemins de Fer*, 11 August 1855, 689; PP Report on Communications, 23 July 1855, 8.

82. Liebart, Session of 22 May 1901, quoted in Helleputte, "Bruxelles-Nord et Bruxelles-Midi," 30.

83. M. de Bassompièrre-Sewrin, "De la Pénétration des chemins de fer dans les villes," *Journal des Chemins de Fer*, 3 December 1854, 847–49.

84. United Kingdom, Parliament, Reports from Commissioners, *Report of Royal Commission Appointed to Investigate the Various Projects for Establishing Railway Termini within or in the Immediate Vicinity of the Metropolis* (London: HMSO, 1846), 21.

85. The city stations within the exclusion zone, Broad Street (1865), Liverpool Street (1871–75), Cannon Street (1866), Holborn Viaduct (1874–77), and Blackfriars (1864–65 and 1886), occupied only four separate sites, Broad Street and Liverpool Street being adjacent to each other. Fenchurch Street (1841 and 1854) was built before the zone was determined and outside of its eastern limit along Bishopsgate (Gordon Biddle and Jack Simmons, eds., *The Oxford Companion to British Railway History from 1603 to the 1990s* [Oxford: Oxford University Press, 1997], 272–73, 283, 289–92).

86. Charles Pearson, *City Improvements and Railroad Termini* (London: Effingham Wilson & J. Ridgway, n.d.).

87. Biddle and Simmons, *Oxford Companion*, 293–99.

88. Ibid., 287–88, 292–93, 352–53, 506.

89. M. Huet, *Les Chemins de fer métropolitains de Londres: Etude d'un réseau de chemins de fer métropolitains pour la ville de Paris, mission à Londres en mai 1876* (Paris: Dunod, 1878), 91, 98, 101.

90. Biddle and Simmons, *Oxford Companion*, 412–13.

91. The medieval fortifications of Philippe Auguste (1180–1223) and Charles V (ca. 1358) were modified by the Valois in the sixteenth century and later expanded on the west by Louis XIII. They were considered ineffective and redundant by Louis XIV, who had them converted into tree-lined boulevards as of 1670. For a concise description of Paris fortifications, see David H. Pinkney, *Napoleon III and the Rebuilding of Paris* (Princeton, NJ: Princeton University Press, 1958), 6–7.

92. "Halles de Paris," *Journal des Chemins de Fer*, 1849, 487; Fl. de Kérizouet, *Projet d'établissement d'un chemin de fer dans l'intérieur de la ville de Paris* (Paris: L. Mathias, 1845). See also René Clozier, *La Gare du Nord* (Paris: J.-B. Baillière, 1940), 61–68; Pierre Lavedan, *Histoire de l'urbanisme à Paris*, rev. ed. (Paris: Hachette, 1993), 476; Pinkney, *Napoleon III*, 79.

93. "Des Gares communes," *Journal des Chemins de Fer*, 23 July 1842, 137.

94. Jean Bastié, *La Croissance de la banlieue parisienne* (Paris: Presses Universitaires de France, 1964), 122.

95. *Journal des Chemins de Fer*, 21 October 1865, 695; 12 July 1862, 555.

96. The *Journal des Chemins de Fer* of 1874 mentions approval from the Conseil d'Etat to build within three years. Bastié, *Croissance*, 122 mentions the Law of 4 August 1875.

97. Mathieu, "Jonction Nord-Midi," 209.

98. "Chemins de fer de la Prusse," *Journal des Chemins de Fer*, 18 September 1869, 613; Ministerium der Öffentlichen Arbeiten and A. F. Leyen, *Berlin und seine Eisenbahnen, 1846--1896* (Berlin: Julius Springer, 1896), 1:238, 452–91.

Chapter 9

1. On growth of network and comparative tables with other countries on the Continent, see Laurent Dechesne, *Histoire économique et sociale de la Belgique depuis les origines jusqu'en 1914* (Liège: Joseph Wykmans, 1932), 422; Michael Mulhall, *Industries and Wealth of Nations* (London: Longmans, 1896), tables; Carl Strikwerda, *A House Divided: Catholics, Socialists and Flemish Nationalists in Nineteenth-Century Belgium* (Lanham, MD: Rowman & Littlefield, 1997), 402.

2. Gustave Abeels, "Les Communications dans et vers la ville aux XIXe et XXe siècles," in *La Région de Bruxelles: Des Villages d'autrefois à la ville d'aujourd'hui*, ed. Arlette Smolar-Meynart and Jean Stengers (Brussels: Crédit Communal, 1989), 237.

3. Janet Polasky, "Un Phénomène typiquement belge: Les Trains ouvriers et leur impact socio-économique," in *Le Temps des trains: 175 ans du train, 75 anniversaire S.N.C.B.*, ed. Bart van den Herten, Michelangelo van Meerten, and Greta Verbeugt (Louvain: Presses Universitaires de Louvain, 2001), 322.

4. Yvon Leblicq, "L'Urbanisation de Bruxelles au XIXe et XXe siècles (1830–1952)," in *Villes en mutation, XIXe-XXe siècles* (Brussels: Crédit Communal, 1982), 385.

5. The four constitutional reforms of 1970, 1980, 1988–89, and 1993 (signed 17 February 1994).

6. Documents parlementaires de la Chambre, session 1908–1909, séance du 28.5.1909, Document no. 161, Annexe A: "Note sur la jonction directe à Bruxelles des parties nord et sud du réseau des chemins de fer belges," pp. 785–875; quoted in Thierry Demey, *Bruxelles: Chronique d'une capitale en chantier*, vol. 1, *Du Voûtement de la Senne à la jonction Nord-Midi* (Brussels: Paul Legrain, 1990), 196.

7. Fernand Brunfaut, *La Jonction* (Brussels: Ad. Goemaere, 1959), 25, 49, 50, 59, 70, 77, 79, 82, 85; Valérie Piette, "Les Brunfaut: Une Famille d'architectes socialistes au service de la jonction," in *Bruxelles et la jonction Nord-Midi*, ed. Serge Jaumain and Chloé Deligne (Brussels: Archives de la Ville de Bruxelles, 2004), 177–90.

8. Demey, *Capitale en chantier*, 1:217–18.

9. Ernest Mahaim, *Les Abonnements d'ouvriers sur les lignes de chemins de fer belges et leurs effets sociaux* (Brussels: Misch & Thron, 1910), vii.

10. Mahaim, *Abonnements d'ouvriers*, 8.

11. Ernest Mahaim, *The Belgian Experience of State Railways* (London: Richard Clay, 1912), 10.

12. Mahaim, *Abonnements d'ouvriers*, 253–59.

13. Polasky, "Trains ouvriers," 324, 326; Janet Polasky, "Transplanting and Rooting Workers in London and Brussels: A Comparative History," *Journal of Modern History* 73, no. 3 (2001): 528–60, quoted from http://www.journals.uchicago.edu/JMH/journal/issues/v73n3/730302/730302/text.htm, pp. 9–10. Mahaim, *Abonnements d'ouvriers*, 5, 6, 8, 10, 204, this last quoting Emile Vandervelde, *L'Exode rural et le retour aux champs*, 2nd ed. (Paris: Félix Alcan, 1903), 155.

14. Mahaim, *Abonnements d'ouvriers*, 11–13. In 1908, the figures were 6,384,243 or 40.98 percent; Strikwerda, *A House Divided*, 274 concurs with this estimate. Dechesne gives the figures: 1870, 14,000; 1880, 355,000; 1900, more than 1,500,000; 1908, 6,300,000 (Dechesne, *Histoire économique et sociale*, 478).

15. Mahaim, *Abonnements d'ouvriers*, cartogramme no. 1 and carte no. 3, pp. 32–67, 80. The work performed by season ticket holders included skilled or unskilled labor in industry, mining, construction, commerce, agriculture, domestic labor, and government work.

16. Mahaim, *Abonnements d'ouvriers*, 68.

17. Ibid., 138, 141–43.

18. Strikwerda, *A House Divided*, 402; Mahaim, *Abonnements d'ouvriers*, 184; Abeels, "Communications," 232.

19. Mahaim, *Abonnements d'ouvriers*, 145–53.

20. Communities between 5,000 and 10,000, +79 percent; between 10,000 and 25,000, +164 percent; between 25,000 and 100,000, +186 percent. Marcel Smets, *L'Avénement de la cité-jardin en Belgique: Histoire de l'habitat social en Belgique de 1830 à 1930* (Liège: Mardaga, 1977), 9.

21. Between 1866 and 1911, growth in towns of more than 100,000 inhabitants in Belgium was from 8.1 percent to 11 percent (1910); in Britain, 23.9 percent (1861) to 37 percent (1911); in France, 7.7 percent (1861) to 14.8 percent (1911); and in Germany, 4.8 percent (1871) to 21.3 percent (1910). Jack Simmons, *The Victorian Railway* (London: Thames and Hudson, 1993), 343.

22. Demey, *Capitale en chantier*, 1:15; Dechesne, *Histoire économique et sociale*, 477. Rural population figures were as follows: 1846, 1,084,000; 1880, 1,199,000; 1895, 1,209,000; and 1910, 1,552,000, for a total Belgian population of 4,337,196 in 1846 and 6,679,282 in 1900.

23. Smets, *Avénement de la cité-jardin en Belgique*, 9.

24. Mahaim, *Abonnements d'ouvriers*, 162–70, 173, 175, 177, 194–95, 199–201. Strikwerda, *A House Divided*, 153, 274; Dechesne, *Histoire économique et sociale*, 478; André-Claude Content, "L'Habitat ouvrier à Bruxelles au XIXe siècle," *Revue Belge d'Histoire Contemporaine* 9, no. 3–4 (1977): 515.

25. Smets, *Avénement de la cité-jardin en Belgique*, 15, 18.

26. B. Seebohm Rowntree, *Land and Labour: Lessons from Belgium*, 2nd ed. (London: Macmillan, 1911), 453; Polasky, "Transplanting," 5.

27. Qualifying workers could borrow up to nine-tenths of the amount required to build a house at less than 4 percent, and taxes were reduced by half (Rowntree, *Land and Labour*, 454). Mahaim, *Abonnements d'ouvriers*, 189 stated more than 75,000. Smets, *Avénement de la cité-jardin en Belgique*, 49 mentions 60,064 certificates issued to testify to workers' eligibility for this housing between 1892 and 1900. Rowntree, *Land and Labour*, 456 lists 25,395 (1890–95), 47,890 (1895–1900), and 68,159 (1900–1905), or 141,444 between 1890 and 1905, twice as mentioned by Mahaim.

28. Smets, *Avénement de la cité-jardin en Belgique,* 19; Rowntree, *Land and Labour,* 428; Victor-Gaston Martiny, "Le Développement urbain," in Smolar-Meynart and Stengers, *Région de Bruxelles,* 178.

29. As opposed to 20 percent in Germany (Mahaim, *Abonnements d'ouvriers,* 194) and up to 29 percent in York, England (Rowntree, *Land and Labour,* 440, 445). In Brussels, rental housing decreased between 1881 and 1895 due to the economic crisis. Louis Verniers, "Esquisse provisoire d'une histoire de la plus-value foncière dans l'agglomération bruxelloise depuis un siècle," *Annales de la Société Royale d'Archéologie de Bruxelles* 41 (1937): 147.

30. Polasky, "Transplanting," 16; Rowntree, *Land and Labour,* 457.

31. The SNCB statistics department would trace activity only as far back as 1997 (telephone communication, 27 September 2002).

32. The peak figures of 46 percent and 46.5 percent in 1956 and 1957, respectively, may reflect increased building activity in preparation for the 1958 World's Fair. SNCB, *Rapport de l'exercice* (Brussels: SNCB, 1913–60).

33. François Befahy, "La Desserte ferroviaire de Bruxelles: Aujourd'hui et demain," paper delivered at the colloquium Bruxelles et la Jonction Nord-Midi: Histoire, Architecture et Mobilité Urbaines, Brussels, 1–2 October 2002. In 1998, 57 million of the 133,923,000 passengers, or 44.8 percent, used commuters' passes (Polasky, "Trains ouvriers," 332).

34. Or from 1,399,000 to 1,632,000 individuals. The census data includes place of residence, place of work, profession, mode of transport, frequency of commute if not daily, and time spent commuting. Van der Haegen, "De Actuele toestand van de binnenlandse pendel in België en meer in het bijzonder deze naar Brussel," *Bulletin de la Société Belge d'Etudes Géographiques* 34, no. 1 (1965): 171–72.

35. Out of 582,500 people employed in Brussels (17.3 percent of the country's employed population of 3,375,000), 190,300 or 32 percent were commuters (Van der Haegen, "Actuele toestand," 178, 192). See also Abeels, "Communications," 232.

36. De Brouckère, statement to Senate on 4 February 1931; cited in Brunfaut, *Jonction,* 77.

37. Van der Haegen, "Actuele toestand," 193, 212–13; Walter De Lannoy and Christian Kesteloot, "Les Divisions sociales et spatiales de la ville," *Contradictions* (Brussels) 58–59 (1990–91): 153–90, esp. 181.

38. Van der Haegen also lists other factors: increased schooling, which prepares a younger workforce for white- rather than blue-collar labor; shorter workdays; five-day workweeks; preference for a green living environment; linguistic conflicts; and high rents in the capital (Van der Haegen, "Actuele toestand," 216).

39. Marcel Mathieu, "La Jonction Nord-Midi: Ses conséquences pour la géographie urbaine de Bruxelles," *Bulletin de la Société Royale Belge de Géographie* 84, fasc. 3–4 (1961): 205, 206–8, 223.

40. Pierre de Maret (Rector of the Université Libre de Bruxelles), "Ouverture du colloque," paper delivered at the colloquium Bruxelles et la Jonction Nord-Midi: Histoire, Architecture et Mobilité Urbaines, Brussels, 1–2 October 2002.

41. Since publication of *Les Abonnements d'ouvriers* in 1910, only Janet Polasky's 2001 article addresses the topic. Polasky, "Transplanting," 23, n. 62.

42. For example, an impending railway strike on 15 March 2002 closed the Royal Library three hours early because there were not enough noncommuting staff members to keep it open (personal observation).

43. Thierry Demey, "Le Rail a influencé le développement de la ville," in *Art et architecture publics: Région de Bruxelles capitale,* ed. Yves Jacqmin et al. (Liège: Mardaga, 1999), 120; Bart van den Herten, Michelangelo van Meerten, and Greta Verbeugt, *Un Tunnel sous Bruxelles: Les 50 ans de la jonction Nord-Midi* (Brussels: Editions Racine, 2002), 26–27.

44. Strikwerda, *A House Divided,* 402; Polasky, "Trains ouvriers," 334; Polasky, "Transplanting," 19. Polasky, "Trains ouvriers," 334 states that "workmen's trains intensified the geographic particularism—local as well as regional—that continues to limit the development of a national identity in Belgium." This suggests that development might be possible, whereas, in fact, the opposite is true. The division of the country along the ethnolinguistic divide has been deepening since the end of World War II and has resulted in a federal monarchy where linguistic issues are contested with tenacity if not animosity.

45. Among the historians whose work attempted to create a Belgian nation and foster nationalism, Henri Pirenne was the most renowned (*Histoire de Belgique,* 7 vols. [Brussels: Henri Lamertin, 1902–32]).

Conclusion

1. Anthony Vidler, "The Scenes of the Street: Transformation in Ideal and Reality, 1750–1871," in *On Streets,* ed. Stanford Anderson (Cambridge: MIT Press, 1978), 29.2. Louis Pasteur began his major discoveries in 1865.

3. H. J. Dyos, "The Slums of Victorian London," *Victorian Studies* 11 (September 1967): 27.

4. Luca Bertolini and Tejo Spit, *Cities on Rails: The Redevelopment of Railway Station Areas* (London: E. & F. N. Spon, 1998), 43. This model is also implied in the program "Les Lieux-mouvements de la Ville," in Paris, which has resulted in a number of publications, such as *Architecture des lieux-mouvements et conception de réseaux* (Paris: Plan Urbain, DRAST, RATP, and SNCF, 1996); Karen Bowie et al., "Polarisation du territoire et développement urbain: Les Gares du Nord et de l'Est et la transformation de Paris au XIXe siècle" (Paris: Plan Urbain, PREDIT, SNCF, and RATP, 1999).

5. Ernest Mahaim, *Les Abonnements d'ouvriers sur les lignes de chemins de fer belges et leurs effets sociaux* (Brussels: Misch & Thron, 1910); Janet Polasky, "Transplanting and Rooting Workers in London and Brussels: A Comparative History," *Journal of Modern History* 73, no. 3 (2001): 528–60.

6. Railways had become state-owned in Belgium and Germany by World War I, and they were state operations in all four countries by the middle of the twentieth century. They have since then been privatized, at least in part, in all four countries.

7. Gordon Biddle and Jack Simmons, eds., *The Oxford Companion to British Railway History from 1603 to the 1990s* (Oxford: Oxford University Press, 1997), 312–13.

8. Jean Bastié, "Supplément," in Pierre Lavedan, *Histoire de l'urbanisme à Paris,* new ed., ed. Jean Bastié (Paris: Hachette, 1993), 661–62.

9. Carroll L. V. Meeks, *The Railroad Station: An Architectural History* (New Haven, CT: Yale University Press, 1956), 5; Karen Bowie, " 'L'Eclectisme pit-

toresque' et l'architecture des gares parisiennes au XIXe siècle" (PhD diss., Université de Paris I Panthéon-Sorbonne, 1985).

10. Karen Bowie, "L'Implantation des gares du Nord et de l'Est dans Paris, 1830–1870: Premiers résultats d'une recherche," in *La Gare: Dedans, dehors* (Paris: Plan Urbain, DRAST, RATP, and SNCF, 1996), 135–42.

11. Meeks, *Railroad Station,* 5.

Selected Bibliography

Only the most significant publications are listed here. All works referred to in the text are acknowledged in endnotes. Included here at the end are three separate sections on the London Euston Road terminals, the Berlin Anhalter Bahnhof, and railway legislation.

Abercrombie, Patrick. "Brussels: A Study in Development and Town Planning." *Town Planning Review* 3–4, no. 2–4 (July, October 1912, January 1913): 2, 97–113; 3, 188–95; 4, 258–72.

Acworth, William Mitchell. *The Railways of England.* London: J. Murray, 1889. Fifth edition, 1900.

Architekten-Verein zu Berlin, ed. *Berlin und seine Bauten.* 2nd ed. Berlin: Ernst & Korn, 1896.

Audet-Perrier, Dominique. *Les Premiers pas des chemins de fer en Charente: Mythes et réalités, 1836–1883.* Paris: Le Croit-vif, 1997.

Baroli, Marc. *Le Train dans la littérature française.* Paris: La Vie du Rail, 1964.

Bastié, Jean. *La Croissance de la banlieue parisienne.* Paris: Presses Universitaires de France, 1964.

Bédarida, François. "Urban Growth and Social Structure in Nineteenth-Century Poplar." *London Journal* 1, no. 2 (1975): 159–88.

Besme, Victor. *Plan d'ensemble pour l'extension et l'embellissement de l'agglomération bruxelloise.* Brussels: Rapport fait au Gouvernement de Brabant, 1866.

Biddle, Gordon, ed. *Britain's Historic Railway Buildings: An Oxford Gazetteer of Structures and Sites.* Oxford: Oxford University Press, 2003.

Biddle, Gordon, and Jack Simmons, eds. *The Oxford Companion to British Railway History from 1603 to the 1990s.* Oxford: Oxford University Press, 1997.

Blackbourn, David. *The Long Nineteenth Century: A History of Germany, 1780–1918.* Oxford: Oxford University Press, 1998.

Bley, Peter. *150 Jahre Eisenbahn Berlin-Potsdam: Aus der Geschichte der ältesten Eisenbahn in Berlin und Preussen.* Düsseldorf: Alba, 1988.

———. *Königlich Preußische Militäreisenbahn: 125 Jahre Berlin-Zossen-Jüterborg.* Düsseldorf: Alba, 2000.

Booth, Charles. *Descriptive Map of London Poverty.* London: Stanford's Geographical Establishment, 1889.

———. *Labour and Life of the People in London.* London: MacMillan, 1902–4.

———. *Life and Labour of the People in London.* 8 vols. London: Macmillan, 1892.

———. *Life and Labour of the People in London*. 2nd ser., Industry. 5 vols. New York: AMS Press, 1970. First published 1892.

———. *Life and Labour of the People in London*. 3rd ser., Religious Influences (1902–4). New York: AMS Press, 1970.

Bowie, Karen. " 'L'Eclectisme pittoresque' et l'architecture des gares parisiennes au XIXe siècle." PhD diss., Université de Paris I, 1985.

———. "La Gare de l'Est à Paris et la réflexion sur les grands projets d'aménagement au siècle dernier." In *Infrastructures, villes et territoires*, edited by Claude Prelorenzo, 73–78. Paris: L'Harmattan, 2000.

———. "Les Gares du Nord et de l'Est au siècle dernier." In *Villes en gares*, edited by Isaac Joseph, 34–44. La Tour d'Aigues: Editions de l'Aube, 1999.

———. "Gares et villes au XIXe siècle: Deux ingénieurs des Ponts et Chaussées et l'implantation des gares du Nord et de l'Est à Paris." *Annales des Ponts et Chaussées* 89 (April 1999): 4–9.

———. *Les Grandes gares parisiennes: Historique, les grandes gares parisiennes au XIXe siècle*. Paris: Délégation à l'Action Artistique de la Ville de Paris, 1987.

———. "L'Implantation des gares du Nord et de l'Est dans Paris, 1830–1870: Premiers résultats d'une recherche." In *La Gare: Dedans, dehors*, 135–42. Paris: Plan Urbain, DRAST, RATP, and SNCF, 1996.

———. "Introduction au rapport de l'ingénieur en chef des Ponts et Chaussées Cabanel de Sermet sur les tracés étudiés et sur celui à adopter pour la première section du chemin de fer de Paris à Strasbourg." *Revue d'Histoire des Chemins de Fer* 23 (2000): 79–137.

———, ed. *La Modernité avant Haussmann: Formes de l'espace urbain à Paris, 1801–1853*. Paris: Editions Recherches, 2001.

———. "The Rothschilds, the Railways, and the Urban Form of 19th Century Paris." In *Die Rothschilds: Eine europäische Familie*, edited by Georg Heuberger, 87–97. Frankfurt: Thorbecke/Boydell & Brewer and Jüdisches Museum, 1994.

Bowie, Karen, and Marie-Noëlle Polino, eds. "Arts et chemins de fer: Actes du IIIe Colloque de l'Association pour l'Histoire des Chemins de Fer en France." *Revue d'Histoire des Chemins de Fer*, 10–11. Paris: AHICF, 1994.

Bowie, Karen, and Simon Texier, eds. *Paris et ses chemins de fer*. Paris: Action Artistique de la Ville de Paris, 2003.

Bowie, Karen, Pauline Prévost-Marcilhacy, P. Laurent, and Pierre Pinon. "Polarisation du territoire et développement urbain: Les Gares du Nord et de l'Est et la transformation de Paris au XIXe siècle." Paris: Plan Urbain, PREDIT, SNCF, and RATP, 1999, http://urbamet.documentation .equipement.gouv.fr/documents/EQUTEX00005329/EQUTEX00005329 .pdf.

Brophy, James M. *Capitalism, Politics, and Railroads in Prussia, 1830–1870*. Columbus: Ohio State University Press, 1998.

Brun, Amédée. *Des Dommages causés par l'exécution de travaux publics de chemins de fer*. Paris: A. Pedone, 1898.

Bruneel, Frédéric. *Avant-Projet de chemin de fer métropolitain avec gare centrale à Bruxelles*. Ghent: Imprimerie C. Annoot-Braeckman, 1893.

Brunfaut, Fernand. *La Jonction.* Brussels: Ad. Goemaere, 1959.

Buls, Charles. "Rapport sur le logement ouvrier." *Bulletin Communal de la Ville de Bruxelle* (1891): no. 2, 650–69.

Camp, Maxime du. *Paris, ses organes, ses fonctions, sa vie dans la seconde moitié du XIXe siècle.* 2nd ed. 6 vols. Paris: Hachette, 1875.

Cannadine, David, and David Reeder, eds. *Exploring the Urban Past: Essays in Urban History by H. J. Dyos.* Cambridge: Cambridge University Press, 1982.

Carlisle, Robert Bruce. *The Proffered Crown: Saint-Simonianism and the Doctrine of Hope.* Baltimore: Johns Hopkins University Press, 1987.

Carmona, Michel. *Haussmann.* Paris: Fayard, 2000.

Caron, François. *Histoire de l'exploitation d'un grand réseau: La Compagnie du Chemin de Fer du Nord, 1846–1937.* Paris: Mouton, 1973.

———. *Histoire des chemins de fer en France,* vol. 1, *1740–1883;* vol. 2, *1883–1937.* Paris: Fayard, 1997, 2005.

Casselle, Pierre. *Commission des Embellissements de Paris: Rapport à l'empereur Napoléon III rédigé par le comte Henri Siméon.* Paris: Commission du Vieux Paris, Rotonde de la Villette, 2000.

———. "Les Travaux de la Commission des Embellissements de Paris en 1853: Pouvait-on transformer la capitale sans Haussmann?" *Bibliothèque de l'Ecole des Chartes* 55 (1997): 645–89.

Cawston, Arthur. *A Comprehensive Scheme for Street Improvements in London accompanied by Maps and Sketches.* London: Edward Stanford, 1893.

Chabat, Pierre. *Bâtiments de chemin de fer: Embarcadères, plans de gare, stations, abris, maisons de garde, remises de locomotives, halles à marchandises, remises de voitures, ateliers, réservoirs etc.* 2 vols. Paris: A. Morel, 1862–66.

Chadwick, Edwin. *Report on the Sanitary Condition of the Labouring Population of Great Britain.* Edited by M. W. Flinn. Edinburgh: University Press, 1964. First published 1842.

Chapman, Brian. "Baron Haussmann and the Planning of Paris." *Town Planning Review* 24, no. 3 (1953): 177–92.

———. *The Life and Times of Baron Haussmann: Paris in the Second Empire.* London: Weidenfeld and Nicolson, 1957.

Chaudun, Nicolas. *Haussmann au crible.* Paris: Edition des Syrtes, 2000.

Chevalier, Louis. *Classes laborieuses et classes dangereuses à Paris pendant la première moitié du XIXe s.* Paris: Plon, 1958.

———. *La Formation de la population parisienne au XIXe s.* Paris: Presses Universitaires de France, 1950.

Chevalier, Michel. *Des Chemins de fer en France.* Paris: H. Fournier, 1838.

———. *Des Intérêts matériels en France: Travaux publics, routes, canaux, chemins de fer.* 2nd ed. Paris: Charles Gosselin et W. Coquebert, 1838.

Choay, Françoise, ed. *Baron Haussmann: Mémoires.* Paris: Seuil, 2000.

Clarke, Linda. *Building Capitalism: Historical Change and the Labour Process in the Production of the Built Environment.* London: Routledge, 1992.

Clozier, René. *La Gare du Nord.* Paris: J.-B. Baillière, 1940.

Cognasson, Patrick. *Gare de l'Est: Porte ouverte sur l'Europe.* Paris: Vie du Rail, 1994.

Content, André-Claude. "L'Habitat ouvrier à Bruxelles au XIXe siècle." *Revue Belge d'Histoire Contemporaine* 9, no. 3–4 (1977): 501–17.

Cooke, M. Emily. *A Geographical Study of a London Borough: St. Pancras.* London: University of London Press, 1932.

Crédit Communal de Belgique. *Bruxelles, construire et reconstruire: Architecture et aménagement urbain, 1780–1914.* Brussels: Crédit Communal, 1979.

Daly, César. "Des Gares de chemin de fer." *Revue Générale d'Architecture* 6 (1845–46): 509–29.

Daumard, Adeline. "Conditions de logement et position sociale." In *Le Parisien chez lui au XIXe siècle,* ed.Adeline Daumard and Jean Favier. Paris: Archives Nationales, 1976.

———. *Maisons de Paris et propriétaires parisiens au XIXe siècle, 1809–1880.* Paris: Cujas, 1965.

De Lannoy, Walter, and Christian Kesteloot. "Les Divisions sociales et spatiales de la ville." *Contradictions* (Brussels) 58–59 (1990–91): 153–90.

Deligne, Chloé. "Discours politique et urbanisme: Réflexion à partir du cas de la jonction Nord-Midi, Bruxelles, 1900–1960." *Revue Belge de Géographie* 122, n.s. 1, fasc. 63 (1998): 29–54.

Delmelle, Joseph. *Histoire des chemins de fer belges.* Brussels: Legrain, 1977.

Demey, Thierry. *Bruxelles: Chronique d'une capitale en chantier.* 2 vols. Brussels: Paul Legrain, 1990–92.

Denford, Steven L. J. *Agar Town: The Life and Death of a Victorian Slum.* Occasional Paper of the Camden History Society. London: Camden History Society, 1995.

Denton, William. *Observations on the Displacement of the Poor, by Metropolitan Railways and by Other Public Improvements.* London: Bell & Dalby, 1861.

Des Cars, Jean, and Pierre Pinon. *Paris-Haussmann: "Le pari d'Haussmann."* Paris: Edition du Pavillon de l'Arsenal, 1991.

Duhem, Gilles, Boris Grésillon, and Dorothée Kohler, eds. *Paris-Berlin: Regards croisés sur deux capitales européennes.* Paris: Anthropos, 2000.

Dunlavy, Colleen. *Politics and Industrialization: Early Railroads in the United States and Prussia.* Princeton, NJ: Princeton University Press, 1994.

Dyos, Harold James, ed. *Exploring the Urban Past: Essays in Urban History.* Cambridge: Cambridge University Press, 1982.

———. "The Growth of a Pre-Victorian Suburb: South London, 1580–1836." *Town Planning Review* 25, no. 1 (1954): 59–78.

———. "Railways and Housing in Victorian London: I, Attila in London; II, Rustic Townsmen." *Journal of Transport History* 2 (1955): 11–21 & 90–100.

———. "The Slums of Victorian London." *Victorian Studies* 11 (September 1967): 5–40.

———. "Some Social Costs of Railway Building in London." *Journal of Transport History* 3, no. 1 (1957–58): 23–31.

———. "The Speculative Builders and Developers of Victorian London." *Victorian Studies* 11 (Summer 1968): 641–90.

———. *Victorian Suburb: A Study of the Growth of Camberwell.* With a foreword by Sir John Summerson. Leicester, UK: Leicester University Press, 1961.

————. "Workmen's Fares in South London, 1860–1914." *Journal of Transport History* 1, no. 1 (1953): 3–19.

Dyos, Harold James, and Michael Wolff, eds. *The Victorian City. Images and Realities.* 2 vols. London: Routledge & Kegan Paul, 1973.

Eichholz, Dietrich. *Junker und Bourgeoisie von 1848 in der Preussische Eisenbahngeschichte.* Berlin: Akademie-Verlag, 1962.

Eisenbahnjahr Ausstellungsgesellschaft mbH, Nürnberg. *Zug der Zeit, Zeit der Züge: Deutsche Eisenbahn, 1835–1985.* Berlin: Siedler, 1985.

Escher, Felix. *Berlin und sein Umland: Zur Genese der Berliner Stadtlandschaft bis zum Beginn des 20. Jahrhunderts.* Berlin: Colloquium Verlag, 1985.

Evenson, Norma. *Paris: A Century of Change, 1878–1978.* New Haven, CT: Yale University Press, 1980.

Ferguson, Niall. *The House of Rothschild.* 2 vols. New York: Viking, 1998.

Freeman, Michael. *Railways and the Victorian Imagination.* New Haven, CT: Yale University Press, 1999.

Fremdling, Rainer. *Eisenbahnen und Deutsches Wirtschaftswachstum, 1840–1879: Ein Beitrag zur Entwicklungstheorie und zur Theorie der Infrastruktur.* Dortmund: Gesellschaft für Westfälische Wirtschaftsgeschichte E.V., 1975.

Gaillard, Jeanne. *Paris: La Ville, 1852–1870.* Paris: L'Harmattan, 1976.

Gall, Lothar, and Manfred Pohl, eds. *Die Eisenbahn in Deutschland: Von den Anfängen bis zur Gegenwart.* Munich: C. H. Beck, 1999.

Gille, Bertrand. *Histoire de la maison Rothschild.* 2 vols. Geneva: Droz, 1965–67.

Girard, Louis. *La Politique des travaux publics sous le Second Empire.* Paris: Armand Colin, 1952.

Gourou, Pierre. "L'Agglomération bruxelloise, éléments d'une géographie urbaine." *Bulletin de la Société Royale Belge de Géographie* 82, fasc. 1–4 (1958): 3–83.

Grinling, Charles Herbert. *The History of the Great Northern Railway, 1845–1922.* London: George Allen & Unwin, 1966.

Guérin Brot, Isabelle, and Jean Pierre Babelon. *Les Débuts du chemin de fer en France, 1831–1870.* Paris: Ministère de la Culture et de l'Environnement and SNCF, 1977.

Gwynn, E. "The Jerry Builder Considered in Relation to the Housing of the Poor." *Public Health* 13, no. 4 (1901): 251–58.

Haegen, van der. "De Actuele toestand van de binnenlandse pendel in België en meer in het bijzonder deze naar Brussel." *Bulletin de la Société Belge d'Etudes Géographiques* 34, no. 1 (1965): 171–216.

Halbwachs, Maurice. *Les Expropriations et le prix des terrains à Paris (1860–1900).* Paris: Cornély, 1909.

————. " 'Gross Berlin': Grande agglomération ou grande ville?" *Annales d'Histoire Economique et Sociale* 6 (1934): 547–70.

————. *La Population et les tracés de voies à Paris depuis un siècle.* 2nd ed. Paris: Presses Universitaires de France, 1928.

Hammer, Karl. *Jakob Ignaz Hittorff: Ein Pariser Baumeister, 1792–1867.* Stuttgart: Anton Hiersemann, 1968.

Handbuch des Eisenbahnwesens in ökonomischer, rechtlichen, administrativer und technischer Beziehung. 5 vols. Stuttgart: Meier, 1873–82.

Hansemann, David Justus Ludwig. *Die Eisenbahnen und deren Aktionäre in ihrem Verhältnis zum Staat.* Leipzig: Renger, 1837.

———. *Über die Ausführung des Preussischen Eisenbahnsystems.* Berlin: Alexander Duncker, 1843.

Harvey, David. "Paris, 1850–1870." In *Consciousness and the Urban Experience: Studies in the History and Theory of Capitalist Urbanization,* edited by David Harvey, 63–220. Baltimore: Johns Hopkins University Press, 1985.

———. *Paris, Capital of Modernity.* New York: Routledge, 2003.

Herbert, Robert. *Impressionism, Art, Leisure and Parisian Society.* New Haven, CT: Yale University Press, 1988.

Hofmann, Albert. "Gross-Berlin, sein Verhältnis zur modernen Grosstadtbewegung und der Wettbewerb zur Erlangung eines Grundplanes für die städtebauliche Entwicklung Berlins und seiner Vororte im zwanzigten Jahrhundert." *Deutsche Bauzeitung* 28, Beilage für Wettbewerbe (2 April 1910): 198.

Holmes, Malcolm J. *Somers Town, a Record of Change.* London: Borough of Camden Libraries and Arts Department, 1989.

Hoyle, Susan Ryley. "The First Battle for London: The Royal Commission on Metropolitan Termini, 1846." *London Journal* 8 (1982): 140–55.

Jaumain, Serge, and Chloé Deligne, eds. *Bruxelles et la jonction Nord-Midi.* Studia Bruxellae 3. Brussels: Archives de la Ville de Bruxelles, 2004.

Joest, Thomas von, and Claudine de Vaulchier. *Hittorff, un architecte du XIXème siècle.* Paris: Musées de la Ville de Paris, 1986.

Jordan, David P. *Transforming Paris: The Life and Labors of Baron Haussmann.* New York: Free Press, 1995.

Kampe, Hans Georg. *Preußische Eisenbahntruppen, 1871–1945: Die Königliche Militäreisenbahn und die Eisenbahnübungsplätze im Süden Berlins.* Berlin: Erwin Meißler, 1998.

Kellett, John Reginald. *The Impact of Railways on Victorian Cities.* London: Routledge & Kegan Paul, 1969.

Klee, Wolfgang. *Preussische Eisenbahngeschichte.* Stuttgart: Kohlhammer, 1982.

Kleihues, Josef Paul, and Christina Rathgeber, eds. *Berlin-New York, Like and Unlike: Essays on Architecture and Art from 1870 to the Present.* New York: Rizzoli, 1993.

Krings, Ulrich. *Bahnhofsarchitektur: Deutsche Grossstadtbahnhöfe des Historismus.* Munich: Prestel, 1985.

Ladd, Brian. *The Ghosts of Berlin: Confronting German History in the Urban Landscape.* Chicago: University of Chicago Press, 1997.

Lamalle, Ulysse. *Histoire des chemins de fer belges.* 2nd ed. Brussels: Lebègue, 1943. Third edition, 1953.

Lambert, Michèle. "Les Problématiques du chemin de fer dans la ville, 1830–1855." *Revue d'Histoire des Chemins de Fer* 5–6 (1991–92): 195–236.

Lardner, Dionysius. *Railway Economy.* London: Taylor, Walton, and Maberly, 1850.

Lavedan, Pierre. *Histoire de l'urbanisme à Paris.* 2nd ed. Paris: Hachette, 1993.

———. "L'Influence de Haussmann: L'Haussmanisation dans l'urbanisme et habitation." *La Vie Urbaine,* n.s. (July-December 1953): 302–17.

Leblicq, Yvon. "L'Evolution de la physionomie de Bruxelles au XIXe siècle." In *Bruxelles, construire et reconstruire*, 12–39, 88–90. Brussels: Crédit Communal, 1979.

Lees, Lynn Hollen, and Andrew Lees, eds. *Cities and the Making of Modern Europe, 1750–1914.* Cambridge: Cambridge University Press, 2007.

Leyen, Alfred von der. *Die Eisenbahnpolitik des Fürsten Bismarck.* Berlin: Julius Springer, 1914.

List, Friedrich. *Schriften, Reden, Briefe.* 10 vols. Berlin: R. Hobbing, 1927–35.

———. *Über eine Sächsisches Eisenbahn-System als Grundlage eines allgemeinen Deutschen Eisenbahn-Systems.* 2nd ed. Mainz: Dumjahn, 1984. First published Leipzig, 1833

Lodge, Martin Christopher Edmund. *On Different Tracks: Designing Railway Regulation in Britain and Germany.* Westport, CT: Praeger, 2002.

Loyer, François. *Paris XIXe siècle: L'Immeuble et la rue.* Paris: Hazan, 1987.

Mahaim, Ernest. *Les Abonnements d'ouvriers sur les lignes de chemins de fer belges et leurs effets sociaux.* Brussels: Misch & Thron, 1910.

———. *The Belgian Experience of State Railways.* London: Richard Clay, 1912.

Malcolmson, Patricia E. "Getting a Living in the Slums of Victorian Kensington." *London Journal* 1 (May 1975): 28–55.

Marcus, Sharon. *Apartment Stories: City and Home in Nineteenth-Century Paris and London.* Berkeley: University of California Press, 1999.

———. "Haussmannization as Anti-Modernity: The Apartment House in Parisian Urban Discourse, 1850–1880." *Journal of Urban History* 27, no. 6 (2001): 723–45.

Mareschal, Jules. *Des Chemins de fer considérés au point de vue social et civilisateur.* Paris: Hachette, 1854.

Martens, Bob. *Der Bahnhofsvorplatz in der Großstadt im 19. und 20. Jahrhundert.* Dissertation der Technischen Universität Wien, no. 46. Wien: VWGÖ, 1988.

Martens, Mina. "Charles Buls, ses papiers conservés aux Archives de la Ville." *Cahiers Bruxellois*, 1957, 252–323; 1958, 30–58.

———, ed. *Histoire de Bruxelles.* Toulouse: Editions Universitaires, 1976.

Martiny, Victor-Gaston. "Faut-il construite des tours à Bruxelles?" *Brabant: Revue Bimestrielle de la Fédération Touristique du Brabant* 3 (1966): 34–40.

Massa-Gille, Geneviève. *Histoire des emprunts de la ville de Paris, 1814– 1875.* Paris: Commission des Travaux Historiques de la Ville de Paris, 1973.

Mathieu, Marcel. "La Jonction Nord-Midi: Ses conséquences pour la géographie urbaine de Bruxelles." *Bulletin de la Société Royale Belge de Géographie* 84, fasc. 3–4 (1961): 161–224.

Mead, Christopher. "Urban Contingency and the Problem of Representation in Second Empire Paris." *Journal of the Society of Architectural Historians* 54, no. 2 (1995): 138–74.

Meeks, Carroll L. V. *The Railroad Station: An Architectural History.* New Haven, CT: Yale University Press, 1956.

Meinke, Bernhard. "Die älteste Stimmen über die militärische Bedeutug der Einsenbahnen, 1833–1842." *Archiv für Eisenbahnwesen* 41 (1918): 921–34, and 42 (1919): 46–74.

Merruau, Charles. *Souvenir de l'Hôtel de Ville de Paris, 1848–1852*. Paris: Plon, 1875.

Ministerium der Öffentlichen Arbeiten and A. F. Leyen. *Berlin und seine Eisenbahnen, 1846–1896*. 2 vols. Berlin: Julius Springer, 1896.

Mistler, Jean. *Gare de l'Est*. Paris: Grasset, 1975.

Mitchell, Allan. *The Great Train Race: Railways and the Franco-German Rivalry*. New York: Berghahn Books, 2000.

———. "Private Enterprise or Public Service? The Eastern Railway Company and the French State in the Nineteenth Century." *Journal of Modern History* 69, no. 1 (1997): 18–41.

Morrell, R. Conyers. *The Story of Agar Town*. London: Premo Press, 1935.

Moureau, François, and Marie Noëlle Polino, eds. *Ecritures du chemin de fer*. Symposium, Sorbonne, 11 May 1996. Paris: Klincksieck, 1997.

Mumford, Lewis. *The Culture of Cities*. New York: Harcourt, Brace, 1938.

Nead, Lynda. *Victorian Babylon: People, Streets and Images in Nineteenth-Century London*. New Haven, CT: Yale University Press, 2000.

Nipperdey, Thomas. *Deutsche Geschichte, 1800–1866: Bürgerwelt und starker Staat*. Munich: C. H. Beck, 1983.

———. *Deutsche Geschichte, 1866–1918*. Munich: C. H. Beck, 1990.

Nock, Oswald Stevens. *The Great Northern Railway*. London: Ian Allan, 1958.

Nothomb, M. *Travaux publics en Belgique, 1830–1839: Chemins de fer et routes ordinaires*. Rapport Présenté aux Chambres Législatives, 12 November 1839. Second edition, 1840.

Novgorodsky, L. "La Jonction Nord-Midi: Liaison ferroviaire à travers la ville de Bruxelles." *La Technique des Travaux* 23, no. 5–6 (1947): 157–74; no. 7–8 (1947): 239–52; no. 9–10 (1947): 281–92; 24, no. 1–2 (1948): 23–37.

Olsen, Donald J. *The City as a Work of Art: London, Paris, Vienna*. New Haven, CT: Yale University Press, 1986.

———. *The Growth of Victorian London*. London: Batsford, 1978.

Ordnance Survey. "Skeleton Ordnance Survey of London and Its Environs." Southampton, UK: Ordnance Map Office, 1851.

Orth, August. "Berlin Centralbahn: Eisenbahnproject zur Verbindung der Berliner Bahnhöfe nach der innern Stadt." Berlin, 1871.

———. *Zur bauliche Reorganisation der Stadt Berlin: Zwei Denkschriften und die am Schinkelfest des Berliner Architekten Vereins 1875 gehaltene Festrede*. Berlin: Ernst & Korn, 1875.

Ottley, George. *A Bibliography of British Railway History*. London: HMSO, 1965.

———. *A Bibliography of British Railway History*. 2nd ed. London: HMSO, 1983.

Ottley, George, Graham Boyes, Matthew Searle, and Donald Steggles, eds. *Ottley's Bibliography of British Railway History, Second Supplement 12957–19605*. York: National Railway Museum in association with Railway & Canal Historical Society, 1998.

Papayanis, Nicholas. *Planning Paris before Haussmann*. Baltimore: Johns Hopkins University Press, 2004.

———. "Urbanisme du Paris souterrain: Premiers projets de chemin de fer urbain et naissance de l'urbanisme des cités modernes." *Histoire, Economie, Sociétés* 17, no. 4 (1998): 745–70.

Pearson, Charles. *City Improvements and Railroad Termini.* London: Effingham Wilson & J. Ridgway, 1851.

Perdonnet, Auguste. *Traité élémentaire des chemins de fer.* 1st ed. 2 vols. Paris: Langlois et Leclercq, 1855–56.

———. *Traité élémentaire des chemins de fer.* 3rd ed. 4 vols. Paris: Garnier, 1865.

Perdonnet, Auguste, and Camille Polonceau. *Portefeuille de l'ingénieur des chemins de fer.* 2nd ed. 4 vols. Paris: E. Lacroix, 1861. Second edition, 1866; new edition, 1873.

Peschaud, Marcel. *Les Chemins de fer allemands et la guerre.* Paris: Charles Lavauzelle, 1927.

Pevsner, Nikolaus. *London, except the Cities of London and Westminster.* The Buildings of England. Harmondsworth, UK: Penguin, 1952.

Pevsner, Nikolaus, and Bridget Cherry. *London 4: North.* The Buildings of England. Harmondsworth, UK: Penguin, 1998.

Picard, Alfred. *Les Chemins de fer français: Etude historique sur la constitution et le régime du réseau.* 6 vols. Paris: J. Rothschild, 1884–85.

Pierres et Rues: Bruxelles, croissance urbaine, 1780–1980. Brussels: Société Générale de Banque and Sint Lukasarchief, 1982.

Pierson, Kurt. *Die Königliche-Preußische Militär-Eisenbahn.* Stuttgart: Motorbuch Verlag, 1979.

Pietra Santa, Prosper de. *Chemins de fer et santé publique: Hygiène des voyageurs et des employés.* Paris: Hachette, 1861.

Piette, Christine. "Rapports sociaux et quartiers parisiens." *Proceedings of the Annual Meeting of the Western Society for French History* 15 (1988): 235–44.

Pinkney, David H. *Napoleon III and the Rebuilding of Paris.* Princeton, NJ: Princeton University Press, 1958.

Pinon, Pierre. *Atlas du Paris haussmannien.* Paris: Parigramme, 2002.

Pirenne, Henri. *Histoire de Belgique.* 7 vols. Brussels: Henri Lamertin, 1902–32.

Polasky, Janet. "Transplanting and Rooting Workers in London and Brussels: A Comparative History." *Journal of Modern History* 73, no. 3 (2001): 528–60.

Polino, Marie-Noëlle, and Ralf Roth, eds. *The City and the Railway in Europe.* Aldershot: Ashgate, 2003.

Pönitz, Carl Eduard. *Die Eisenbahnen als militärisch Operationslinien betrachtet und durch Beispiele erläutert.* Adorf: Verlagsbüreau, 1842.

Ranieri, Liane. *Léopold II urbaniste.* Brussels: Hayez, 1973.

Ratcliffe, Barrie M. " 'Classes laborieuses et classes dangereuses à Paris pendant la première moitié du XIXe siècle': The Chevalier Thesis Reexamined." *French Historical Studies* 17 (1991): 542–74.

———. "Urban Space and the Siting of the Parisian Railway Station, 1830–1847." *Proceedings of the Western Society for French History* 15 (1988): 224–34.

Réau, Louis, Pierre Lavedan, Renée Plouin, Jean Hugueney, and Robert Auzelle. *L'Oeuvre du Baron Haussmann.* Paris: Presses Universitaires de France, 1954.

Reden, Friedrich Wilhelm von. *Die Eisenbahnen Deutschlands.* Berlin: Mittler, 1843.

Reynaud, Léonce, and Edouard Collignon, eds. *Les Chemins de fer au XIXe siè-cle*. Paris: Presses de l'École Nationale des Ponts et Chaussées, 1988. First published 1883.

———. *Les Travaux publics de la France*, vol. 2, *Les Chemins de fer*, by Edouard Collignon. Paris: J. Rothschild, 1883.

Ribeill, Georges. *La Révolution ferroviaire: La Formation des compagnies de chemin de fer en France, 1823–1870*. Paris: Belin, 1993.

Richards, Jeffrey, and John M. MacKenzie. *The Railway Station*. Oxford: Oxford University Press, 1986.

Röll, Victor von, ed. *Enzyklopädie des Eisenbahnwesens*. 2nd ed. 10 vols. Berlin: Urban & Schwarzenberg, 1912–23.

Roth, Ralf. *Das Jahrhundert Der Eisenbahn: Die Herrschaft Über Raum Und Zeit, 1800–1914*. Ostfildern: Jan Thorbecke Verlag, 2005.

Rouleau, Bernard. *Le Tracé des rues de Paris: Formation, typologie, fonctions*. Paris: CNRS, 1975.

Rowntree, B. Seebohm. *Land and Labour: Lessons from Belgium*. 2nd ed. London: Macmillan, 1911.

Saalman, Howard. *Haussmann: Paris Transformed*. New York: Braziller, 1971.

Schivelbusch, Wolfgang. *The Railway Journey: Trains and Travel in the 19th Century*. New York: Urizen Books, 1979.

Schneider, Donald David. *The Work and Doctrine of Jacques Ignace Hittorff, 1792–1867*. 2 vols. New York: Garland, 1977.

Schreiber, von. *Die Preussische Eisenbahnen und ihr Verhältnis zum Staat, 1834–1874*. Berlin: Ernst & Korn, 1874.

Schwabe, H. *Berliner Südwestbahn und Centralbahn, beleuchtet vom Standpunkte der Wohnungsfrage und der industriellen Gesellschaft*. Berlin: J. Guttentag, 1873.

Sedgwick, John. *An Essay on the Rights of Owners and Occupiers of Property Required by a Railway Company to Compensations, and the Way to Obtain It*. London: George & James W. Taylor, 1862.

Sheppard, Francis. *London: A History*. Oxford: Oxford University Press, 1998.

Showalter, Dennis E. *Railroads and Rifles: Soldiers, Technology, and the Unification of Germany*. Hamden, CT: Archon Books, 1975.

Simmons, Jack. *The Railway in England and Wales, 1830–1914*, vol. 1, *The System and Its Working*. Leicester, UK: Leicester University Press, 1978.

———. *The Victorian Railway*. London: Thames and Hudson, 1991.

Smets, Marcel. *L'Avénement de la cité-jardin en Belgique: Histoire de l'habitat social en Belgique de 1830 à 1930*. Liège: Mardaga, 1977.

Smolar-Meynart, Arlette, and Jean Stengers, eds. *La Région de Bruxelles: Des Villages d'autrefois à la ville d'aujourd'hui*. Brussels: Crédit Communal, 1989.

Stengers, Jean. *Bruxelles: Croissance d'une capitale*. Antwerp: Fonds Mercator, 1979.

Strauven, Francis. "Art Nouveau to Art Deco: Horta's Later Development from a Historical Perspective." In *Horta: Art Nouveau to Modernism*, edited by Françoise Aubry and Jos Vandenbreeden, 209–224. Ghent: Ludion Press, 1996.

Strikwerda, Carl. *A House Divided: Catholics, Socialists and Flemish Nationalists in Nineteenth-Century Belgium.* Lanham, MD: Rowman & Littlefield, 1997.

Summerson, John. *Victorian Architecture in Britain: Four Studies in Evaluation.* New York: Columbia University Press, 1969.

Sutcliffe, Anthony. *The Autumn of Central Paris: The Defeat of Town Planning, 1850–1970.* London: Edward Arnold, 1970.

————, ed. *Multi-Storey Living: The British Working-Class Experience.* London: Croom Helm, 1974.

————. *Paris: An Architectural History.* New Haven, CT: Yale University Press, 1993.

Taylor, Ronald. *Berlin and Its Culture: A Historical Portrait.* New Haven, CT: Yale University Press, 1997.

Teisserenc-de-Bort, Pierre-Edmond. *Des Principes généraux qui doivent présider au choix des tracés des chemins de fer.* Paris: Schneider et Langrand, 1843.

————. *Les Travaux publics en Belgique et les chemins de fer en France.* Rapport adressé à M. le Ministre des Travaux Publics. Paris: L. Mathias, 1839.

Terade, Annie. "Le Nouveau quartier de l'Europe et la Gare Saint-Lazare." *Revue d' Histoire des Chemins de Fer: Les Chemins de fer dans la ville* 5–6 (1991–92): 237–60.

Then, Volker. *Eisenbahnen und Eisenbahnunternehmer in der Industriellen Revolution: Ein Preussisch/deutsch-englischer Vergleich.* Göttingen: Vandenhoeck & Ruprecht, 1997.

Tourneux, Félix. *Encyclopédie des chemins de fer et des machines à vapeur.* Paris: J. Renouard et cie, 1844.

Turnock, David. *A Historical Geography of Railways in Great Britain and Ireland.* Brookfield, VT: Ashgate, 1998.

United Kingdom, Parliament, House of Commons. *First Report of the Commissioners Appointed by Her Majesty to Inquire into and Consider the Most Effectual Means of Improving the Metropolis, and of Providing Increased Facilities of Communication within the Same.* London: HMSO, 1844.

United Kingdom, Parliament, Reports from Commissioners. *Report of Royal Commission Appointed to Investigate the Various Projects for Establishing Railway Termini within or in the Immediate Vicinity of the Metropolis.* London: HMSO, 1846.

United Kingdom, Parliament. *Report of the Royal Commission on the Housing of the Working Classes.* London: HMSO, 1884–85.

United Kingdom, Parliament. Parliamentary Papers. *Metropolitan Railway Commission.* 1846, xvii (719).

————. Parliamentary Papers. *Select Committee on Artisans and Labourers' Dwellings.* Minutes of Evidence, 7, 1882.

————. Parliamentary Papers. *Select Committee on the Condition of Labourers Employed in the Construction of Railways, etc. Railway Labourers and Labourers on Public Works.* Report of the Select Committee. London: Charles Knight, 1846.

Valance, Georges. *Haussmann, le grand.* Paris: Flammarion, 2000.

Vandenberghen, J. *La Jonction Nord-Midi*. Histoire de la Traction Electrique en Belgique 4. Brussels: SNCB, 1997.

———. *La Naissance et l'évolution des chemins de fer de l'état belge et des réseaux concédés*. Brussels: SNCB, 1985.

van den Herten, Bart, Michelangelo Van Meerten, and Greta Verbeugt, eds. *Un Tunnel sous Bruxelles: Les 50 ans de la jonction Nord-Midi*. Brussels: Editions Racine, 2002.

Van Loo, Anne. "L'Haussmannisation de Bruxelles: La Construction des boulevards du centre, 1865–1880." *Revue de l'Art* 106, no. 4 (1994): 39–49.

Van Zanten, David. *Building Paris: Architectural Institutions and the Transformation of the French Capital, 1830–1870*. Cambridge: Cambridge University Press, 1994.

Verniers, Louis. "Démographie et expansion territoriale de l'agglomération bruxelloise depuis le début du XIXe siècle." *Bulletin de la Société Belge d'Etudes Géographiques* 5 (May 1935): 79–123.

———. "Esquisse provisoire d'une histoire de la plus-value foncière dans l'agglomération bruxelloise depuis un siècle." *Annales de la Société Royale d'Archéologie de Bruxelles* 41 (1937): 113–69.

———. "Les Transformations de Bruxelles et l'urbanisation de sa banlieue depuis 1795." *Annales de la Société Royale Archéologique de Bruxelles* 37 (1934): 84–222.

Verniquet, Edme. *Atlas du plan général de la ville de Paris*. Dessiné et gravé par Bartholomé et Mathieu. Paris: Chez l'auteur, 1795.

Villedeuil, Pierre-Charles Laurent de. *Bibliographie des chemins de fer: Index chronologique, 1771–1846*. Paris: Librairie Générale, 1906.

Villes en mutation, XIXe-XXe siècles. Brussels: Crédit Communal, 1982.

Weber, Max Maria von. *Nationalität und Eisenbahn-Politik*. Vienna: A. Hartleben, 1876.

———. *Die Schule des Eisenbahnwesens*. 3rd ed. Leipzig: Weber, 1873.

Weber, Max Maria von, and Richard Hoch, eds. *Schule des Eisenbahnwesens*. 4th ed. Leipzig: Weber, 1885.

Weinreb, Ben, and Christopher Hibbert, eds. *The London Encyclopaedia*. London: Macmillan, 1983.

Whitehead, Jack. *The Growth of Camden Town, AD 1800–2000*. London: Jack Whitehead, 1999.

Williams, Roy. *The Midland Railway: A New History*. Newton Abbot, UK: David & Charles, 1988.

Willms, Johannes. *Paris, Capital of Europe: From the Revolution to the Belle Epoque*. New York: Holmes & Meier, 1997.

Wohl, A. S. *The Eternal Slum: Housing and Social Policy in Victorian London*. Studies in Urban History 5. Montreal: McGill-Queen's University Press, 1977.

———. "The Housing of the Working Classes in London, 1815–1914." In *The History of Working-Class Housing: A Symposium*, edited by Stanley D. Chapman, 15–51. Totowa, NJ: Rowman and Littlefield, 1971.

Yelling, J. A. *Slums and Slum Clearance in Victorian London*. London: George Allen & Unwin, 1986.

Zeldin, Theodore. *France, 1848–1945.* 2 vols. Oxford: Oxford University Press, 1973–77.

Ziegler, Dieter. *Eisenbahnen und Staat im Zeitalter der Industrialisierung: Die Eisenbahnpolitik der Deutschen Staaten im Vergleich.* Stuttgart: Franz Steiner Verlag, 1996.

London: Euston Road Terminals

In this section, works are given in chronological order for each station. Works containing entries on more than one station are included in the general bibliography.

Euston

Bourne, John Cooke, and John Britton. *Drawings of the London and Birmingham Railway . . . with an Historical and Descriptive Account by John Britton.* London: J. C. Bourne, 1839.

Ormandy, Fisher. *Report upon the Cattle Traffic of the London and North Western Railway for the Year 1849.* London: Printed by the Order of the Committee, 1849.

Taylor, William, in association with the Institution of Civil Engineers. "Observations on the Street Paving of the Metropolis; with an Account of a Peculiar System Adopted at the London and North-Western Railway Station, Euston-Square." *Institution of Civil Engineers: Minutes of Proceedings* 9, no. 825 (26 February 1850): 214–33.

Handbook to London As It Is. London: John Murray, 1851.

Conder, F. R. *The Men Who Built Railways: A Reprint of F. R. Conder's Personal Recollections of English Engineers.* Edited by Jack Simmons. London: Thomas Telford, 1983. First published 1868.

Walford, Edward. *Old London,* vol. 5, *Paddington Green to Seven Sisters.* London: Village Press, 1878.

Billington, J. D. "Mr. Dombey Travels by Rail." *Dickensian* 28 (1932): 205–8.

Smith, G. Royde, and Midland and Scottish Railway. *Old Euston: An Account of the Beginning of the London and Birmingham Railway and the Building of Euston Station.* London: Country Life, 1938.

Godfrey, Walter H., and J. R. Howard Roberts, eds. *Survey of London,* vol. 21, *Tottenham Court Road and Neighborhood: The Parish of St. Pancras, Part III.* London: London County Council, 1949.

Pevsner, Nikolaus. *London Except the City and Westminster.* The Buildings of England. Harmondsworth, UK: Penguin, 1952.

Summerson, John Newenham. *The Architectural History of Euston Station.* London: British Transport Commission, 1959.

Block, Geoffrey D. M. "London's Oldest Rail Terminus." *Country Life* 127 (17 March 1960): 554–56.

Robbins, Michael. "A Note on the Camden Round-House: From R. B. Dockray's Diary." *Journal of Transport History* 7 (1965): 158–59.

Curtis, J. S. *Old Euston.* Shepperton, England: Ian Allan, 1965.

Smithson, Alison, and Peter Smithson. With foreword by Nikolaus Pevsner. *The Euston Arch and the Growth of the London, Midland and Scottish Railway.* London: Thames and Hudson, 1968.

"Euston Station: London's Oldest Terminus Rebuilt as an Envelope for a £15m. Total Travel Concept Centre." *Building* 25, no. 43 (October 1968): 103–10.

Moorcroft, R. L. "Station Reconstruction at Euston, London." *Architect's Journal* 148, no. 51 (18–25 December 1968): 1455–64.

Haresnape, Brian. *Railway Design since 1830.* London: Ian Allan, 1968–69.

Jackson, Alan A. *London's Termini.* Newton Abbot, UK: David & Charles, 1969.

Hobhouse, Hermione. *Lost London.* London: Macmillan, 1971.

Nock, O. S. *Railway Archaeology.* Cambridge, UK: Patrick Stephens, 1981.

Course, Edwin. *London's Railways Then and Now.* London: Batsford, 1987.

Jenkinson, David. "Old Euston." *Railway South East* 1 (Winter 1987–88): 50–54.

________. "Memories of Euston." *Back Track* 3 (1988): 74–80.

Ransom, P. J. *The Victorian Railway and How It Evolved.* London: Heinemann, 1990.

Ellaway, K. J. *Euston.* Oldham, UK: Irwell Press, 1994.

Woodford, Peter, ed. *From Primrose Hill to Euston Road.* London: Camden History Society, 1995.

King's Cross

Mackie, Charles. *Itinerary of the Great Northern Railway from London to York.* New ed. London: W. H. Smith, 1854.

Stanford's New London Guide. London: Edward Stanford, 1860.

Handbook to London As It Is. London: John Murray, 1866.

Johns, C. A. "One Hundred Year at King's Cross." *Railway Magazine* 98 (1952): 649–57, 734–39, 759.

Roberts, Howard, and Walter H. Godfrey, eds. *Survey of London,* vol. 24, *King's Cross Neighbourhood: The Parish of St. Pancras, Part IV.* London: London County Council, 1952.

Jackson, Alan A. *London's Termini.* Newton Abbot, UK: David & Charles, 1969.

Townsend, Peter Norman. *Top Shed: A Pictorial History of the King's Cross Locomotive Depot.* London: Ian Allan, 1975.

Wrottesley, John. *The Great Northern Railway.* London: Batsford, 1979–81.

Greater London Council. "King's Cross New Road Scheme." London: Greater London Council Public Relations Branch, 1984.

Simmons, Jack. "Suburban Traffic at King's Cross, 1852–1914." *Journal of Transport History,* ser. 3, 6, no. 1 (1985): 71–78.

Duckworth, Stephen P., and Barry V. Jones. *King's Cross Development Site: An Inventory of Architectural and Industrial Features.* London: English Heritage, Historic Buildings and Monuments Commission for England, 1988.

Hawkins, Chris. *The Great British Railway Station: Kings Cross.* Pinner, Middlesex: Irwell Press, 1990.

Hunter, Michael, and Robert Thorne, eds. *Change at King's Cross: From 1800 to the Present.* London: Historical Publications, 1990.

Essex-Lopresti, Michael. *Exploring the Regent's Canal.* Studley, Warwicks: Brewin Books, 1994.

Davies, Philip. "All Change at St. Pancras." *English Heritage Conservation Bulletin* 30 (November 1996): 12–13.

Duncan, Andrew. *Secret London.* London: New Holland, 2000.

St. Pancras

Midland Counties' Railway Companion: With Topographical Description of the Country through which the Line Passes, and Time, Fare, and Distance Tables, Corrected to the 24th August. Nottingham: R. Allen, 1840.

Barlow, William Henry. "Description of the St. Pancras Station and Roof, Midland Railway, March 29, 1870." *Institution of Civil Engineers Proceedings* 30, no. 1,253 (1869–70): 78–105, plates 8–9.

Williams, Frederick S. *The Midland Railway: Its Rise and Progress, a Narrative of Modern Enterprise.* London: Bemrose, 1877.

Walford, Edward. *Old London,* vol. 5, *Paddington Green to Seven Sisters.* London: The Village Press, 1878.

Scott, George Gilbert. *Personal and Professional Recollections.* London: Sampson Low, Marston, Searle & Rivington, 1879.

Noble, John. *The Midland Railway Company.* Sutton: Sharpe, 1881.

Acworth, W. M. "The Midland Railway." *Murray's Magazine,* March 1888, 306–23.

Stretton, Clement E. *The History of the Midland Railway.* London: Methuen, 1901.

Roberts, Howard, and Walter H. Godfrey, eds. *Survey of London,* vol. 24, *King's Cross Neighbourhood: The Parish of St. Pancras, Part IV.* London: London County Council, 1952.

Ellis, Cuthbert Hamilton. *The Midland Railway.* London: Ian Allan, 1953.

Ferriday, Peter. "The Grandest Folly of Them All: The Architecture of St. Pancras Station and Hotel." *Country Life,* 18 November 1965, 1314–17.

Barnes, E. G. *The Rise of the Midland Railway, 1844–1874.* London: George Allen & Unwin, 1966.

Summerson, John. "Red Elephant in Euston Road." *Illustrated London News,* 7 October 1967, 17–19.

Simmons, Jack. *St. Pancras Station.* London: George Allen & Unwin, 1968. Revised edition, 2003).

Jackson, Alan A. *London's Termini.* Newton Abbot, UK: David & Charles, 1969.

Channon, Geoffrey. "A Nineteenth-Century Investment Decision: The Midland Railway's London Extension." *Economic History Review* 25 (1972): 448–70.

Kaukas, Bernard. "St. Pancras Revisited." *London Journal* 8 (1982): 191–203.

Whitehouse, Patrick, and David St. John Thomas. *LMS 150: The London Midland & Scottish Railway.* Newton Abbot, UK: David & Charles, 1987.

Williams, Roy. *The Midland Railway: A New History.* Newton Abbot, UK: David & Charles, 1988.

Bradley, Simon. *St. Pancras Station.* London: Profile, 2007.

Berlin Anhalter Bahnhof

Entries in this section are presented in chronological order.

Comité der Berlin-Sächsischen Eisenbahn-Gesellschaft. *Rundschreiben an die Herren Actien-Zeichner zum Bau der Berlin-Sächsischen Eisenbahn.* Berlin: Weidle, 1838.

Petersen and Rosenbaum. *Bericht an das Comité der Berlin-Sächsischen Eisenbahn-Gesellschaft über die Vorzüge der Allerhöchst genehmigten, direkt von Berlin ausgehenden Berlin-Sächsischen Eisenbahn, vor einem von Potsdam über Roslau nach Köthen projectirten Anschluß an die Magdeburg-Köthen-Halle-Leipziger Eisenbahn.* Berlin: Weidle, 1838.

Nowack. "Karte der Berlin-Anhaltischen Eisenbahn." Berlin: Simon Schropp, 1843.

"Das neue Empfangsgebäude der Berlin-Anhaltischen Eisenbahn." *Deutsche Bauzeitung* 14 (11 December 1880): 531–32.

Pinkenburg, G. "Umbau des Anhalter Bahnhofes zu Berlin." *Zeitschrift des Architekten und Ingenieurvereins zu Hannover* 30 (1884): 21–32, 105–8, 145–48, 237–44, 317–20.

Architekten-Verein zu Berlin, ed. *Berlin und seine Bauten.* 2nd ed. Berlin: Ernst & Korn, 1896.

Ministerium der Öffentlichen Arbeiten and A. F. Leyen. *Berlin und seine Eisenbahnen, 1846–1896.* Berlin: Julius Springer, 1896.

Börsch-Supan, Eva. *Berliner Baukunst nach Schinkel, 1840–1870.* Munich: Prestel, 1977.

Berlin, Anhalter Bahnhof: Bausubstanz der Gründerjahre als Museumsobjekt. Berlin: Museum für Verkehr und Technik, 1980.

Maier, Helmut. *Berlin Anhalter Bahnhof.* Berlin: Aesthetik und Kommunikation, 1983.

Kliem, Peter G., and Klaus Noack. *Berlin Anhalter Bahnhof.* Berlin: Ullstein, 1984.

Lausch, H., R. Mohrmann, R. Rosenkranz, A. Schwipps, S. Stern, "Bürgerinitiative Schöneberger Südgelände," and Stiftung Naturschutz Berlin. *Das verborgene Grün von Schöneberg: Der Naturpark Südgelände.* Berlin: Verlag Konstanze Freihold, 1985.

Gottwaldt, Alfred Bernd. *Der Anhalter Bahnhof und seine Lokomotiven.* Düsseldorf: Alba, 1986.

Knothe, Rainer. *Anhalter Bahnhof: Entwicklung und Betrieb, Zeugen und Zeugnisse aus über Hundert Jahren.* Berlin: Aesthetik und Kommunikation, 1987.

Bley, Peter. *150 Jahre Berlin-Anhaltische Eisenbahn.* Düsseldorf: Alba, 1990.

Ries, Henry. *Menschen am zerstörten Anhalter Bahnhof: Fotografien, 1948.* Berlin: Museum für Verkehr und Technik, 1990.

Gottwaldt, Alfred Bernd. "The Railway Buildings of Berlin." In *Common Roots—Separate Branches,* edited by Rob Shortland-Ball, 37–42. London: Science Museum, 1994.

Gottwaldt, Alfred Bernd, and Stefan Nowak. *Berliner Bahnhöfe: Einst und jetzt.* Düsseldorf: Alba, 1994.

Gottwaldt, Alfred Bernd. *Eisenbahn-Zentrum Berlin, 1920–1939: Bahnhöfe, Lokomotiven und Zuge.* Berlin: Jaron Verlag, 1997.

Legislation

General

Guillaume, Achille. *De la Législation des rails: Routes au chemins de fer en Angleterre et en France.* Paris: Carilian-Goeury, 1838.

Meylan, Jacques. *Le Domaine ferroviaire en droit comparé (Droits Français, Allemand et Suisse).* Geneva: Librairie Droz, 1966.

Rosenthal, E. "Enteignung." In *Enzyklopädie des Eisenbahnwesens,* 2nd ed., edited by Victor von Röll, 4:342–61. Berlin: Urban & Schwarzenberg, 1912–23.

Britain

Bigg, J., ed. *Bigg's General Railway Acts: A Collection of the Public General Acts for the Regulation of Railways.* London: J. Bigg, Waterlow, 1845–1911.

———. *Bigg's General Railway Acts: A Collection of the Public General Acts for the Regulation of Railways.* 16th ed. London: J. Bigg, Waterlow, 1912.

Browne, John Hutton Balfour, and Henry Studdy Theobald. *The Law of Railway Companies.* 4th ed. London: Stevens, 1911.

Kostal, R. W. *Law and English Railway Capitalism, 1825–1875.* Oxford: Clarendon Press, 1994 (1997 paperback with corrections).

Parris, Henry. *Government and the Railways in Nineteenty-Century Britain.* London: Routledge, 1965 (esp. chap. 4, "The Invasion of Land," 144–80).

Williams, O. Cyprian. *The Historical Development of Private Bill Procedure and Standing Orders in the House of Commons.* 2 vols. London: HMSO, 1948.

France

Adam, Jean-Paul. *Instauration de la politique des chemins de fer en France.* Paris: Presses Universitaires de France, 1972.

Daru, Napoléon. *Des Chemins de fer et de l'application de la loi du 11 juin 1842.* Paris: L. Mathias, 1843.

Vigouroux, E. *Législation et jurisprudence des chemins de fer et des tramways.* Paris: E. Thorin, 1886.

Prussia and Germany

Bähr, O., and W. Langerhans. *Das Gesetz über die Enteignung von Grundeigenthum von 11. Juni 1874.* Berlin: Fr. Kortkampf, 1875.

Beschorner, Julius Hermann. *Das deutsche Eisenbahnrecht mit besonderer Berüksichtigung des Actien und Expropriationsrechtes.* Erlangen: Ferdinand Enke, 1858.

Bessel, August, and Eduard Kühlwetter. *Das Preussische Eisenbahnrecht.* Cologne: Franz Carl Eisen, 1855.

Bohlmann, O. *Die Praxis in Expropriationssachen: Beiträge zur Beurtheilung der bezüglichen Kontroversen des Preussischen, wie auch des gemeinen Rechts.* 2nd ed. Berlin: Weber, 1881.

Eger, Georg. *Das Gesetz über die Enteignung von Grundeigenthum vom 11. Juni 1874.* 2nd ed. 2 vols. Breslau: J. U. Kern, 1902.

Fritsch, Konstantin. *Das deutsche Eisenbahnrecht; Grundriß des Reichs und des Preußischen Rechts.* Berlin: Verlag der Verkehrswissenschaftlichen Lehrmittelgesellschaft bei der Deutschen Reichsbahnen, 1927.

———. *Handbuch der Eisenbahngesetzgebung in Preussen und dem Deutschen Reiche.* Berlin: Julius Springer, 1906.

Hansemann, David Justus Ludwig. *Kritik des Preussischen Eisenbahn-Gesetzes vom 3. November 1838.* Aachen: J. A. Mayer, 1841.

Koffka, Emil. *Kommentar zum Gesetz über die Enteignung von Grundeigenthum vom 11. Juni 1874. . . .* 2nd ed. Berlin: Franz Vahlen, 1913.

L . . . *Die Preussischen Eisenbahn-Unternehmungen und die Allerhöchste Verordnung von 24. Mai [1844].* Berlin: Enslin, 1844.

Mayer, Otto. *Le Droit administratif allemand.* 4 vols. Paris: Giard & Brière, 1904.

Preussens Eisenbahngesetzgebung: Eine Zusammenstellung der bisher erschienen, die Eisenbahn-Unternehmungen betreffenden Gesetze und Ministerial-Rescripte. Glogau: Karl Flemming, 1844.

Reden, Friedrich Wilhelm von. *Législation des chemins de fer en Allemagne.* Paris: L. Mathias, 1845.

Schrötter, J. A. *Das Preussische Eisenbahnrecht in seiner heutigen Gestalt umfassend das Gesetz über die Eisenbahn-Unternehmungen, vom 3. November 1838. . . .* Berlin: H. W. Müller, 1883.

Seydel, Friedrich. *Das Gesetz über die Enteignung von Grundeigenthum vom 11. Juni 1874.* Berlin: Carl Heymanns Verlag, 1882.

Siegfried, Heinrich. *Das Gesetz über die Enteignung von Grundeigenthum: Erläutert unter Benutzung des amtlichen Motive sowie der Kommissionsberichte und Verhandlungen der beiden Häuser des Landtages.* Berlin: Gustav Hempel, 1874.

Weber, Max Maria von. *Bemerkungen zum vorläufigen Entwurf eines deutschen Reichseisenbahngesetzes.* Leipzig: Teubner,1875.

Belgium

de Laveleye, A. *Expropriation par zones pour cause d'utilité publique.* Brussels: E. Guyot, 1863.

Gendebien, Jules. *Législation et jurisprudence des chemins de fer en Belgique (1834–58).* Brussels: Bruylant, 1858.

Index

Titles of publications and foreign terms are in italics, illustrations in boldface.

Bruneel, Frédéric   152, 155, 158, 170, 182, 240n33
Brunfaut, Fernand (1886–1972)   145, 158, 161, 170–71, 241n36
Brussels   5, 44, 181
  belt line   147, 148
  Besme plan   183
  Charleroi Canal   146, 239n7
  city planning   161–64
  communes   145, 146, 175
  Gare Centrale   145, 148, 150–53, 156–58, 162–64, 169, 176–77, 185–86
  Gare du Midi (orig. Gare des Bogards)   143, 146, 148–50, 152–53, 158, 160, 169, 176
  Gare du Nord   143, 146, 148–50, 152–53, 158
  Helleputte report   158
  home owmership and subsidy   44–45, 169, 174–75, 245n27
  Junction   45, 126, 143–77, **154**, 179, 181, 183, 240n35, 241n36, 241n41, 241n44
    list of projects   189–94
  Mont des Arts (orig. Montagne de la Cour)   151–53, 162
  Notre-Dame de la Chapelle   152–53, 156, 159, 160, 162–63
  Office National pour l'Achèvement de la Jonction Nord-Midi (ONJ)   155–56, 158–60, 170, 241n40
  particularism   5, 170, 247n44
  pentagon   143, **144**, 145, 146
  public image   5, 143, 146–47, 149, 152, 155, 160, 162–64, 169
  Putterie   152–53, 155, 157–59, 240n30
  Royal Library   151, 161–62
  Saint-Gilles   145, 146, 148, 163
  Saint-Josse-ten-Noode   145, 146
  Saint-Roch neighborhood   151, 158
  Senne River vaulting   26, 44, 147, 149–50, 161, 163, 179
  SS. Michel and Gudule   156, 159
  tolls   146
  V+   164

The Builder   33, 34, 92, 166
building materials supply   13
Buls, Charles (1837–1914)   44, 151, 159–61, 163, 240n29

Cabanel de Sermet, Pierre-Sophie (1801–75)   98, 111, 182
cahiers des charges (schedule of conditions)   23, 116–17, 125
canals   8, 9, 197n20
Channel Tunnel   125, 182
Channel Tunnel Rail Link (CTRL)   53, 60
Chartres   14–15
Cheap Trains Act (1883)   42, 124
Civil War (U.S.)   109, 123
Cocquerill, John   85, 88, 187
Commission des Embellissements de Paris   70, 72, 79, 103–5, 115, 215n7–8, 216n19
commuting   30, 41–43, 45, 59, 94, 106, 138–40, 168, 181, 208n85
  in Belgium   169–77
  reduced fares   39, 41–42, 166, 169–77, 208n87, 246n32–34
  workmen's trains   30, 41, 43, 169, 172
Compagnie du Chemin de Fer du Nord   15, 22, 76, 85–88, 91, 93, 96, 101–3, 107, 125, 167, 187
Compagnie dy Chemin de Fer de l'Est (orig. Chemin de Strasbourg)   20, 22, 90, 96, 99, 104, 107, 111, 114, 125
Congrès Internationaux d'Architecture Moderne (CIAM)   161, 163, 184
Corbusier, Le   100 (Voisin Plan) 161
Cubitt, Lewis (1799–ca.1883)   56
cut-and-cover construction   155–56, 158, 160, 166, 241n40

de Bassompièrre-Sewrin, M.   20, 49, 165
de Lamartine, Alphonse (1790–1869)   9, 112–13